A·N·N·U·A·L E·D·I·T·I·O·N·S

COMPUTERS IN EDUCATION

Tenth Edition

W9-BUI-768

02/03

Editors

John J. Hirschbuhl
University of Akron

John J. Hirschbuhl is the founder of the Center for Computer-Based Education, an assistant to the associate vice president for information services, and professor of education at the University of Akron. He is currently a consulting scholar for the IBM Corporation and a senior vice president of development and operations at Computer Knowledge International, Inc. He received his Ph.D. from Pennsylvania State University and his B.S. and M.A. from Temple University. Dr. Hirschbuhl has published over 100 articles in professional journals on computer-based education and training, and he has consulted with many of the *Fortune* 500 companies and academic institutions.

Dwight Bishop
University of Akron

Dwight Bishop, primary developer in the University of Akron's Multimedia Lab, has created commercial and academic software. He has instructed courses in computer-based education, multimedia authoring, multimedia screen design, and statistics. Mr. Bishop has 7 years of experience as a personnel consultant (training and selection). He received his B.A. from the University of North Carolina, his M.S. from Purdue (I/O psychology), and his M.A. (computer-based education) from the University of Akron.

McGraw-Hill/Dushkin
530 Old Whitfield Street, Guilford, Connecticut 06437

Visit us on the Internet
http://www.dushkin.com

Credits

1. Introduction
Unit photo—© 2001 by Sweet By & By/Cindy Brown.

2. Curriculum and Instructional Design
Unit photo—Courtesy of Pamela Carley.

3. Classroom Applications and Software Evaluations
Unit photo—Courtesy of Apple Computer, Inc.

4. Teacher Training and Resources
Unit photo—McGraw-Hill/Dushkin photo.

5. Multimedia
Unit photo—Courtesy of Tom Way/IBM Microelectronics.

6. Special Issues
Unit photo—© 2001 by Sweet By & By/Cindy Brown.

7. The Internet and Computer Networks
Unit photo—AP/Wide World Photo by Carlos Osorio.

8. Distance Learning
Unit photo—Courtesy of Apple Computer, Inc.

Copyright

Cataloging in Publication Data
Main entry under title: Annual Editions: Computers in Education. 2002/2003. 10/E
    1. Computer-managed instruction—Periodicals. 2. Computer-assisted instruction—Periodicals. 3. Computers and civilization—Periodicals. I. Hirschbuhl, John J., *comp*. II. Bishop, Dwight, *comp*. III. Title: Computers in education.
ISBN 0-07-247880-2   371.3'9445'05   87–654373   ISSN 1094-2602

© 2002 by McGraw-Hill/Dushkin, Guilford, CT 06437, A Division of The McGraw-Hill Companies.

Copyright law prohibits the reproduction, storage, or transmission in any form by any means of any portion of this publication without the express written permission of McGraw-Hill/Dushkin, and of the copyright holder (if different) of the part of the publication to be reproduced. The Guidelines for Classroom Copying endorsed by Congress explicitly state that unauthorized copying may not be used to create, to replace, or to substitute for anthologies, compilations, or collective works.

Annual Editions® is a Registered Trademark of McGraw-Hill/Dushkin, A Division of The McGraw-Hill Companies.

Tenth Edition

Cover image © 2002 PhotoDisc, Inc.

Printed in the United States of America   1234567890BAHBAH5432   Printed on Recycled Paper

Members of the Advisory Board are instrumental in the final selection of articles for each edition of ANNUAL EDITIONS. Their review of articles for content, level, currentness, and appropriateness provides critical direction to the editor and staff. We think that you will find their careful consideration well reflected in this volume.

Editors/Advisory Board

EDITORS

John J. Hirschbuhl
University of Akron

Dwight Bishop
University of Akron

ADVISORY BOARD

George M. Bass
College of William and Mary

Curtis Bring
Moorhead State University

Andrew J. Brovey
Valdosta State University

Anthony A. DeFalco
Long Island University

Richard D. Howell
Ohio State University

John E. Jacobson
University of Missouri
Kansas City

Sandra L. Leslie
Belmont Abbey College

Fredric Linder
Virginia Commonwealth University

Thomas E. Love
Malone College

John Mitterer
Brock University

Landra L. Rezabek
University of Wyoming

Bonnie L. Shapiro
University of Calgary

Vicki Sharp
California State
University, Northridge

Rosemary W. Skeele
Seton Hall University

Sharon E. Smaldino
University of Northern Iowa

John E. Splaine
University of Maryland
College Park

Stephen J. Taffee
Educational Consultant

Susan B. Turkel
Queens College

Marvin Westrom
University of British Columbia

Staff

EDITORIAL STAFF

Ian A. Nielsen, Publisher
Roberta Monaco, Senior Developmental Editor
Dorothy Fink, Associate Developmental Editor
Addie Raucci, Senior Administrative Editor
Robin Zarnetske, Permissions Editor
Marie Lazauskas, Permissions Assistant
Diane Barker, Proofreader
Lisa Holmes-Doebrick, Senior Program Coordinator

TECHNOLOGY STAFF

Richard Tietjen, Senior Publishing Technologist
Jonathan Stowe, Director of Technology
Janice Ward, Software Support Analyst
Ciro Parente, Editorial Assistant

PRODUCTION STAFF

Brenda S. Filley, Director of Production
Charles Vitelli, Designer
Mike Campbell, Production Coordinator
Laura Levine, Graphics
Tom Goddard, Graphics
Eldis Lima, Graphics
Nancy Norton, Graphics
Juliana Arbo, Typesetting Supervisor
Karen Roberts, Typesetter
Jocelyn Proto, Typesetter
Cynthia Vets, Typesetter
Larry Killian, Copier Coordinator

To the Reader

In publishing ANNUAL EDITIONS we recognize the enormous role played by the magazines, newspapers, and journals of the public press in providing current, first-rate educational information in a broad spectrum of interest areas. Many of these articles are appropriate for students, researchers, and professionals seeking accurate, current material to help bridge the gap between principles and theories and the real world. These articles, however, become more useful for study when those of lasting value are carefully collected, organized, indexed, and reproduced in a low-cost format, which provides easy and permanent access when the material is needed. That is the role played by ANNUAL EDITIONS.

The tenth edition of *Annual Editions: Computers in Education* is designed to provide you with the latest information and trends regarding computers and the roles they play in people's lives. Today's fast-moving society has focused on a mass move toward a media-laced Internet whose World Wide Web carries streamed audio and video and other digital technologies, such as phone mail systems, online database access, teleconferencing systems, and interactive multimedia systems. These technologies provide an electronic pipeline that can reach anyone anywhere on Earth.

Streamed media and interaction have become windows to the universe, and they are providing an interconnectedness that is inherent to learning. This technology is providing a globel education wideband network for the twenty-first century. We are now zipping our way along the worldwide digital highway on our way to educational and training materials that stimulate us to interact with realistic simulations and to key information that enables us to conceive new and more powerful ways of thinking about and solving sophisticated problems. This communication is providing homes, schools, universities, and businesses with a wide broadband communication system. We now have the needed bandwidth and links online to bring the community, home, school, and business together in lifelong interactive educational experiences.

Digital video has become a common application on today's Internet. Through it we can influence the lives of people all over the globe through collaborative teaching and learning in an authentic setting. Current instructional management systems are capable of delivering, managing, and assessing learning results in order to maximize the effectiveness of online teaching/learning systems. We are now realizing the long-sought benefits of technology within the education and training systems of the United States.

This volume addresses the question, "How are the U.S. education and training communities riding the back of current technologies in order to make it a better-educated and more competitive nation in this twenty-first century global economy?" We have reviewed the current literature and selected key statements that respond to the issue.

In addition, there is an abundance of articles dealing with distance learning, networking, the Internet, and interactive multimedia applications for the classroom, laboratory, and the home. There is a pressing need for a publication that brings togehter this wealth of pertinent information on the successful implementation of current technology into schools, homes, and businesses as well as the new hardware/software applications that have made this possible. The *Annual Editions* format uniquely meets this need.

This anthology addresses the current issues confronting computer-using educators and trainers. Both need to know about the current classroom applications and software evaluations. It also provides a close-up look at integrating technology into the curriculum, teacher training, interactive multimedia, the Internet, and distance learning applications.

This volume is designed for use by educators involved in preservice and inservice education of educators, trainers, and administrators. It is also intended for parents, students, school board members, and others concerned with the use and impact of technology on today's education and training activities. Efforts have been made to include articles without references to specific hardware or software that may become quickly outdated.

As always, it is expected that you will have suggestions for improving future editions of *Annual Editions: Computers in Education*. You can help shape the next volume by completing and returning the postage-paid *article rating form* located on the last page of this book.

John J. Hirschbuhl
Editor

Dwight Bishop
Editor

Contents

UNIT 1

Introduction

Six selections examine the current state of computer implementation of the learning environment and the clash between earlier Industrial Age and present Information Age education.

The concepts in bold italics are developed in the article. For further expansion please refer to the Topic Guide, the Glossary, and the Index.

UNIT 2

Curriculum and Instructional Design

Five articles provide information on employing microcomputer-based software in the classroom.

Overview   62

UNIT 3

Classroom Applications and Software Evaluations

Six selections provide criteria for the selection and implementation of instructional software in the classroom.

The concepts in bold italics are developed in the article. For further expansion please refer to the Topic Guide, the Glossary, and the Index.

UNIT 4

Teacher Training and Resources

Six selections examine the problems associated with staff development and teacher education to ensure teacher computer compentency in the classroom.

The concepts in bold italics are developed in the article. For further expansion please refer to the Topic Guide, the Glossary, and the Index.

UNIT 5

Multimedia

Five selections demonstrate how educators have harnessed the power of multimedia to improve their students' education.

UNIT 6

Special Issues

Five selections discuss the need for computer equipment in some schools, the status of women in the technology field, the impact of computer use in early child development, and distribution rights of Internet data.

The concepts in bold italics are developed in the article. For further expansion please refer to the Topic Guide, the Glossary, and the Index.

UNIT 7

The Internet and Computer Networks

Five articles address several issues about the Internet and other networks, including the need to build critical skills that enable students to benefit from using the Net and using the Internet as a ready-reference resource.

The concepts in bold italics are developed in the article. For further expansion please refer to the Topic Guide, the Glossary, and the Index.

UNIT 8

Distance Learning

Four articles discuss the value of interactive technologies within a distance learning environment.

This topic guide suggests how the selections in this book relate to the subjects covered in your course.

The Web icon (⌾) under the topic articles easily identifies the relevant Web sites, which are numbered and annotated on the next two pages. By linking the articles and the Web sites by topic, this ANNUAL EDITIONS reader becomes a powerful learning and research tool.

3

◉ AE: Computers in Education

The following World Wide Web sites have been carefully researched and selected to support the articles found in this reader. The sites are cross-referenced by number and the Web icon (◉) in the topic guide. In addition, it is possible to link directly to these Web sites through our DUSHKIN ONLINE support site at *http://www.dushkin.com/online/*.

The following sites were available at the time of publication. Visit our Web site—we update DUSHKIN ONLINE regularly to reflect any changes.

Introduction

1. Agency for International Technology
http://www.ait.net
AIT is a nonprofit education organization established in 1962 to develop, acquire, and distribute quality technology-based resources. It provides leadership to the educational technology policy community as well as instructional television programs.

2. Goals 2000
http://www.ed.gov/pubs/goals/progrpt/index.html
The reform initiative started by the U.S. Department of Education has a progress report to share.

3. History of Computers in Education
http://www.csulb.edu/~murdock/histofcs.html
This site explores the history of computers and the history of computers in education. A time line lists the dates in which important events took place and gives a brief explanation of the impact of technology on education.

Curriculum and Instructional Design

4. CTW
http://www.ctw.org/home/content/0,2946,,FF.html
Children's Television Workshop enjoys a visionary role in innovative family programming. Its new media property is custom-made for today's families. The Workshop delivers a unique approach to the Internet, melding technology and edutainment to bring families together to learn and have fun.

5. Education Place
http://www.eduplace.com/index.html
Houghton Mifflin's home page contains activities for students, parents, and teachers, which include weekly author interviews and child-written book reviews. It has links to excellent education topics and organizations with synopses of research (for instance, phonics instruction).

6. Teaching With Electronic Technology
http://www.wam.umd.edu/~mlhall/teaching.html
This collection of World Wide Web sites addresses the use of electronic technologies in the classroom, which range from general and theoretical resources to instructive examples of specific applications to teaching and learning.

Classroom Applications and Software Evaluations

7. Beginner's Guide to HTML
http://www.itc.univie.ac.at/docs/html-primer.html
This is a primer for producing documents in HTML, the markup language used by the World Wide Web.

8. Classics for Young People
http://www.ucalgary.ca/~dkbrown/storclas.html
A growing number of children's literature classics are out of copyright and are among the books available in full text here.

9. ENC Online
http://www.enc.org
The Eisenhower National Clearinghouse includes science and math resources, lesson plans, a search engine, and more.

10. NASA Spacelink
http://spacelink.msfc.nasa.gov/home.index.html
This aeronautics and space resource for educators contains a variety of space travel information, including travel throughout the galaxy with information and images.

11. The Nine Planets
http://seds.lpl.arizona.edu/billa/tnp/
This planetary tour through the solar system has sound and video clips and links to related sites.

12. Scholastic Network
http://www.scholastic.com
Here is a selection of Scholastic products, including Global Community, Magic SchoolBus, contests, Scholastic publications, and new school-home Software Clubs for Grades PreK–8.

13. Teachers Helping Teachers
http://www.pacificnet.net/~mandel/
Provides basic teaching tips, new teaching methodology ideas, and forums for teachers to share. Download software and participate in chat sessions. Features educational resources on the Web, with new ones added each week.

14. The TeleGarden
http://www.usc.edu/dept/garden/
Interact and view a remote garden filled with living plants. Members care for the garden through a robot arm.

15. Volcano World
http://volcano.und.nodak.edu
Study extinct and live volcanoes worldwide. There are activities for children and adults, and lesson plans for teachers.

Teacher Training and Resources

16. Boulder Valley School District Home Page
http://www.bvsd.k12.co.us
This is the site of a district-developed home page containing planning ideas and links to educational resources for teachers and students.

17. Getting U.S. Teachers Online
http://quest.arc.nasa.gov/online/table.html
This NASA resource provides online service providers, listed by state, as well as other access options for K–12 teachers.

18. The History Channel
http://www.historychannel.com
The History Channel offers a section on classroom study guides and ideas for and from educators, along with many other helpful features and related links.

DUSHKIN ONLINE

19. Teachers Guide to the Department of Education
    http://www.ed.gov/pubs/TeachersGuide/
Government goals, projects, grants, and other educational programs are listed here as well as links to services and resources.

Multimedia

20. CNN Interactive
    http://cnn.com
The latest news, including pictures and archival links, is available here, along with the Infoseek search engine.

21. Mighty Media
    http://www.mightymedia.com
The mission of this privately funded consortium is to empower youth, teachers, and organizations through the use of interactive communications technology.

22. Mustang List of Lesson Plans
    http://mustang.coled.umn.edu/lessons/lessons.html
This source leads to many other sites that contain electronic lesson plans, including online interdisciplinary projects.

23. MSNBC Cover Page
    http://www.msnbc.com
As the only news organization to embrace three media technologies—broadcast, cable, and the Internet—MSNBC brings you up-to-the-minute news from around the globe.

24. NASA Aerospace Education Services Program
    http://www.okstate.edu/aesp/AESP.html
This site leads to cross-curricular projects, science, technology, space, literature, math, language, astronomy, writing projects, museum links, and space image libraries.

25. The Science Learning Network
    http://www.sln.org
This collection of museum sites includes movies, teachers' projects, news, and links to other science education material.

Special Issues

26. Consortium for School Networking
    http://www.cosn.org
This site provides information and discussion on how to implement networks in schools. It offers online resources and forums.

27. Educators Net
    http://www.educatorsnet.com
Billed as the "World's No.1 Education Search Engine," this site has over 7,200 reviewed listings and acts as a guide to education-related resources and businesses on the Internet.

28. ERIC Clearinghouse on Teaching and Teacher Education
    http://www.ericsp.org
This ERIC site has links to lesson plans and sites on applying technology, as well as essays on teaching with technology.

The Internet and Computer Networks

29. Online Internet Institute
    http://oii.org
A collaborative project between Internet-using educators, proponents of systemic reform, content area experts, and teachers who desire professional growth, this site provides a learning environment for integrating the Internet into educators' individual teaching styles.

30. The Teachers' Network
    http://www.teachnet.org
Bulletin boards, classroom projects, online forums, and Web mentors are featured, as well as the book, *Teachers' Guide to Cyberspace*, and a course on how to use the Internet.

31. WebCrawler
    http://webcrawler.com
This is a fast search engine that analyzes the full text of documents, allowing the searcher to locate keywords that may have been buried deep within a document's text.

32. Yahooligans! The Web Guide for Kids
    http://www.yahooligans.com
An excellent site for children, this resource can be used if you wish to limit access by your students but still allow independent searching.

Distance Learning

33. The Chronicle of Higher Education: Distance Education Page
    http://www.chronicle.com/distance/
This site, maintained by *The Chronicle of Higher Education*, provides daily updates, articles, and resources concerning distance education.

34. Distance Learning on the Net
    http://www.hoyle.com/distance.htm
Distance learning and education is the subject of this home page. Included are descriptions of distance education Web sites along with links that lead to further distance learning and education resources on the Net.

35. Yahoo! Distance Learning Site Listings
    http://dir.yahoo.com/Education/Distance_Learning/
Yahoo! lists a few dozen sites that contain important information and resources concerning distance education. You may also select from a number of catagories, including Course Online, Online Teaching and Learning, Adult and Continuing Education, and Colleges and Universites.

We highly recommend that you review our Web site for expanded information and our other product lines. We are continually updating and adding links to our Web site in order to offer you the most usable and useful information that will support and expand the value of your Annual Editions. You can reach us at: *http://www.dushkin.com/annualeditions/*.

www.dushkin.com/online/

Unit Selections

1. **Lamar Alexander: A Transformative Power,** Stefanie Sanford
2. **High-Tech Teaching,** Felicia E. Halpert
3. **Technology & Literacy: Raising the Bar,** Decker Walker
4. **Early Childhood Classrooms in the 21st Century: Using Computers to Maximize Learning,** Susan W. Haugland
5. **What Students Want to Learn About Computers,** Judith O'Donnell Dooling
6. **Technology Use in Tomorrow's Schools,** Barbara Means

Key Points to Consider

❖ How will instructional technology change the way we learn? Why?

❖ What effect will the Internet/Intranet have on schools and learning? At what levels?

❖ What is the greatest obstacle to proper use of technology in the classroom?

❖ How would you use technology in a distance learning environment?

❖ What steps can we take, when integrating computers into the learning place, to maximize children's learning?

 **Links** | **www.dushkin.com/online/**

1. **Agency for International Technology**
   http://www.ait.net
2. **Goals 2000**
   http://www.ed.gov/pubs/goals/progrpt/index.html
3. **History of Computers in Education**
   http://www.csulb.edu/~murdock/histofcs.html

These sites are annotated on pages 4 and 5.

Today, electronic technology is used widely at home, in the workplace, and in the schools. The ubiquitous presence of technology available to the next generation will markedly raise educational expectations. Students and teachers have increasing access to almost limitless amounts of information on the World Wide Web. The onrush of new telecommunication applications is forcing educators to adopt and utilize these new technologies and to measure their impact on learning in both classroom and distance-based learning environments. The Internet, PowerPoint, and online management tools such as WebCT and Blackboard are at the center of in-class and distance learning environments. These mainstream technologies combined with student demands for new technology-based instructional delivery are transforming schools and colleges and the way students of all ages learn. Teachers are improving their efficiency in utilizing alternate delivery systems that are designed to meet the needs of students in the classroom or those who wish to learn in either a synchronous or asynchronous mode.

The articles selected for this unit track the concerns and dreams of educational leaders who have come face to face with the promises and problems connected with the current and future implementation of instructional technology into the mainstream curriculum.

In the unit's first article, Stefanie Sanford provides an interview that pictures Lamar Alexander as a thoughtful leader in the education field for over the past quarter of a century. In this interview he speaks passionately about the role of education and opportunities that can be brought to institutions by bringing choice and technology into our nation's school systems.

In the next article, "High-Tech Teaching," Felicia Halpert presents a scenario of how children learn when they are in charge of finding the information they need on the Internet. She points out that they try much harder, spend more time, and outperform those who try to learn without using computers. Her conclusion is that students feel in control and are taking responsibility for their own learning.

In the following article, "Technology & Literacy: Raising the Bar," Decker Walker discusses how the ubiquitous presence of technology available to the next generation will markedly raise educational expectations. Walker believes information technology will influence society and education as much as print technology has, and the effect won't take hundreds of years to appear. Susan Haugland believes that *how* computers are used with young children is more important than if computers are used at all. She provides four steps required to integrate computers into the learning place in order to maximize children's learning. She provides a "how to" for using computers to empower young children and enhance their learning experience.

The next article "What Students Want to Learn About Computers" encompasses a review of a survey of students, parents, and administrators. The author discusses their wants and needs. Key to satisfying the wants is the ability of educators to integrate technology into the curriculum as a tool for teaching and learning. The author also points out the importance of the redefinition of the role of the teacher. In the next article, "What Students Want to Learn About Computers," Judith O'Donnell Dooling describes the chemistry of how to blend technology, teaching, and learning.

Finally, Barbara Means discusses how students and teachers have increasing access to almost limitless amounts of information on the World Wide Web. In "Technology Use in Tomorrow's Schools," she provides a panorama of how educational use of the computer has grown from the 1980s into this century. She points out that we still fall short of providing a seamless, convenient, robust, and reliable technology support structure for all students and teachers.

LAMARALEXANDER:
A TRANSFORMATIVE POWER

BY STEFANIE SANFORD

LAMAR ALEXANDER has been a thought leader in the education field for over a quarter of a century. From growing up as the child of two educators, to serving as governor of Tennessee for two terms and chairing a path-breaking educational policy effort at the National Governor's Association prior to back-to-back runs for the presidency in 1996 and 2000, quality education has been the passion of this Renaissance man. He focused on K-12 improvements as U.S. secretary of education and served as president of the University of Tennessee. Alexander currently serves as founder and chairman of the board of Simplexis, an educational technology company that helps streamline administrative buying processes in K-12 institutions. He speaks passionately about the role of education and opportunities that can be brought to institutions by bringing choice and technology into our nation's school systems.

Q: **What is your vision for the role of technology in education?**

Judy Breck, who works for big chalk.com, is writing a book where she uses a wonderful metaphor for what technology means for education today. The elite families of England used to send their children on a grand tour of Europe, knowing that the most important thing they could do as parents was help their children acquire as much knowledge as possible. That's true of all civilizations. Philip of Macedonia hired Aristotle to teach his son. But now, because of technology, knowledge like that is available to everyone—to every child. You don't have to have Philip of Macedonia as

From *Converge Magazine*, March 2001, pp. 24, 26, 28. © 2001 by Converge Magazine. Reprinted by permission.

a father or Aristotle as a teacher to have the knowledge of the world open to you. The business of organized education is to help children acquire as much knowledge as they can, and perhaps more importantly, develop a love for acquiring knowledge.

Q: There is considerable talk in some venues about technology's capacity to "transform" classroom education— even transcending our old notions of "classroom instruction." How do you see these tools affecting the educational experience?

Technology does have transformative power, primarily because it is a change or educational reform without much controversy. We've worked for 20 years for other kinds of reforms: charter schools, school choice, longer school days and a longer school year. All of these proposals run into massive resistance from teacher unions and busy parents. Many parents think that the education they had is good enough for their children, so they are nervous about big changes to the old ways of doing things. But technology slips in under the door and through the window and doesn't threaten teachers and principals. Instead, these tools empower them and put them in charge.

Look at technology in schools compared to other educational reform efforts. In all of our efforts in injecting choice into K-12, even having both presidential candidates fight over who is more supportive of charter schools—and yet we only have about 200 nationwide. Education technology is relatively new on the scene, and we've just about wired all the schools in the nation.

But really, there are a couple of transformations. The first is the access to a world of knowledge. The second is that technology tools make school structure easier to change, and can result in efficiencies that will yield more money to be spent on teaching and learning. For example, the Simplexis idea is based on the reality that about 15 percent of all school dollars are spent on buying things—probably $70 billion per year goes to things other than teachers and instruction. It goes to buy things like erasers, school buses and biology class frogs. If you can show a 10 percent cost savings in these purchases, that is a significant amount of extra money to go to a school's core mission—the classroom.

Q: You have a long and impressive career working on education at all levels. In my lifetime, there seems to have always been a "crisis" in education. Do you agree? What is the crisis? Is it the same as it was 10, 20 or 30 years ago? Do these difficulties change over time?

I do think there has always been a crisis—at least people have always thought so. My father ran for school board right after World War II because he

thought our district in Maryville, Tenn., was in crisis and needed new leadership. He and a slate of new people ran, won and brought in a new superintendent. That was 50 years ago. But that crisis is a little different than the one today. Today, the world is changing quickly, and the definition of what we need to know is a lot higher. Now, if you are working in the Saturn plant in Tennessee, there is no blue-collar job there anymore. To work there, you need to know algebra and statistics, and how to communicate in a sophisticated way. Simply, to live in our world, you need to know a lot more than you used to. Suddenly, the standards are higher, and the institutions we use to help children learn are changing more slowly than other institutions in our economy. The Army has changed. Hospitals have changed. Road-building, the stock market, everything has changed, but schools have stayed the same. That means that the primary educational crisis is a political one of not changing our schools so that teachers and students can meet these standards.

"All education takes is good teachers, involved parents and a good environment."

Q: Do you see the private sector as the primary engine of innovation and improvement in education? Do you see an appropriate federal/state government role in education/technology?

The role of the private sector should empower teachers and principals and create an environment where they can do their jobs. All education takes is good teachers, involved parents and a good environment. The private sector helps create a good environment. For example, if Simplexis can help a school official buy buses, frogs and equipment faster and more cheaply, then the private sector is doing their part. If a company like bigchalk.com can provide a lesson plan that helps a teacher run a better classroom, then they have done their part. A company like Co-nect can work with a Memphis school district to help teachers integrate technology into their classroom instruction. The Edison project can help principals and school boards manage schools better. All of these companies are trying to create products that will let education professionals do their jobs better.

As for government, the state and local governments' roles are pretty straightforward: setting high standards; attracting and keeping the best teachers; and paying the bills. The federal government's job is to provide as much money as it can with as little control as possible. That sounds hard, but that is essentially what they have been doing in the technology area. Through E-rate and other technology funds, the federal government has put between $4 and 5 billion into helping schools equip themselves and connect to the Net. And they are doing that with a minimum amount of control and regulation.

In addition to that commitment to technology funding, the federal government should also do for K-12 what they have done in higher education—provide scholarship money to minority and low-income students to attend the school of their choice—like a GI bill for kids. Young people have been using Department of Education loans and grants to go to NYU or Notre Dame, but for some reason, some can't stand the notion that a young kid might use federal funds to go to a Catholic high school. If we did that in K-12, we would animate the competition among schools to draw students and provide opportunity for a better education for those at the lower end of the economic ladder. For 50 years, we have poured lots of federal dollars into higher education through direct financial aid. We should do the same for K-12.

Q: What are your most vivid memories of your own education? The most influential teacher you ever had?

That's easy. There are two. First, my piano teacher and second, my senior English teacher who made me stand up in front of the class and write the word "just" 1,000 times. "Just" is a colloquialism of my area, and she said, "If you grow up saying 'just' all the time, you'll never amount to anything!"

STEFANIE SANFORD (*stefanie.sanford@bus.utexas.edu*) IS A CONSULTANT AND FREELANCE WRITER BASED IN AUSTIN, TEXAS. SHE HOLDS AN M.P.A. FROM THE KENNEDY SCHOOL OF GOVERNMENT AT HARVARD UNIVERSITY.

High-Tech Teaching

Studies show that kids who use computers in class come out ahead. Here's how to make sure your child's school is teaching him what he needs to know.

BY FELICIA E. HALPERT

Michael Meharg's fifth-grade students have shared weather data with first-graders in Australia and written poems with eighth-graders in Israel. They've received information about the north pole from a team dog-sledding across the Arctic and collaborated with children around the world to write and publish a book. And thanks to a computer, the Internet, and their teacher's passion for technology, they did all this without ever leaving their school in rural Alpena, Michigan.

Thousands of American schools are incorporating computers into the classroom. According to the National Center for Education Statistics, the percentage of U.S. public schools with Internet access skyrocketed from 35 percent in 1994 to 78 percent in 1997. Although critics say that U.S. investment in educational technology has been both too costly and too rapid—the Department of Education spent nearly $600 million on it in 1998 alone—Linda Roberts, the director of the department's Office of Educational Technology, says the investment has clearly benefited students. "In district after district, we've found that students spend more time reading, writing, and problem solving when technology is involved," she says.

In fact, a 1997 report issued by the President's Committee of Advisors on Science and Technology found that students who used computers in class outperformed those taught without them by anywhere from 25 to 41 percent.

Why does technology boost academic performance? No one has pinpointed the exact reasons, but teachers say that students are consistently more enthusiastic if a project involves working on the computer. "When kids are

Logging on to Learn

- For an ecology project, Jane Hager's fourth-grade class, in Waukegan, Illinois, used the Web to find up-to-the-minute statistics on the status of certain endangered animals and even tracked the recovery of animals affected by the Exxon Valdez oil spill.
- Michael Meharg's students, in Alpena, Michigan, asked kids in schools around the world to vote on the most popular school lunch and compiled the data they collected into a graph.
- In a nationwide elementary-school project, students wrote down signs of spring in their area and e-mailed their observations to a central site. Then they compared their data with reports from schools in other areas. "They learned that spring moves from south to north in a much more graphic way than they would have learned from a textbook," says Gail Lovely, a technology and learning consultant in Los Angeles.

- Libby Adams, a computer-resource teacher in Kansas City, Missouri, recently helped a third-grade class use a multimedia program to create a slide show on African Americans in sports. She also helped first-graders use multimedia and word-processing software to write their own "counting book" for math class.

in charge of finding the information they need on the Internet, it's amazing how much harder they try," says Libby Adams, a computer-resource teacher at Troost Academy, an elementary school in Kansas City, Missouri. "I think it's because they feel in control and are taking responsibility for their own learning—plus, it's just plain fun."

Clearly, technology is here to stay, and more than likely, your child's school has already incorporated it into the classroom to some degree: A recent Gallup poll showed that 99 percent of today's kids have used a personal computer, most often at school. But there's a lot more to a good technology program than a few computers. Here are

From *Parents,* March 1999, pp. 105-106. © 1999 by Felicia E. Halpert. Reprinted by permission.

some ways to evaluate whether your child's school is headed in the right direction:

•Where are the computers located?

Ideally, they should be in each classroom, where they'll become integrated into the daily learning environment. If your child's school can't wire every room, the next-best thing is to have a centralized "computer room" instead.

•How are students using their computer time?

"Technology should not take time away from learning the basics; it should enhance the existing curriculum," says Roberts, of the Department of Education. For example, when Libby Adams' third-grade class was working on a project about communities, the students used software to create maps of their own neighborhoods.

Projects like this work within an existing lesson plan but add a dimension of immediacy that textbooks can't provide. "Technology in the classroom is at its best when it allows students to create something, do their own research, or interact with people, regardless of distance," says Gail Lovely, a technology and learning consultant in Los Angeles. Conversely, she says, "skill-drill" programs that boost reading and math are fine for at-home use but are not an optimal use of school time, since they don't encourage collaborative learning.

•Are the teachers computer-savvy, and do they have technical support?

Training teachers to use the technology is key. "Despite all the investment in buying computers," says Roberts, "too few resources are provided for professional development." Teachers have to do a great deal more than surf the Web. "It takes a lot of planning to keep all the kids busy with meaningful activities related to the lesson when only three of them at a time are actually using the computer," says Lovely. Most teachers don't have the expertise or time to find the best online projects, Websites, and software,

and if they don't have help, the computers may not be used effectively.

Ideally, your child's school should have a media specialist to provide this support, but many schools can't afford one. The next-best thing, according to Lovely, is for several schools to share a specialist. "If that's not possible either, I recommend that schools train a few of their own teachers," she says. Once the trainees tell their fellow teachers about the possibilities, enthusiasm will grow.

•Is your child's school taking advantage of grants?

The price tag for computers, software, staff training, Internet access, and wiring can quickly add up. Fortunately, a lot of that money is available from the government and private businesses. The E-Rate, a 1996 national initiative to make Internet access affordable for schools and libraries, has already given out "technology discounts" worth more than $1 billion. Some districts hire technology directors to oversee the equipment and apply for such grants. For most schools, though, a grant writer is a luxury they can't afford, so they rely on interested teachers and parents instead.

In the end, whether your child learns at home or in school, writing, researching, and communicating on

How Parents Can Get Involved

You can help boost the computer program in your child's school, even if you don't know a URL from a megabyte. Here's how:

- **Join the club.** Many schools have technology committees, which often welcome parents' input. The committee may decide which grades to target for computer-aided learning, what kinds of projects the kids should focus on, or which grants to apply for.

- **Make a donation.** If you work for a technology-oriented company, or if your office is getting new computers, ask about the possibility of giving equipment or software to your child's school.

- **Follow up with your child at home.** If you have a family computer, encourage her to play skill-building or educational games, which are not only fun but will also challenge her to think, calculate, and solve logic problems.

the computer are skills that will benefit him far down the road. "The world our kids inherit is going to be very different from ours," says Lovely. "And you can bet that computers will have an even bigger role in it than they do now."

Felicia E. Halpert is executive editor of Scholastic Network, an Internet curriculum for kindergarten through eighth grade.

Technology & Literacy:
Raising the Bar

Future generations will value the ability to use information technology as highly as we value the abilities to read and write today.

Decker Walker

Widespread use of information technology will markedly raise educational expectations. Today, we believe that all educated people should read and write well, but this expectation is only about 200 years old. Before the development of the printing press, mass production, mechanization, and industrialization that made cheap printed material possible, expectations for literacy were much lower. Widespread literacy was unthinkable.

Information technology will influence society and education as much as print technology has, and the effect won't take hundreds of years to appear. Already, information technology is transforming the workplace. Within one generation—30 years—our ideas of what every educated person should be able to do will change drastically, too. A few of today's educational expectations may fall by the wayside, but for the most part, we will add the new expectations to the old ones. This heightened public expectation will raise the bar for literacy.

Information technology will soon be as readily available as paper and pencil. Many people worry what will

> Information technology will influence society and education as much as print technology has.

happen when students don't have a calculator, but nobody worries what will happen when they don't have a pencil and paper. The technologies of print are so ubiquitous that depending on them doesn't worry us. It will be the same with calculators and word processors. To understand technology's impact, we must imagine a world in which everyone can get calculators, word processors, and video cameras as easily as they get pencils, paper, and books today. I believe that such a world will arrive within a generation.

New Tools, Expanded Capabilities

Many people find it hard to believe that information technology will be as intuitive and easy to use as paper and pencil. Today's computers are so difficult to learn and to use that only professionals find it worthwhile to spend hundreds of hours mastering them. Will everybody take the time? Let's not forget that pencils and paper are easy to use only because we have spent hours learning and practicing in school! Learning to use a word processor is not more difficult than learning to write by hand. But even if learning to create electronically takes more time, the results are worth the trouble because the things we create with information technology are much more useful than their print counterparts.

Say you write a story with a pencil. Want to send it to Aunt Margaret in Poughkeepsie? You need an envelope, a stamp, and several days. Want to enlarge the letters so that Aunt Margaret can read them? Either you write it all again or you need a fancy copy machine. Want to send it to all your relatives? You need a copier and lots of envelopes and stamps. Change your mind and want to rewrite? You'll have to start over again. When you write electronically, you can do all these things and many more in sec-

From *Educational Leadership,* October 1999, pp. 18-21. © 1999 by the Association for Supervision and Curriculum Development. Reprinted by permission.

onds at almost no cost. Similar conclusions apply to numbers that we calculate by hand versus with a spreadsheet, to drawings or diagrams, even to sounds we make acoustically versus digitally. Creating something in a digital electronic representation gives a result that is more easily stored, copied, shared, revised, and combined with other things. Hence, the electronic form and the ability to create it will be more highly valued and thus worthwhile to learn.

Many people find it hard to accept that using technology will challenge students more. They believe that technology, by making things easier and doing things automatically, will reduce demands on students and lead to less effort and thought. For instance, spell checkers will ruin students' spelling. Perhaps they will, though it's also possible that immediate correction may make students even better spellers. Still, even when using technology reduces skills that have been automated, it also enables people to do new and more challenging things. Getting good at revising when one writes with a word processor is a greater challenge than becoming a better speller. Some people will want to do the new things that the technology enables them to do because these abilities will bring extra value to their lives. When other people recognize this extra value, they will want it for themselves. And when nearly everybody does these more powerful things, the public will expect all educated people to do them.

New Expectations

In the next generation, Americans will expect educated people to

- Use several symbol systems;
- Apply knowledge in life;
- Think strategically;
- Manage information; and
- Learn, think, and create as part of a team.

Educational innovators have advocated these criteria as general expectations for all educated people in past generations, but in the next generation, most people will need them to live satisfactory lives. Here's why.

Using symbol systems. Today, a basic, worldwide expectation is that educated people should be able to read and write in a common language. In the next generation, educated people will be expected to master several symbol systems.

Using information technology, everyone will be able to send and receive messages in visual and graphic forms, such as drawings, photographs, and diagrams. Everyone will be able to send and receive messages by using logical, mathematical, and scientific notations, such as graphs, charts, tables, equations, and computer languages. Everyone will be able to send and receive messages that make sophisticated use of sounds—voices, background music, sound effects—as well as movement—animation, films—and, ultimately, programmed interactions—today's computer games.

Now that sending and receiving these messages are as easy as e-mail, educated people need to be competent producers and critical consumers of messages expressed in these symbol systems. Computer programs already give teachers and students the tools for composing interactive multimedia messages that include video, active tables made with spreadsheets, graphs generated automatically from tables of data, and much more. Many new curriculums emphasize the ability to go back and forth between different representations of the same situations. We can trace much of the widespread enthusiasm for multisensory education and multiple intelligences to a dawning awareness of the multimedia expressive possibilities of information technology.

Applying knowledge. Past generations expected educated people to show what they knew by repeating what they had learned. The problem has always been that merely repeating what we've learned is much easier than using that knowledge to solve an unfamiliar problem. Alfred North Whitehead called this *inert knowledge,* and in the United States, in particular, inert knowledge gets no respect. Colonials made fun of the inept schoolmaster Ichabod Crane. The bombastic orator spouting high-sounding, empty words is a stock character in U.S. literature, famously caricatured in *Huckleberry Finn* and gently chided in *The Wizard of Oz.*

In past generations, school and society were unable to provide the material means and guidance that students needed to learn to apply their knowledge flexibly to a range of concrete situations. It was all educators could do to provide a book and a chalkboard and to teach verbal lessons. With information technology, students learning about the growth of cities, say, can manage the growth of a simulated city. Students learning about genetics can apply their knowledge in computer programs that simulate breeding.

The next generation will need educated persons who can do more than talk about such subjects. The person who understands the world but cannot use that understanding to reshape it is at a disadvantage. Educated people will be expected to creatively use what they know; to express themselves; to design, build, and invent.

Thinking strategically. Fundamental to using knowledge in life is using strategic thinking. Today, as in past generations, educators sometimes assign problems that require students to apply their learning to a new situation, but problem solving is seldom sufficient to enable students to use their knowledge flexibly and creatively in real-life situations. In life, problems don't appear already formulated. Finding the problems is the first challenge. Once we've found them, real-life problems are usually much more complicated than textbook problems. Seldom will a few steps lead to the solution. Instead, they require a strategy, a broad plan of attack that envisions many steps in sequence. We may need to break down each step in turn into further steps.

Tackling such problems seems unrealistic when students must approach them with only their wits and pencil and paper. Our compromise has been to let students learn to solve neat little problems in school and then work up to complicated problems in college and on the job. But age 18 is a little late to begin developing the resourcefulness and the strategic-thinking skills needed for tackling really complex problems, and 12 years of solving neatly formulated problems is not good preparation.

Today, students and teachers can use information technology to scaffold work on complex, authentic problems. Students collaborate with their peers and with adult scientists to collect and analyze data on such problems as acid rain, stream pollution, and indoor air pollution.

In the next generation, educated people will be expected to tackle big, authentic problems and use their knowledge to plan and carry out solutions. When anyone can use powerful tools to solve little problems, the ability to think strategically becomes important. Strategic thinking requires finding the little problems hidden in the messy big ones, formulating those problems, developing a plan of attack, and selecting and sequencing the neat little problems so that taken together, they solve the big messy one. Strategic thinking also requires taking stock of goals, resources, and knowledge; moving confidently between the details of a problem and the broad plan of action; and explaining what and why every step of the way.

Managing information. In past generations, educators struggled to transmit the culture and to give students the power to learn by reading. Just providing books, libraries, teachers, and school buildings stretched resources to the limit. Today, students in the most remote hamlet can find lifetimes of knowledge online. The abilities to read and to acquire knowledge are now not enough. People must determine what they really need to know and check whether they already know it in some way that they do not immediately recognize. If not, they must find out what relevant knowledge is out there, where it is, how long it will take to acquire it,

Today, students in the most remote hamlet can find lifetimes of knowledge online.

and how difficult acquiring it will be. Having located the needed pieces of knowledge, the educated person of the next generation will have to validate and apply them. This is what we mean by managing information.

Today, many teachers coach students in using the bibliographic resources available over the Internet and the World Wide Web. Increasing numbers of high school students are participating in research and action projects that involve them in the knowledge-management problems of professionals. In the next generation, all educated people will be competent researchers and knowledge managers, keeping track of what they know and don't know and finding ways to learn what they need.

Learning, thinking, and creating together. In past generations, teachers worked hard on self-management skills. They trained students in self-control and self-discipline—to behave politely, obey rules, manage time, meet deadlines. The next generation will also need social and organizational skills. The more challenging and rewarding tasks in an information age will be too big and too complex for a single person to do, no matter how talented and well disciplined. No single person can design a computer or build a plane or make a movie. Big, complex jobs require lots of people with varied skills and knowledge, and mobilizing and coordinating these people require social and organizational skills.

In the next generation, people will use technology to support teamwork and collaboration at a distance. Students and teachers will work in distributed teams, coordinating their

work and following long-term plans. Already, bold experiments in project-based learning foster productive collaborative work in classrooms.

Raising the Bar: What Does It Mean for Educators?

Educational systems are hard-pressed to meet today's expectations, so raising the bar so far in one generation will put enormous pressure on an already troubled institution. We don't need a crystal ball to see that we're in for rough times. Educators will be caught between rising educational expectations and strong opposition to both the information society and its educational imperatives.

Opponents will vigorously resist pressures to use more technology. Traditionalists will demand more attention to common knowledge, basic skills, and print literacy. Critics of technology will urge more attention to goals beyond symbols, such as direct experience, feelings, intuition, human relationships, and humanitarian or spiritual concerns. Both visions will compete vigorously with the new expectations. We can expect some wild fights.

Students who are struggling with and failing to meet today's expectations—disproportionately poor, minority, and at-risk students—will face an even tougher challenge. Teachers—who may be the first in their families to attend college, who studied for years to master the technologies of print, and who taught for years in overcrowded and poorly equipped schools—will hear the next generation say that their skills no longer qualify them as fully educated people. School systems whose leaders have toiled for years to bring all students up to high standards will hear from the next generation that these standards are not high enough.

It's highly doubtful that more effort and resources alone will enable schools to meet the new expectations. New approaches will also be needed. The new expectations themselves point to possible new directions. Students should be more motivated to work on authentic problems, and most students will welcome the chance to assume more responsibility for their learning, to work in teams, and to assemble portfolios of their work. Thus, students' talents and energies can play a bigger role in their schooling and propel them to new heights of achievement. Students can also support one another. Peer tutoring is an effective technique, and more can surely be done to help students learn from one another.

Also, the technology that created the problem can help solve it. For instance, technologies that support translation from one symbol system to another should help students leverage knowing some symbol systems into learning others. Telecommunications will allow scientists and other professionals to supplement and support teachers. The technologies of collaboration allow new forms of advisement. Each child could have a team of advisors, including the child's parents and teachers and other consultants who know the child. Using collaboration tools, the team could coordinate its work and advise and monitor the child's learning more effectively. Electronic portfolios of student work might make up for the fact that today's tests do not measure students' ability to use dynamic symbol systems; apply knowledge in life; think strategically; manage information; and learn, think, and create with other students.

Although the new expectations generated by an increasingly technological society pose many challenges, they also provide many opportunities. The next generation should be an exciting time to work in education!

Decker Walker is a Professor at Stanford University, School of Education, 485 Lasuen Hall, Stanford, CA 94305–3096 (e-mail: decker@Stanford.stanford.edu).

Early Childhood Classrooms in the 21st Century: Using Computers to Maximize Learning

Susan W. Haugland

The twenty-first century has arrived! Every parent, teacher, and administrator faces new opportunities and challenges. More young children than ever before are in child care—many for as long as 10 hours a day. And school-age children are often in programs before and after school. One of the biggest issues facing our country is caring for and educating these young children who spend so much of their day with us.

The new century finds electronic technology used widely at home and in the workplace. Computers are also finding their way into more and more schools. And so they should. To become productive adults in an increasingly computer-oriented society, children should have the opportunity to become comfortable with computers early in their lives.

Because young children spend so much of their day in child care and school, the early childhood classroom is an excellent place for children to begin using computers. Through children's early exposure, computer use can become second nature.

When used effectively, computers make an excellent learning tool, imparting to children knowledge and skills far beyond expectation. With computers children become deeply engaged in the learning process; they beg to learn. The challenge to teachers in the new century is to find ways to use electronic technology as an exciting tool that sparks the learning process.

Using computers to facilitate learning

Many of my colleagues and I have discovered that, as with any learning resource, *how* computers are used with your children is more important than *if* computers are used at all (Haugland 1998; O'Riordan 1999; Papert 1999). Integrating computers into classrooms may make a significant difference in children's developmental gains or it may have no effect at all or actually reduce children's creativity (Haugland 1992). Computers clearly have a powerful influence on children, and thus how we use them is especially important. To integrate computers and maximize children's learning, four steps are critical: selecting developmental software, selecting developmental Websites, integrating these resources into the curriculum, and selecting computers to support these learning experiences.

Selecting developmentally appropriate software

NAEYC's "Position Statement on Technology and Young Children—

Ages Three through Eight" (1996) indicates, "Market researchers tracking software trends have identified that the largest software growth recently has been in new titles and companies serving the early childhood educational market" (p. 11). Indeed there is a tremendous array of software choices. It is easy to become distracted by glitzy packaging and promises from manufacturers, losing sight of what is truly important: providing children with a sound educational tool for learning.

Using the Haugland Developmental Software Scale (1997a), I have identified more developmental software to date than any classroom or child could ever utilize. However, it represents only 25% of the software evaluated. The challenge is finding these gems among the vast quantity of software on the market.

Teachers, administrators, and parents have two options for selecting developmentally appropriate software. First, they can utilize the Haugland scale to evaluate software themselves. Specific instructions for administering the scale are outlined step-by-step in *Young Children and Technology: A World of Discovery* (Haugland & Wright 1997).

Most educators and parents prefer not to evaluate software themselves. *Young Children and Technology* and the Website Children and Computers (http://childrenandcomputers.

From *Young Children,* January 2000, pp. 12-18. © 2000 by the National Association for the Education of Young Children. Reprinted by permission.

com) provide descriptions, scores, publishers, and prices of developmental software. The Website also lists the Developmental Software and Web Site Awards for the previous three years by curriculum area. (Websites were added this year.) In addition, the Website features bimonthly four reviews of the latest developmental software and children's Websites.

A valuable goal for a school's computer study group is to use the Haugland Developmental Software Scale (1997a) to review all classroom software for its developmental appropriateness. Teachers must be involved in the process and understand why such a review is important. After the review has been completed, the study group can provide to all teachers a list of the inappropriate software to be removed from the school. Teachers with objections should have an opportunity to discuss how the software is used in their classrooms and why they believe it to be developmentally appropriate. Then the group can discard the nondevelopmental software.

Selecting developmental Websites

Many rich educational opportunities await children on the Internet, and its potential is primarily untapped. While the Internet has been researched less extensively than software (due to its more recent development), it provides children with a variety of learning opportunities that appear to enhance problem solving, critical thinking skills, decision-making, creativity, language skills, knowledge, research skills, the ability to integrate information, social skills, and self-esteem.

The sheer volume of Internet sites is overwhelming. Also, they have not been screened by anyone. Some sites are developmentally appropriate, while others are simply terrible. The Haugland/Gerzog Developmental Scale for Web Sites (1998) is a tool for evaluating the appropri-

ateness of Websites before exposing young children to them. The scale is scored in the same manner as the software scale. The Children and Computers Website also includes a listing of a variety of developmental appropriate Websites for children.

There are four types of children's Websites: information, communication, interaction, and publication.

Information sites

Enhanced with sound and videos, information sites are rich reference resources that teachers and parents can use to model or assist children in answering questions, making new discoveries, and building knowledge. For example, a virtual trip to the zoo gives children opportunities to see pictures, hear animal sounds, and view movies of animals exploring their natural habitats. The National Zoo (http://www.si.edu/natzoo/) from the Smithsonian Institute is such a Website. A virtual tour of a dinosaur museum (http://www.wf.carleton.ca/Museum/7.html) is another possibility. In another, a classroom in Miami, Florida, took an online tour of Italy to learn more about the children's electronic pen pals from Rome.

Communication sites

At communication sites children interact with friends, relatives, or classrooms across the street, in another city, or even across the globe. Using simple e-mail addresses, children and classroom groups write letters, compose stories, create poems, or work on a class project such as a virtual monster. At the virtual monster Website (http://www.2cyberlinks.com/monster.html), four classrooms provide descriptions of one physical feature each of a creature. Then they draw their monsters—composites of the four features—and compare the results! Afterward some of the classrooms continue to learn cooperatively, ex-

ploring other topics such as weather patterns, summaries of their favorite stories, and so on.

Also through e-mail children can ask "experts" questions in various disciplines. Two examples are Ask Dr. Math (http://forum.swarthmore.edu/dr.math/) and Ask an Astronaut (http://www.nss.org/askastro/home.html). These provide classrooms not only with the answers to questions, but also with the opportunity to explore a variety of occupations.

Interaction sites

Interaction sites are similar to software programs, using sound, animation, sound effects, and high-quality, realistic graphics. Unfortunately they sometimes run slowly. The Internet, however, is improving. Edmark's Kid Desk: Internet Safe (1998) provides descriptions of sites for children three to eight years of age. A tremendous variety of Internet sites are arranged by topic. As you explore them you will find some to be more developmentally appropriate than others.

Publication sites

The Internet can be used as a resource for actually publishing children's work. Even three-year-olds can understand that when their work is displayed on the Internet everyone in the world can see it. Imagine their pride! Motivation for learning is sparked as they create new pictures and stories. There are a number of Websites that post children's work, such as KidPub (http://www.kidpub.org/kidpub/).

Connecting software and Websites to the curriculum

For computers to have an impact on children's learning and for teachers to tap into the rich benefits, computer activities need to mesh with children's educational goals. Only when computers are integrated into the curriculum do children demonstrate gains in conceptual understanding, develop abstract thinking, increase verbal skills, and have gains in problem solving (Haugland 1992). When teachers begin to view computers as valuable teaching tools, children become excited about learning, and computer activities begin to replace traditional curricular units or activities. Computers then free the teacher to engage with children in hands-on learning.

An effective approach. How do teachers connect children's learning at the computer to their overall curriculum? Teachers can accomplish this most easily by selecting software or Websites that match their learning objectives for the year. To begin, they may decide to focus on one curricular area such as language, math, or social studies and select several software programs or Websites that facilitate their objectives. This process of slowly integrating computers into classrooms is manageable for teachers and takes into account that resources may be limited.

Worst-case scenario. Contrast this approach with the logical steps one school followed to integrate computers. This school (kindergarten through eighth grade) began by hiring a technology specialist who, working with others, developed a technology plan. Training seminars were provided on simple computer operation, connecting to the Internet, Microsoft Word, and Kid Pix Studio. Then two computers were purchased for every classroom and a technology lab was created, equipped with 14 learning stations and a state-of-the-art projection system.

Parents were clearly impressed with all of this new equipment!

I visited the school to see how the computers were being used. Fifty percent of the classrooms were not using the computers, and most of the children hated using the high-tech lab room. How could this be? What had gone wrong?

A World of Caution

While the potential of the Internet is tremendous, some precautions need to be addressed. Anyone can place anything on the Internet, some of which may be very harmful to young children. A screening device is essential, such as Kid Desk: Internet Safe (1998), Net Nanny (http://www.netnanny.com), or Cyber Patrol (http://www.cyberpatrol.com).

It is critical that children understand they cannot share any personal information such as their last name, address, phone number, or parents' names for their own safety. I feel most comfortable if children use a pen name when on the Internet—the name of their dog, cat, or favorite stuffed animal.

Half of the teachers could not see how the software connected to their curriculum. My guess is that they viewed it as play rather than learning. Also, when software was not being used in the computer lab, teachers could not use it in their classrooms without the approval of the technology specialist. This took the responsibility and the control from the teachers because computers and software had clearly become the job of the technology specialist.

Why did children not respond more positively to the lab? Children indicated, "It is so boring." How could that be?

First, two-thirds of the software were drill and practice, nondevelopmental programs. Second, children were not allowed to explore and discover the software. Instead they were told to follow step-by-step what the technology specialist did, which was projected on the screen. In addition, children were asked to focus on their own computers and not interact with others. This clearly was not a community of learners!

Despite all the money this school had invested, it had a long road ahead before computers would become a valuable learning tool. The disappointing results at this school emphasize the essential role teachers must play in integrating technology into the curriculum so that computers can have a significant impact on children's learning.

Selecting computers

Vast changes have occurred in computers. From Apple IIs and IBM 286s, we have forged ahead to Power Macs and Pentiums, all with GBs of ROM (read-only memory permanently stored on the computer) running faster than ever. And we use CDs (compact disks) as opposed to diskettes. CDs hold huge quantities of information and programming. These changes in computers have enabled software and the Internet to function in ways that we never dreamed possible.

These dramatic changes present challenges to teachers, parents, and administrators as they select computers. New, high-quality software frequently cannot run on older machines. Thus, when selecting computers try to anticipate your computer needs for the next three years. This ensures that the computers you purchase will keep pace with the curriculum. Also select computers that have the ability to be upgraded. While the price of computers is falling so rapidly that you will probably decide in the future to purchase new machines, it is still important to have that option. Ultimately, upgrading may be all you can afford.

The most frequent question I am asked about computer selection is, "Which brand of computer do you recommend?" Three factors are helpful in making this decision: software compatibility, access to maintenance and repair, and promotional sales events.

While most software is hybrid, meaning it can run on either a Macintosh or a Pentium, there is some quality software that runs only on one machine, usually the Pentium.

Integrating Computers and Four-Year-Olds

Sean, an early childhood teacher, always begins the school year by taking pictures of his four-year-olds class. This year he uses the Jam Camera (1999), a digital camera. As he takes the pictures, he displays them on two computers. Children come over to the computers frequently to talk about the pictures. Gradually the children dictate information and stories about them. The pictures and stories are displayed throughout the classroom so children can see themselves, learn about each other, and begin to develop a sense of group unity. Eventually they are transferred into a classbook.

Knowing that children's writing abilities are limited, Sean next introduces Thinking Out Loud (1998), which consists of six stories. Children sequence pictures from a story and then dictate story ideas for each page. They then go back and expand these ideas into a story, again dictating into a microphone. Finally, children select the music to accompany each picture based on faces that depict the mood of the music.

Sean has read aloud all of the six original stories to the children at group time, and now when children finish their stories they are invited to share them.

Next, additional language programs are introduced, including I Spy (1998) and Paint, Write, and Play (1996). As children become familiar with this software, related Internet sites are made available, enabling the children to publish their stories or discover more about nature, the desert, and cities, all of which are featured in these two software programs. (For specific Websites, visit http://childrenandcomputers.com.)

While Sean's strategies represent just one approach, his introduction and use of computers in the classroom is seamless, totally integrated with the daily curriculum. The number and kind of computer resources he uses will undoubtedly change, but for now this gradual approach is manageable.

Reviewing software demands is an important first step.

The ease with which computers can be maintained and repaired is key. Once, a computer in my classroom totally shut down (crashed). When I took the computer for repair, the shop discovered that, even though I was using a virus protector, the computer had 99 viruses. Without ease of repair this computer would have been out of the classroom for at least a month. With easy access to repair, it was back in the classroom in two days.

Watch for promotions and sales. The computer industry is currently very competitive. Some companies provide special promotions for schools, particularly when schools are purchasing multiple computers.

Because computer software and Internet requirements change so quickly, I am not providing a list of optimal computer specifications. They could be out of date within six months! Instead, I suggest you anticipate how you will be using computers in the next three years. Then review your requirements with several computer companies. Another option is to visit PC World at http://www.pcworld.com; this site provides basic tips on buying computers, printers, promotions, and other useful information.

Maximizing the benefits from computers

The software and Websites have been selected, teachers have planned how to integrate software into their curriculum, and the computers are up and running! To maximize the benefit computers have on children's learning, three components are important: access, availability, and parent collaboration.

Children's access to computers

Children use computers in basically two locations, school and home.

In the classroom. Nearly 64% of Americans report that they have major concerns about the fact that most schools don't have the equipment, training, or funding to effectively use computers and technology in educating children (Milken Exchange & P. D. Hart 1998, 9). "In classrooms with one or two computers, 4 in 10 teachers say they rely on [computers] to a moderate or great extent. In classrooms with six or more computers, the figure rises to 7 in 10 teachers" (O'Riordan 1999, 3). Caperton and Papert (1999, 8) project that if the country spent one dollar a day for each child in school, every child would have a computer!

Home computers and family income. Children's access currently is probably greater at home than at school (O'Neil 1995). More than 60% of all computers purchased last year went to households with kids (Family Forum 1999, 1). Eighty percent of chil-

Strategies for Facilitating Equitable Access

1. Become an advocate, stressing the importance of providing access to computers in libraries, schools, and after-school programs for children without home computers.

2. Establish a software and computer lending library enabling children to have home computer use. An important task of a study group could be securing funding.

3. Become an advocate by expressing to computer companies your disappointment in gender biases and the amount of violence included in their software. Parents' letters and calls make a difference because software publishers view the home market as crucial. Review the software young children are using to ensure that it is as appealing to girls as it is to boys.

4. Encourage children to work together in small groups on projects. Plan the composition of these groups so that boys and girls are working together on the computer toward a common goal.

Strategies for Improving Computer Availability

1. Assess every teacher's interest in integrating computers into the classroom. If teachers have little or no interest, remove the computers from their classrooms and relocate them. There is no sense in computers gathering dust when they would be used frequently in other classrooms. Assure teachers when you remove the computers that they will be returned whenever they are interested in computer integration.

2. Close labs and utilize any support staff as technology mentors to all teachers using computers in their classrooms. Move the lab computers to classrooms where teachers are using computers as an integral teaching resource.

3. Recruit mentors and interested parents to help teachers get their classrooms "computing," not only increasing the time children spend at the computer, but also meshing it with the curriculum.

4. Provide rewards for teachers who create a community of learners and use computers effectively in the classroom. Inform all the teachers at the beginning of each year as to what these rewards will be.

dren whose households earn $75,000 or more have home computers, while only 20% of children whose households earn less than $30,000 have home computers (Milken Exchange 1998, 31). This inequity of children's access to computers outside the classroom is a serious issue.

Computer use and gender.   Also of concern is gender equity. When boys and girls are four and five years old, the amount of time they spend at computers is not significantly different (Haugland 1992). Yet when children reach fourth grade, significant differences emerge: boys spend more time at computers than do girls.

Software manufacturers must carefully examine the role their products play in supporting gender differences. Males, or male voices, lead the majority of software, and themes such as spaceships are used to deliver unrelated content, both of which are more appealing to boys. To tackle this problem, see "Strategies for Facilitating Equitable Access."

Availability

An issue closely connected to accessibility is availability. Just because computers are in homes and schools does not necessarily mean children use them. Children may in reality use computers at home or school

rarely, or children may use computers whenever they desire.

Where?   A 1995 study of computers in schools found that only 35% of the computers were in teachers' classrooms (O'Neil 1995). Research indicates that placing computers in classrooms rather than in labs is more effective in learning, leading to significant gains in math, reading, and language arts (Milken Exchange 1998). Papert (1999) supports these findings, stressing that until teachers integrate computers into their curriculum, computers will not have a significant impact on the education of young children.

When?   Equally important, who decides when children use the computers? In developmentally appropriate settings children make many choices regarding when and how long they use learning resources. Computers should be no different. Some days children will spend significant quantities of time as they research a topic or create and illustrate a story. Other days they will be more interested in reading or running the ticket counter at the airport. Children's computer time ebbs and flows similarly to other learning activity times.

How?   What is important is that every child in the classroom be con-

fident with the computer and view it as a viable source for learning. When you arrange your computer center, place extra chairs at each computer. This encourages cooperative learning at the computer, and children who are hesitant about using the computer may become enticed by a friend who is doing something really exciting. The extra chairs also facilitate peer tutoring. Children seek help from others in the classroom whom they have seen using a program successfully.

For preschool and kindergarten classrooms, I recommend an initial training period during which every child is invited individually or in a small group to use the computer and explore software until he or she has used four or five programs. If children come in groups, make sure sometime during the session each child has hands-on experience. While this requires a significant investment of adult time, you will reap many benefits throughout the year.

First, it ensures that all the children in your room use the computer, including those who are hesitant or afraid they cannot possibly operate this big, adult machine. Otherwise, children using computers in your classroom may be only those children who are experienced, confident, or have a home computer.

Second, training establishes a pattern of turn taking.

Third, it encourages children to use a variety of software, not just a program they see advertised or the first program they happen to try and like.

After the initial training period, treat the computer like any other learning resource.

Provide a waiting list next to the computers where children can sign up or place their name card (if they cannot write), then proceed to other activities. When a computer is available, a waiting child is given the option to use the computer. Thus, children can spend their time learning instead of waiting.

Parent collaboration

Working closely with parents regarding home computer use is also

Strategies for Assisting Parents with Home Computer Use

1. One school e-mailed me that they had downloaded all the evaluations from the Children and Computers Website and placed them in a binder for parents to review when selecting software. *Young Children and Technology* (Haugland & Wright 1997) includes 150 reviews of developmental software, including pictures of all the programs.

2. Provide parents with a list of the software children use in the classroom. Suggest that parents explore their children's interest in using any of these programs at home. As children build skills, they become valuable classroom tutors.

3. Provide a workshop for parents using computers at home to discuss critical issues. You may find that parents want to form a support group to share resources and ideas.

important. With the explosion of software for the home market (O'Neil 1995), parents see new opportunities for educating their children. They need guidance to help them select appropriate computer experiences (Haugland 1997b). Parents will benefit from collaborating with you on selecting quality software, supervising computer experiences, monitoring computer time, and using the Internet.

Conclusion

Computers empower young children. They enable them to become totally immersed in the joys of learning. The key is *how* computers are used. Selecting developmental software and Websites is essential. As computers are connected with young children and integrated into their curriculum, the benefits to children become clear. If computer experiences are not developmentally appropriate, children would be better served with no computer access.

As children explore developmentally appropriate software and Websites, important issues emerge, such as access, availability, and parent collaboration. Our goals should be to have multiple computers in classrooms (five or more) so that children can easily access these tremendous learning tools and teachers can effectively integrate computers into their curriculum. Parent collaboration provides an important opportunity to increase computer access and provide children empowering learning experiences, at home and at school.

References

Caperton, G., & S. Papert. 1999. *Vision for education: The Caperton-Papert platform.* Available online at http://www.mamamedia.com/areas/grownups/new/education/papert_001.htm.

Family Forum. 1999. Computers in the home. Available online at http://www.parenting.qa.com/cgi-bin/detailcomputers/5203.core.tipsfact/

Haugland, S. 1992. Effects of computer software on preschool children's developmental gains. *Journal of Computing in Early Childhood* 3 (1): 15–30.

Haugland, S. 1997b. Children's home computer use: An opportunity for parent/teacher collaboration. *Early Childhood Education Journal* 25 (2): 133–35.

Haugland, S. 1997a. *The developmental scale for software.* Cape Girardeau, MO: K.I.D.S. & Computers.

Haugland, S. 1998. Children and computers [Website]. Online at http://childrenandcomputers.com

Haugland, S., & G. Gerzog. 1998. *The developmental software scale for web sites.* Cape Girardeau, MO: K.I.D.S. & Computers.

Haugland, S. W., & J. L. Wright. 1997. *Young children and technology: A world of discovery.* New York: Allyn & Bacon.

I spy [software]. 1998. New York: Scholastic Multimedia.

Jam camera [hardware]. 1999. Tulsa, OK: KB Gear Interactive.

Kid desk: Internet safe [software]. 1998. Redmond, WA: Edmark.

Milken Exchange. 1998. *West Virginia study results.* Available online at http://www.milkenexchange.org/research/wvirginia_article.html.

Milken Exchange & P. D. Hart Research Associates. 1998. Key survey findings. In *Public Opinion Poll—1998,* 2. Available online at http://www.milkenexchange.org; click on Publications.

NAEYC. 1996. Position statement on technology and young children—Ages three through eight. Washington, DC: Author.

O'Neil, J. 1995. Teachers and technology: Potentials and pitfalls. *Educational Leadership* (Annual): 10–11.

O'Riordan, K. 1999. *Report reviews current research on education technology.* Available online at http://www.milkenexchange.org/;click on Articles.

Paint, write, and play [software]. 1996. Minneapolis, MN: The Learning Company.

Papert, S. 1999. *Child power: Keys to the new learning of the digital century* (See "Education's 19th-Century Thinking in a 21st-Century World"). Available online at http://www.connectedfamily.com/

Thinking out loud [software]. 1998. Pleasantville, NY: Sunburst Communication.

Susan W. Haugland *is a professor emeritus in child development at Southeast Missouri State University. She is president of K.I.D.S. & Computers, Inc., which provides teacher training and children's computer classes, evaluates software, and publishes evaluations on a Website and in a quarterly newsletter.*

What Students Want to Learn About Computers

A survey of students, parents, and administrators suggests that they want and need new approaches to teaching and learning with computer technology.

Judith O'Donnell Dooling

On a typical morning in early spring, the computer lab at Woodbury Middle School in Woodbury, Connecticut, hums with activity. Clustered around computer work centers in pairs or small groups, 25 students are completing the 8th grade memory book. The book integrates language arts, computer technology, and videoclips.

After taking a few minutes at the beginning of the period to explain some computer technology skills that students will need to use that day, computer teacher Jeff Turner moves around the room to monitor the students' work. When students ask him questions, he usually counters with another question to encourage problem solving. Sometimes he refers students to one of the project's Famous Persons—students who have emerged as tech experts in the skills needed to complete that day's work. Famous Persons, who are sometimes students with special learning needs or who have struggled in traditional academic subjects, rotate as the need for specific expertise changes.

When the class period ends, students reluctantly close up their work. At lunchtime, however, when the computer lab is open to students, many

8th graders return to work on the memory book. Over the last few years, the computer lab has become one of the school's most active and popular spots.

Computer Technology in Schools

Student involvement with computers at Woodbury Middle School reflects the growing importance of computer technology in today's schools and classrooms. Over the last 20 years, computer technology has assumed an increasingly prominent role, and schools have gradually responded by helping children develop the computer technology skills needed in the global workplace. The Report on the Effectiveness of Technology in Schools (Software & Information Industry Association, 1999) estimated that by 1994, U.S. public and private schools, colleges and universities, and post-secondary training centers had purchased and installed 18.1 million computers. Despite this effort to acquire hardware, we have been less successful in identifying what computer skills should be taught in school and how computers can be used as a tool for teaching and learning.

Many schools are figuring out how computer technology can play a central role in teaching and learning. In addition to decisions about selecting, purchasing, and organizing computers and software, schools are wrestling with developing a computer technology curriculum, scheduling computer time, and providing professional development for teachers. With limited time and many instructional needs, fitting computer technology into the way we have traditionally conceived teaching and learning means another "add-on."

Many schools are figuring out how computer technology can play a central role in teaching and learning.

For computer technology in school to be successful, we need to change our approach. At Woodbury Middle School, for example, teachers use specific strategies for teaching and learning with and about computers. The

From *Educational Leadership*, October 2000, pp. 20-24. © 2000 by the Association for Supervision and Curriculum Development. All rights reserved. Reprinted by permission.

school was one of six that participated in a recent study I conducted for my doctoral dissertation on students' beliefs about computer technology and experiences in using computer technology (O'Donnell Dooling, 1999).

As a middle, and later an elementary, school principal, I was concerned that we effectively address all children's computer technology learning needs. Computers have entered the school curriculum largely in response to societal changes, and many children arrive at school with extensive knowledge about using computers. I also noted a gender difference in children's voluntary access to computers during open lab time. Despite existing data on gender differences in math and science, I found little research on gender differences in computer technology and I wanted data that would inform my practice.

I chose to study children in grades 4 through 7 because the research on gender differences in computer technology had focused primarily on older students. I wanted to see how and when gender differences in computer technology emerged. I looked for participants from three elementary and three middle schools that were in the same socioeconomic stratification categorized by the state department of education. One hundred and seventy-six teachers, 9 administrators, and 1,427 students (with parental permission) volunteered to participate in the study.

Some of what we learned from the study confirmed perceptions widely held by many educators. Other findings offered unexpected and helpful insights into children's and teachers' experiences with computer technology. The study also led to connections with other schools that use innovative strategies for teaching and learning with computer technology.

What Students Said

Through inventories, surveys, and handwritten technology autobiographies, the students who participated in the computer technology study provided rich and detailed descriptions of how they first learned about computers, how capable they felt about using computers, their experiences with computers in and out of school, and their expectations for future computer use. The descriptions were surprisingly consistent across grades 4 through 7 and participating schools. Among the broad conclusions of the study were the following:

Boys and girls frequently learn about computers from more experienced persons, starting at an early age. Experiences with computers began early for most children, often at home. Children most frequently cited their fathers as the family member who taught them about computer technology, but students also mentioned mothers, siblings, extended family members, neighbors, friends, and parents' coworkers. According to the students in the study, one-on-one instruction with a more experienced person provided powerful and lasting learning experiences. One 6th grade girl recalled a computer experience from early childhood:

> I sat on my dad's lap and he would tell me what to click or press. I guess that is the way I learned to use computers because from that period on, I was able to use computers. Since my dad was always helping me, I was able to remember what to do.

Students in grades 4 through 7 also enjoy learning about computer technology through independent exploration. Roughly 30 percent of participating students said that they most preferred to learn about computers by simply trying to figure things out by themselves, or with the support of a text or manual. One 6th grade girl noted, "I personally prefer to explore the computer on my own. I learn by doing, not by listening." Concern for peers motivated a 5th grade boy who preferred to learn about computers alone: "That way, if I don't get it, I won't be embarrassed or shy. Also, if I get it faster than the others, they won't feel bad."

Students generally expressed confidence in their ability to use computers, but there is evidence of gender differences in these beliefs. Both boys and girls rated their capacity for using computer technology successfully as strong. They believed that they were capable of learning to use computers effectively and that computers were meant for everyone. However, reflective of similar patterns in math and science, some students (more boys than girls, and up to 10 percent of a given student population) believed that computers were a male domain. One 4th grade boy said, "girls shouldn't use computers. It's too technical. Girls will probably screw it up."

The effectiveness of computer technology experiences at school depends on the student's prior knowledge, the teacher, access to hardware and software, and scheduling. For children who had not had rich computer technology experiences outside school, the classroom and the computer lab became gateways to computer technology, with positive and negative effects. At school, students began to see the computer as a tool rather than as entertainment. A 5th grade girl reported that "at home, I thought of computers as a toy. But as we began to use them in school, I knew they were helpful in many other ways." Nonetheless, a 6th grade girl lamented the schedule, noting "in school this year, I didn't have a computer at home and I didn't really like computers because we had so many things to do and so little time."

The classroom teachers' expertise and enthusiasm for computer technology also had a direct impact on students. "My [classroom] teacher is a computer fanatic," wrote a 4th grade boy. "She gives my class many assignments on the computer. My computer teacher teaches us about new, advanced technology. Both of them give us support."

Finally, children who had rich computer experiences outside school held teaching and learning about technology in the classroom and computer lab to a high standard, particularly if instruction occurred within a traditional model. As a 6th grade boy wrote, "Teachers are too slow when teaching about computers. Whenever there is a person still failing or not doing well in an area, everyone is stopped where they are and we all work on that area until [the person] has caught up."

Not all computer learning at school happens during formal instruction. During class, lunch, and recess, children exchanged tips and shortcuts for using software, gave recommendations for purchasing computer games, and argued the relative merits of hardware upgrades. More subtle learning also took place when students observed how school personnel regulated access to computers. Schools need a careful plan for granting access to classroom computers and the computer lab to prevent inequities. In the words of one 4th grade girl, "My school has at least two [computers] to a classroom. I never get to use the school computers because all the boys in my class hog them."

Students believe that computers are helpful and that they will use them more in their future workplaces than in school. Boys and girls believed that computers were essential to their future success. According to a 4th grade girl, "Whether you work at McDonald's or the White House, you'll use computers." However, students less frequently cited the need to use computers for schoolwork. One 6th grade boy stated, "I don't think I will use computers a lot in school because I haven't used computers a lot yet."

What Teachers Said

The computer technology study also sought the perceptions and experiences of teachers through responses to inventories, surveys, and interviews. Collectively, participants in the study and in follow-up research reported several common themes:

Within any school or grade, the level of teacher proficiency with computer technology varies greatly. In some cases, the students may know more than the teacher. Both classroom teachers and computer teachers

acknowledged the broad spectrum of teachers' computer skills, as well as the discrepancy between the technology skills of the teacher and those of some students. One middle school teacher wrote, "It takes some time to overcome 'computer phobia.' Having a computer in my classroom has led

Schools need a careful plan for granting access to classroom computers and the computer lab to prevent inequities.

me to experiment, learn, teach myself, and have students teach me."

Students bring to school considerable experience with computers, but these skills are often software-specific and game-oriented. Teachers noted that students' skills are understandably linked to the students' individual experiences. As a result, students often acquired competence in the basic functions of computer and software programs, leaving the school to teach about more complex computer tools and techniques. In addition, student expertise was frequently associated with computer games, resulting in skills with limited educational applications.

Computer curriculums may vary substantially from school to school. Teachers, students, and administrators most often perceived the computer curriculum at their school to be a recent work-in-progress that focused on basic skills, especially keyboarding. Schools more experienced in integrating computers with other curriculum areas viewed computers as tools. They believed that curriculum integration was both instructionally effective and efficient, and they valued authentic learning experiences with technology.

If we want children to learn technology, they've got to use technology. At Shepaug Valley Middle/High

School in Washington, Connecticut, computer teacher Ted Roth arranged the computer lab hardware on mobile carts. Half the time, the computers remained in the computer lab for whole-class demonstrations. The remaining time, children used the computers for grade-level assignments in classrooms. Woodbury Middle School computer teacher Jeff Turner also advocated the importance of hands-on learning. "Kids have to play with, smell, and touch computers."

What Schools Might Do

As schools seek needed hardware and software, educators are working to develop new models for teaching and learning with computers. The practices of schools that participated in the computer study and several other schools involved in follow-up research offer ideas.

Integrate curriculum to use computer technology as a tool for teaching and learning. Students appreciate learning experiences that are authentic and relevant. When computer skills are taught on a need-to-know basis within the context of a content-area assignment, students can apply and reinforce their new knowledge immediately. Jeff Turner says that if he provides direct instruction for more than five minutes, "I'm wasting students' time." Instead, tackling one or two new computer skills a day helps students build complex knowledge gradually.

This approach results in remarkable student performance. At Middlebury Elementary in Middlebury, Connecticut, 2nd graders use art software to produce scientific drawings of penguins during their study of Antarctica, and 4th graders chart and graph the growth of their paperwhite bulbs using spreadsheets. At Shepaug Valley Middle/High School, 8th graders publish a newspaper to complete their study of the Great Depression, and 12th graders submit an exit portfolio which demonstrates eight district computer technology competencies. The work contained in the portfolio must include diverse, authentic classroom assignments from grades 9 through 12.

Redefine the role of the teacher. Computer teachers are assuming the role of facilitator. They still explain and model computer skills for students, but they often invite others into the classroom to share in instruction. They welcome divergent thinking and are quick to acknowledge that they are learners, too.

Students can also be teachers. Computer teachers, such as Dar New at Silver Beach Elementary School in Bellingham, Washington, and Ted Roth at Shepaug Valley Middle/High School, train interested students to assist teachers and other students with computer instruction. New has trained seventy-five 4th and 5th grade Tech Tutors and assigned them to each K–3 classroom to assist staff and students. They also work with senior citizens who come to the school to learn about computer software and the Internet. High school students on Roth's Tech Team meet during the week to learn new skills and problem-solving strategies. Then the students assist teachers and students during class and accompany Roth when he presents teacher inservice programs.

From a child's birth, parents are teachers. Beyond the computer skills that they share at home, parent volunteers can provide one-on-one coaching in the computer lab. At Middlebury Elementary, while the computer teacher instructs the class, two trained parent volunteers and the classroom teacher assist students as they use new skills to complete classroom assignments.

Provide all school staff with ongoing professional development linked to authentic work. As with students, teachers and staff should learn computer skills as they perform real work. At Middlebury Elementary School, computer teacher Sallie McMullen's inservice course teaches staff to use presentation software for classroom instruction and to create teaching materials, lesson plans, grading systems, and performance tasks. When Oxford Center School staff in Oxford, Connecticut, began to plan their computer technology inservice time, they worked with a parent who assisted with the training and arranged for sessions to be held at his place of employment, a local telephone company.

Elicit the support of administrators, parents, and the community. Given the fast-paced rate of computer technology evolution, helping our children develop competence in this area is a daunting challenge. Although children come to school with some measure of computer knowledge, many variables influence whether they will learn more about computers at school. A successfully passed budget, a donation of hardware from the business community, a parent volunteer, and a principal's efforts to fine-tune the schedule all directly shape the computer experiences of our students in school.

Back at Woodbury Middle School, Jeff Turner is already looking beyond the 8th grade memory book to where the computer curriculum might lead. He envisions student work in interdisciplinary portfolios that include animation, sound effects, and video. He'd like to connect students more closely to the community by doing such work as developing touch-screen menus for local restaurants. He's considering creating a town Web site that would feature oral histories by local senior citizens. If the enthusiasm of this teacher and his students indicated things to come, the future of computer technology in school—and of our students and communities—looks very bright, indeed.

References

O'Donnell Dooling, J. (1999). A study of gender differences in beliefs toward computer technology and factors which influence these beliefs in grades 4, 5, 6, and 7. *Dissertation Abstracts International, 60*(6), 1989A. (University Microfilms No. ATT 9936826).

Software & Information Industry Association. (1999). *Report on the effectiveness of technology in schools.* (Study item No. CLD9988). Washington, DC: Author.

Judith O'Donnell Dooling is Principal of Middlebury Elementary School, P.O. Box 1093, Middlebury, CT 06762; (203) 758-2401; jdooling@region15.org.

Technology Use in Tomorrow's Schools

From word processing software to the Internet to portable, hand-held devices, computer technology use in schools is growing. How will it look in the future?

Barbara Means

Students and teachers have increasing access to almost limitless amounts of information on the World Wide Web. In addition, the trend toward using such general-purpose application packages as word processing, spreadsheet, and database software for school assignments has grown considerably since the 1980s. Nearly 50 percent of teachers in a recent national survey, for example, had required word processing during the previous school year (Becker, 1999). Students also are increasingly involved in building Web pages and multimedia presentations to show their solutions to problems or to demonstrate what they have learned in their research. Educators are using network technology to support collaborations—locally and at great distances—among students, experts, and teachers. The percentage of classrooms participating in network-based collaborations is still relatively small, however.

Despite great strides in incorporating technology into U.S. schools, we still fall short of providing a seamless, convenient, robust, and reliable technology support structure for all students and teachers. Today's desktop computers and Internet usages are not the educational ideal (Roschelle, Hoadley, Pea, Gordin, & Means, in press). Many educators lament the relative paucity of up-to-date computers and network connections in classrooms, but a look into almost any classroom with a sizable number of computers reveals all kinds of problems related to the computers' size, weight, shape, and requirements for multiple cords and wires. Similarly, today's World Wide Web is disorganized, of uneven quality, and overrun with advertising. In too many cases, students and teachers are either not using the technology available to them or are using technology to accomplish tasks that could be done offline more quickly and with less effort extraneous to the learning content (Healy, 1998).

Nevertheless, our experience with the less-than-ideal technological infrastructure available in today's schools suggests important directions for the 21st century. The insights gained from these experiences, coupled with advances in research on human learning and the technological improvements that can be expected in the coming decade, give rise to cautious optimism concerning technology's role in the schools of tomorrow.

The Roots of Educational Technology

Mastery learning approaches dominated the early days of computer use to teach academic subjects, with skills and subject matter broken down into byte-sized bits for discrete skill practice or knowledge transmission. These efforts to teach content through computers were supplemented by courses in computer literacy and, at the high school level, computer programming.

In the late 1980s, these practices gave way to an emphasis on incorporating general-purpose technology tools, such as word processors and spreadsheets, into learning in the academic content areas. General office applications became more common in the classroom than software explicitly designed for instructional purposes. The emphasis on adopting general tools for educational purposes received a further boost from the rise of the World Wide Web and search engines for locating Web sites on almost any topic. Such slogans as *connecticut the classroom to the world* and *the world at your fingertips* reflect today's emphasis on access to a much broader information base through the Web.

From *Educational Leadership,* December 2000/January 2001, pp. 57-61. © 2000 by the Association for Supervision and Curriculum Development. All rights reserved. Reprinted by permission.

Although classrooms continue to lag behind the business and entertainment sectors in terms of capitalizing on network technologies, the rate of increase in Internet access within U.S. schools during the final decade of the 20th century was phenomenal. In 1990, few U.S. schools had Internet connections, and many of these were low-speed, dial-up modem connections from a single computer. By 1994, the percentage of schools with Internet access was significant—35 percent—and by 1999, the percentage had risen to 95 percent. As with computers, we stopped counting school connections and started looking at the availability of Internet access within individual classrooms.

In 1994, only 3 percent of U.S. classrooms had Internet access. In 1996, President Clinton announced a set of national educational technology goals, including providing Internet access to every classroom in the United States. By 1997, the proportion of connected classrooms had grown to 27 percent. Sixty-three percent of U.S. public school classrooms had Internet access by 1999, according to National Center for Education Statistics data (2000), resulting in part from the E-rate—the telecommunications discount to schools and libraries passed in 1996.

Technology for Meaningful Learning

As access to technology grows, educators must decide how best to use it. *How People Learn,* a recent report from the National Research Council (Bransford, Brown, & Cocking, 1999), applies principles from research on human learning to issues of education. The report explores the potential of technology to provide the conditions that research indicates are conducive to meaningful learning: real-world contexts for learning; connections to outside experts; visualization and analysis tools; scaffolds for problem solving; and opportunities for feedback, reflection, and revision.

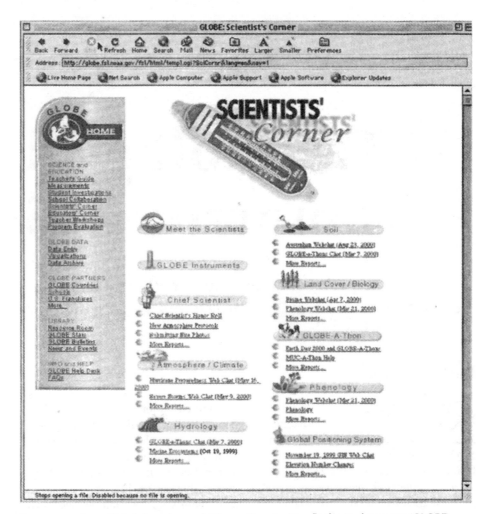

Programs such as Global Learning and Observations to Benefit the Environment (GLOBE) turn students into collaborating scientists.

A few examples illustrate how technology can provide these capabilities. The Global Learning and Observations to Benefit the Environment (GLOBE) program helps elementary and secondary school students learn science by involving them in real scientific investigations, such as measuring soil and water quality. Students follow detailed data collection protocols for measuring characteristics of their local atmosphere, soil, and vegetation. Using GLOBE Internet data-entry forms, thousands of students submit data to a central archive, where it is combined with data from other schools to develop visualizations—a data map showing measured values and their geographic locations—that are posted on the Web. The scientists who developed the data collection protocols and depend on the students' data for their research

visit classrooms, exchange e-mail with students, and participate with students in scheduled Web chats (Means and Coleman, 2000).

Hands-On Universe, a program of the University of California at Berkeley's Lawrence Hall of Science, gives students the opportunity to use image processing software to investigate images from a network of automated telescopes. Automated telescopes now capture many more images from outer space than professional astronomers have time to analyze. Hands-On Universe enlists students to review images from space and to help search for supernovas and asteroids as they acquire astronomy concepts and research skills. Hands-On Universe lets students use the same kinds of software tools as scientists, albeit with more user-friendly interfaces, to examine and classify

The rate of increase in Internet access within U.S. schools during the final decade of the 20th century was phenomenal.

downloaded images. Hands-On Universe students have discovered a previously unknown supernova and published their work in a scientific journal.

Teachers have also found advantages in using technology supports for student collaboration within their own schools and classrooms. Knowledge Forum—formerly Computer-Supported Intentional Learning Environments (CSILE)—for example, provides a communal database, with text and graphics capabilities. Students create text and graphics "nodes" about the topic they are studying, labeling their contributions by the kind of thinking represented: "my theory for now" or "what we need to learn about next." Other students can search and comment on these nodes. With teacher support, students can use Knowledge Forum to share information and feedback, to accumulate knowledge over time, and to exercise collaboration skills. The communal hypermedia database provides a record of students' thoughts and electronic conversations over time (Scardamalia & Bereiter, 1996), allowing teachers to browse the database to review their students' emerging understanding of key concepts and their interaction skills (Means & Olson, 1999).

ThinkerTools software, another visualization and analysis tool, helps middle school students learn about velocity and acceleration. Students begin with what the program developers call "scaffolded inquiry activities"—problems, games, and experiments that help students understand motion, first in one direction and then in two directions. As students progress, they are exposed to more complex simulations, culminating in their learning of the principles underlying Newtonian mechanics. In a carefully controlled study, middle school students who had used ThinkerTools outperformed high school physics students in their

ability to apply principles of Newtonian mechanics to real-world situations (White & Frederiksen, 1998).

Although such examples of technology-enhanced learning activities are prominent in the education literature, they do not represent mainstream educational practice in the United States. A national survey of 4,100 teachers found that in the 1997–98 school year, the most commonly assigned use of technology was still word processing—required by nearly 50 percent of the teachers (Becker, 1999). Thirty-five percent of the teachers asked students to use CD-ROMS for research. Internet research or information gathering was the third most common teacher-directed student use of computers. Nearly 30 percent of all the teachers—and more than 70 percent of the teachers with high-speed Internet connections in their classrooms—had their students conduct Internet research (Becker, 1999). Internet assignments had become slightly more common than games and software drills, which 29 percent of the teachers had assigned. Interactive uses of the Internet were relatively infrequent. Only 7 percent of the teachers reported having their students use e-mail three times or more during the school year and even fewer had their students work with students at a distance in cross-classroom projects.

What's Next?

Despite their relative scarcity, such uses of technology and learning principles in carefully designed instructional activities foretell future innovations that are likely to have the advantage of much more seamless, unobtrusive technology supports. Today's desktop computers and the networks they run on offer a huge array of potential uses—everything from keeping track of student grades to supporting the manipulation of dig-

itized images—but they are bulky, expensive, and awkward to use in a classroom.

Many technology trend watchers believe that the 21st century will see a move away from such strong reliance on general-purpose computing devices toward lower-cost, portable, hand-held devices, often connected through global networks and tailored for specific applications (Norman, 1998). Major equipment manufacturers are investing in wireless technologies, wireless personal area networking has emerged, and the popularity of both hand-held computing devices and cell phones is growing rapidly. Nowhere is the potential impact of these trends greater than in our nation's schools.

Students could carry and use lightweight, low-cost learning appliances rugged enough to fit in their backpacks as they move from class to class, school to home, or between school-based and community-based learning settings. When used with wireless networks, high-powered servers, and teacher workstations, these low-cost devices are likely to provide more narrow but more effective functionality than today's desktop computers and to be much easier to use. Computing and networking will be taken for granted as part of the school environment. Teacher workstations will be able to exchange information with student devices and with school- or district-level servers. Complex, memory-hogging programs can reside on servers and be pulled down to local computers or appliances on an as-needed basis.

Tomorrow's Classroom

Given the possibilities of new technologies, what might tomorrow's classroom look like? A MathPad, for example, might be an educational appliance—smaller and lighter than to-

Schools will become one among many kinds of organizations offering formally organized distributed learning.

day's hand-held devices, with capability for stylus input, display, and mathematical calculations and graphing. Such devices might feature short-range radio communication capabilities linking the hand-held device to other hand-helds or to another computing device, such as a teacher workstation, a share-board display system, or sensors built into the environment.

Given this emerging technology infrastructure, we can envision such educational activities as the following. Middle school students in an environmental science class monitor local haze using a sun photometer to measure attenuation of sunlight caused by haze, smoke, and smog. Seven small groups of students take their photometer readings at their schools' softball field each day at noon, and the readings are automatically sent to their MathPads. The students' MathPads contain a template for displaying the readings of all seven groups, so the students can send their readings to one another.

Upon returning to the classroom, one group transmits the completed template for today's readings to the class's shareboard computer, and the teacher begins a class review and discussion of the data on the wall-sized display. The teacher and students call up software that incorporates prompts to help them judge the reasonableness of the measurements the student groups have taken. The teacher plots each group's reading on a graph showing measurements over the last six months as a point of departure for discussing the distinction between accuracy and precision.

The teacher then introduces the next assignment: work in small groups to investigate haze data from their own and other schools. Controlling the display from her workstation, the teacher connects through the Internet to the online Haze Project database and reminds the students of the contents of the database and strategies for navigating the database Web site. To make sure they know how to read the data tables, the teacher asks several comprehension questions, having students submit answers with their MathPads and checking the students' responses on her workstation to make sure no one is lost. She directs students to return to their small groups to explore the data archive before deciding on a research question for a project that will take them several weeks and culminate in presentations for their class and submission of their work to the Haze Project's online student journal. Students may choose to collaborate with students at other schools through e-mail and real-time online discussions using software that allows them to share and manipulate data graphs.

As in today's GLOBE and Hands-on Universe projects, the Haze Project students of tomorrow participate in the real-world context of ongoing scientific investigation. Connections to a larger world become second nature. The students' data and analyses are part of much larger projects with real stakeholders. Students contribute to and learn from a community of investigators. Visualization and analysis tools on the students' MathPads and the teacher's workstation help the students see patterns in their data. Prompts built into the data-recording software scaffold students' efforts to check the reasonableness of the data they have collected. The technology also supports access to similar data sets and conferencing with others involved in the Haze Project, two activities that provide opportunities for reflection, analysis, and revision. The teachers' ability to exchange information with individual student MathPads lets students receive quick feedback on their lines of reasoning and allows the teacher to adjust instruction to meet students' needs.

In terms of the technology itself, a combination of small quantities of expensive equipment (one or a few central workstations for each classroom and a top-notch display facility) and large numbers of inexpensive devices (such as the MathPads themselves) is likely to be more cost-effective than current technology expenditures. The most challenging technical requirement is that of compatibility so that different pieces of equipment can communicate.

Challenges Ahead

Is this scenario realistic? One could easily predict a very different impact of technology on education. The increasing availability of Web-based alternative learning resources coincides with a decline in public confidence in the efficacy of schools and increasing interest in alternatives, such as voucher programs, charter schools, and home-schooling. Over the next two decades, public school will likely have to compete for resources and for students—not only with private schools and homeschooling options—but with Internet-based alternatives as well. I doubt that brick-and-mortar schools will become obsolete, if only for their utility as places for students to spend their time, but they will become one among many kinds of organizations offering formally organized, distributed learning.

The increased pressure of competition should stimulate schools to improve. Schools that incorporate the technology of the future can offer the best combination of traditional face-to-face instruction—role modeling, socialization, and morale building—and projected benefits of learning with new technologies: increased participation in systems of distributed learning that engage broader communities, learning-enhancing representations of concepts and data, a restructuring of teaching and learning roles, and more meaningful assessment practices.

My vision for educational technology use is at least as dependent on improvements in teacher preparation and professional development around pedagogy, content, and assessment practices as it is on technological advances. My vision is technologically feasible—the question is whether our education system, and society in general, will support and promote the policies, resources, and practices needed to make it a reality.

Author's note: This article is a version of the chapter "Technology in America's Schools: Before and After Y2K," which appeared in the *ASCD Yearbook 2000,* edited by Ron Brandt. Preparation of the chapter was supported in part by National Science Foundation grant CDA-9729384. The opinions expressed are those of the author and do not necessarily reflect the policy or opinions of the Foundation.

References

Becker, H. J. (1999). *Internet use by teachers: conditions of professional use and teacher-directed student use.* Irvine, CA: Center for Research on Information Technology and Organizations.

Bransford, J. D., Brown, A. L., & Cocking, R. R. (Eds.). (1999). *How people learn: Brain, mind, experience, and school.* Washington, DC: National Academy Press.

Healy, J. (1998). *Failure to connect: How computers affect our children's minds—for better and worse.* New York: Simon & Schuster.

Means, B., & Coleman, E. (2000). Technology supports for student participation in science investigations. In M. J. Jacobson & R. B. Kozma (Eds.), *Innovations in science and mathematics education* (pp. 287–319). Mahwah, NJ: Erlbaum.

Means, B., & Olson, K. (1999). Technology's role in student-centered classrooms. In H. Walberg & H. Waxman (Eds.), *New directions for teaching practice and research* (pp. 297–319). Berkeley, CA: McCutchan.

National Center for Education Statistics. (2000). *Internet access in U.S. public schools and classrooms: 1994–1999.* (NCES No. 2000086). Washington, DC: U.S. Government Printing Office.

Norman, D. A. (1998). *The invisible computer: Why good products can fail, the personal computer is so complex, and information appliances are the solution.* Cambridge, MA: MIT Press.

Roschelle, J., Hoadley, C., Pea, R. Gordin, D., & Means, B. (in press). Changing how and what children learn in school with computer-based technologies. *The Future of Children.*

Scardamalia, M., & Bereiter, C. (1996, November). Engaging students in a knowledge society. *Educational Leadership, 54*(3), 6–10.

White, B. Y., & Frederiksen, J. R. (1998). Inquiry, modeling, and metacognition: Making science accessible to all students. *Cognition and Science, 16,* 90–91.

Barbara Means is Codirector of the Center for Technology in Learning, SRI International, 333 Ravenswood Ave., Menlo Park, CA 94025; barbara.means@sri.com.

Unit Selections

7. **Project TEAMS: Integrating Technology Into Middle School Instruction,** Robert A. Reiser and Sarah M. Butzin
8. **Using the Internet to Improve Student Performance,** Angela M. Guptill
9. **Working With WebQuests: Making the Web Accessible to Students With Disabilities,** Rebecca Kelly
10. **Designing Instruction for Emotional Intelligence,** Richard Goldsworthy
11. **An Illusory Dilemma: Online to Learn or In Line With Standards,** Judi Harris

Key Points to Consider

❖ Imagine that you are assigned to design an Internet-enhanced writing course for high school students. How would you use the Internet and the World Wide Web to aid students in the writing process?

❖ How can we make the World Wide Web more accessible to students with disabilities?

❖ Describe how one would create and implement a technology-based instructional model. How would the model support the curriculum? What is the model's ultimate goal?

 **Links**   # www.dushkin.com/online/

4. **CTW**
   http://www.ctw.org/home/content/0,2946,,FF.html
5. **Education Place**
   http://www.eduplace.com/index.html
6. **Teaching With Electronic Technology**
   http://www.wam.umd.edu/~mlhall/teaching.html

These sites are annotated on pages 4 and 5.

A curriculum is a plan for action that includes strategies for achieving desired goals. Curriculum design is the organizational pattern or structure of a curriculum. There is a broad level that involves basic value choices. There is a specific level that involves the technical planning and implementation of curricular elements. The curricular elements include needs, student characteristics, problems, goals, objectives, content, learning activities, and evaluation procedures. These elements can be used as a blueprint for developing instructional strategies and human interfaces in various learning situations. For example, interactivity is a learning activity that can be used in various learning environments. Interface design and usability assessment provide learners with a comfortable way to manipulate data and other learning objects and in so doing increase learning facilities and thus increasing learner interaction and performance.

In addition, it is necessary to provide adaptive learning facilities that use graphical user interfaces with learning opportunities that meet the learner on the appropriate plane. In order to provide such a curriculum, teachers and designers must infuse technology-based learning tools into teacher-designed lesson plans. If this can be done, each school could contribute to the creation of a technology-based, interactive instructional curriculum library.

Articles in this unit provide specific strategies and tactics for designing, developing, integrating, and delivering curriculum-driven, Internet-based learning. It begins with Robert Reiser and Sarah Butzin's "Project TEAMS: Integrating Technology Into Middle School Instruction." They describe an instructional model and an instructional approach in which technology does play an integral part in the middle school curriculum. The authors point out that in addition to its emphasis on the use of technology, the TEAMS instructional approach also focuses on the use of active learning and interdisciplinary instruction.

In "Using the Internet to Improve Student Performance," Angela M. Guptill details how teachers can use the Web to draw associations between prior knowledge and new information, collect and classify information, and predict outcomes based on a Web site search. The author shows how technological resources have made it possible to develop lessons that promote critical, analytic, higher-order thinking skills and real-world problem solving that are frequently found in assessments today.

Next, Rebecca Kelly describes a Web-based teacher-created lesson plan that incorporates research, problem solving, and the application of skill and knowledge. The lesson is especially helpful in meeting the needs of students with disabilities within general education classrooms. The lesson also provides multiple representations of information, multiple means of expression, and multiple means of engagement.

In the next article, "Designing Instruction for Emotional Intelligence," Richard Goldsworthy focuses on the development of instruction that incorporates affective goals, objectives, and strategies into educational programs and practices. The article provides a framework for systematically addressing key areas of social competence in development efforts.

Finally, "An Illusory Dilemma: Online to Learn or In Line With Standards" focuses on telecollaboration and teleresearch Internet-supported, curriculum-based learning. The article not only describes the processes but also details the activity structures that go into the two processes. These structured approaches seem to help students address many content and process standards at the same time and in engaging, pedagogically sound ways.

Project **TEAMS** Integrating Technology into Middle School Instruction

Technology Enhancing Achievement in Middle School

By Robert A. Reiser and Sarah M. Butzin

For years, leaders in the field of instructional technology have urged that media hardware and software should be an integral part of the instruction that is delivered in schools (Reiser & Ely, 1997). The purpose of this article is to describe the Project TEAMS (Technology Enhancing Achievement in Middle School) instructional model, an instructional approach in which technology does play an integral part in the middle school curriculum. In addition to its emphasis on the use of technology, the TEAMS instructional approach also focuses on the use of active learning and interdisciplinary instruction. These elements of the TEAMS model will also be described.

Why Project TEAMS Was Developed

Project TEAMS began in 1993 at Florida State University, as a research and development project funded by an Excellence in Education grant from the John S. and James L. Knight Foundation. The development of TEAMS was inspired by parents whose children had participated in a successful technology-based elementary school program called Project CHILD (Computers Helping Instruction and Learning Development), also developed at Florida State University (Butzin, 1997). These parents had seen the enthusiasm toward school and the academic success their children had achieved in Project CHILD. They wanted the momentum to continue and constantly asked, "When are you going to have something for middle school?"

The developers were also concerned that the use of technology in many middle schools was limited to lab-based programs, rather than integrated into classroom instruction. Many middle school teachers seemed locked in traditional roles of delivering whole group, text-based instruction. Students were often locked into passive roles of watching, waiting, and withering.

Across the nation, an active "Middle School Movement" was advocating refreshing ideas and specific recommendations to restructure junior highs into middle schools, rethink the curriculum, reorganize the classroom and redefine the role of teachers. Important national reports such as Turning Points (Carnegie Corporation, 1989) had recommended teacher teaming and more age-appropriate instruction for the early adolescent child.

Other educators were beginning to explore the importance of thematic teaching and integrated instruction. In this regard, we were particularly influenced by James Beane's notion that broad topics such as transitions, caring, identities, and conflict resolution, which come directly from personal adolescent concerns, could be the basis for connecting academic content (Beane, 1990).

From *TechTrends*, March 1998, pp. 39-44. © 1998 by TechTrends. Reprinted by permission.

These topics served as the overarching themes for each of our nine-week units at the sixth grade level.

Finally, we realized the importance of the middle grades in determining a child's future. We wanted to find ways to renew the excitement of learning that so many children seem to lose early in their school careers. Technology, along with exploratory hands-on activities, seemed a logical way to engage middle school students more fully.

Today's students are eager to become technologically literate. They easily relate to electronic media in their fast-paced world outside the classroom. Technology can also provide quality learning time that motivates, provides feedback, and guides students on the correct learning path. Therefore, technology integration became the centerpiece in Project TEAMS.

How are TEAMS Instructional Units Organized?

The TEAMS curriculum is comprised of four nine-week thematic units. In each unit the subject areas of science, mathematics, social studies, and language arts are tied together around one of the global themes mentioned earlier (transitions, caring, identities, and conflict resolution). During each unit, students engage in several "rotations" to learn specific skills related to the unit content.

A typical TEAMS rotation extends over a period of approximately two weeks. The first two or three days of the rotation consists of whole group instruction, during which time the skills that the students are expected to learn during that rotation are introduced and discussed. During the next five or six days, the students work in small groups at various learning stations in the classroom, practicing the unit skills. Groups rotate from station to station on a daily basis until all of the groups have engaged in the activities at all of the stations. After this is accomplished, the class works together as a whole group for one or two days, reviewing what they learned and practiced at the various stations. Each rotation then concludes with some type of assessment of student learning. This end-of-rotation assessment activity is one of several types of assessments employed in a TEAMS classroom. Others include having the teachers assess the quality of the work students do at stations, and having the students assess their own performance during each rotation.

There are at least four learning stations set up for each rotation. There is a *Technology Station* for computer-based learning, an *Exploration Station I* for creative activities involving student-generated products, an *Exploration Station II* for learning in a game-like format, and a *Text Station* for written work. For example, a language arts rotation designed to help students identify the main ideas in a passage includes the following station activi-ties, each of which is designed to be undertaken by several pairs of students working together on the task:

- a technology station where students use a piece of software that puts them in the role of newspaper reporters identifying the main ideas in, and writing headlines for, given newspaper stories;
- an exploration station where students create telegrams that summarize key ideas that they must transmit to other students;
- a second exploration station where students must identify whether given sentence strips describe a main idea or provide supporting details; and
- a text station where students read text passages from their science and geography texts and identify the main idea in each passage.

In addition to the four types of stations described above, teachers often add a fifth station of their own choosing. This station may involve the use of another form of technology, such as a videodisc, or a computer connected to the Internet, or may involve the use of text-based, or exploration-type activities. By having a fifth station in the classroom, teachers with a large number of students are able to keep each of the small groups in their class down to a fairly modest size.

The activity that students will undertake at a particular station is described in simple language on a "task card" located at that station. Although teachers are free to create their own station activities and task cards, the TEAMS model provides teachers with many suggestions for station activities. Indeed, the program materials include over 40 sample task cards in each of the four major subject areas.

Station activities provide students with the opportunity to be self-directed, active learners, either working independently or cooperatively in small groups. Prior to the day students begin their station work, the teacher will typically provide a quick overview of the activities that will take place at each station. The following day, at the beginning of the class period, group members examine a wall chart to determine which station their group will be working at on that day. The group members then proceed to that station, where they read the task card that describes the station activity. The group members then organize the group so that they can work together, or independently, to accomplish it. Sometimes the group will decide upon individual roles and responsibilities. In other cases, designation of roles and responsibilities may be decided upon by a team captain (a title which rotates among group members on a regular basis).

During station work, the teacher shifts to the role of coach and facilitator. While the students work at station activities, the teacher circulates around the room, guiding, probing, checking, and encouraging students as needed. Sometimes the teacher may have a Teacher Sta-

Table 1. Grade 6 Caring Unit: Sample Interdisciplinary Station Rotations

	SCIENCE	SOCIAL STUDIES	MATHEMATICS	LANGUAGE ARTS
ACADEMIC TOPIC	Positive and negative consequences of human actions on Earth's ecosystem.	Environmental consequences of changing the physical characteristics in various world locations.	Use direct measures and compare given characteristics such as length, weight, volume.	Comparison and contrast in reading and writing.
WHOLE GROUP	Overview of concepts and vocabulary; view and take pro/con notes on video *Two Sides of Fire* on controlled burning.	Overview of concepts and vocabulary; view and take pro/con notes on the Three Gorges Dam project in China.	Overview of concepts and vocabulary; view videodisc *Adventures of Jasper Woodbury: A Capital Idea* -recycling theme.	Overview of concepts and vocabulary; introduce Venn diagrams.
TECHNOLOGY STATION	*Biology Concepts - Ecology* software	Internet research on Three Gorges Dam project	*MathKeys: Area of Triangles* software.	Use word processing software to revise comparison/contrast sentences.
EXPLORATION I STATION	Make an endangered species poster	Draw a picture showing before and after effects of the Three Gorges Dam project.	Review the Jasper videodisc and solve the problem as a group.	Use C-C Clue Cards and Game Board to identify comparison or contrast sentences.
EXPLORATION II STATION	Oil spill clean up hands-on activity	Pro and Con Bingo identifying Three Gorges Dam issues.	Measure and compare a variety of common objects.	Find and insert Missing Pieces (comparison/contrast words) in four given passages, three of which focus on content currently covered in the other major subject areas.
TEXT STATION	Use pro/con notes from whole group to write a comparison/contrast paper about controlled burns.	Read about an endangered species; draw a picture and a map showing location(s) where it is found.	Complete "Polygon Perimeters" worksheet	Read a given passage with a caring theme and construct a Venn diagram to compare and contrast content.

tion to work with a small group of students who need extra attention.

Key Elements of the TEAMS Model

As mentioned earlier, Project TEAMS is an approach for integrating instructional technology, interdisciplinary instruction, and active learning into the middle school curriculum. Now that we have provided an overview of how a TEAMS classroom operates, we would like to focus on how these three elements are part of the TEAMS approach.

The use of instructional technology as an integral part of the instructional process lies at the center of the TEAMS approach. Unlike many other instructional approaches where technology is peripheral to everyday classroom activities, technology plays a key role in the TEAMS approach. Computer hardware and software are used during every rotation to provide students with instruction and practice on the skills they are learning. Other forms of instructional technology, such as the Jasper Woodbury videodiscs (Cognition and Technology Group at Vanderbilt, 1993), are also employed. We have reviewed software provided by numerous publishers and have identified software programs that support the acquisition of most of the skills taught in the curriculum.

In those cases where existing software has not been available, we have used the Internet, spreadsheets, word processing programs, and databases to provide students with technology-based practice activities.

We also believe that students and teachers are most likely to view technology as an integral part of the instructional process if that technology is based in the classroom, rather than a media lab. Thus, we have worked with administrators and teachers to ensure that at least four computers are located in each of the TEAMS classrooms. On occasion, this has meant moving some computers out of labs or out of classrooms where they were not being used. In most cases, by having at least four computers in each TEAMS classroom, and by having students work in pairs at the computer station, all the students in a class are able to engage in a technology-based activity during each rotation.

Active learning, the second key element of the TEAMS approach, is supported by the extensive use of station activities. Unlike traditional classrooms, where most of the instruction involves the teacher leading the entire class in lecture and discussion sessions, under the TEAMS approach a large percentage of the instructional time is devoted to having students work independently or in small groups at the various learning stations described earlier. Teachers and students have reported that this is one of the most positive features of the TEAMS approach and has resulted in students being on task to a greater extent than when they are receiving whole group instruction.

The third key element of the TEAMS approach, the use of interdisciplinary instruction, is supported in a variety of ways. These include summer planning workshops and weekly planning meetings where the teachers from the four major subject areas meet to identify overlapping or related areas of interest and study. In many cases, such meetings have resulted in teachers implementing a simple resequencing of required coursework so as to highlight connections across subject areas. For example, the sixth grade science and social studies (geography) teachers at one school decided to coordinate their study of weather and weather mapping, and the mathematics teacher offered to have the students work on the calculations necessary for weather reporting during this same time period.

In addition to identifying logical connections across subject areas, TEAMS teachers are also encouraged to identify how their subject matter relates to the overarching themes of each nine-week unit in the TEAMS curriculum. As mentioned earlier, these themes are based on the personal concerns of middle school children and deal with such areas as conflict resolution and transitions. We believe that by having each teacher spend some time focusing on these overarching themes, students will be better able to identify the relationships across subject areas, as well as identify how that subject area may be relevant to his or her everyday concerns.

Table 1 provides an overview of the whole group instruction and station activities in all four major subject areas for a two-week rotation during the unit with "caring" as its theme. As can be seen, many of the activities during the rotation focus on caring for the environment. By examining the activities described in the table, you should be able to note connections across subject areas as well as to the overarching "caring" theme.

Development Implementation, and Results

In the 1995–96 school year, after two years of development and formative evaluation, the TEAMS model was fully implemented at the sixth grade level at one middle school. Since that time the TEAMS model and accompanying TEAMS materials have been revised and expanded upon, to the point where we now have, at the sixth and seventh grade levels, a fully developed set of instructional materials and a training process that enables teachers to implement the TEAMS model effectively. The model is now being implemented at the sixth grade level in four middle schools in Florida. Three of the schools are located in low-to-middle-income urban areas and the fourth school is in a relatively poor rural community. The TEAMS approach is also being implemented at the seventh and eighth grade levels at one of the schools.

Research is currently being conducted to evaluate the effects of Project TEAMS on academic achievement and other school-related outcomes. Two reports examining the effects of Project TEAMS have already been prepared. The first (Riggin & Gill, 1997) focused on the effects of Project TEAMS at one school during the 1995–96 school year; the second (Cooksy & Gill, 1997) focused on the effects of TEAMS at three schools during 1996–97. Results from the 1996–97 evaluation include the following:

- **Student Attitudes.** Most students reported that they had positive attitudes toward school and learning. Their teachers generally concurred.
- **Self-directed Learning Abilities.** Students rated themselves highly on several measures of self-directed learning that TEAMS attempts to foster (e.g., looking for information from sources other than the teacher, establishing individual learning goals, staying on task). Teachers at two of the three schools concurred with the students' opinions, while teachers at the third school were less positive.
- **Working in Groups.** Most students indicated that they liked working in small groups, found them useful, and felt they learned while working in them. Their teachers generally concurred.
- **Computer Skills.** Students gave themselves high ratings in computer skills, a set of skills that Project TEAMS is designed to foster. The students' teachers generally concurred.

• **Learning.** At two of the three schools where the evaluation took place, improvements (from fifth grade to sixth grade) in the standardized test performance of TEAMS students were compared to improvements among students in a comparison group. Student scores on the overall test, as well as on the mathematics and language portions, were examined. At the middle school where TEAMS has been in place the longest, TEAMS students improved their scores on the overall achievement test, as well as the mathematics portion, to a significantly greater extent than a matched comparison group from other schools in the same county. However, at a second middle school in its first year of implementation, the improvement in TEAMS students' scores in mathematics and on the overall test were significantly less than that of a group of non-TEAMS students at the same school. It should be pointed out, however, that whereas approximately one-fourth of the TEAMS students at the second school were classified as exceptional education students, none of the students in the comparison group at that school were classified as such.

Conclusion

As we indicated at the outset of this article, Project TEAMS was undertaken to incorporate a variety of innovative practices into middle school instruction, and thereby improve the quality of middle school education. The project has placed particular emphasis on using instructional technology as an integral part of the instructional process. The TEAMS project is now into its sixth year, and while we certainly have not accomplished nearly all of the goals we set, we are confident that we have made good progress in improving the quality of middle school education in the schools where Project TEAMS has been implemented. We invite others who are interested in making similar changes in middle school instruction to contact us for more information.

References

Beane, J. (1990). *A middle school curriculum: From rhetoric to reality.* Columbus, OH: National Middle School Association.

Butzin, S. (1997). Whatever happened to Project CHILD? *Learning and Leading with Technology, 24* (6), 24–27.

Carnegie Corporation. (1989). *Turning points: Preparing American youth for the 21st century.* Washington, DC: Carnegie Council on Adolescent Development.

Cognition and Technology Group at Vanderbilt (1993). Anchored instruction and situated cognition revisited. *Educational Technology, 33* (3), 52–70.

Cooksy, L.J. & Gill, P. (1997). *Project TEAMS evaluation report: School year 1996–97.* Tallahassee, FL: Department of Educational Research, Florida State University.

Reiser, R.A., & Ely, D.P. (1997). The field of educational technology as reflected through its definitions. *Educational Technology Research and Development, 45* (3), 63–72.

Riggin, L.J.C. & Gill, P. (1997). *Project TEAMS evaluation report:: School year 1995–96.* Tallahassee, FL: Department of Educational Research, Florida State University.

Robert A. Reiser and Sarah M. Butzin are codirectors of Project TEAMS. Dr. Reiser is a professor in the Instructional Systems program at Florida State University. Dr. Butzin is executive director of the Institute for School Innovation. More information about Project TEAMS is available at the following Web site: www.ifsi.org.

USING THE INTERNET
to Improve Student Performance

Angela M. Guptill

Use a search of the Web to draw associations between prior knowledge and new information

Individual or team collection of information

Classify information

Predict outcomes based on Web site search

Refine online search, as needed

Activities like these are essential parts of Internet-based lessons, and the activities are related to a well-known standard that teachers have relied on for years: *Bloom's Taxonomy.* These particular activities can be categorized as "application of knowledge," and teachers can assess the breadth and depth of their own lessons—and the performance of their students—by using a checklist like this one. This article shows how.

Challenges of New Technologies

Technology in the classroom creates new opportunities and challenges for educators. Skill-and-drill computer programs are being replaced by access to sites on the World Wide Web that allow students to use collaboration and multi-media to gather and demonstrate knowledge. Technological resources have made it possible to develop lessons that promote critical, analytic, higher-order thinking skills and real-world problem-solving that are frequently found on assessments today (Blasi, Heinecke, Milman, &

Washington, 1999). With the proper tools to monitor student performance, special educators have the opportunity to target individual needs and monitor progress as students progress through the curriculum using the Internet as a resource.

Challenges of the Standards Movement

As the focus on learning standards and outcomes prevails, educator concern has shifted from the multiple-choice standardized test to performance-based assessments. The possibilities for developing and strengthening higher-order thinking skills using the Internet has increased with the availability of interactive sites and classroom collaboration found on the Internet. Although research is inconclusive about the effect of technology on student performance, studies suggest that several outcome areas may be enhanced. According to Blasi et al. (1999), "These areas include higher order thinking skills, more sophisticated communi-

Access to sites on the World Wide Web allows students to use collaboration and multimedia to gather and demonstrate knowledge.

From *Teaching Exceptional Children*, March/April 2000, pp. 16-20. © 2000 by *The Council for Exceptional Children*. Reprinted by permission.

Teachers and students can use the Internet to obtain feedback from other students—world-wide—as well as to provide feedback to others.

cation skills, research skills, and social skills" (p. 5).

This focus has challenged educators to develop lesson plans using the Internet that target the development of higher-order thinking skills required on many state assessments. For instance, the World Wide Web can be used as a source of information for teachers and students to enhance classroom instruction and present knowledge using multimedia. Educators can evaluate these outcomes, but it is more complicated than the standardized testing route. According to Blasi et al. (1999), "Standardized tests are an efficient means for measuring certain types of learning outcomes but educators must ask if these are the outcomes valuable for the new millennium" (p. 3).

Honey, McMillan, and Spielvogel (1995) have emphasized the real-world applications of modern technology: "Evidence indicates that when used effectively, technology applications can support higher-order thinking by engaging students in authentic, complex tasks within collaborative learning contexts" (p. 3). The availability of interactive sites and collaboration with other teachers and classrooms across all subjects and grades has made lesson planning easier (see Figures 1 and 2). More difficult has been the assessment of student performance using critical, higher-order, and problem-based inquiry skills. "It is clear that teaching and learning processes are embedded within complex systems. The challenge is to develop evaluation models that reflect this complexity" (Blasi et al., p. 4).

Benefits and Outcomes of Internet-Based Instruction

What are the benefits of Internet-based instruction, and what type of outcomes can be realized over traditional instruction? According to Owston (cited in Pea & Roschelle, 1999), the Web can improve learning in three ways: "(a) by appealing to the learning styles of students, presumably increasing their motivation to learn; (b) by offering greater convenience through asynchronous communication; and (c) by providing a fertile ground for developing higher order thinking skills which are required to overcome the

Figure 1 Sample Internet Lesson Plan

The Structure of Matter　　　　**Grade 8**

Unit Goals:
- Students will analyze the structures of matter by accessing their Hyperstudio stack titled "The Structure of Matter" and finding 3 Web sites that provide supporting information.
- Utilize Language Arts Skills—Complete Web site evaluation forms for 3 Web sites. Use information to prepare a newspaper article on the structure of matter. Send a copy to the assigned collaborative classroom. Respond to feedback and provide feedback to your collaborative partner.
- Prepare a multimedia presentation using your findings and the findings of your collaborative partner.
- Students will utilize technology skills—accessing programs, evaluating Web sites, toggle between programs, collaborate with other classrooms, prepare multimedia presentation.

Length of Unit: 8-12 days
Students should be able to:
- Classify objects by their properties
- Understand that matter exists in 3 states: solids, liquids, gases
- Understand the difference between chemical change and physical change (demonstrated through the newspaper article and presentation)
- Successfully collaborate with partner and provide feedback
- Prepare and present multimedia presentation
- Respond to questions from classmates and collaborative partner

Materials:
- Classroom computer lab with Internet access
- Software: Hyperstudio
- Web site evaluation form
- Technology taxonomy for assessment
- Web addresses for collaboration with other classrooms

Note: Adapted from lesson presented by Joint Jerome School District 261(1999). Available: http://www.d261.k12.id.us/tip/index.htm.

general lack of organization of knowledge in the Web" (p. 23).

And don't forget the real-world applications: "The Internet can help learners explore the world beyond the classroom by providing access to vast resources and information, promoting scientific inquiry and discovery,

Classroom Collaboration

To share classroom ideas, projects, and communicate with teachers and students from around the world try . . . http://www.epals.com/index.html

This Web site allows educators to locate classrooms to collaborate with by grade, location, and subject area.

and allowing students to communicate with experts" (Honey et al., 1995, p. 5).

Developing Internet-Based Lessons and Assessments

Access to the Internet provides educators with the opportunity to develop and implement lessons similar to the one that appears in Figure 1—a technology/science/language arts lesson selected from the Internet

The Internet can help learners explore the world . . . by providing access to vast resources and information.

Figure 2 Lesson Development and Assesment

1. For a lesson plan such as that in Figure 1, locate a collaborative classroom with a site on the Internet. This is a classroom working on the same topic in the same grade. Students can send and receive information (see http://www.epals.com/index.html).
2. Use a Web site evaluation form. Such a form gives the student the opportunity to critically analyze the information present on each Web site for timeliness and accuracy. These skills are addressed in the evaluation section of the technology taxonomy in Figure 3. See Web Site Evaluation form (Figure 2a).
3. Before presenting the lesson, assess whether it will provide students with the opportunity to progress up the technology taxonomy (Figure 3). Each lesson should facilitate demonstration of higher-level thinking skills.
4. Conduct performance measurement. At least quarterly, monitor the progress each student has made. This includes an assessment of progress using technology to develop critical-thinking and higher-order thinking skills. Careful documentation and charting of performance and progress is helpful for the student, parent, and the teacher. Use the technology taxonomy in Figure 3 to measure individual growth and performance.

Figure 2a Web Site Evaluation: Junior High School

Student Information

Name: _____ Today's Date: _____

Topic: _____

Presentation of Information

URL of Web Page: _____
Name of Web Page: _____
Date the Web Page Was Made: _____
E-Mail Address of Author: _____
Was it easy to locate the Web Page ?   __ Yes   __ No
Did the Web Page give you a list of other good sites?
   __ Yes   __ No
Did the pictures and sound help you to understand the information?
   __ Yes   __ No
Did you find any spelling errors?   __ Yes   __ No
If yes, explain what errors you found:

Did you think that the information that you found was accurate?
Explain why or why not.

Notes

Notes:

Would you recommend this site to a classmate?   __Yes   __ No

---

> *"When used effectively, technology applications can support higher-order thinking by engaging students in authentic, complex tasks within collaborative learning contexts."*

(http://www.d261.k12.id.us/tip/index.htm). The lesson was adapted to cover all levels on the "technology taxonomy" (adapted from *Bloom's Taxonomy*) in Figure 3. The lesson challenges students to use higher-level thinking skills as they use the World Wide Web to perform assignments and participate in activities.

Educators can select similar lessons and adapt them for their own use (see Figure 2). Teachers can measure students' progress on the lesson by completing the "technology taxonomy" (Figure 3). This assessment model can be used to chart progress as students perform activities incorporated in the lesson using the Internet to access the World Wide Web.

Another boon to evaluation is the use of the Internet to obtain feedback from other students—worldwide—through collaboration, as well as to provide feedback to others. Teachers can access Web sites that provide instructional guidelines and can visit chat rooms that address Internet use in the classroom (see box, "Internet Resources").

Internet Resources for Educators

Awesome Library for Teachers, Students, and Parents
   http://www.neat-school-house.org/awesome.html
Yahooligans!
   http://www.yahooligans.com/
The Global Classroom
   http://www/globalclassroom.org/projects.html
Index to Internet Lesson Plan Sites for K–12 Educators
   http://falcon.jmu.edu/~ramseyil/lesson.htm
Links to Educational Web Sites
   http://windsor.k12.co.us/links.htm
Internet Resources: Education Resources
   http://www.mcneese.edu/depts/library/int/educ.htm

Figure 3 Technology Taxonomy

Measuring Student Performance

Competence	Learning Hierarchy/Computer Application
Knowledge	• Search and reinforce . . . • Knowledge of major ideas • Knowledge of dates, events, places • Technological and academic concepts
Comprehension	• Surf (and sift) through information on the Web, and read for understanding • Identify valuable Web sites, record sites • Group Web sites into categories • Interpret, compare, and contrast facts • Predict consequences—use interactive Web sites to develop understanding of concepts • Contact experts to clarify understanding • Interpret information, provide perspectives
Application	• Draw together associations between prior knowledge and a search of the Web • Individual or team collection of information • Classify information • Predict outcomes based on Web site search • Refine online search, as needed • Select photographs, quotations, sound clips, virtual reality tours for use in presentation • Select format of presentation: newspaper, collage, Web page
Analysis	• Organization of information . . . (text, graphics, sound clips) • Sort and discern quality information from outdated or biased information • Find solutions to questions using collaboration and investigations with peers and experts
Synthesis	• Combine information from different Web sites • Modify information to meet assignment guidelines • Create and design Web sites, interactive projects, visual displays, and written text • Prepare essays, projects, visual displays, interactive presentations • Compose meaningful text from information gathered • Explain findings/synthesize findings
Evaluation	• Assess value and quality of presentation • Compare and discriminate between information from different sites • Verify value of information from various sources • Recognize the difference between subjective vs. objective information • Support information with prior knowledge • Summarize findings

Measuring individual growth and performance of students is a necessity when working with students with disabilities. To measure these elements when incorporating the use of technology into lessons, a taxonomy checklist is useful. This makes it possible to visualize student progress and provides excellent documentation.

Note: Adapted from *Bloom's Taxonomy* (adapted from Learning Skills Program, 1999. Available: http://www.coun.uvic.ca/learn/program/hndouts/ bloom.html).

Teachers can use the technology taxonomy in Figure 3 to check their lessons before class to ensure that learners gain exposure to each level of the taxonomy.

Internet for Success

The Internet is an educational tool that can be used to expand learning opportunities and develop higher-order thinking skills. By adapting lessons found on the Web, collaborating with other classrooms, and obtaining feedback from other teachers and students, teachers can greatly expand their instructional strategies. Using a visual checklist such as the technology taxonomy (Figure 3) makes it possible to bring a level of classroom accountability to the application of advanced technology. It also serves as an instrument to measure individualized progress that may be incorporated in quarterly student progress reports to parents. Using the supports available on the Internet (see boxes), teachers have opportunities to develop lessons that provide students with effective instruction and enriched experiences.

References

Blasi, L., Heinecke, W., Milman, N., & Washington, L. (1999). New directions in the evaluation of the effectiveness of educational technology. The Secretary's Conference on Educational Technology 1999 [online]. Available: http://www.ed.gov/Technology/Techconf/1999/whitepapers/paper8.html.

Honey, M., McMillan, K., & Spielvogel, R. (1995). Critical issue: Using technology to improve student achievement. The Center for Children and Technology [online]. Available: http://www/ncrel.org/sdrs/areas/issues/methods/technlgy/te800.htm.

Joint Jerome School District #261. (1999). Technology Integration Project: The structure of matter. Available: http://www/d261.id.us/tip/index.htm.

Learning Skills Program, Bloom's Taxonomy [online]. Available: http://www.coun.uvic.ca/learn/program/hndouts/bloom.html.

Pea, R., & Roschelle, J. (1999). Trajectories from today's WWW to a powerful educational infrastructure. Educational Researcher, 26, 22–26.

Angela M. Guptill *(CEC Chapter #402), special education teacher, Shaker Junior High School, North Colonie Central School District, Latham, New York, and candidate, Certificate of Advance Study in Educational Administration, State University of New York at Albany.*

Address correspondence to the author at 1260 Loudon Road, Apt. #C3, Cohoes, NY 12047 (e-mail: ANG111@aol.com).

This article was made possible in part by a grant from the AAUW Educational Foundation.

Working with WebQuests

Making the Web Accessible to Students with Disabilities

Rebecca Kelly

Searching the Internet is becoming an every-day practice for most students. Students with disabilities, however, are sometimes put at a disadvantage when attempting to complete this task. One practice that has become invaluable to me as a special education/inclusion teacher is the use of the WebQuest format. This article describes how students are boosting their learning through teacher-led lessons on the World Wide Web.

One such type of lesson, the WebQuest, is especially helpful in meeting the needs of students with disabilities within general education classrooms. Students with special needs sometimes experience information overload when first learning about computer programs; consequently, they need lists or steps to follow. According to research, independent activity—including well-defined search options—works best with specified steps that help reinforce these skills (Hawes, 1998). (See box, "What is a WebQuest?")

Essential WebQuest Principles

The Center for Applied Special Technology (CAST) has suggested the following principles of universal design for learning: multiple representations of information, multiple means of expression, and multiple means of engagement (Orkwis & McLane, 1998; Stahl, 1999). These principles are met with the flexibility and design of the WebQuest and can be incorporated in the creation stage of the lesson. With the special education teacher's knowledge of his or her students' needs, two of the IDEA requirements can

also be met with regard to accommodations and access to the general education curriculum. First, teachers can address goals of the individualized education program (IEP) to focus on accommodations and modifications to support the child's success in the general curriculum (Goldberg, 1999). Teachers can incorporate instructional support into the design of the WebQuest in the form of readability, larger text, and simpler directions. Also, because schools and teachers are required to help the child be involved in and progress within the general education curriculum, the WebQuest format offers the op-

portunity to incorporate basic skills with higher-order thinking skills and other enrichment activities with peers without disabilities.

Creating a Draft Web Page

The first step in designing a WebQuest is creating a draft of the Web page. This can be accomplished by the teacher alone or with the input of the students. The initial information should include the classroom objectives; in addition, IEP objectives and state standards should be identified at the initia-

---

What Is a WebQuest?

The WebQuest is a teacher-created lesson plan in the form of a simple World Wide Web page with active, preselected Internet links and a specific purpose for students. It is designed to provide students with an independent or small-group activity that incorporates research, problem-solving, and application of basic skills. It can be created at no cost to the teacher and can be constructed on a computer with a minimum 486 processor that has Internet access. The lesson then provides guided research using the Internet while incorporating skills such as problem-solving skills.

The WebQuest is a lesson design originated by Bernie Dodge of San Diego State University (http://edweb.sdsu.edu/webquest/webquest.html). The design incorporates the combination of sequenced steps and preselected, linked Web sites to guide the student through the lesson. The original model includes six components—Introduction, Task, Process, Resources, Evaluation, Conclusion—that guide students through the lesson. The components may be renamed or rearranged to meet the needs of the students. The WebQuest can be used as preceding information for a unit, extension of an idea expressed within the unit, or a culminating project.

WebQuest received the 1999 Project IDEA (Identifying and Disseminating Educational Alternatives) award from the Delaware Department of Education and the Exceptional Children and Early Childhood Group.

From *Teaching Exceptional Children*, July/August 2000, pp. 4-13. © 2000 by The Council for Exceptional Children. Reprinted by permission.

With the WebQuest, teachers can address IEP goals and focus on accommodations and modifications to support the child's success in the general curriculum.

tion of the WebQuest. State standards (Table 1) shape the lesson and IEP goals and objectives fine-tune it.

Once the teacher has determined when in the course of the unit of study the students will use the WebQuest, the objectives are easier to determine. Although it does take time for the teacher to create this type of lesson, it pays off in the classroom with an engaging, cooperative lesson that flows smoothly and incorporates a variety of skills. (For further information, see box, "Hints for Web Page Creation.")

Collaborative problem-solving fits in nicely with the WebQuest lesson and is a proven way to identify barriers related to inclusion and to create ways to overcome these barriers. The cooperative learning and adapted curriculum approaches of the WebQuest format tend to increase the success of inclusive classrooms (Hobbs & Westling, 1998).

A WebQuest S.O.S.

One example is "S.O.S.—Salvaging One Sunken Ship," a WebQuest created in coordination with my eighth-grade students' American History, English, and reading classes (http://www.k12.de.us/delmar/school/

projects/webquest/sos/sos.html) (see Figure 1). About half of the students in this class of 22 had reading and written-expression goals on their IEPs, with documented levels ranging from second grade to sixth grade. This group also included students identified with disabilities in the areas of expressive and receptive language, learning disabilities, hearing impairments, and mild mental retardation.

According to Holloway (1999), the major reasons for the lack of reading comprehension among remedial readers are poor motivation, lack of experience, and egocentricity. Teachers can help regain motivation and improve the students' reading performance by connecting reading activities with realistic experiences and real-life applications. In addition, the incorporation of self-directed activities, such as the WebQuest lessons, invites collaborative learning and allows for varied forms of self-expression (Holloway, 1999). When working with students in an inclusive classroom, teachers need to create a learning environment that accommodates the needs of the students with disabilities without bringing undue attention to those students.

Teamwork and cooperative learning are also important goals; but teachers must still provide modifications, as stated in student IEPs. The teamwork is modeled for the students by the coordination between the general education teacher and the special education teacher. In the case of the S.O.S. WebQuest, I solicited the help of the reading specialist in the creation stage of the lesson. The reading specialist assisted with the selection of a relevant historical fiction book at a lower reading level; she also provided several Internet links regarding shipwrecks and the International Ice Patrol that she had collected over the past few years. With her material and my background in educational technology and special education, we proceeded forward with our integrated WebQuest.

WebQuest Components

The integrated WebQuest unit usually takes about four to five class periods (about 50 minutes each) to complete. The unit usually has six components: Introduction, Task, Resources, Process, Evaluation, and Conclusion.

The first period should be used as an overview of the contents and usage of the WebQuest, with next two to three sessions involved in searching the Web sites linked to the WebQuest page. The final period or two can be spent working on the solution or problem-solving activity noted in the Task part of the lesson.

Introduction

The WebQuest's Introduction provides an overview and essential background information of the lesson. In our S.O.S. WebQuest, it explained that the sinking of the *Lusitania* and the *Titanic* were different incidents but that they share some similarities. It also explained that students can gain a better understanding of the events by reading historical fiction, such as *Dark Crossing* by Joanne Suter. In the Planner (Figure 2) that I created to help make effective WebQuests, this section is set up by the classroom teacher and should reflect the subject area standards, as well as any unit concepts the students should be aware of before starting the WebQuest.

The Task

The next section of the WebQuest is the Task. It can also be referred to as the Problem because it states the student's role in solving a specific problem or situation. For example, the S.O.S. WebQuest states that the students assume the role of a deep sea salvager who has been awarded a grant to explore and possibly raise either the *Lusitania* or the *Titanic*. Part B of the Planner shows a checklist that teachers and students can use as a "brainstorming" exercise that helps them choose activities. The Planner also reinforces the five *W*'s (who, what, when, where, and why), which serve to round out the activities.

In the S.O.S. example, students must research each location and the details of the ship and its sinking to help gain facts as they create an informed opinion. Students are then charged with writing a letter to the chairman of the grant committee, by providing a rationale for whichever ship the student selects to raise and by using persuasive letter-writing style and language to prove a point. Because letter writing was a skill the students were familiar with, but needed to work on, the teachers agreed on the students' selection.

Table 1. Delaware State Standards Addressed by the WebQuest "S.O.S.—Salvaging One Sunken Ship"

Subject	Standard
English/Lang. Arts.—Standard 1	Students will use written and oral English appropriate for various purposes and audiences.
English/Lang. Arts—Standard 2	Students will construct, examine, and extend the meaning of literary, informative, and technical texts through listening, reading, and viewing.
English/Lang. Arts—Standard 3	Students will gain access, organize, and evaluate information gained by listening, reading, and viewing.
Social Studies/History—Standard 2	Students will gather, examine, and analyze historical data.

Hints for Web Page Creation

Once the teacher or the students have written the draft of a WebQuest page or other home page, the page creation begins. If you do not have a page editor that allows you to easily create Web pages, do not fear. Netscape Communicator has a component called Netscape Composer, a user-friendly page editor, that is downloadable and available at no cost (see below). Using the page editor, you can create the WebQuest page, beginning with heading, text, and even pictures. With a few simple steps, a URL address becomes an active link to the Internet. You can also create tables to present information in a neat, organized way.

Once you or the students have created the page in HTML format, you have two choices. First, the page can be placed into a folder on the computer, saved to a disk, and then uploaded via the school's server. The second choice involves saving the document to a classroom computer's hard drive. The links will still work the same, but that specific computer is the only machine that can access the file.

How to Access Netscape Composer

Netscape Composer includes a What-You-See-Is-What-You-Get (WYSIWYG) document-creation tool, with drag-and-drop hyperlink and image capability. Its functions are similar to word-processing commands.

Step 1. Go to http://home.netscape.com/download

Step 2. If Using Windows 95, follow appropriate directions to download Netscape 4.6 Communicator. Composer is one of its components.

Step 3. The file takes 32 MB memory. The file size is 14.6 MB.

Step 4. For instructions on how to use, the Composer NetHelp file can be downloaded or printed out (about 35 pages).

Resources

The third WebQuest section, Resources, consists of Internet links that the teacher preselects. Depending on the computer literacy level of the students, students may use this opportunity to search for relevant sites and record the information in the Planner. Compiling the Resources can take a lot of time; teachers may want to weed out any sites with extremely difficult readability or organization of information. By having these links, students do not need to worry about typing in a cumbersome URL address to a Web site; they simply click on the hypertext link on the Resources page. This section can also be built in to the Process to aid students who have difficulties breaking the sequence of the steps to use the preselected links.

Process

Process, the fourth component of the WebQuest, consists of steps that guide the students toward reaching their goal. The S.O.S. WebQuest provided five steps clearly describing what the student was expected to do. Simplification of language due to low reading ability is very easy to incorporate in this stage. The steps can be broken down into as many as needed for the student to be successful. Students can also be helpful in creating this section with the guidance of the teacher in breaking down the sequence of the activity so that all students understand the task. If the Process steps are photocopied onto a transparency, all students can join in the discussion of how to make the steps easier to understand. Again, ownership of the activity helps increase student participation and success. English class became the scene for the Process and final Evaluation components of the S.O.S. WebQuest.

Evaluation

The next step, the Evaluation, tells students how they will be graded on completion of the lesson. For example, the S.O.S. WebQuest Evaluation section states that students will receive a grade consisting of 25% for the *Lusitania* research index cards, 25% for the *Titanic* research index cards, and 50% for the letter to the grant committee. I have

Initial drafts of the WebQuest online unit should include the classroom objectives, IEP objectives, and state standards of learning.

found that student input in the planning of this stage also helps reinforce the importance of each part of the activity. The letters were assessed based on a rubric that mirrors the state standards. Adherence to IEP goals and objectives was also measured and recorded at the appropriate times during the activity.

Conclusion

The last part of a WebQuest is the teacher-written Conclusion. Here, the teacher states the cross-curricular objectives that the student has successfully accomplished with the completion of the activity. The Conclusion also revisits the academic standards that apply to the students' work.

Standards and WebQuest

WebQuest lessons offer connections to the curriculum standards while maintaining flexibility necessary to meet students' special needs. Teaching to the content standards requires certain instructional approaches. New standards require students to apply, demonstrate, or use specific knowledge of skills, rather than just retain facts or demonstrate basic rote knowledge (e.g., see Table 1). Higher-order thinking and problem-solving skills are targeted, and more group projects and student collaborations seem to help in the instructional process (McLaughlin, Nolet, Phim, & Henderson, 1999). A one-computer classroom can encourage the class to work together to solve the problem posed. On the other hand, a computer lab facilitates using the approach with small groups of two or three students or with individuals.

Benefits to Students

We found many benefits to students from participating in the WebQuest. Homebound students with Internet access can be involved by including a link to the teacher's e-mail in case of questions concerning the lesson. In one case, a teacher sent the URL of the WebQuest to the mother of a student who requested information on missed assignments because of illness. The mother later said that she found the format easy to follow and that she had understood the directions and was able to help her son complete the activity. He returned to school the next week with his activity completed and was not behind in the classwork.

Positive feedback received from students stated that they not only enjoyed the Internet search part of the lesson, but asserted that the project was "something that made sense." Many students commented that even though "having to think is hard—filling in the blanks is easier." They agreed they un-

Figure 1. Text from Screenshot of WebQuest: S.O.S.—Salvaging One Sunken Ship

Created by Rebecca Kelly and Dr. Joanne Czernick with the help of their eighth grade Reading class, Delmar Jr. High School, Delmar, Delaware, February 1999

INTRODUCTION—TASK—RESOURCES—PROCESS—EVALUATION—CONCLUSION

INTRODUCTION

The sinking of the Lusitania (1915) and the Titanic (1912) are different incidents which occurred in history; however, these events share some similarities. In addition to reviewing historical accounts, students may read fictional accounts such as "Dark Crossing" by Joanne Suter (Lusitania) to gain a better understanding of the events and how they reflect a historical era as well as affect it.

TASK

You are a deep sea salvager who is interested in finding the wrecks of famous ships that have sunk. You have been awarded a grant by the International Maritime Society (IMS) that will provide resources to explore, and possibly raise, only one sunken ship. You have narrowed your choice down to two ships: the Lusitania or the Titanic. You need to research each location and the details of each sinking to help you gain facts to create opinion.

You will write a letter to the chairman of the IMS, giving your rationale for raising the ship of your choice. You will need to persuade them that your efforts will be worthwhile.

RESOURCES

Use the following links to find your information.

For the Lusitania

RMS Lusitania
Lusitania
Cunard Line's Lusitania
RMS Lusitania

For the Titanic

The Titanic Gallery
RMS Titanic—the Story Told
RMS Titanic's Final Resting Place
The Titanic Information Site

THE PROCESS

1. Within your small group of 2–4, label two sets of four large index cards with the following headings on the top left side of the card: Location, Time/Date of Incident, Historical Facts, and Questions Still Unanswered.
2. On the top right corner, label one set, "The Lusitania" and one set, "The Titanic."
3. Using the links in the Resources section above, find the following information to put on the cards for both ships. (You may want to divide up the work within your group due to time limitations.)
- Location: possible types of information include, but are not limited to: size of ship originally, size of wreckage, latitude and longitude.
- Time/Date of Incident: possible information might include: time of day the ship sank, the season and weather conditions, what year it sank.
- Historical Facts: include information such as: how many people aboard, how many survived, lifestyles of the people, importance of the ship, famous people aboard, significance of the actual sinking.

- Questions still unanswered: this includes questions that historians, other researchers, and your group have after looking over the data.
4. After collecting all of the data, you must make your decision about which ship should be salvaged or raised. Make a list of supporting arguments on your own sheet of notebook paper.
5. Using the arguments you have listed, write a business letter to the Chairman of the IMS, 200 State Street, Washington, DC 10003, giving your rationale for raising the ship of your choice. You will need to persuade them that your efforts will be worthwhile. Hand this letter in to your teacher when you are finished.
- Extra Credit: While doing your research you found out about the International Ice Patrol. You may want to reference in an extra paragraph about how the ICP can help you in your salvage operation. To go to the International Ice Patrol site, <u>click here</u>.

EVALUATION

You will receive one grade on this Web Quest assignment—25% for your Lusitania research index cards, 25% for your Titanic research index cards, and 50% for your letter to the IMS. The letter will be graded according to the rubric used in English class for a letter. Remember, content, construction, and mechanics of the letter will all be taken into consideration.

CONCLUSION

With the completion of this WebQuest, I hope you have gained experience in doing research to gain facts and to construct a persuasive argument. It is also hoped that the information you found has given you a new or expanded insight about how events shape history. In addition, the letter writing part was meant to reinforce writing skills including persuasive writing, supporting details, and, of course, mechanics. Hopefully, it will encourage you to ask questions and seek out the answers.

Last updated February 1999
Special thanks to students in 2nd period Reading for their assistance in constructing this page: S. Hargrove, B. Harris, J. Horseman, J. LeKites, D. Timmons, S. Hopkins, D. Heath, M. Stewart, A. Bailey, K. Carey, A. Henry, M. Norman, T. Phippin, M. Waddler, M. Jones, and R. Niblett.

Based on a template from THE WEBQUEST PAGE

Figure 2. WebQuest Planner (1 of 3)

Topic _____

Part A - Introduction (by teacher)

*To set up what material needs to be covered or known prior to the activity; also sets the stage for the activity and how it relates to content covered in the classroom

Part B – Task

Type of activity (check all that apply)

- ❑ Oral expression
    - ❑ Individual presentation
    - ❑ Group presentation
    - ❑ Skit or play
    - ❑ Other
- ❑ Written expression
    - ❑ Report format
        - ❑ Character essay
        - ❑ Narrative (like someone is telling a story)
        - ❑ Compare/contrast essay
        - ❑ Persuasive essay
        - ❑ Other
    - ❑ Article format
    - ❑ Letter
    - ❑ Poem
    - ❑ Diary entry(ies)
    - ❑ Other
- ❑ Artistic expression
    - ❑ Artwork (either on computer or to be scanned)
    - ❑ Photography (either digital or to be scanned)
    - ❑ Other

Looking at the things you have checked above, think about a situation in which resources from the Internet could help you solve your problem or create a response. Include the following:

***Who (what role will the student play)* –**

***What (what duties will he/she have to do)* –**

When (either what era is this taking place or what time frame might you be working with)-

***Why (what are you trying to accomplish)* –**

Figure 2. WebQuest Planner (2 of 3)

Part C - Resources

1. Title of site to be used for information:_____

    URL address: http://_____

2. Title of site to be used for information:_____

    URL address: http://_____

3. Title of site to be used for information:_____

    URL address: http://_____

4. Title of site to be used for information:_____

    URL address: http://_____

5. Title of site to be used for information:_____

    URL address: http://_____

6. Title of site to be used for information:_____

    URL address: http://_____

7. Title of site to be used for information:_____

    URL address: http://_____

8. Title of site to be used for information:_____

    URL address: http://_____

9. Title of site to be used for information:_____

    URL address: http://_____

10. Title of site to be used for information:_____

    URL address: http://_____

Figure 2. WebQuest Planner (3 of 3)

Part D - The Process
List the directions of how to accomplish the task(s) listed in Part B.

1._____

_____

2._____

_____

3._____

_____

4._____

_____

5._____

_____

Part E – Evaluation
How will the results be graded?

- ❑ By the teacher
- ❑ By the students
- ❑ By both teacher and students
(rubrics can be generic or specific, depending on the project or product created)

Part F – Conclusion (by the teacher)
To show the purpose and connections of the activity to the state standards and to general IEP goals, if applicable

Student Assignments

Part B   Part C   Part D

Teachers can help regain motivation and improve students' reading performance by connecting reading activities with realistic experiences and real-life applications.

derstood the subject better after looking at it from a new perspective and that it was a type of lesson that they would like to do again.

In addition, the general education teachers involved liked the level of engagement and diversity the WebQuest offered. In the case of the S.O.S. WebQuest, the student writing samples showed deeper thought than previous letter-writing exercises in class. Student interest was also evident when some even offered to help type the WebQuest on Netscape Composer and helped find and save images from the Internet for inclusion into the Web page itself. Duration of the WebQuest is at the teacher's discretion and can last from a few days to a few weeks, depending on the class size, ability, and class time schedule.

Special Education/Inclusion Accommodations for WebQuest

Both special and general education teachers can easily include accommodations and modifications in this type of lesson format. Because the WebQuest is text based, read-aloud programs such as the *Kurzweil 3000* allow the page contents to be read to students with visual or learning difficulties. In addition, the size of the type can be enlarged easily during the creation stage to promote easier readability. As previously noted, the author of the lesson can match the readability level with that of students with low reading levels. The lesson can also be adjusted to meet the reading and written expression goals of an IEP or to easily mirror state standards in a particular area. It is also a perfect vehicle to foster active participation in a project that spans several curricular areas. When using WebQuests in addition to other technology-based approaches, such as PowerPoint, my eighth-grade inclusion class improved their reading levels (Kelly, 1999). After comparing the reading levels as recorded on my students' IEPs from spring 1998 to spring 1999 with those of special education students in another eighth-grade inclusion class without the implementation of technological approaches, my group showed an average increase of 2.3 grade levels, whereas the other class showed an increase of 1.2 grade levels over the same time with the same general education teachers. The only variable that changed between the two groups was the implementation of creative technology-based approaches, such as the WebQuests, to improve and promote reading and written expression.

As a special education teacher in an inclusive classroom, I have observed the engagement of all students in the learning process through the use of the WebQuest design—including students with visual impairments, hearing impairments, learning disabilities, and no disabilities. Each student

The WebQuest Planner reinforces the five W's (who, what, when, where, and why) for students as they conduct their online research.

brings his or her best to the lesson and is able to participate in class without watering down the content. The WebQuest is not only a *design*, it is a *device* through which participation without frustration makes learning fun, exciting, and accessible to all students—which is just as it should be.

References

Goldberg, L. B. G. (1999). Making learning accessible. *Exceptional Parent, 29*(11), 34–40.

Hawes, K. S. (1998). Reading the Internet: Conducting research for the virtual classroom. *Journal of Adolescent & Adult Literacy, 41,* 563–565.

Hobbs, T., & Westling, D. L. (1998). Promoting successful inclusion through collaborative problem solving. *TEACHING Exceptional Children, 31*(1), 12–18.

Holloway, J. H. (1999). Redefining literacy: Improving the reading skills of adolescents. [Online]. *Educational Leadership, 57*(2). Available: http://www.ascd.org/readingroom/edlead/9910/holloway.html

Kelly, R. (1999). Getting everybody involved: Cooperative PowerPoint creations benefit inclusion students. *Learning & Leading with Technology, 27*(1), 10–14.

McLaughlin, M. J., Nolet, V., Phim, L. M., & Henderson, K. (1999). Integrating standards: Including all students. *TEACHING Exceptional Children, 31*(3), 66–71.

Orkwis, R., and McLane, K. (1998). *A curriculum every student can use: Design principles for student access.* Reston, VA: The Council for Exceptional Children.

Stahl, S. (1999). *Adapting curricula to address diverse learner needs.* Dover, DE: Sixth Annual Inclusion Conference (Center for Applied Special Technology).

Rebecca Kelly, *Special Education Teacher/ Special Education Building Coordinator, Delmar Middle and High Schools, Delmar School District, Delmar, Delaware.*

Address correspondence to the author at 405 Delaware Avenue, Delmar, DE 19940 (e-mail: rkelly@delmar.k12.de.us).

Designing Instruction for Emotional Intelligence

Richard Goldsworthy

"What has received relatively little attention by instructional technologists and designers is **the development of instruction that incorporates affective goals, objectives, and strategies into educational programs and practices**" (Martin & Briggs, 1986, p. xi, emphasis in original).

The importance of helping both children and adults grow socially and emotionally has received heightened attention in the past few years. In the corporate world, interpersonal skills, the "soft skills" of corporate training, are being recognized as at least as important, and often even more so, than technical and "cognitive" skills. These soft skills include maintaining motivation in the face of adversity, sustaining self-confidence, working with others in often pressure-intensive work environments where group work is essential to success, and in general responding in appropriate ways to social situations. They go beyond—and, perhaps, make possible—the traditional soft skills of selling, customer support, and conflict resolution. They are as important to finding a job and being successful as they are to the performance of specific job responsibilities. Goleman (1995, 1998) has argued, in fact, that EQ, or Emotional Quotient, is far more important to occupational and personal success than IQ.

In the worlds of our children, violence, conflict, and aggression are receiving increased attention in homes and schools, especially after such tragic events as the shootings in Littleton, CO, and the upswing of weapons-focused violence in educational institutions in the United States.

There exists a long history of researchers trying to understand the roots of conflict, particularly aggressive and violent behavior, and to create prevention and isolated intervention programs that reduce levels of conflict and aggressive behavior in schools. Calls for the inclusion of social processes as an overt part of school curriculum and as an important part of understanding any learning (see, e.g., Goodenow, 1992) are likely to extend such efforts beyond the realm of stand-alone interventions into daily school practices as the lines between "cognitive" and "affective" aspects of life become increasingly blurred, and as instructional and curricular designers recognize that learning specifically and activity generally are already socially contextualized.

As a result of the heightened recognition of social aspects of learning in both the corporate and educational worlds, the instructional design (ID) field faces the challenge of creating effective instruction that goes beyond using socially significant interaction in service to cognitive goals, as represented in the field's present emphasis on the use of collaborative and cooperative learning activities in the form of project- and problem-based learning. In addition to recognizing the importance of social activities in traditionally cognitive instructional goals and the often overlooked corollary that we must support learners' participation in those social activities, we must go further and develop educational activities that directly focus on supporting our learners in developing social competence.

This article provides a framework for systematically addressing key areas of social competence in development efforts. This framework is drawn from recent theoretical and practical research and development efforts on emotional intelligence and related efforts from cognitive and developmental psychologists. First, I will briefly ad-

From *Educational Technology*, September/October 2000, pp. 43-48. © 2000 by Educational Technology. Reprinted by permission.

dress a few sources of information regarding the ID field's treatment of socioemotional learning, then introduce the Emotional Intelligence Framework and draw upon several past and ongoing technology-based efforts to illuminate avenues of development. The article closes with a call for future development efforts.

The Background

The ID field has long addressed, although often obliquely, issues of social competence and emotional intelligence. We have long hand-waved at the "affective domain," pointing to its importance as part-and-parcel of learning in general. It should be noted, however, that all too frequently, the affective domain has been treated as a poor relation, necessary to effective learning but not the focal point of our endeavors.

Early on, Krathwohl, Bloom, and Masia (1964) developed what is perhaps the most detailed account of the affective domain for this field in their attempts to produce a set of taxonomic objectives for the socioemotional realm. Such seminal writers on instructional design as Dick and Carey (1990), Gagné (1985), and others have included a place for the affective, usually motivational. A recent volume edited by Reigeluth (1999) sought to recanvas instructional design theories and included a section on the affective domain with chapters reporting work ranging from character education to attitudinal instruction. The 1995 *Handbook of Research for Educational Communications and Technology* (Jonassen), however, has only one chapter specifically addressing the affective domain and that focuses on attitude change. Only a handful of chapters mention emotion in any sense, and motivation is discussed by only a few authors, generally in terms of technology as an impetus for generating it. Skinner's work, *The Technology of Teaching* (1962), directly addresses the issues of emotion, self-control, and motivation more than many of our contemporaries today.

Perhaps the most extensive work in our field to address the issue of emotion and affect in learning and the learning of emotional skills is that of Martin and Briggs (1986). In their work, they highlighted the problem of treating the affective and cognitive (and psychomotor, for that matter) domains as conceptually distinct. While noting that most theorists acknowledge these domains are integrated naturally in real-world learning, Martin and Briggs pointed out that in ID research and development practice, these domains have, despite this recognition, been treated, for the most part, separately. The present article's opening quotation concerning the problem of the affective domain is from their work of almost 15 years ago, yet relatively little has changed in the field in regard to their lament. Their work, however, provides an excellent resource today for those interested in working with

socioemotional issues and educational design in an integrated, rather than conceptually isolated, manner.

So, the ID field has not been totally blind to issues emotional and social. However, I would argue that we have all too often treated human socioemotionality as at best a tool for the more weighty matters of technical, cognitive, or performance competence. Sometimes it is seen as a necessary but inconvenient part of instruction in those other competencies. And, at worst, it is conceptualized as a distraction from the "really" important objectives of learning. Our treatment of the socioemotional issues of learning is evolving, however, as we strive both to specifically address issues of social competence and capitalize on the socially situated nature of all learning in order to increase the effectiveness of instruction. In our efforts to do so, emotional intelligence, a loose theoretical construct originally proposed by Salovey and Mayer (1990) and later popularized by Goleman (1995), serves well.[1]

In a break from a tradition that stretches back to Plato and casts the emotions in a role to be subordinated by cognition, several researchers and writers, including Dewey (1966), Gardner (1983), Goleman (1995, 1998), LeDoux (1996), and Salovey and Mayer (1990), have emphasized the importance of the emotions as central to the self and, importantly, as *educable*. According to these theorists, social competence or emotional intelligence is malleable; that is, capable of growth over the lifespan. This stands in sharp distinction to IQ, which typically is cast as relatively static (for a detailed discussion of this and other issues of the relevance and validity of IQ, see Gould's (1996) excellent work.) Since these views and work by instructional designers in the affective domain assume that emotional intelligence is teachable, or at the very least learnable, how can we support it? What are its components? What does emotional intelligence include?

A complete canvassing of the field is needed, for it includes areas as diverse as personal psychology, social psychology, cognitive science, social skills development, social problem solving, social information processing, conflict resolution, peace education, and group dynamics.

In this article, for convenience, I subsume aspects of all of the above under the rubric of Emotional Intelligence—"the capacity for recognizing our own feelings and those of others, for motivating ourselves, and for managing emotions well in ourselves and our relationships" (Goleman, 1998, p. 317)—and focus on presenting a distillation of key areas of social competence on which we instructional designers could and should be working. I present this distillation in the form of the Emotional Intelligence Framework (EIF) in the hope that others will begin to systematically address this emergent yet ambiguous field. I will follow the discussion of the EIF with a report of work we and others are doing in developing technological tools to support emotional intelligence.

Table 1. The Emotional Intelligence Framework.

1. Emotional Intelligence is not static; it can and should be taught.

2. Emotion and cognition are highly interrelated and should be treated as such.

3. Emotional Intelligence has six components:
   (3.1)   Self-awareness of emotion.
   (3.2)   The ability to handle emotion appropriately.
   (3.3)   The ability to motivate oneself by harnessing emotion.
   (3.4)   Awareness of emotional responses in others.
   (3.5)   The ability to relate to and manage emotional relations with others.
   (3.6)   Knowledge and practice of appropriate, situation-specific social skills—specific social skills, such as negotiation, making eye contact, etc., in support of the Emotional Intelligence Framework (EIF), 3.1–3.5.

4. These six components (3.1–3.6) recur at various levels of complexity throughout an individual's life and, therefore, emotional development is lifelong and somewhat cyclical.

The Emotional Intelligence Framework (EIF)

I have proposed the EIF (see Table 1) as part of an effort to review work in our field that addresses social competence in any manner using the computer or other technologies. This review was done as a background effort for work I have performed under a grant from the National Institute of Mental Health to create multimedia software to support children, specifically those diagnosed with Attention Deficit/Hyperactivity Disorder (ADHD), in their development of social skills. The review itself is in submission, and I would be happy to share it with interested readers. The first stage of the multimedia for social skills research effort is summarized below and reported fully by Goldsworthy, Barab, and Goldworthy (in press). The EIF has four broad principles:

1. Emotional Intelligence Is Not Static.   The principle that emotional intelligence can be taught has already been addressed. It simply reminds us that we should never assume anything regarding our learners' social competence. They learn new social habits, good and bad, on a daily basis. It may take a long time to extinguish a socially maladaptive behavior, but it can be done. Developing new habits of heart and mind is also time-intensive and requires practice and support. But we must remember that our EQ grows, and therefore we as designers must take it into account, both when assessing the readiness of our learners and in individualizing our instruction.

2. Emotion and Cognition Are Tightly Interwoven.
The principle that emotion and cognition are highly interrelated and should be treated as such is most forcefully brought home by LeDoux's (1996) work on the interrelation of the emotional and rational in the brain. For our work as instructional design theorists and practitioners, this realization has implications for how we conceive instruction. If we think of emotion and cognition as separate processes in a pluralistic mind, then we are likely to discuss how our rationality can constrain or control our emotions. I follow Damasio's work in *Descartes' Error* (1994) in preferring to conceive of the emotions as a duality; that is, as two intermixed sides of our self, as opposed to a dualism through which competing sides of a bifurcated self compete for control. The recognition that all cognition is already, in some regard, socioemotionally situated brings home the importance of including affective elements in all our instruction, not as a nice addition, but rather as a necessary element in any affective learning environment. Collaborative learning and those educational strategies that capitalize upon it are effective not solely because they bring the collective brain power of a group to a problem, but also, and perhaps primarily, because the social act of working in a group is the heart and soul of learning.

3. Emotional Intelligence Has Six Content Components.
(3.1) Self-awareness of emotion includes recognizing the physiological signs of an emotional response as well as knowing one's own typical emotional responses to specific and general trigger situations. This ability is distinct from but related to one's ability to handle emotion effectively (3.2) and to harness emotion to motivate oneself toward some near or far term goal (3.3). Moving beyond these more intrapersonal skills, socially competent people have an awareness of emotional responses in others (3.4). That means they can recognize the verbal and nonverbal signs of an emotional response in others. They can feel empathy for others, put themselves in someone else's shoes, and consider how the other person may be responding and why. This fundamental empathic skill grounds the ability to relate to and manage emotional relations with others (3.5). That means knowing how to respond appropriately in a given emotional milieu. In order to achieve these more broadly based competencies (3.1–3.5), people need to learn to perform specific, targeted social skills (3.6), skills such as making eye contact, remaining calm, entering a conversation, and negotiating. These skills then support the Emotional Intelligence Framework.

4. Emotional Intelligence Development Is Iterative.
The six components of Section 3 recur at various levels of complexity throughout an individual's life and, there-

fore, emotional development is lifelong and iterative—as an individual improves (or, unfortunately, devolves) in one area, there is a cyclic effect on other areas. As in Senge's (1990) discussion of organizational behavior, emotional intelligence is bound to cycles both virtuous and vicious. Thus, if an individual loses his or her job, for example, he or she may lose self-esteem, which may lead to a drinking problem, which further decreases self-esteem and lessens the likelihood of finding a new job, *ad infinitum*. Such problems are the focus of programs such as JOBS that seek to help people in transition by supporting their emotional intelligence (Goleman, 1998, pp. 255–257).

EI and Instructional Design

My own group is interested primarily in examining the use of technology to enhance educational and training curricula and programs focused on aspects of socioemotional competence. It would be, of course, unfortunate for designers to think that technology alone can solve EI problems, or even that it should be the main avenue of distribution/implementation for most EI instructional design efforts.[2] However, in our experience, technology can play several important roles in supporting the development of learners' emotional intelligence, particularly as an instructional distribution medium rich with performance and situation examples and as a source of real- and near-time support of social performance.

For this article, I will discuss a few present uses of technology to support emotional intelligence, suggest some other possible uses, and then close by proposing directions for developers to take to further enrich this nascent field.

Bubble Dialogue (see Figure 1) developed by the Language and Hypermedia Research Group at the University of Ulster, has been used to support social development in therapeutic (Jones & Selby, 1997), conflict resolution (Jones, Price, & Selby, 1998), and educational settings (Cunningham, McMahon, & O'Neill, 1992; McMahon, O'Neill, & Cunningham, 1992). Bubble Dialogue has been described as an "open-ended" software package that is relatively content-free. One of its strengths lies in enabling learners to role-play. Two individuals, co-located at a single computer, are able to put words into the mouths and thoughts into the minds of an onscreen character. As can be seen in Figure 1, these utterances and thoughts are displayed, following the conventions of cartoons, as thought and speech balloons. The program can be used in either creation or review model. In the latter, users can review and change or annotate previous panels of dialogue. In the former, they cannot. Users can easily move between modes. The dialogue between two characters can be saved for later reflective discussion.

Figure 1. In Bubble Dialogue, learners role-play characters within a story. Learners may choose what characters say and think, thereby affording them the opportunity to consider not only what is said, but its socioemotional significance as well.

As a tool for distancing an individual from an emotional event, thereby enabling, for example, a teacher or therapist to make public the thoughts of a patient and then analyze them, Bubble Dialogue shows much innovation. Other uses of such a tool might include pre-scripting a story, complete with dialogue, and having learners fill in the thought balloons to indicate what the characters on screen are actually thinking while engaged in the narrative. Such a task would demonstrate and, with feedback, practice the emotional intelligence skill of empathy, of taking on the perspective of other characters, and, additionally, of recognizing what emotions might be appropriate for a person in a given situation.

Other technology efforts might target the choice of what to perform and effective performance of targeted social skills. Hagiwara and Myles (1999), for example, sought to teach autistic elementary children to wash their hands after going to the bathroom. They used a social story-based multimedia intervention. The results, which must be tempered by validity and reliability concerns, were positive. Others have attempted to teach more complex soft skills, such as selling, as did Kass, Burke, Blevis, and Williamson (1993/1994) in their development of Yello, a scenario-based multimedia tool for teaching advertising executives to sell telephone Yellow Page spots. Yet others have focused directly on social skills through the use of interactive video. For example, Carrol, Bain, and Houghton (1994), in a study of 72 children with Attention Deficit/Hyperactivity Disorder, found that an interactive video condition (as compared to linear video) received significantly higher levels of attention and that subjects demonstrated increased comprehension of the social behaviors being modeled, including making positive self-statements, initiating conversation, and responding to interpersonal social interactions (e.g., handling anger).

In our own work (see Goldsworthy, Barab, & Goldsworthy, in press), we have used QuickTime videos embedded in multimedia shells to teach children social problem solving, a complex process underlying emotional intelligence and involving the gathering of information, analysis of possible recourses, implementation of a solution, and reflection upon performance. The program stepped users through the analysis of several socially significant scenarios depicted in the 2–3 minute videos (see Figure 2). Questions regarding the video are given and feedback, when possible, delivered. Responses, both open-ended and multiple choice, could be delivered to the teacher for group discussion. In a controlled, three-group (computer, therapist, and control conditions) pre-post experimental evaluation of the tool, we found learners with ADHD developed an increased competence in their social problem solving as compared to the control group. No significant differences were found between the therapist-directed and the computer-based instruction. We are now also examining interactive video and the Web as a means for teaching conflict resolution skills through scenario-based education and online and offline group activities. A further project under way involves the development of a real-time game to help children develop empathy capability, and aggression and impulse control.

Using the Emotional Intelligence Framework, designers can think about other projects that might be useful. Under EIF 3.4, for example, we want to have folks able to recognize emotional responses in others. Support for developing this skill might range from something as simple as displaying canonical emotional reactions to learners, having them label the emotion, and providing feedback. In fact, some work similar to this has been done with special needs populations. There is a wealth of correlational and developmental assessment research in the area of affect recognition, but little work exists on training this ability, and none, that I could find, on the use of computers to do so. In work along this line of inquiry, however, videos of emotionally charged situations has been used to assess learners' ability to recognize the emotional content of a situation irrespective of the dialogue. This has been done by filtering the verbal content in order to obfuscate the meaning but not the tone of conversation (see Goleman, 1998, especially p. 18 and p. 239). In general, work on verbal and non-verbal recognition of emotion has been primarily basic research and assessment focused as opposed to practical efforts toward training—the exception being, again, special needs populations.

In terms of real- and near-time support of people, we could be developing tools to serve as reminders or as debriefing prompts. Embedded in a Palm device, such a just-in-time tool might aid learners of all ages in reflecting on performance. Others may be interested in how the functions of a support group, for example Alcoholics Anonymous, might be transi-

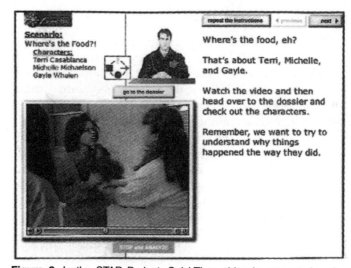

Figure 2. In the STAR Project, QuickTime video is presented and a mentor, top-center, guides the learner through analysis. The videos are 2–3 minutes, scripted scenes with significant social problems.

tioned to a more distributed and readily available environment, such as a Web-based support group, in order to perhaps enable those without local access to such resources to benefit from the community support they engender.

In addition to using the EIF to support the many ways technology can be used to support EI in our instructional development, it may be helpful to break out technology into educational subtypes. I have previously proposed four Lenses on Learning (Goldsworthy, 1999). These straightforward categories for thinking about technology enable us to systematically consider various ways in which our instructional design may incorporate technology. They include *learning from technology* in which we embed the content, in this case socioemotional, inside instruction delivered by the computer (or other medial). We may also design our educational environment to explicitly consider the *learning around technology*, wherein we pay specific attention to the educational opportunities of our technological and non-technological design components engender. When focused on *learning through technology*, the designer is specifically addressing opportunities for learner growth as mediated by technology. Bubble Dialogue is an example of stand-alone learning through technology, whereas networked collaboration and network-enabled project-based learning are more distributed examples. Finally, *assessment by technology* enables us to automate many aspects of information-gathering from and feedback to our learners. A designer may combine an EIF component with careful consideration of the affordances of these four aspects of educational technologies in order to propose and develop an effective technology-enhanced learning environment. By using the two frameworks together, we are more able to consider the big picture of our development efforts regardless of our target audience.

A Call to Arms

There is a clear need to recognize the social nature of all learning, the importance of targeting specifically socioemotional competencies, and the rich potential for growth the ID field has within these two combined areas. The Emotional Intelligence Framework set forth herein and the sample development efforts described provide a place from which designers may springboard into this exciting and very challenging area. We must recognize the socioemotional aspects of learning activities and design accordingly. We must design activities and programs specifically addressing aspects of EI. Finally, we must apply what this field has to offer in terms of formative design and situated assessment of learning to the development of more effective affective educational efforts.

References

Carrol, A., Bain, A., & Houghton, S. (1994). The effects of interactive versus linear video on the levels of attention and comprehension of social behavior by children with attention disorders. *School Psychology Review*, 23(1), 29–43.

Cunningham, D. J., McMahon, H., & O'Neill, W. (1992). Bubble dialogue: A new tool for instruction and assessment. *Educational Technology Research and Development*, 40(2), 59–67.

Damasio, A. (1994). *Descartes' error: Emotion, reason, and the human brain.* New York: Putnam.

Dewey, J. (1966). *Democracy and education.* New York: The Free Press.

Dick, W., & Carey, L. (1990). *The systematic design of instruction* (3rd ed.). New York: HarperCollins.

Elias, M., & Tobias, S. (1996). *Social problem solving: Interventions in the schools.* New York: Guilford.

Gagné, R. M. (1985). *The conditions of learning and theory of instruction* (4th ed.). New York: Holt, Rinehart, and Winston.

Gardner, H. (1983). *Frames of mind: The theory of multiple intelligences.* New York: Basic Books.

Goldsworthy, R. (1999). Lenses on learning and technology: Roles and opportunities for design and development. *Educational Technology*, 39(4), 59–62.

Goldsworthy, R., Barab, S., & Goldsworthy, E. (in press). Supporting ADHD Learners Development of Social Problem-Solving Skills. *Journal of Special Education Technology.*

Goleman, D. (1995). *Emotional intelligence.* New York: Bantam Books.

Goleman, D. (1998). *Working with emotional intelligence.* New York: Bantam Books.

Goodenow, C. (1992). Strengthening the links between educational psychology and the study of social contexts. *Educational Psychologist*, 27(2), 177–196.

Gould, S. J. (1996). *The mismeasure of man.* New York: W. W. Norton.

Hagiwara, T., & Myles, B. W. (1999). A multimedia social story intervention: Teaching skills to children with autism. *Focus on Autism and Other Developmental Disabilities*, 14(2), 82–96.

Healy, J. M. (1999). *Failure to connect.* New York: Touchstone.

Jonassen, D. H. (1995). (Ed.). *Handbook of research for educational communications and technology.* New York: Macmillan.

Jones, A., & Selby, C. (1997). The use of computers for self-expression and communication. *Journal of Computing in Childhood Education*, 8(2/3), 199–214.

Jones, A., Price, E., & Selby, C. (1998). Exploring children's responses to interpersonal conflict using Bubble Dialogue in a mainstream and EBD school. *Computers and Education*, 30(1–2), 67–74.

Kass, A., Burke, R., Blevis, E., & Williamson, M. (1993/1994). Construction learning environments for complex social skills. *Journal of the Learning Sciences*, 3(4), 387–427.

Krathwohl, D. R., Bloom, B. S., & Masia, B. B. (1964). *Taxonomy of educational objectives: The classification of education goals.* Handbook II: Affective domain. White Plains, NY: Longman.

LeDoux, J. (1996). *The emotional brain: The mysterious underpinnings of emotional life.* New York: Simon & Schuster.

Martin, B. L., & Briggs, L. J. (1986). *The affective and cognitive domains: Integration for instruction and research.* Englewood Cliffs: Educational Technology Publications.

McMahon, H., O'Neill, W., & Cunningham, D. J. (1992). "Open" software design: A case study. *Educational Technology*, 32(2), 43–55.

Reigeluth, C. M. (1999). *Instructional-design theories and models: A new paradigm of instructional theory, volume 2.* Mahwah, NJ: Lawrence Erlbaum Associates.

Salovey, P., & Mayer, J. D. (1990). Emotional intelligence. *Imagination, Cognition, and Personality*, 9(3), 185–211.

Salovey, P., & Sluyter, D. J. (1997). *Emotional development and emotional intelligence: Educational implications.* New York: Basic Books.

Senge, P. M. (1990). *The fifth discipline: The art and practice of the learning organization.* New York: Doubleday.

Skinner, B. F. (1962). *The technology of teaching.* New York: Appleton-Century-Crofts.

Notes

1. Additionally, Salovey and Sluyter's (1997) edited book on the educational implications of aspects of emotional intelligence is of particular salience to us as designers, as may be the work of Elias and Tobias (1996) on designing technological and non-technological interventions for social problem solving.

2. Goleman argues that EI is social and should, therefore, be taught through social means. He doesn't exclude technology but advises its mix with personal contact, something most of us recognize. Healy (1999), on the other hand, warns of the potential ill-effects of computer use by young children. As with most things, moderation is the key.

Richard Goldsworthy is Director of Research and Development at The Academic Edge, Inc., Bloomington, Indiana (e-mail: rick@academicedge.net).

An Illusory Dilemma

Online to Learn or In Line with Standards?

Curriculum-based telecomputing need not be in competition for time spent addressing curriculum standards. Online activities can assist students' subject-area learning, as the example projects in this article demonstrate.

By Judi Harris

An exceptionally creative and talented elementary school teacher told me a story recently that saddened but did not surprise me. This teacher has been helping her students use computers as learning tools in many ways and for many years. In particular, her students have been doing rich, multidisciplinary, curriculum-based telecollaborative and teleresearch projects for more than six years. Yet in May, this talented teacher's principal told her that the students in their school would "not be using the Internet" during the 2000–01 school year because their low achievement test scores required more "concentrating on the basics."

Perhaps you, like me, are shaking your head now, perplexed by this all-too-familiar misconception that in-school use of the Internet (and even computers in general) by students is somehow an "add-on," an "extra," or even a new curriculum." Combined with increasing pressure in many places for higher scores on standardized tests, we can understand why Internet-based work in the classroom can be seen as dispensable. Love & McVey (2000) described this tension as:

> additional demands associated with current standardized testing practices. Clearly there is a need to document student learning and to hold schools accountable. However, the often unreasonable pressure of preparing children for statewide tests has led to some instructional choices that may be of questionable worth in terms of the children's long-term educational attainment. (p. 2)

Though it's true that some Internet enriched learning activities seem disassociated from curriculum standards, we must remember that *tools don't constitute curriculum.* Rather, tools should be used in service of students' learning needs.

Telecollaboration and Teleresearch

Internet-supported, curriculum-based learning can take many forms, but essentially it is either *online collaboration,* also called "telecollaboration," or *online research,* also called "teleresearch." Telecollaborative learning activities are those in which students communicate electronically with others. Teleresearch learning activities are those in which students locate and use online information. Online collaboration and research are frequently combined in larger-scale educational projects. Both can use text, still or animated images, and sound. Both can be synchronous or asynchronous.

© 2000, ISTE (International Society for Technology in Education), 800.336.5191 (U.S. & Canada) or 541.302.3777 (Int'l), iste@iste.org, www.iste.org. All rights reserved.

Both can reproduce what students already do when they collaborate and do research using more traditional learning approaches. Yet to make these new opportunities worth the time, effort, and other resources necessary to bring them into the classroom, it is important to use the new tools in new and powerful ways.

Collaborative online learning activities can offer many educational benefits to their participants. The nature of these benefits depends, in large part, on the specifics of each activity's design and how well what the activity makes possible educationally matches the needs and preferences of participating students. In general, telecollaboration is most appropriate when students can be well served by:

- being exposed to multiple points of view, perspectives, beliefs, interpretations, and/or experiences
- comparing, contrasting, and/or combining similar information collected in dissimilar locations
- communicating with a real audience using written language
- expanding their global awareness

Online research can offer an ever-expanding wealth and variety of current information to learners. Whether this abundance helps or hinders students' subject-area learning depends, like online collaboration, on the activity's design and students' information-seeking and appraising skills. In general, teleresearch is most appropriate when students can be well served by:

- accessing information not available locally
- viewing information in multiple formats (e.g., text, graphics, video)
- comparing and contrasting differing information on the same topic
- considering emerging and very recent information (e.g., interim reports of research studies in progress)
- delving deeply into a particular area of inquiry

What kinds of learning activities can help students meet curriculum standards while incorporating telecollaboration and teleresearch in powerful ways? The scope and variety of curriculum-based telecomputing activities can be understood according to their structures and purposes.

Activity Structures and Purposes

Activity structures are flexible frameworks that help teachers efficiently and effectively create curriculum-based telecollaboration. They are a special type of thinking tool for teachers—a form of design assistance. They help us capture what is essential about the structure of a learning activity and communicate that in such a way as to encourage the creation—not replication—of context-appropriate environments for learning.

I have identified 18 telecollaborative activity structures to date, and I have grouped them into three categories.

- *Interpersonal Exchanges* are activities in which individuals talk electronically with other individuals or groups, or in which groups talk with other groups.
- *Information Collection and Analysis* activities involve students collecting, compiling, and comparing different types of interesting information.
- *Problem Solving* activities promote critical thinking, collaboration, and problem-based learning.

Curriculum-based teleresearch activities are categorized differently, according to their apparent learning *purposes* rather than their structures. The purposes include:

- practicing information-seeking and evaluating skills
- exploring a topic of inquiry or finding answers to a particular question
- reviewing multiple perspectives on a topic
- collecting data
- assisting in authentic problem solving

- publishing information syntheses or critiques for others to use in teleresearch

More information about each of these structures and purposes, along with examples of classroom-tested, curriculum-based activities that illustrate them, can be found at *Virtual Architecture*'s (Harris, 1998) Web home: http://ccwf.cc.utexas.edu/~jbharris/ Virtual-Architecture/. Please see the articles describing telecollaboration and teleresearch in terms of structures and purposes at http://ccwf.cc.utexas.edu/ ~jbharris/Virtual-Architecture/Foundation/index.html.

Time and Space

Have you noticed that the only time there seems to be a profusion of space in a house (or apartment, or classroom, or office) is when we first move in? Somehow, as time passes, our roommates and possessions—or, perhaps, our expectations—multiply in such a way so that soon we feel we need more space. As teachers, we face a similar situation with the biggest challenge to powerful educational use of the Internet: *time*. Somehow, as the years pass, we realize that we must add more to what our students experience in our classrooms. Fortunately, Internet tools and resources are not (or, shall I say: *should not be*) additions to our curricula; rather, they can be used as "instruments of construction." So, at least theoretically, once we have developed the skills prerequisite to using Internet tools and resources effectively within the curriculum, adding online components shouldn't take additional time or space.

Are some of you starting to smell snake oil? If you have used online facilities as part of your teaching already, does it seem that doing so took more, rather than less, time and energy? Part of this expenditure of precious resources may have to do with developing technical expertise, arranging network access, and so on. Yet beyond that, it does seem that curriculum-based telecomputing projects take longer, doesn't it?

The reasons behind this relationship probably have more to do with the *types* of telecomputing projects that we see as worthwhile in terms of time, effort, and resources needed. Although I know of no research results that have reported this discovery, from talking with many telecomputing teachers and from being involved in many curriculum-based projects myself, I suspect that what we see as worthy projects are student-centered, active, problem-based, multi-modal, and interdisciplinary. Planning for and implementing such rich educational experiences requires more time, energy, and resources than traditional, didactic, unimodal teaching. Use of the Internet isn't really what occupies more time and space in our schedules; teaching well does.

But the very real limitations of curricular crowding and time shortage still need to be addressed. Unfortunately, unlike a family that may be able to move to a larger house when its members perceive a need for additional space, there's not much hope of any of us getting more space in our students' schedules. Might it be possible, then, for each project to effectively *combine* curricular goals, telecollaborative activity structures, and teleresearch purposes? Let's take a look at some example projects to see how it is done.

Musical Plates

The Musical Plates project (http://k12science.ati.stevens-tech.edu/curriculum/musicalplates/, Figure 1) is a multidisciplinary exploration of earthquakes and plate tectonics that helps secondary students learn actively in science, mathematics, language arts, and instructional technology. Students are introduced to this problem-based project by reading a scenario about a geologist's work assignment (Figure 2). They use real-time earthquake and volcano data, accessed using the Internet, to respond to the situation. In addition, they assert data-based hypotheses about how earthquakes and

Once we have developed the skills prerequisite to using Internet tools and resources effectively within the curriculum, going online shouldn't take additional time or space.

volcanic eruptions affect the plants and animals in differing natural habitats and how local, national, and global human communities respond to such natural events. Participants are encouraged to publish their work online at the site for others to use.

Seen from a design standpoint, this rich project offers students engaging teleresearch opportunities to accomplish all six purposes listed previously. More importantly, students satisfy multiple requirements in each of four curriculum areas. The project's creators have cited these specifically according to two national, five state, and one local sets of standards (http://k12science.ati.stevens-tech.edu/curriculum/musicalplates/standards.html). For example, the New Jersey Core Curriculum Content Standards that students satisfy by participating fully in the Musical Plates project include:

> 3.2: All students will actively listen in a variety of situations in order to receive, interpret, evaluate, and respond to information obtained from a variety of sources.
>
> 3.3: All students will compose texts that are diverse in content and form for different audiences for real and varied purposes.
>
> 3.5: All students will view, understand, and use nontextual visual information and representations for critical comparison, analysis, and evaluation.

Advocates for the Millennium

This imaginative five-week project (www.angelfire.com/mi/llennium3/, Figure 3) from Alberta, Canada, helps students in Grades 3–9 explore ideas related to millennia through work in language arts, social studies, and information and communication technology. Much of this project is telecollaborative; students engage in activities structured as global classrooms, keypal exchanges, telementoring, information exchanges, and electronic publishing. Teleresearch is used to help students explore millennium-related topics from multiple points of view; for example, students can make predictions, create inventions, or research important people from the past 1,000 years.

The project, now in its third year, adopts a new theme annually but is scheduled similarly each time. During the spring of 2000, for example, the project commemorated the International Year of the Older Person with weekly activities including the following:

> Week Two: The Past
> Research an important person of the last 1,000 years. Research is placed on a circle that will go on a 1,000-year timeline.
>
> Week Three: The Present
> Students record the stories of their own grandparents or a grandparent they have adopted. Students complete PowerPoint presentations on the millennium.
>
> Week Four: The Future
> Futuristic poetry, predictions, stories, and descriptive writing. What will the future look like? Where will you be? What does a car or a house of the future look like? Be creative!

Curriculum standards that the project satisfies are listed by grade level and discipline (www.angelfire.com/mi/llennium3/lacurobj.html). For eighth graders, for example, 14 language arts, 19 information and communication technology, and more than 50 social studies standards are addressed in the context of just this one project.

Fairy Tale Cyber Dictionary

In this simple yet powerful project for very young students (www.op97.k12.il.us/instruct/ftcyber/index.html, Figure 4), each participating teacher

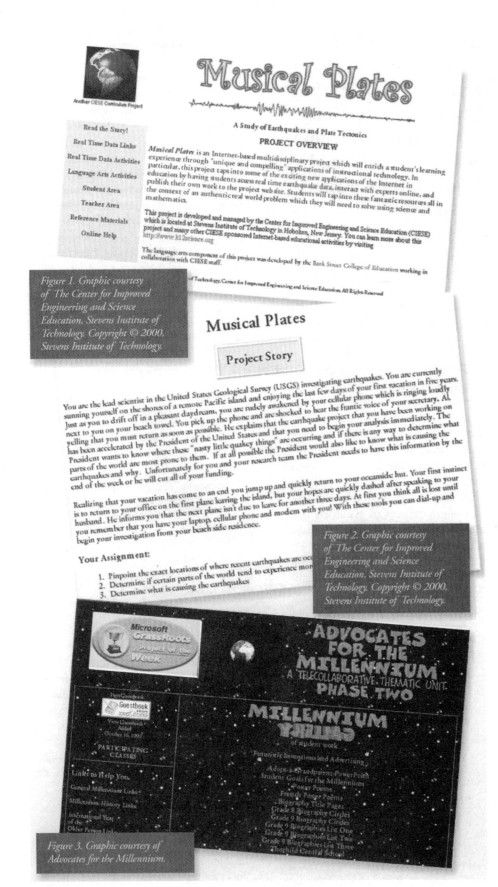

Figure 1. Graphic courtesy of The Center for Improved Engineering and Science Education, Stevens Institute of Technology. Copyright © 2000, Stevens Institute of Technology.

Figure 2. Graphic courtesy of The Center for Improved Engineering and Science Education, Stevens Institute of Technology. Copyright © 2000, Stevens Institute of Technology.

Figure 3. Graphic courtesy of Advocates for the Millennium.

chooses a familiar fairy tale to read aloud to his or her class. As a group, students then retell the story in their own words and with their own art-work, either writing or dictating their version of the tale. There's a clever challenge in this particular project's design: In retelling the fairy tale, students are asked to choose and include words beginning with each letter of the alphabet that communicate important aspects of the story.

For example, when kindergarten students in Kapa'a Elementary School in Kapa'a, Kauai, Hawaii, retold the story of "Jack and the Beanstalk," they created the sample shown in Figure 5. When you select a letter, you

> ## Use of the Internet isn't really what occupies more time and space in our schedules; teaching well does.

see the students' captioned illustration of a word from the fairy tale beginning with that letter (Figure 6).

Participating classes' fairy tales are posted at the project's site for all to enjoy. Although it was not described in the posted plans for the project, I suspect that students visiting this cyber-collection use the student- written and -illustrated tales to review alphabet and spelling skills.

The Fairytale Cyber Dictionary project demonstrates that multiple curriculum standards can be addressed even in short-term projects with the simplest of designs. As you can see, this project addresses listening comprehension, word analysis, spelling, memory-building, sequencing, linguistic problem-solving, and graphic skills.

What Dilemma?

The point, I hope, is clear: Participating in one well-designed project can help students address many content and process standards at the same

Enter Here

Figure 4. Graphic from the Fairy Tale Cyber Dictionary. Reprinted with permission.

Jack and the Beanstalk

Kindergarten - Kapa'a Elementary School - Kapa'a, Kauai, Hawaii

Figure 5. Graphic from the Fairy Tale Cyber Dictionary. Reprinted with permission.

A B C D E F G H I J K L M N O P
Q R S T U V W X Y Z

Pick a letter, dick a letter!

(The sentences put together into a story)

Jack and the Beanstalk

Jack traded his cow for five magic beans. Jack's mother threw the magic beans out the window. The vine grew. Jack looked out the window and he saw a giant beanstalk. Jack was excited when he saw the beanstalk. The beanstalk grew and grew and grew. Jack went up the beanstalk.

Jack climbed the beanstalk. Jack climbed the beanstalk and saw a castle. Jack sneaked into the castle. The giant's wife gave Jack some breakfast in the kitchen.

The castle door slammed. Jack went in the oven. Jack hid in the oven.

The giant was eating at the table. The harp played beautiful music with no one playing it. The giant told the hen to lay a golden egg. The hen layed magic golden eggs.

The giant took a nap and his snores shook the castle. The giant snored, "zzzzzzzzzzzz."

J is for Jack.
Jack climbed the beanstalk.

Figure 6. Graphic from the Fairy Tale Cyber Dictionary. Reprinted with permission.

time and in engaging, pedagogically sound ways. Although there is yet no generalizable evidence that doing so will help improve standardized test scores, it would stand to reason that *if the testing instruments are reliable, valid, and matched to relevant curriculum standards,* the benefits of such project-based learning should also be reflected in higher test scores. If they aren't, perhaps we should question the *tests* before we question the ways in which creative teachers are helping their students learn. Use of Internet tools and resources in curriculum-based ways not only directly addresses curriculum standards but can also do so in a time-efficient and learner-centered way.

References

Harris, J. (1998). *Virtual architecture: Designing and directing curriculum-based telecomputing.* Eugene, OR: International Society for Technology in Education.
Love, R., & McVey, M. (2000). Teachers' use of the Internet. *Teachers College Record* [Online serial]. Available: www.tcrecord.org/printidkwparam.asp?@IdNumber=10538.

Judi Harris (judi.harris@mail.utexas.edu), associate professor in Curriculum and Instruction and area coordinator for Instructional Technology at the University of Texas at Austin, directs the Electronic Emissary (emissary.ots.utexas.edu/emissary). She has authored more than 150 articles and four books, most recently the 1998 books Virtual Architecture: Designing and Directing Curriculum-Based Telecomputing *(published by ISTE) and* Design Tools for the Internet-Supported Classroom *(published by ASCD).*

Unit 3

Unit Selections

Key Points to Consider

❖ Locating software that meets a particular set of objectives can be a challenge. Describe how you would search for specific application packages. Discuss what criteria you would use to determine whether you should purchase the program or develop your own.

❖ What are some strategies you can use to effectively integrate technology into the classroom?

❖ How can technology be used to provide a context for which grounded constructions may emerge?

 **Links** **www.dushkin.com/online/**

These sites are annotated on pages 4 and 5.

Software is the fuel that brings computers to life; it is also the magic that makes Internet interactive multimedia happen. It contains the grain of creativity that causes us to wonder, "How did they do that?" Internet-based multimedia can capture the learner's imagination and help demonstrate ideas. However, it must be chosen with a certain criteria in mind, such as the purpose for using it, who will be using it, and whether it will be effective in satisfying the learner's needs. We must guard against being persuaded by combinations of immediate access, sound, graphics, video, and animation that stimulate our senses but fail to meet the objectives of our curriculum or the needs of our learners. Using systematic evaluation techniques found in these articles, we have the mindtools that are needed to meet the learner's needs.

In the lead article, David Jonassen, Chad Carr, and Hsiu-Ping Yueh describe how common computer software applications can be used as knowledge construction mindtools. The authors state that technologies should not support learning by attempting to instruct the learners, but rather should be used as knowledge construction tools that students learn with, not from. They describe how learners function as designers, and the computers function as mindtools for interpreting and organizing their personal knowledge.

Next, Sasha Barab, Kenneth Hay and Thomas Duffy describe five ways in which technology can be used to foster authentic learner inquiry. They explain how technology can be used to provide a fertile context from which grounded constructions may emerge. They envision using such technological resources as providing multimedia environments to be explored in a context where the learner is engaged in authentic inquiry.

Sherry Roberts's article "Kids as Computers" describes how a teacher combined small group design and role-playing with an information-processing model to teach students computer literacy. The students learned how the information processing cycle works. In this process each group member becomes a step in the information processing cycle. This model strategy is also the answer to classroom management concerns. The article provides many activities that lead to the development of concepts and skills such as decision making, problem solving, and conflict resolution.

In "Learning to Use Your Mind Effectively in a Technology-Based Classroom," Pamela Keel presents the structure of teaching technology. She presents methods that differentiate and allow students to take

their research and projects to individual levels that are matched to their own experiences. The article outlines the steps needed to achieve specific learning objectives. The processes involved in this strategy closely resemble the components of project management. Students are grouped into teams, assigned projects, and expected to complete a quality project by a specific due date.

Next, Lynn McNally and Cindy Etchinson specify seven practical strategies for integrating technology into the classroom in a smooth and effective manner. The approach uses a variety of software applications as classroom management tools. The article details ways for both teachers and students to use technology tools for classroom management. It accomplishes a shared sense of classroom ownership and responsibility in a collaborative classroom setting.

Finally, James Donlevy and Tia Rice Donlevy describe a series of free, online workshops developed by Channel Thirteen/WNET New York and Disney Learning Partnerships to help teachers explore issues in education. The issues include multiple intelligences, constructivism, academic standards, cooperative and collaborative learning, and assessment. Curriculum redesign, inquiry-based learning, and the role of parents and the community are important components as well in this review of important issues in education.

Computers as Mindtools for Engaging Learners in Critical Thinking

By David H. Jonassen, Chad Carr, and Hsiu-Ping Yueh

Traditionally, instructional technologies have been used as media for delivering instruction, that is, as conveyors of information and tutors of students. When used in this way, information is stored in the technology. During the instructional process, learners perceive and try to understand the messages stored in the technology as they *interact* with it. Interaction is often limited to pressing a key to continue the information presentation or responding to queries posed by the stored program. The technology program judges the learner's response and provides feedback, most often about the correctness of the learner's response. Technologies that have been developed by instructional designers are often marketed to educators as validated and teacher proof, removing any meaningful control of the learning process by the learners or the teachers. In this article, we argue that technologies should not support learning by attempting to instruct the learners, but rather should be used as knowledge construction tools that students learn with, not from. In this way, learners function as designers, and the computers function as *Mindtools* for interpreting and organizing their personal knowledge.

Mindtools are computer applications that, when used by learners to represent what they know, necessarily engage them in critical thinking about the content they are studying (Jonassen, 1996). Mindtools scaffold different forms of reasoning about content. That is, they require students to think about what they know in different, meaningful ways. For instance, using databases to organize students' understanding of content organization necessarily engages them in analytical reasoning, where creating an expert system rule base requires them to think about the causal relationships between ideas. Students cannot use Mindtools as learning strategies without thinking deeply about what they are studying.

Using Computers as Mindtools

Many computer applications have been developed explicitly to engage learners in critical thinking. Others can be repurposed as Mindtools. There are several classes of Mindtools, including semantic organization tools, dynamic modeling tools, information interpretation tools, knowledge construction tools, and conversation and collaboration tools (Jonassen, in press). We shall briefly describe and illustrate some of these (space limits prevent illustrations of all Mindtools). For a report of research on Mindtools, see Jonassen and Reeves (1996).

Semantic Organization Tools

Semantic organization tools help learners to analyze and organize what they know or what they are learning. Two of the best known semantic organization tools are databases and semantic networking (concept mapping) tools.

Databases. Database management systems are computerized record keeping systems that were developed originally to replace paper-based filing systems. These electronic filing cabinets allow users to store information in organized databases that facilitate retrieval. Content is broken down into records that are divided into fields which describe the kind of information in different parts of each record.

Databases can be used as tools for analyzing and organizing subject matter (i.e. Mindtools). The database shown in Figure 1 was developed by students studying cells and their functions in a biology course. The

 From *TechTrends*, March 1998, pp. 24-32. © 1998 by TechTrends. Reprinted by permission.

Figure 1. Content database.

cell type	location	function	shape	tissue systems	specialization	related cell
Astocyte	CNS	Supply Nutrients	Radiating	Nervous	Half of Neural Tissue	Neurons, Capillaries
Basal	Stratum Basale	Produce New Cells	Cube, Columnar	Epithelial	Mitotic	Epithelial Cells
Basophils	Blood Plasma	Bind Imm.E	Lobed Nuclei	Connective, Immune	Basic, Possible Mast	Neutrophil, Eosinophil
Cardiac Muscle	Heat	Pump Blood	Branched	Muscle	Intercalated discs	Endomysium
Chondroblast	Cartilage	Produce Matrix	Round	Connective		
Eosinophil	Blood Plasma	Protazoans, Allergy	Two Lobes	Connective, Immune	Acid, Phagocytos (Prote	Basophil, Neutrophil
Ependymal	Line CNS	Form Cerebralspinal Fluid	Cube	Nervous	Cilia	
Erythrocytes	Blood Plasma	Transport O2, Remove CO2	Disc	Connective	Transport	Hemocytoblast, Proeryt
Fibroblast	Connective Tissue	Fiber Production	Flat, Branched	Connective	Mitotic	
Goblet	Columnar Epithelial	Secretion	Columnar	Epithelial	Mucus	Columnar
Keratinocytes	Stratum Basal	Strengthen other Cells	Round	Epithelial		Melanocytes
Melanocytes	Stratum Basale	U.V. Protection	Branched	Epithelial	Produce Melanin	Keratinocytes
Microglia	CNS	Protect	Ovoid	Nervous	Macrophage	Neurons, Astrocytes?
Motor Neuron	CNS(Cell Body)	Impulse Away from CNS	Long, Thin	Nervous	Multipolar, Neuromuscul	Sensory Neuron, Neurog
Neutrophil	Blood Plasma	Inflammation, Bacteria	Lobed Nuclei	Connective, Immune	Phagocytos, Neutral	Basophils, Eosinophil
Oligodendrocyte	CNS	Insulate	Long	Nervous	Produce Myaline Sheath	Neurons
Osteoblast	Bone	Produce Organic Matrix	Spider	Connective	Bone Salts	Osteoclasts
Osteoclast	Bone	Bone Restoration	Ruffled Boarder	Connective	Destroy Bone	Osteoblasts
Pseudostratified	Gland Ducts, Respira	Secretion	Varies	Epithelial	Cilia	Goblet

database can then be searched and sorted to answer specific questions about the content or to identify interrelationships and inferences from the content, such as, "Do different shaped cells have specific functions?" Constructing content databases requires learners to develop a data structure, locate relevant information, insert it in appropriate fields and records, and search and sort the database to answer content queries. A large number of critical thinking skills are required to use and construct knowledge-oriented databases.

Semantic Networking. Semantic networking tools provide visual screen tools for producing concept maps. Concept mapping is a study strategy that requires learners to draw visual maps of concepts connected to each other via lines (links). These maps are spatial representations of ideas and their interrelationships that are stored in memory, i.e. structural knowledge (Jonassen, Beissner, & Yacci, 1993). Semantic networking programs are computer-based, visualizing tools for developing representations of semantic networks in memory. Programs such as SemNet, Learning Tool, Inspiration, Mind Mapper, and many others, enable learners to interrelate the ideas that they are studying in multidimensional networks of concepts, to label the relationships between those concepts, and to describe the nature of the relationships between all of the ideas in the network, such as that in Figure 2.

The purpose of semantic networks is to represent the structure of knowledge that someone has constructed. So, creating semantic networks requires learners to analyze the structural relationships among the content they are studying. By comparing semantic networks created at different points in time, they can also be used as evaluation tools for assessing changes in thinking by learners. If we agree that a semantic network is a meaningful representation of memory, then learning from this perspective can be thought of as a reorganization of semantic memory. Producing semantic networks reflects those changes in semantic memory, since the networks describe what learners know. So, semantic networking programs can be used to reflect the process of knowledge construction.

Dynamic Modeling Tools

While semantic organization tools help learners to represent the semantic relationships among ideas, dynamic modeling tools help learners to describe the dynamic relationships among ideas. Dynamic modeling tools include spreadsheets, expert systems, systems modeling tools, and microworlds, among others.

Spreadsheets. Spreadsheets are computerized, numerical record keeping systems that were designed originally to replace paper-based, ledger accounting systems. Essentially, a spreadsheet is a grid or matrix of empty cells with columns identified by letters and rows identified by numbers. Each cell is a

Figure 2. A mind map.

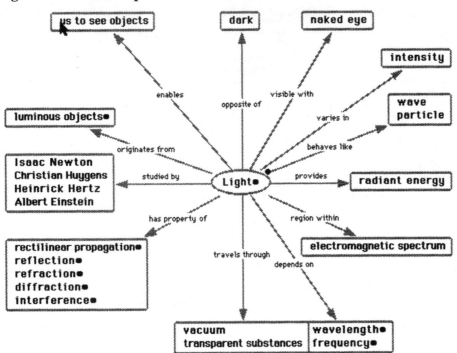

placeholder for values, formulas relating values in other cells, or functions that mathematically or logically manipulate values in other cells. Functions are small programmed sequences that may, for instance, match values in cells with other cells, look up a variable in a table of values, or create an index of values to be compared with other cells.

Spreadsheets were originally developed and are most commonly used to support business decision making and accounting operations. They are especially useful for answering "what if' questions; for instance, "What if interest rates increased by one percent?" Changes made in one cell automatically recalculate all of the affected values in other cells. Spreadsheets are also commonly used for personal accounting and budgeting.

Spreadsheets also may be used as Mindtools for amplifying mental functioning. In the same way that they have qualitatively changed the accounting process, spreadsheets can change the educational process when working with quantitative information. Spreadsheets model the mathematical logic that is implied

by calculations. Making the underlying logic obvious to learners should improve their understanding of the interrelationships and procedures. Numerous educators have explored the use of spreadsheets as Mindtools. Spreadsheets frequently have been used in mathematics classes to calculate quantitative relationships in various chemistry and physics classes. They are also useful in social studies instruction and have even supported ecology. Spreadsheets are flexible Mindtools for representing, reflecting on, and calculating quantitative information. Building spreadsheets requires abstract reasoning by the user; they are rule-using tools that require that users become rule-makers. Spreadsheets also support problem solving activities, such decision analysis reasoning, which requires learners to consider implications of various conditions and entails higher order reasoning.

Expert Systems. Expert systems have evolved from research in the field of artificial intelligence. An expert system is a computer program that simulates the way human ex-

perts solve problems, that is, an artificial decision maker. They are computer-based tools that are designed to function as intelligent decision supports. For example, expert systems have been developed to help geologists decide where to drill for oil; bankers to evaluate loan applications; computer sales technicians how to configure computer systems; and employees to decide among a large number of company benefits alternatives. Problems whose solutions require decision making are good candidates for expert system development.

Most expert systems consist of several components, including the knowledge base, inference engine, and user interface. There are various "shells" or editors for creating expert system knowledge bases, which is the part of the activity that engages critical thinking. Building the knowledge base requires the learner to articulate causal knowledge.

The development of expert systems results in deeper understanding because they provide an intellectual environment that demands the refinement of domain knowledge, supports problem solving, and monitors the acquisition of knowledge. A good deal of research has focused on developing expert system advisors to help teachers identify and classify learning disabled students.

Systems Modeling Tools.
Complex learning requires students to solve complex and ill-structured problems as well as simple problems. Complex learning requires that students develop complex mental representations of the phenomena they are studying. A number of tools for developing these mental representations are emerging. Stella, for instance, is a powerful and flexible tool for building simulations of dynamic systems and processes (systems with interactive and interdependent components). Stella uses a simple set of building block icons to construct a map of a process (see Figure 4). The Stella model in Figure

Figure 4. Conceptual map of the Beast

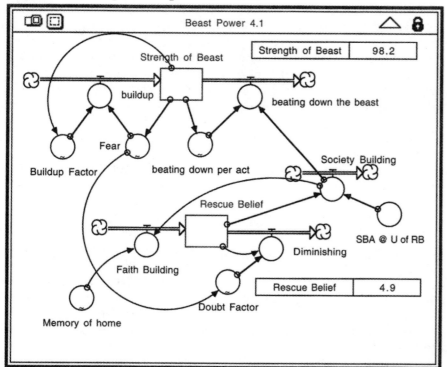

4 was developed by an English teacher in conjunction with his tenth grade students to describe how the boys' loss of hope drives the increasing power of the beast in William Golding's novel, *The Lord of the Flies.* The model of beast power represents the factors that contributed to the strength of the beast in the book, including fear and resistance. Each component can be opened up, so that values for each component may be stated as constants or variables. Variables can be stated as equations containing numerical relationships among any of the variables connected to it. The resulting model can be run, changing the values of faith building, fear, and memory of home experienced by the boys while assessing the effects on their belief about being rescued and the strength of the beast within them. Stella and other dynamic modeling tools, such as Model-It from the Highly Interactive Computing Group at the University of Michigan, probably provides the most complete intellectual activity that students can engage in.

Microworlds. Microworlds are exploratory learning environments or discovery spaces in which learners can navigate, manipulate or create objects, and test their effects on one another. Microworlds contain constrained simulations of real-world phenomena that allow learners to control those phenomena. They provide the exploratory functionality (provide learners with the observation and manipulation tools and testing objects) needed to explore phenomena in those parts of the world. Video-based adventure games are microworlds that require players to master each environment before moving onto more complex environments. They are compelling to youngsters, who spend hours transfixed in these adventure worlds. Microworlds are perhaps the ultimate example of active learning environments, because the users can exercise so much control over the environment.

Many microworlds are being produced and made available from educational research projects, especially in math and science. In mathematics, the Geometric Supposer and Algebraic Supposer are standard tools for testing conjectures in geometry and algebra by constructing and manipulating geometric and algebraic objects in order to explore the relationships within and between these objects (Yerulshamy & Schwartz, 1986). The emphasis in those microworlds is the generation and testing of hypotheses. They provide a testbed for testing students' predictions about geometric and algebraic proofs.

The SimCalc project teaches middle and high school students calculus concepts through MathWorlds, which is a microworld consisting of animated worlds and dynamic graphs in which actors move according to graphs. By exploring the movement of the actors in the simulations and seeing the graphs of their activity, students begin to understand important calculus ideas. In the MathWorlds activity illustrated in Figure 5, students match two motions. By matching two motions they learn how velocity and position graphs relate. Students must match the motion of the green and red graphs. To do this, they can change either graph. They iteratively run the simulation to see if they got it right! Students may also use Math-World's link to enter their own bodily motion. For example, a student can walk across the classroom, and his or her motions would be entered into MathWorld's through sensing equipment. MathWorld would plot the motion, enabling the student to explore the properties of his or her own motion.

Information Interpretation Tools

The volume and complexity of information are growing at an astounding rate. Learners need tools that help them to access and process that information. A new class of intelligent information search engines are scanning information resources, such as the World Wide Web, and locating relevant resources for learners. Other tools for helping learners make sense of what they find are also emerging.

Visualization Tools. We take in more information through our visual modality than any other sensory system, yet we cannot output ideas visually (except in mental images and dreams), which cannot be shared visually except using paint/draw programs. While it is not yet possible to dump our mental images directly from our brains into a computer, a very new and growing class of visualization tools are mediating this process by providing us tools that allow us to reason visually in certain areas. Visualization tools help humans to represent and convey those mental images—usually not in the same form they are generated mentally, but as rough approximations of those mental images.

There are no general-purpose visualization tools. They tend to be specific to the kinds of visuals you wish to generate. An excellent example of a visualization tool is the growing number of tools for visualizing chemical compounds. Understanding chemical bonding is difficult for most people, because the complex atomic interactions are not visible. Static graphics of these bonds found in textbooks may help

learners to form mental images, but those mental images are not manipulable and cannot be conveyed to others. Tools such as MacSpartan enables students to view, rotate, and measure molecules using different views (see Figure 6) and also to modify or construct new molecules. These visualization tools make the abstract real for students, helping them to understand chemical concepts that are difficult to convey in static displays.

Knowledge Construction Tools

Papert has used the term "constructionism" to describe the process of knowledge construction resulting from constructing things. When learners function as designers of objects, they learn more about those objects than they would from studying about them.

Hypermedia

Hypermedia consists of information nodes, which are the basic unit of in-

formation storage and may consist of a page of text, a graphic, a sound bite, a video clip, or even an entire document. In many hypermedia systems, nodes can be amended or modified by the user. The user may add to or change the information in a node or create his or her own nodes of information, so that a hypertext can be a dynamic knowledge base that continues to grow, representing new and different points of view. Nodes are made accessible through links that interconnect them. The links in hypermedia transport the user through the information space to the nodes that are selected, enabling the user to navigate through the knowledge base. The node structure and the link structure form a network of ideas in the knowledge base, the interrelated and interconnected group or system of ideas.

While hypermedia systems have traditionally been used as information retrieval systems which learners browse, learners may create their own hypermedia knowledge bases that reflect their own understanding of ideas. Students are likely to learn more by constructing instructional materials than by studying them. Designing multimedia presentations is a complex process that engages many skills in learners, and it can be applied to virtually any content domain. Carver, Lehrer, Connell, & Ericksen (1992) list some of the major thinking skills that learners need to use as designers, including project management skills, research skills, organization and representation skills, presentation skills, and reflection skills.

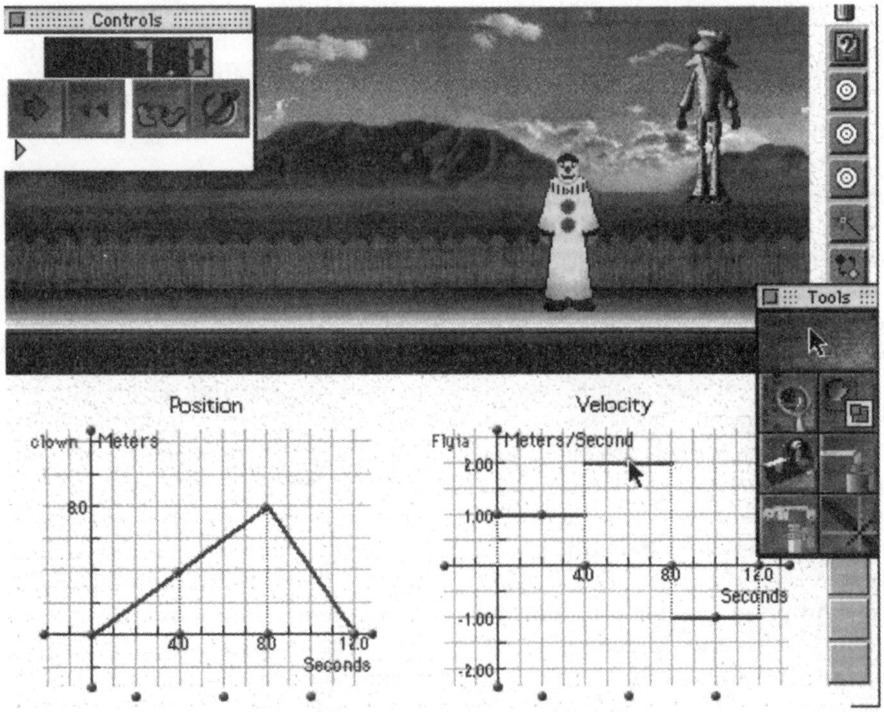

Conversation Tools

Newer theories of learning are emphasizing the social as well as the constructivist nature of the learning process. In real world settings, we often learn by socially negotiating meaning, not by being taught. A variety of synchronous and asynchronous computer-supported environ-

Figure 5. Experiment in Math World

Figure 6. Tool for visualizing chemical compounds

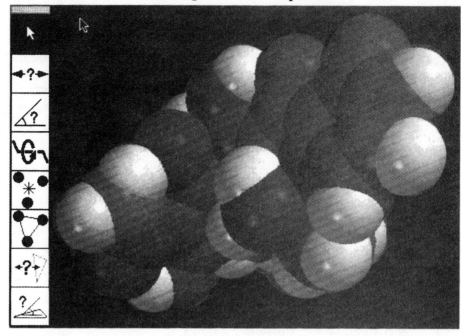

ments are available for supporting this social negotiation process. On-line telecommunications include live conversations, such as Chats, MOOs, and MUDs and videoconferencing, and asynchronous discussions, including electronic mail, Listservs, bulletin boards, and computer conferences. These many forms of tele-communications can be used for supporting interpersonal exchanges among students, collecting information, and solving problems in groups of students (Jonassen, Peck, & Wilson, 1998).Interpersonal exchanges may include keypals, global classrooms, electronic appearances, electronic mentoring, and impersonations (Harris, 1995). Examples of information collections include information exchanges, database creation, electronic publishing, electronic field trips, and pooled data analysis. Problem-solving projects include information searches, parallel problem solving, electronic process writing, serial creations, simulations, and social action projects.

Online communication presumes that students can communicate, that is, that they can meaningfully participate in conversations. In order to do that, they need to be able to interpret messages, consider appropriate responses, and construct coherent replies. Many students are not able to engage in cogent and coherent discourse. Why? Because most students have rarely been asked to contribute their opinions about topics. They have been too busy memorizing what the teachers tell them. So it may be necessary to support students' attempts to converse. A number of online communication environments have been designed to support students' discourse skills, such as the Collaboratory Notebook (O'Neill & Gomez, 1994). The Collaboratory Notebook is a collaborative hypermedia composition system designed to support within- and cross-school science projects. What is unique about the Collaboratory is that it focuses on project investigations rather than curricular content. During a project, the teacher or any student can pose a

question or a conjecture (Figure 7), which can be addressed by participants from around the country. The Collaboratory provides a scaffolding structure for conversations by requiring specific kinds of responses to messages. For instance, in order to support the conjecture in Figure 7, learners can only "provide evidence" or "develop a plan" to support that conjecture. This form of scaffolded conversation results in more coherent and cogent conversations.

Collaborative conversations are becoming an increasingly popular way to support socially co-constructed learning. Many more sophisticated computer-supported conferencing environments are becoming available to support learner conversations.

Rationales for Using Technology as Mindtools

Why do Mindtools work? That is, why do they engage learners in critical, higher-order thinking about content?

Learners as Designers

The people who learn the most from designing instructional materials are the designers, not the learners for whom the materials are intended. The process of articulating what we know in order to construct a knowledge base forces learners to reflect on what they are studying in new and meaningful ways. The common homily, "the quickest way to learn about something is to have to teach it," explains the effectiveness of Mindtools, because learners are teaching the computer. It is important to emphasize that Mindtools are not intended necessarily to make learning easier. Learners do not use Mindtools naturally and effortlessly. Rather, Mindtools often require learners to think harder about the subject matter domain being studied while generating thoughts that would be impossible without the tool. While they are thinking harder, learners are also thinking more meaningfully as they construct their own realities by designing their own knowledge bases.

Knowledge Construction, Not Reproduction

Mindtools represent a constructivist use of technology. Constructivism is concerned with the process of how we construct knowledge. When students develop databases, for instance, they are constructing their own conceptualization of the organization of a content domain. How we construct knowledge depends upon what we already know, which depends on the kinds of experiences that we have had, how we have organized those experiences into knowledge structures, and what we believe about what we know. So, the meaning that each of us makes for an experience resides in the mind of each knower. This does not mean that we can comprehend only our own interpretation of reality. Rather, learners are able to comprehend a variety of interpretations and to use each in constructing personal knowledge.

Constructivist approaches to learning strive to create environments where learners actively participate in the environment in ways that are intended to help them construct their own knowledge, rather than having the teacher interpret the world and ensure that students understand the world as they have told them. In constructivist environments, like Mindtools, learners are actively engaged in interpreting the external world and reflecting on their interpretations. This is not "active" in the sense that learners actively listen and then mirror the one correct view of reality, but rather "active" in the sense that learners must participate and interact with the surrounding environment in order to create their own views of the subject. Mindtools function as formalisms for guiding learners in the organization and representation of what they know.

Learning with Technology

The primary distinction between computers as tutors and computers as Mindtools is best expressed by Salomon, Perkins, and Globerson (1991) as the effects of technology versus the effects with computer technology. Learning with computers refers to the learner entering an intellectual partnership with the computer. Learning with Mindtools depends on the mindful engagement of learners in the tasks afforded by these tools and that there is the possibility of qualitatively upgrading the performance of the joint system of learner plus technology. In other words, when students work with computer technologies, instead of being controlled by them, they enhance the capabilities of the computer, and the computer enhances their thinking and learning. The result of an intellectual partnership with the computer is that the whole of learning becomes greater than the sum of its parts. Electronics specialists use their tools to solve problems. The tools do not control the specialist. Neither should computers control learning. Rather, computers should be used as tools that help learners to build knowledge.

Figure 7. Scaffolded computer conference from CoVis

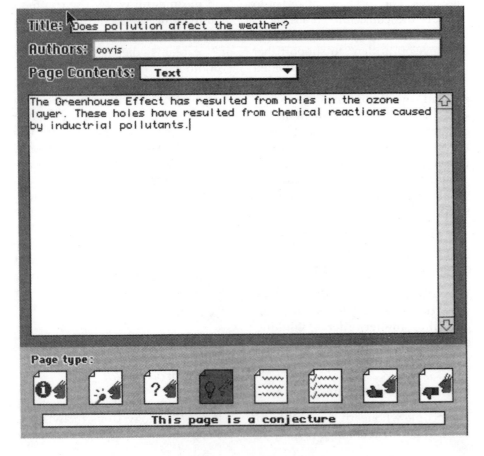

(Un)intelligent Tools

Educational communications systems too often try to do the thinking for learners, to act as tutors and guide the learning. These systems possess some degree of "intelligence" that they use to make instructional decisions about how much and what kind of instruction learners need. Derry and LaJoie (1993) argue that "the appropriate role for a computer system is not that of a teacher/expert, but rather, that of a mind-extension "cognitive tool" (p. 5). Mindtools are unintelligent tools, relying on the learner to provide the intelligence, not the computer. This means that planning, decision-making, and self-regulation of learning are the responsibility of the learner, not the computer. However, computer systems can serve as powerful catalysts for facilitating these skills assuming they are used in ways that promote reflection, discussion, and problem solving.

Distributing Cognitive Processing

Computer tools, unlike most tools, can function as intellectual partners which share the cognitive burden of carrying out tasks (Salomon, 1993). When learners use computers as partners, they off-load some of the unproductive memorizing tasks to the computer, allowing the learner to think more productively. Our goal as technology-using educators should be to allocate to the learners the cognitive responsibility for the processing they do best, while requiring the technology to do the processing that it does best. Rather than using the limited capabilities of the computer to present information and judge learner input (neither of which computers do well) while asking learners to memorize information and later recall it (which computers do with far greater speed and accuracy than humans), we should assign cognitive responsibility to the part of the learning system that does it the best. Learners should be responsible for recognizing and judging patterns of information and then organizing it, while the computer system should perform calculations, and store and retrieve information. When used as Mindtools, we are engaging learners in the kinds of processing that they do best.

Cost and Effort Beneficial

Mindtools are personal knowledge construction tools that can be applied to any subject matter domain. For the most part, Mindtools software is readily available and affordable. Many computers come bundled with the software described in this article. Most other applications are in the public domain or available for less than $100. Mindtools are also reasonably easy to learn. The level of skill needed to use Mindtools often requires limited study. Most can be mastered within a couple of hours. Because they can be used to construct knowledge in nearly any course, the cost and learning effort are even more reasonable.

Computers can most effectively support meaningful learning and knowledge construction in higher education as cognitive amplification tools for reflecting on what students have learned and what they know. Rather than using the power of computer technologies to disseminate information, they should be used in all subject domains as tools for engaging learners in reflective, critical thinking about the ideas they are studying. Using computers as Mindtools (employing software applications as knowledge representation formalisms) will facilitate learning more readily than any computer-based instruction now available. In this article we have introduced the concept of Mindtools and provided brief descriptions and some examples. More information and examples are available on the World Wide Web (http://www.ed.psu.edu/~mindtools).

References

Carver, S. M., Lehrer, R., Connell, T., & Ericksen, J. (1992). Learning by hypermedia design: Issues of assessment and implementation. *Educational Psychologist, 27*(3), 385–404.

Derry, S.J., & LaJoie, S.P. (1993). A middle camp for (un)intelligent instructional computing: An introduction. In S.P. LaJoie & S.J. Derry (Eds.), *Computers as cognitive tools* (pp. 1–14). Hillsdale, NJ: Lawrence Erlbaum Associates.

Harris, J. (1995, February). Organizing and facilitating telecollaborative projects. *The Computing Teacher, 22* (5), 66–69. [Online document: http://www.ed.uiuc.edu/Mining/February95–TCT.html]

Jonassen, D.H. (1996). *Computers in the classroom: Mindtools for critical thinking.* Columbus, OH: Merrill/Prentice-Hall.

Jonassen, D.H. (in press). *Mindtools for engaging critical thinking in the classroom.* 2nd Ed. Columbus, OH: Prentice-Hall.

Jonassen, D.H., Beissner, K., & Yacci, M.A. (1993). *Structural knowledge: Techniques for representing, assessing, and acquiring structural knowledge.* Hillsdale, NJ: Lawrence Erlbaum Associates.

Jonassen, D.H., Peck, K.L., & Wilson, B.G. (1998). *Learning WITH technology: A constructivist perspective.* Columbus, OH: Prentice-Hall.

Jonassen, D.H., & Reeves, T. C. (1996). Learning with technology: Using computers as cognitive tools. In D.H. Jonassen (Ed.), *Handbook of research for educational communications and technology* (pp. 693–719). New York: Macmillan.

O'Neill, D. K., & Gomez, L. M. (1992). The Collaboratory notebook: A distributed knowledge building environment for project learning. Proceedings of ED MEDIA, 94. Vancouver B.C., Canada.

Perkins, D.N. (1986). *Knowledge as design.* Hillsdale, NJ: Lawrence Erlbaum.

Salomon, G. , Perkins, D.N., & Globerson, T. (1991). Partners in cognition: Extending human intelligence with intelligent technologies. *Educational Researcher, 20*(3), 2–9.

Yerulshamy, M., & Schwartz, J. (1986). The geometric supposer: Promoting thinking and learning. *Mathematics Teacher, 79,* 418–422.

David H. Jonassen is a professor in Instructional Systems at Pennsylvania State University.

Chad Carr is a doctoral student in Instructional Systems at Pennsylvania State University.

Hsiu-Ping Yueh is an assistant professor in the Department of Agricultural Extension at National Taiwan University.

Grounded Constructions and How Technology Can Help

By Sasha A. Barab, Kenneth E. Hay, and Thomas M. Duffy

Currently, there is an increasing number of educators abandoning predominantly lecture-based modes of instruction and moving towards more learner-centered models in which students, frequently in collaboration with peers, are engaged in problem solving and inquiry. This movement is facilitated by current technologies that function less like books, films, or journals and more like laboratories, workshops, and studios where students can immerse themselves within contexts that challenge and extend their understandings. These novel technologies facilitate the development of rich learning environments that encourage exploration and discovery, supporting students in the construction of personally meaningful and conceptually functional understandings. Drawing heavily on examples from our own research, in this article we discuss five ways that we have used technology for stimulating and/or supporting authentic learner inquiry. Rather than using technology simply as a medium for delivering pre-specified content, our research is predicated on the belief that technology can be used to provide a fertile context from which grounded constructions may emerge.

Background

Whereas traditional perspectives describe knowing and thinking as isolated activities that occur primarily within the context of the cerebellum, many current theorists argue that thinking is *situated;* that is, being in part a product of the content, activity, and culture in which it is developed and applied (Brown, Collins, & Duguid, 1989). *Situated cognition* is a recent term for a family of research efforts that explain cognition, including problem solving, sense making, understanding, transfer of learning, and creativity, in terms of the relationship between learners and the properties of specific environments. From a situated perspective it becomes impossible, and irrelevant, to separate the learner, the material to be learned, and the context in which learning occurs. A contrast can be made with schema theories in which knowledge is considered to be solely contained within the learner (represented in memory as schemata or mental models), and with behaviorist theories in which cognition plays a less central role.

Certain assumptions inherent to theories of situated cognition (e.g., the inseparability of content and context or the codetermined nature of knowing) have implications for developing effective instructional contexts. For example, a logical extension from the contention that content cannot be separated from context is the belief that impoverished contexts (i.e., contexts that present knowledge stripped of the occasions and conditions in which it is used) produce impoverished knowledge. In such environments, learning becomes the memorization of seemingly abstract, self-contained entities, not useful tools for understanding and interacting with the world.

From *TechTrends,* March 1998, pp. 15-23. © 1998 by TechTrends. Reprinted by permission.

In contrast to some of the more traditional uses of technology in the classroom (e.g., using computer-assisted instruction to support drill-and-practice, or using word processors or calculators to increase productivity), our research has focused on technology as a tool for facilitating learner inquiry within rich environments that situate the content being learned. In these environments knowledge is not a thing (a product) delivered to students; rather, knowing is a situated activity (a process) supported by the use of technological tools. In other words, the tools that we have been researching establish opportunities for rich interactions with the potential to support learners in building understandings. These understandings are not abstract concepts but "grounded constructions" that are situated in and built out of learner experiences (Barab, Cherkes, Swenson, Garret, & Shaw, 1998). We use the term *grounded construction* to capture the notion that understandings are contextualized within the particular environment in which they are being constructed, and cannot be pre-structured and handed (delivered) to the learner (wholecloth). This notion of *situatedness* is especially relevant in that the ill-structured problems and complex phenomena that we have been studying may involve multiple strategies, solutions, and understandings, all of which are equally valid, and whose appropriateness must be evaluated in terms of whether they are progressive (functional) for the task at hand (Bereiter, 1994; Honebein, Duffy, & Fishman, 1993). Additionally, they are functional for a particular context and not objective truths that necessarily apply to all contexts.

Founded in this situated perspective, our research has pointed toward five uses to which educators may apply technology so as to support learners in developing grounded constructions (see Table 1). These five uses are not features inherent to the technology, as if technology were a self-contained entity; rather, they refer to uses or roles that technology can afford within particular contexts. They are best conceived of as situated potentials that are actualized (and given shape) within the larger context of learner inquiry—a process that requires the guidance of an effective facilitator.

Information Resource

Creating information resources for learners is, arguably, growing to become the dominant use of technology. However, these resources, if we are going to maximize their effectiveness, should not be treated as isolated tools introduced in a vacuum without consideration of learner goals. Rather, we envision such technological resources as providing multimedia environments to be explored in a context where the learner is engaged in authentic inquiry.

Strategic Teaching Framework[1] (STF) (Duffy, 1997) is an information resource we developed to aid teachers in adopting a learner-centered approach to teaching that involves three elements or skills: the use of problem centered inquiry, the use of collaborative groups to generate and evaluate alternative hypotheses, and the use of teacher questioning to coach and model inquiry skills. Rather than viewing the goal as one of designing an environment to "train" teachers in implementing these three skills, our objective was to establish a set of resources that facilitate teacher inquiry and allow teachers to visit classrooms where they can study how expert teachers used these strategies as a tool for both planning and reflecting on their own teaching practices.

The design of STF involved producing videos of three learner-centered teachers as each taught a whole class period with their students. The teaching was not

Table 1. Five Uses for Technology

GENERAL USE	ROLE
Information Resource	provide information to support learner inquiry (e.g., hypermedia, WWW, interactive CD ROMs)
Content Contextualization	situate the material to be learned within a rich context (e.g., anchored instruction, experiential simulations)
Communication Tool	facilitate collaborative and distributed learning (e.g., asynchronous conferencing tools, teleapprenticeships)
Construction Kit	provide concrete tools for building phenomena/understandings (e.g., LOGO, HTML & VRML editors, HyperStudio)
Visualization/Manipulation Tool	present phenomena for scrutiny and manipulation (e.g., visualization tools, model-based simulations)

Figure 1. Conceptual Database in STF

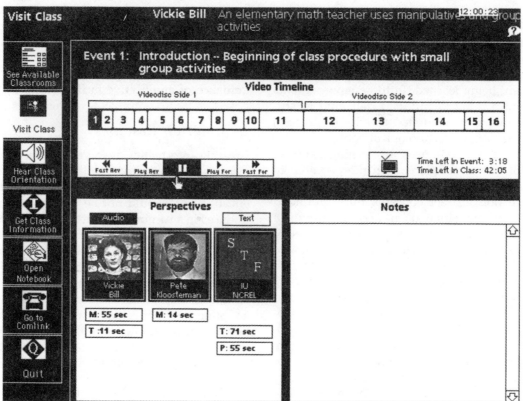

scripted; the goal was to capture the authentic practices of these teachers. Each STF teacher uses all three key elements (problems, groups, and questioning) in teaching—but uses them in different ways, thus offering alternative perspectives to the teachers and, perhaps more importantly, de-emphasizing teaching as a specific procedure. The videos are available on a CD-ROM, allowing the teacher to study the practices in detail. The teachers can also pause the video and obtain three different perspectives on the teaching activity being studied: those of the teacher in the video, those of a teacher educator, and those of an educational researcher. In addition to the video database, there is a conceptual database, containing articles and video clips organized around conceptual issues.

STF is designed to support teachers who are motivated to develop a new perspective on and new strategies for teaching. The intent is for STF to support both planning and reflection. That is, the design goal is to have the teachers first study the video, situating themselves in the classroom and analyzing the learner-centered teaching practices. Then, as questions develop, they can turn to the conceptual database for a more detailed discussion of the issues. (See Figure 1.)

STF has been evaluated in both pre-service (Lambdin, Duffy, and Moore, 1997) and in-service (Chaney, Tammy, & Duffy, 1997) teacher environments. In both cases, the guided use of STF was found to significantly impact teachers' conceptual perspective and teaching practices.

However, it is clear from both studies that the role of a facilitator in promoting the change process is central. The facilitator is central both in asking leading edge questions as the learners analyze the STF teachers, and in facilitating the process of reflecting on the learners' own teaching practices as they begin the change process. In other words, STF does not do it alone; it requires on-site support in situating the materials so that teachers are aided in engaging in the inquiry process. Central to the conception of STF is that teachers will first watch the classroom teacher and then explore the database of conceptual material. As a result, their understanding of the information contained in the articles would be contextualized (grounded) to actual teachers engaged in actual practice, thus creating direct connections with a real life situation out of which teachers can build grounded constructions.

Content Contextualization

Using Anchors. The approach of "anchored instruction" offers potential insights into how theories of situated cognition can impact instructional practice (CTGV, 1990; 1993). Anchored instruction refers to instruction in which the material to be learned is presented in the context of an authentic event that serves to anchor or situate the material and, further, allows it to be examined from multiple perspectives. The work of the CTGV (1990; 1992; 1993) has primarily focused on video-based "macrocontexts," intended to overcome inert knowledge by anchoring learning—which involves meaningful problem-solving activities—to the macrocontext. In contrast to the disconnected sets of "application problems" located at the end of textbook chapters, macro-contexts refer to stories that take place in semantically rich, open-ended environments. In these macrocontexts students begin with a higher-order problem and then use top-down strategies to generate the necessary sub-goals to reach the final state. This top-down processing helps students learn the lower level skills (i.e., mathematical algorithms and facts) in a manner that also gives them insights into the relationships between the skills being learned and the reciprocal opportunities for using them.

"Rescuing Rocky," a computerized lesson developed to study the power of anchors, provides an example of anchored instruction (Barab, Fajen, Kulikowich, & Young, 1996; Barab & Young, 1998). This lesson begins with a one-minute QuickTime™ video clip suggesting that a monkey, Rocky, is dying of Simian AIDS contracted in a government lab experiment. The video clip informs viewers that a cure for AIDS has been discovered by a scientist in the Brazilian rain forests, but her research data and the area of rain forest where she had been working had been destroyed by fire. However, just prior to the disaster a scientist had written a letter to a colleague giving clues to an AIDS cure. These clues provide general descriptions which, when properly combined with specific information in the lesson, allow participants to develop a cure for Rocky. Having read the letter, viewers receive control over which information they would like to explore.

The computerized lesson contains text, pictures, videos, and animated stories about HIV, SW, the immune system, immigration, plants and animals of the rain forest, and other information related to the rain forest. Students are expected to learn particular information so that they can pass through customs and travel to the rain forest where they experiment with various plants and insects to develop a cure. Solving the anchor problem requires students to learn about viruses, immunizations, AIDS, customs, international laws, exchange rates, deforestation, plants and animals of the rain forest, ethics, and chemical interactions—content typically associated with multiple disciplines. However, students do not learn these concepts as objective facts to be memorized; rather, they become important tools whose proper understanding and application are essential for, and directly tied to, completing the task of saving Rocky.

Students learning the content to address the anchor problem scored higher on achievement questions and evidenced more transfer than did students who studied the information without the anchor. More importantly, students learning in the context of an engaging anchor made connections among the various disciplinary concepts, even seeing relations between the computerized lesson and other lessons, and between the lesson and personal experiences. For example, one student told us that his mother worked in the "underground" helping to make available various medicines for AIDS patients who were not able to afford the expensive new combinations of drugs (Barab & Young, 1998).

Experiential Simulations. The use of simulations provides another example of situating learning within a rich context in which students build an appreciation for the use of the content they are learning. Our focus is on *experiential* rather than *model-based* or *symbolic* simulations (the latter are discussed later in this article). An experiential simulation, "establishes a certain psychological reality, and places the participants in defined roles in that reality" (Gredler, 1996). However, here the learner himself is situated within a context in which the content being learned is applied. We[2] have been looking at the use of a suite of simulations (Fernandez and Body, 1997) designed to situate the learners in workplace roles, including bank teller, hotel manager, environmental worker, and bank manager. The simulations are designed for use on low-end computers typically found in middle and high schools. This is not vocational training; rather, the goal is to develop problem solving and basic literacy skills as well as knowledge of work ethics and responsibilities. For example, in the bank teller simulation, a customer asks for a transaction to be completed. The student uses bank manuals, account information, an analysis of the materials submitted by the customer, and other resources to determine if and how the transaction should be completed and must decide what to tell the customer. In order to facilitate classroom implementation, when the time comes to make a decision, the students are presented multiple-choice options. They must select from the options and then justify their answers.

Our research suggests that the simulations are very engaging (Duffy, Greene, Farr, and Mikulecky, 1996). We interviewed middle school children who could describe scenarios they worked with six months earlier. We also observed numerous classes in at-risk schools in which the students, working in teams of three, were all absorbed in working on the "problem." The simulations situate the learner in a real life event, providing a context from which students can build grounded constructions of the content and, more importantly, the process of problem solving. The central learning goal of the simulations is to help the students develop effective problem solving strategies—to become reflective practitioners if you will, engaging in critical thinking during the process of working on the problem and reflecting on both the process and the content learning that occurred through working on the scenario. With this end in mind, the teacher should play a central role in coaching the students in the problem solving strategies and in facilitating the reflective process.

However, based on interviews and observations, it is clear that teachers did not have a clear perspective on their role. Indeed, they tended to think of the simulations as "doing" the teaching rather than simply providing a context for learning (Hawley, Lloyd, Mikulecky, & Duffy, 1997). In response to this need, our current research with simulation environments has two components. First, we are developing resource materials to help teachers develop strategies for assessing and coaching problem solving skills as the students work with the simulations. Second, we are evaluating the effect of three different strategies for interacting with students (encouragement, directive, inquiry) on the students' problem solving activities in both near-and far-transfer tasks (Hawley, Chaney, & Duffy, 1997).

Communication Tool

An example of technology being used as a communication device to support the development of grounded constructions was the *Apprenticeship Notebook,* created to aid students participating in the Scientist's Apprentice Camp (SAC). SAC was designed to match inquisitive, highly motivated middle school students and teachers with researchers in the School of Science at Indiana University/ Purdue University Indianapolis (Hay & Barab, 1998). Participants worked in groups of four with the expert guidance of a practicing scientist as they conducted scientific research. They were presented with an authentic research problem and had hands-on experience with state of the art instrumentation and equipment. However, findings and general perception of the previous year suggested that simply putting students into scientists' labs was not effective. Scientists focused on mastering basic factual knowledge and therefore tended to lecture to the campers for the first days of the camp. Also, students tended to use much of the laboratory time for asking questions so that they could put together their presentations delivered on the final day of the camp.

The *Apprenticeship Notebook* had five components: Overview, Science Chat, Links, Schedule, and Notebook. Although the other components served as information resources, or as a type of "public" journal in the case of the Notebook section, the component of prime importance here is the Science Chat. The Science Chat is an asynchronous conferencing area where students could talk among themselves, or with their teachers and scientists. This chat section allowed students to pose questions to the scientists outside of the laboratory time:

What is a rotation vector and periodic function?
—Jackie

Do the bats send out the sonar signals voluntarily or not?
—Pat

Do all clear solutions absorb the same amount of light???
—Tom

Similar to what a teacher would do in a lecture setting, scientists often used these questions to test student understanding. For example, as a follow- up to Tom's "clear solution" question (above), Dr. R. asks,

What do you think happens to color or transparency of a solution that absorbs light from all regions of the visible spectrum (still clear) but absorbs more white light than . . . say, water?

The important observation here is that this didactic instruction is being conducted outside of the lab and at the conveyance of the scientist, thus maximizing the hands-on work where they need to be with the scientist physically.

However, the Chat section also created a "reflective zone" that was away from the excitement of the laboratory, making it possible for students to reflect on the laboratory experience with each other. For example:

Q: What are some of the differences between lasers and flashlights?—Tony

A: . . . a flashlight spreads its light out from a long distance. A laser has a small concentrated beam of light . . . —Fred

A: . . . a laser light is much more concentrated . . . —Pat

A: . . . lasers take the same amount of light and puts it in a smaller area . . . —Tom

Q: What do you think our hypothesis is going to be?—Rob

A: Our hypothesis will be about the watershed and how the wetlands will clean it up.

And after time to think and formulate questions, this reflective zone gave student opportunities and a comfortable social distance to ask the scientist difficult questions that were not simply factual, but extensions into the heart of the scientific practice. For example:

Q: How can a cube come out looking like two mountains on a sonar graph?—Tim

Q: Wouldn't the sonar signal you recorded have to send out several of these signals to get the full picture of the object instead of just one?—Terry

Q: If we had phase information, do the 3D or 2D graphs look like the target image?

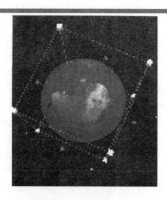

Figure 2. Screenshot of a student adding the 23 degree tilt on the Earth.

It should be noted that Tim's question goes to the very heart of the group's (bat sonar) research. This group investigated whether bat sonar is a replacement for human vision or a totally different way of perceiving the spatial world. His confusion is an attempt to say, "Why don't the graphs (derived from radar signals bouncing of a cube) look like a cube?"

Construction Kit

Technology-based learning environments can also provide a context for students to build phenomena and, as a result, rich understandings of complex phenomena. In one project this summer, high school students attended a camp (Future Camp) that used state-of-the-art virtual reality (VR) equipment to design one of three VR worlds (Barab & Hay, 1998). In these projects it was the responsibility of the students to determine the direction of the project, with the teacher mentors available as a resource for the students. As students designed their VR worlds, they were forced to grasp many difficult concepts to which they did not have previous understandings (see Figure 2). Students were not handed solutions, but had to continually manipulate the tools and draw inferences from these interactions. We believe that it is within these interactions, grounded within the particular context in which the students were immersed, that the seeds of deep understanding are sown.

For example, in the VR Solar System Project (one of the three VR group projects) group members quickly had to grapple with issues of scale. Size, distances, and time scales were easily manipulated and created many conceptual difficulties. Planet sizes constituted the first conceptual challenge confronting the group. Creating the sun, Jupiter, the moon, and placing them next to each other gave students immediate feedback on the relative size of the heavenly bodies of our solar system. However, conceptual difficulties quickly developed when they went to place them in relative positions to the Sun. One student asked "how can we get the Earth and Jupiter's orbit on one screen and be real-like?" As he later consulted a resource he quickly came to the conclusion about how the solar system is illustrated: "This picture is wrong, there is no way they could get Mercury, Earth and Saturn all in the same picture. The distances are too great. . . . My science book lied."

As evident in the campers' exclamation that the "textbooks lied" and in the pre-test/post-test measures, students of the current educational practices have an extremely distorted view of the scale of the solar system. We argue that the process of building an interactive, dynamic, virtual model of the solar system created a powerful and unique learning opportunity. This is but one of the many concepts that learners grappled with while building their VR worlds. We suggest that learning in these student-determined environments allows learners to develop their own reasoned interpretations of their interactions with the world they are building.

Although the camp was grounded in a learner-centered pedagogical base, the teachers' adherence to this style was varied. Teachers who became resources for the learners had groups that were more active, productive, and ultimately evidencing higher scores on post measures than did those teachers who failed to retreat to let students direct the projects (Barab & Hay, 1997). In post interviews the directive teachers expressed frustration at the students' lack of ability; it did not occur to them that by continually holding the student's "hand" (computer mouse) they were not allowing the students to extend their functioning and develop those abilities they were accused of not having.

Visualization/Manipulation Tool

Visualization Tools. The impact of the Information Age on scientists has been enormous. With advances in data collection methods, scientists can routinely collect and archive gigabytes and even terabytes (that's billions and trillions bytes) of data on various phenomena. Finding ways of representing this data so that it can be used to gain insights into the real-world phenomena from which it was derived has proven to be a significant task. Scientific visualization is the new area of science that has emerged in response to this challenge. With advances in graphic computers, the data is mapped onto a computer display so that the scientist can see the data set holistically, making patterns and emerging trends more apparent. Scientific visualization makes the abstract numbers come alive for the scientists.

Another issue that visualization has overcome for scientists, and can for students as well, is making abstract more concrete. To do this scientists use "contextual cues techniques" in their visualizations. These techniques contextualize the data set into their original context. For example, weather data can be contextualized with underlying maps, CAT scans can be contextualized in a transparent model of a human, and water temperature can be contextualized in 3D representations of rivers and oceans. Unlike traditional graphs that map data back onto an abstract X–Y coordinate system, scientific visualizations map data onto their original contexts. Visualization also offers educators an experiential base that is not possible through other means. For example, it is possible for educators to use thermometers to help students understand the notion of temperature at a single point. However, the experience of temperatures across the U.S. at any given time and over time is an entirely different matter. It is not possible for a learner to have direct experience with the phenomena spread out over a large area, except with the aid of visualizations. With the aid of visualization tools the experience becomes one that covers the entire U.S., or the world for that matter, over days or years.

Authenticity is another issue that visualization provides, which is consistent with situated learning theory. These data are identical with the data that practicing scientists are using. There is no boiling down of content into textbook exercises; rather they are put into the same complex, dynamic, real-time position as the other scientists. Finally, visualization opens up the process of science to learners in a profound way. Visualizations are used more and more to illustrate science and influence science policy to the general public. If the citizens of tomorrow are not visualization savvy they will have no voice on scientific matters of public interest.

In a collaborative project with The Children's Museum of Indianapolis, we are developing an interface that gives learners the ability to use the visualization tools that real scientists use (Hay, 1997). The *Digital Weather Station* takes on the challenge of putting the power of professional level atmospheric visualization and simulation tools into the hands of children as young as six years old (see Figure 3). We do this in several ways. First, we create a "learner-centered," as opposed to "user-centered," interface onto the tools. In other words, rather than assuming the user knows the content and has the skills to use the tool, a learner-centered interface allows users without the knowledge or skills to effectively use the tool and learn with it. We are currently in the process of setting up a context or problem that is appropriate for museum use and will situate the use of the *Digital Weather Station.*

Although this particular project requires the use of a high-end computer and visiting the Indianapolis Children's Museum, we are working towards incorporating the Web to make, at the very least, pre-computed standard visualizations available to learners at a distance. Thus, users may simply go to the site and make a database query as to which visualization they would like to explore. In the weather arena, there are already available sites such as the CoVis and BlueSkies projects, which are specifically designed for educators and students. The upside to this approach of making available pre-computed standard visualizations is that the visualization comes quickly. The downside is that learners are strictly limited to the types of visualizations that have been pre-determined by someone else. There is little opportunity to do "exploratory visualization" to see what is out there. Standard representations are meant to visualize certain aspects of the data; they do that very well, but leave little room for exploration.

Visualization is a powerful technology to provide students with an authentic base of experience in abstract domains. It can contextualize those abstractions, and foster scientific understanding for the public debate in the information age. And we expect it to come into the hands of classroom teachers in the near future.

Model-Based Simulations. Whereas experiential simulations provide a context for learning (i.e., a tool for situating learning), model-based simulations provide phenomena for exploration (i.e., a world for inquiry). The latter are consistent with Perkins' (1991) notion of *phenomenaria,* which refers to learning environments with the "specific purpose of presenting phenomena and making them accessible to scrutiny and simulation" (p. 47). One example is the popular SimCity software in which students are required to use their knowledge about the development of cities (i.e., knowledge of transportation systems, population issues, ramifications of taxation, ramifications of pollution, etc.) to develop and maintain a virtual city. This process allows students to make decisions (e.g., raising taxes) and examine the effects it has on their city, ultimately providing insights into various phenomena that are related to the historical development of a city. For example, by raising taxes students will see the direct effects it has on the SIMS (virtual residents), who, depending on other conditions (such as pollution, schools, crime, and others) will remain or move out of the city.

Another example is *Odyssey of Discovery: Science,* which is a teacher-developed tool that provides an interactive learning environment where students build science process skills while being introduced to fundamental concepts. Each of these dynamic environments provides a three-dimensional world where students make their own discoveries and build scientific inquiry skills. Students can explore a fossil bed, find a spacecraft in the solar system, learn about the properties of matter, and measure the Earth's circumference using ancient methods. In a "virtual aquarium," students work with a fresh water ecosystem in which they can manipulate temperature, PH, and acidity and then add various plants and fish. Some of these plants and fish will survive, depending on the water conditions, and some will die. However, the underlying principles and laws that determine whether a particular species lives or dies is not explicitly stated; rather it must be derived through an examination of the outcomes that result from the manipulation of various variables.

It is this latter attribute in which understanding is emergent (situated) that separates phenomenaria from more didactic learning environments. In these environ-

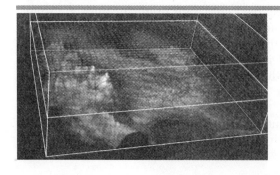

Figure 3. Screenshot taken from the Digital Weather Station.

ments students have the primary role of being investigators, manipulating variables and hypothesizing as to why specific results arise. These software provide the environment (backdrops) for this inquiry to occur, making certain phenomena not readily apparent (either due to the abstract nature of the content as in the weather project, or unethical and impractical to investigate as in Odyssey of Discovery: Science or Chelsea Bank software) more visible and available for manipulation to the learner.

Closing Thoughts

In this article we introduced the notion of grounded constructions, arguing that the goal of instruction is to establish learning environments that situate or contextualize the content being learned. These learner-driven constructions need to be conceived as grounded within those contexts in which they are derived. This is not meant to imply that learners cannot be supported in making connections between what they learned and other contexts; rather, that the initial understandings need to be grounded within a context of inquiry that provides meaning to that which is learned. Without this initial grounding learners may never come to appreciate the real-world applicability of that which they are learning. To this end we described five educational uses to which teachers may apply technology:

- provide information to support learner inquiry;
- facilitate collaborative and distributed learning;
- situate the material to be learned within a rich context;
- provide concrete tools for building phenomena/ understandings; and
- present phenomena for scrutiny and manipulation.

The goal in creating these environments is to stimulate and sustain students as they investigate various phenomena. The technology allows the learners to study these various phenomena through the participation in activities from which specific concepts emerge and are given meaning. The power of providing learners with rich experiences in a context where they can engage in activities and observe the resultant effects is central to the situated perspective, which has guided much of our research. The benefit of these technological tools is that they provide the learner with a host of actual "experiences" that contextualize and provide legitimacy to learning.

It is important to note that the technology is not the total experience; rather it is a tool or resource with the potential to support learners who are engaging in a rich learning experience. Our research has found that the potential of any of these technologies is dependent on the presence of a teacher/facilitator who helps the learner establish and appreciate the technology in relation to the

greater context in which it is situated. The role of this teacher/facilitator is not to *tell* students right answers and correct procedures, but rather to *guide* students as they direct their own learning process (Vygotsky, 1978). In other words, technology is simply a tool that teachers can use to aid in the development of robust learning experiences for students. However, we believe that within the proper context, emergent technologies can serve as a rich tool for supporting learning and holds exciting promise for educators.

References

Barab, S. A., Cherkes-Julkowski, M., M., Swenson, R. Garrett. S., & Shaw, R. E. (1998, May). *Principles of self organization: Ecologizing the learner-facilitator system.* To be presented at the annual meeting of the American Educational Research Association, San Diego, CA.

Barab, S. A., & Hay, K. E. (1998, May). *Constructing knowledge and virtual worlds: Knowledge diffusion in future camp 97.* To be presented at the annual meeting of the American Educational Research Association, San Diego, CA.

Barab, S. A., Fajen, B. R. Kulikowich, J. M., & Young, M. F. (1996). Assessing hypermedia navigation through Pathfinder: Prospects and limitations. *Journal of Educational Computing Research, 15*(3), 185–205.

Barab, S. A., & Young, M. F. (1998, February). *Perception of the raison d'être of content information: The purpose and mechanisms of Anchored Instruction.* To be presented at the annual meeting of the Association for Educational Communications Technology, St. Louis, MO.

Bereiter, C. (1994). Implications of postmodernism for science, or, science as progressive discourse. *Educational Psychologist, 29,* 3–12.

Brown, J. S., Collins, A., & Duguid, P. (1989). Situated cognition and the culture of learning. *Educational Researcher, 18,* 32–42.

Cognition and Technology Group at Vanderbilt. (1990). Anchored instruction and its relationship to situated cognition. *Educational Researcher, 19,* 2–10.

Cognition and Technology Group at Vanderbilt. (1993). Anchored Instruction and situated cognition revisited. *Educational Technology,* March Issue, 52–70.

Chaney, T., & Duffy, T. (1997). *Impacting teacher attitude and teacher practice: The case for strategic teaching frameworks.* Manuscript under review.

Duffy, T. (1997). Strategic Teaching Framework: An instructional model for a constructivist learning environment. In C. Dulls & A. Romiszowski (Ed.), *Instructional development state of the art. Volume 3: Paradigms.* Englewood NJ: Educational Technology Press.

Duffy, T., Greene, B., Farr, R. & Mikulecky, L. (1996). *Cognitive, social, and literacy competencies: The Chelsea Bank simulation project.* Year One Final Report submitted to the Andrew W. Mellon and Russell Sage Foundations. Bloomington, IN: Indiana University.

Fernandez, C., & Body, K. (1997, March). *Workplace simulations: The Classroom Inc. design and implementation strategy.* Paper presented at the annual meeting of the American Educational Research Association. Chicago, IL.

Hawley, C., Lloyd, P., Mikulecky, L., & Duffy, T. (1997, March). *Workplace simulations in the classroom: The teacher's role in supporting learning.* Paper presented at the annual meeting of the American Educational Research Association. Chicago, IL.

Hawley, C., Chaney, T., & Duffy, T. (1997) *Workplace simulations: The teachers role in supporting the development of problem solving skills.* Manuscript in preparation.

Hay, K. E. (1997, October). *Educational application of virtual reality: A rational and case studies of 3D visualization and world building.* Presented at the Indiana University Virtual Reality Conference, Bloomington, IN.

Hay, K. E. & Barab, S. A. (1998, May). *Building worlds: Tools of virtual practice.* To be presented at the annual meeting of the American Educational Research Association, San Diego, CA.

Hay, K. E. & Barab, S. A. (1998, May). *Electronic performance support system: Supporting science apprenticeships.* To be presented at the annual meeting of the American Educational Research Association, San Diego, CA.

Honebein, P., Duffy, T., & Fishman, B. (1993) Constructivism and the design of learning environments: Context and authentic activities for learning. In T. Duffy, J. Lowyck, & D. Jonassen (Eds.), *Designing environments for constructivist learning*. Heidelberg: Springer-Verlag.

Lambdin, D., Duffy, T., & Moore, J. (1997) Using an interactive information system to expand preservice teachers' visions of effective mathematics teaching. *Journal of Technology and Teacher Education, 5*, 171–202.

Land, S. M., & Hannafin, M. J. (1996). A conceptual framework for the development of theories-in-action with open-ended learning environments. *Educational Technology Research and Development, 44*, 37–53.

Perkins, D. (1991). Technology meets constructivism: Do they make a marriage? *Educational Technology, 31*, 18–23.

Vygotsky, L. (1978). *Mind in society: The development of higher psychological processes*. Cambridge, MA: Harvard University Press.

Whitehead, A. N. (1929). *The aims of education and other essays*. New York: MacMillan.

Notes

1. The development of Strategic Teaching Framework was a joint project of Indiana University and the North Central Regional Educational Laboratory. Thomas Duffy, Beau Jones, and Randy Knuth were lead designers.

2. This research was funded in part by a grant from the Andrew W. Mellon Foundation and the Russell Sage Foundation, "Assessing learning and supporting the teacher as coach" in Chelsea Bank simulations. T. Duffy, R. Farr, B. Greene, and L. Mikulecky, principal investigators.

Sasha A. Barab is an assistant professor in Instructional Systems Technology and Cognitive Science at Indiana University, Bloomington.

Kenneth E. Hay is an assistant professor in Instructional Systems Technology and Cognitive Science at Indiana University/Purdue University at Indianapolis.

Thomas M. Duffy is a full professor in the Instructional Systems Technology Department and Cognitive Science at Indiana University, Bloomington.

Kids as Computers

By Sherry J. Roberts

I teach computers and career education on a rotating nine-week schedule. I thought, "How can my students possibly have time to know, understand, and be able to apply all these concepts?" With the required content and the short time frame, I realized I needed to "teach smarter," but the question was still how?

The answer came to me while I was in a professional development session. I needed to use group work and more innovative ways to present information. Combining a concept that is sometimes difficult for students to understand with a classroom management concern, I developed a plan that would not only help students understand how the information processing cycle works but also eliminate time lost on task.

Working in Groups

Middle school students are sociable; they enjoy working in groups. Considering this, I formed cooperative groups, changing both classroom climate and instruction. I divided students into groups of four or five, modeling

---

A teacher combines small group design and role-playing with an information-processing model to teach students computer literacy. In the process, she realizes classroom management benefits.

---

the individual roles on information processing cycles.

Assigning Responsibilities

In computer application class, it's important that students learn how the information processing cycle works. Students need to understand how all parts of a computer system work together to produce results. This can be a difficult concept for them to grasp, especially when you explain how some

---

of the devices can function in more than one step of the cycle.

The idea of making each group member *become* a step in the information processing cycle seemed possible. With the class divided into groups, I assigned each member a step with specific responsibilities as follows: Input, Process, Output, and Storage.

Input was responsible for bringing to the group such things as handouts, instructions, texts, and disks. Being responsible for bringing information into the group exemplified what Input might do as a part of the information processing cycle, both for a computer and for the group. Because many input devices can also be classified as storage devices, Input would take over Storage's responsibilities if Storage was absent. For instance, if Storage was absent, Input would be responsible for putting away the group's work or texts.

Process took over once Input brought data to the group. Process was the group manager. Getting the group started, keeping them on task, and maintaining order were all Process responsibilities. Process executed commands—much like what happens

© 2001, ISTE (International Society for Technology in Education), 800.336.5191 (U.S. & Canada) or 541.302.3777 (Int'l), iste@iste.org, www.iste.org. All rights reserved.

during this stage of the information processing cycle.

Output followed Process. This group member was responsible for such things as speaking for the group, turning in materials, and retrieving printouts. Seeing Output at work in the group helped students understand the role of these devices in the information processing cycle. Previously, they could not see how output could be either a hard copy or a soft copy. This process made the concept of hard copy and soft copy clearer. Whenever there was a printout, Output was responsible for turning this hard copy in to the instructor. If someone needed to speak for the group, or a group visual was presented, Output was responsible for this "soft copy."

Storage is the final component of both the group and the information processing cycle. Storage was responsible for putting everything in its place. This group member was accountable for seeing that books were returned, disks were put back in the workbasket, and the group area was clean. As with input, storage devices can function two ways. A storage device can also be an input device. In the group, this means that Storage would assume Input's responsibilities if Input was absent. This helped students understand these devices in the information processing cycle.

As students participated in these groups, they saw that their jobs were dependent on each other. It was also an opportunity to stress how some of the roles could hold more than one job. For example, Input could also become Storage or vice versa.

Being a part of this classroom management process, modeled on the information processing cycle, gave students a concrete example of how this system works in the computer. Knowing how the computer functions is an important concept in computer literacy. Being a part of the cycle helped students apply the concept of how the computer functions and transfer their learning to a practical application. In business education, students need to be able to apply what they are learning to skills they are going to need in the real world. Learning to work or function together as a group is part of how they will work or function in the world of business.

Classroom Management

This model strategy was also the answer to classroom management concerns. Establishing groups and making each student responsible for a part of the group's process proved to be successful in many ways. First, many times we were in a lab setting with some 30 students. Too many students moving around can pose problems. With only one member of each group up at any one time, these problems were virtually eliminated. Second, within the framework of the group setting, I was able to teach such concepts as working cooperatively, effectively, and efficiently as a team. Third, a surprising result from using the group management was a decrease in absenteeism. Students were less likely to be absent from class because they *did* assume responsibility for their jobs in the group, and they also wanted that positive response received for a job well done.

Examples of Group Activities

Because students stayed in their groups for the entire nine-week class, they developed working bonds that made learning activities more productive in the classroom. Group activities often involved using computers and other technology devices. One such activity involved the group preparing a Microsoft® PowerPoint® presentation about the devices involved in each of the parts of the information processing cycle. Group members worked together to prepare a presentation and handouts for their group to use as a study guide. Output produced the printout of this study guide and gave it to each group member. Output turned in a disk for a group grade on the activity.

Another activity involved making a presentation on their choice of one of the career clusters. Each group had the opportunity to make decisions about how they would present their information to the class. The presentation needed to include some form of technology. Some groups chose to make brochures about their cluster or posters using Brøderbund's PrintShop or Microsoft Word. Other groups chose to make visual presentations using PowerPoint and the classroom projector.

Each group was required to make a study guide about their career cluster. Once the group gave their career cluster presentation to the class, group members gave the class a handout, or hard copy, about the cluster for students to use as a study guide. Output turned in the soft copy.

In sixth grade, students worked in groups on a "Think, Write, Pair, Share" activity to learn the keys on the keyboard. Each group worked on all the words they could think of for the left-hand keys in this activity. Process was still responsible for keeping the group on task to complete the activity. Output was responsible for turning in the final hard copy and speaking to the class.

To begin the activity, I wrote the left-hand keys on the board in the order they appear on the keyboard. Students had one minute to think of all the words they could using only those letters, one minute to write down all those words, and two minutes to work with one partner in their group to mix the two lists into one big list. After the two minutes, they had five minutes to work together as a group to compile all the words that could be keyed in using only these letters. Another day we did this same activity with only the right-hand letters—a more difficult task! In doing this activity, I found that students remembered the keys more easily and felt a sense of accomplishment in knowing the keyboard. Not only does this activity help students learn the location of keys on the keyboard, but it also shows them the effectiveness of working together to complete a task.

Conclusions

Thinking back on the use of this strategy, I realize it reached far beyond classroom management and the concept of the information processing cycle. By "teaching smarter," I taught my students not only the concept of the information processing cycle, but also many other concepts and skills such as decision making, problem solving, and conflict resolution. Learning was increased because of the shared responsibility of all group members to work together. Through innovative classroom management, students were also motivated to accept responsibility.

The group-oriented classroom proved successful. Students enjoyed participating in groups and worked well together when they understood their roles. The benefits of group work are many—particularly as we prepare today's students for tomorrow's workforce. As adults, they will often work in teams and be assigned roles as members of the team. This classroom experience provided students an opportunity to develop skills in areas such as consensus, decision making, responsibility, researching, and problem solving.

The experience provided me with a possible answer to my question, "How can my students possibly have time to know, understand, and be able to apply all these concepts?" For this to happen, I must respond to students' needs as learners (e.g., group work), provide resources in a more innovative and motivating manner, and give students responsibility for their own behaviors and learning.

Sherry Roberts (sherry.roberts@eku.edu) is currently a visiting instructor at Eastern Kentucky University in Richmond, teaching in the Department of Management, Marketing, and Administrative Communication. She is also a consultant in technology integration with Roberts' Educational Consultants, Inc. Reach Ms. Roberts by e-mail.

Subject: Technology education, computer application

Audience: Teachers, teacher educators

Grade Level: 6–8 (Ages 11–14)

Technology: Presentation and word processing software

Standards: *NETS•S 1.* Read about the NETS Project at www.iste.org—select Standards Projects.)

Learning to Use Your Mind Effectively in a Technology-Based Classroom

My approach to teaching the use of technology in the classroom? Let me see. . . . I need to first examine my approach to teaching in general.

Pamela Keel

Teaching is a complex art—a behavioral art. I teach multi-media—computer graphics, presentation software, Web site design, video and music production, 3D animation, and game programming—to high school students.

The key to academic success comes from challenging the minds of students. Because I believe everyone is an individual, my philosophy of education supports differentiating curriculum within the classroom. Technology lends itself to this philosophy.

The Coalition of Essential Schools, founded by educator Theodore Sizer, is a "national network of schools that increases student achievement by supporting the rethinking of priorities and the redesign of curriculum, instruction, and assessment" *www.essentialschools.org*. The first time I read its *Common Principles*, a philosophy for learning, I was moved to the point of tears. Someone had actually put into eloquent language what I secretly believed education to be about. Someone else felt like me! For years I have observed my colleagues teaching in classrooms with straight rows of desks, complaining about students not trying hard enough, and reaching into last year's files to plan this year's lessons. I do not teach that way and have often felt out of place. In the *Common Principles*, issues are addressed that are often

From *Understanding Our Gifted,* Spring 2000, pp. 23-25. Reprinted with permission from Open Space Communications. 800-494-6178, www.openspace.com.

neglected by educational policies and procedures. Teaching students to learn to use their minds well in an environment conducive to trust, decency, and non-anxious expectation is the mandate of the Coalition.

I have talked with hundreds of Coalition colleagues over the last 10 years regarding educational practices and have discovered that often well-intentioned educators have difficulty implementing true reform, even though we have all agreed that reform is critical. We talk about implementing the *Common Principles* in our schools, but while the conversations are enthusiastic and stimulating, frequently the "talking" does not lead to the "doing." We grab an extra cookie at the end of the meeting, make sure we "signed in" so we receive credit for our attendance, and make a date to "talk again." If we take the risk to allow our vision to guide our curricular decisions, our students learn to use their minds well, and standards are met in a more natural process.

Teaching technology using methods that differentiate and allowing students to take their research and projects to individual levels are natural extensions of my educational philosophy. Using the *Common Principles* as my guide, I hope to see students come to class on time, greet their peers cheerfully, ponder their daily goals, and set about to accomplish these goals enthusiastically. At the end of each class, reflection time allows students to record the positives and negatives of their day and the things they need to change. Contact time with the teacher and peers consists of asking for and giving creative advice, sharing strokes of genius, and lamenting what "they should have done." I visualize students on the telephone, making multimedia contacts and inviting those contacts to speak to the class. I visualize that the teacher is a background figure in a forum designed for self-motivated projects and learning so stimulating that the need for a power figure is unnecessary. I see my students becoming charismatic presenters, comfortable discussing technical aspects of their work while keeping their audience entranced. Public exposure and presenting at other schools is vital to this process. The business community may recruit my students based on their confident interviews and outstanding portfolios, and the students can apply their academic experiences to the business world.

Using a goal-setting process known as "working backwards," I have outlined steps to achieve the desired end. Following is a list of student expectations, as they relate to the business world:

- Be on time
- Troubleshoot your own problems
- Use appropriate language
- Stay on task
- Take pride in your work
- Show respect to yourself, your peers, and the instructor
- Learn to use your mind well
- Request a conference if there is an issue you need to discuss
- Game-playing or inappropriate use of the Internet are not allowed.

The students have not enthusiastically received these classroom expectations. Although they have been exposed to most of these expectations throughout school, they have been accustomed to a classroom where the teacher is in the position of power. I try to be patient and consistent in enforcing these new expectations. If these students are going to become marketable in the multimedia industry, all of these expectations are minimum requirements. Students have had to learn that they are capable of resolving their own problems.

There are approximately 30 multimedia software packages in the multimedia lab. Many are industry standards such as Adobe Photoshop and Newtek Lightwave. The students have not followed written tutorials for any of the software, preferring to "learn by playing." I have implemented a structured process where each student follows a written tutorial and has each lesson in that tutorial checked off when completed. They develop technical reading skills and perseverance by working through each structured tutorial lesson. I frequently prompt students to ask their peers for help in order to develop an atmosphere of teamwork and trust. At the end of the tutorial (generally 10–15 lessons), the students complete a tutorial documentation sheet designed to refine their evaluation skills. This gives me an opportunity to work with them on their written expression and technical writing skills. The documentation requires students to assess the effectiveness of the tutorial, and a section asks them to evaluate their performance on the tutorial. This allows me to observe each student's comfort level with personal introspection, a workplace skill fundamental to upward mobility.

Following successful completion of the tutorial, students are asked to come up with three business-based projects. They have to define the client, the goal of the project, and how that project demonstrates mastery of the software's potential. Students write this information on a planning sheet and then have a conference with me. Deadlines are set, and the student is left to his or her own devices to create a project. Once the project is finished, the student is required to submit a written report describing the planning process, layout/design choices, techniques used, and a self-evaluation. A classroom presentation completes the process.

Presentations serve several purposes for students.

- They must feel proud enough of their work to hold it up for peer review
- They must develop "think on their feet" skills in order to answer questions
- They have to be comfortable discussing technical aspects of their work
- They must learn to accept critical feedback.

The trust evident in the classroom during a presentation is truly touching as students thoughtfully phrase their feedback in a gentle yet purposeful manner. The presentation brings formal closure to the tutorial-project-report cycle. It also serves as a celebration, particularly if the presenting student has demonstrated exemplary mastery of the software's capabilities. At times, spontaneous applause erupts, and smiles are exchanged all around as students appreciate the work of their peers. It is a special time and true to my philosophy. The teacher takes a back seat.

There are several procedures I implement in the classroom that are designed to add to the creative, thoughtful atmosphere.

- Music sets the tone. When the atmosphere is charged, classical music calms things down. When the students drag, a pop radio station or more up-beat CDs are appropriate.
- The first 10 minutes of every day are devoted to journaling. Sometimes the topic is mandatory, and other times it is optional. Journal time has been developed in order to give students time to transition to a classroom setting, leaving their "baggage" at the door. They are given the option of sharing their journals with the class. Their poetry and imaginative writings continue to astound me.
- Students take control of the classroom opening and closing procedures. There is a supervisor in charge of signaling the start of daily cleanup, and every class vacuums, dusts, cleans computer screens, and puts chairs back where they belong. Taking care of the classroom instills ownership and pride, and the shared cleanup brings closure to a hard day's work.

Short-term goals for the class include:

- A teambuilding activity in the form of a day-hike in the foothills which will be filmed and edited into a documentary by the students
- Visitations to nearby schools so that students may present their work and educate other students about career options in multimedia
- A field trip to watch the IMAX release of *Fantasia* in order to study cartoon animation
- An integration project with a neighboring high school humanities class to introduce the concept of computer art
- In-class speakers representing the multimedia industry and art institutes.

Long-term goals include:

- Updating computers and software in order to keep pace with industry standards
- Participation in state, national, and international multimedia competitions.

My approach to teaching the use of technology in the classroom calls for rethinking our approach to education. I adopt fundamental business practices in setting student expectations, such as team building activities, accepting personal responsibility for learning, formalized conferencing, etc. Students may enter my class with a preconceived notion of what to expect, which often differs greatly from reality. I expect a lot from my students. While they may struggle to reach those expectations, their sense of accomplishment and pride as they show visitors around our room leaves me feeling very warm inside. After all, teaching is an art, is it not?

Computers may be our tools, but the human interaction factor is a much more powerful force in our classroom. I believe in personal empowerment, and I have seen it work with all children, whether they are labeled "at-risk," "gifted," or "average."

Reference

Sizer, T. (1984). *Horace's compromise: The dilemma of the American high school.* Boston: Houghton Mifflin.

Pamela Keel is the Multimedia Instructor at the Technical Education Center, Boulder Valley School District, Colorado.

Strategies of Successful Technology Integrators: Part I

Streamlining Classroom Management

How do you create a coherent curriculum that includes effective technology use, excites your students about learning, and helps them score well on standardized tests?

By Lynn McNally
and Cindy Etchison

Problem: Your school has the computers (some in the classroom and some in a lab), and they are on a network with access to printers and the Internet. Now, how do you combine 24 students, these machines, and your curriculum? Then, how do you ensure that all students feel excited about school and score well on state-required standardized tests?

Feeling a little overwhelmed? Welcome to teaching today.

But teachers are not the only ones who feel overwhelmed. The world has become a much more hectic place than it was 20 or even 10 years ago, and we all feel we have too much to do.

Hard work used to be the standard by which we could all succeed, but hard work alone cannot do it for us anymore. We need to *work smart—* or for all the grammarians out there, *work smartly*. One way for educators to work smart is to find and follow some strategies for integrating technology into the classroom in a smooth and effective manner.

Enter "The Strategies of Successful Technology Integrators" developed by

two overworked technology resource teachers (TRTs) from Loudoun County, Virginia. Loudoun County, just west of Washington, D.C., is the third fastest growing county in the United States. An explosion of high-tech companies locating here—such as America Online and WorldCom— has brought us technology-savvy residents who are very aware of the advantages of technology use and who want those advantages for their children.

We share the same dream with our colleagues and many of our students' parents—to help teachers and students effectively integrate digital tools into the classroom in a way that transforms learning.

As a means of achieving that goal, we took a long look at the National Educational Technology Standards for Students (NETS•S), which call for students to responsibly use technology tools for communications, research, problem solving, and productivity in the pursuit of learning. We also looked at our available hardware and

software along with our experiences in the classroom. We came up with seven down-to-earth, practical, every-day strategies that fulfill the promise of that dream and can easily be used by all teachers.

In this article, we present the first strategy, which addresses school and classroom management. The second article will present three strategies for tapping the power of software tools, and the third will give three strategies for using the network to its fullest. The goal is to help educators save time that can then be spent with our clients (i.e., our students) and to help facilitate learning for all.

Strategy one: Use a variety of software applications as classroom management tools.

© 2000, ISTE (International Society for Technology in Education), 800.336.5191 (U.S. & Canada) or 541.302.3777 (Int'l), iste@iste.org, www.iste.org. All rights reserved.

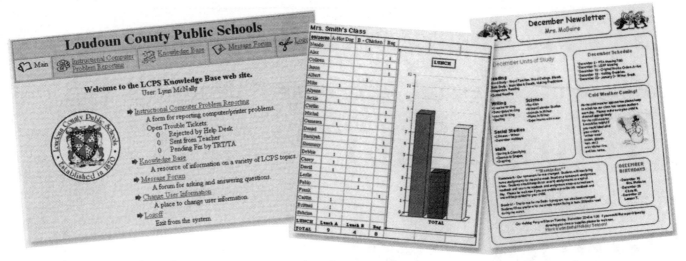

Figure 1. Loudon County teachers submit technical problems online.

Figure 2. Lunch preferences can be compiled easily in a spreadsheet.

Figure 3. Class newsletters are a great way to get students involved.

Streamline Management Tasks.

Just as business has used software applications to save time and increase the productivity of their employees, so can schools. The day-to-day management of records and information in a school system is an important task in every school employee's life. Anything that helps streamline all of those duties is one way for all of us to begin to work smart.

The all-powerful database and spreadsheet programs that help businesses can help us, too. We know that the administrative tasks of attendance and school record keeping can be streamlined with administrative software packages. Additionally, as we purchase and use more electronic materials in our schools, the management of inventory and maintenance records becomes an increasingly crucial task.

Moving toward a Web-based solution for maintaining these inventories can save school systems thousands of dollars. The reporting, dispatching of technicians, and tracking of computer and network problems through a Web-based, back-end database (keyed to an inventory database) can streamline the process and, at the same time, provide school systems with the much-needed data to justify budget requests for additional personnel or services.

For example, in Loudoun County; classroom teachers having a problem with a computer or other piece of equipment (printer, digital camera,

etc.) go to their intranet. They use a technical support page, on which they enter the serial number of the device and a brief description of the problem (Figure 1). The technology resource teacher in the building intervenes with training (if it is a training issue rather than a technical malfunction) or initiates a series of troubleshooting procedures. The TRT then documents the steps taken to solve the problem and, if the problem still exists, calls (through the same Web-interfaced database) for a technician who reads the history of the problem and proceeds to initiate a fix or replacement. Often, the description of the problem and the trouble-shooting procedures taken by the TRT tell the technician exactly what the problem is, and he or she is able to arrive at the school with the needed parts.

Another important management tool used by many teachers is a gradebook program, which can more easily allow the tracking of both qualitative and quantitative assessments of students. A networked database could compile different teachers' grades for all students and automatically generate an electronic report card.

A networked database would also greatly assist in the creation and deployment of individualized education plans (IEPs). A customized database can allow teachers to more easily build customized IEPs and quickly generate test data, printed plans, per-

mission letters, mailing labels, and status reports. And more important is having that database on a network so that all the key players who touch the life of that child can access this significant information.

Include Students.

The network-based solutions described previously are imperative if we are to use technology to work smart, but let's not forget some of the simpler solutions for classroom management. These tools include word processing, spreadsheet, database, and draw and paint programs. Using them also helps a teacher start to look at the computer as a resource to manage everyday activities, and when the teacher uses the computer, it sends a message to students: "Look, I use the computer to get my work done. You can, too.

> **When the teacher uses the computer, it sends a message to students: "Look, I use the computer to get my work done. You can, too."**

Figure 4. A word-processed Word Wall allows students to share their knowledge—and the words are readable by all.

Figure 5. Student artwork can be used for many things, including to label their storage space in the classroom.

Figure 6. Personalized certificates can be much more meaningful than purchased awards.

In elementary schools, classroom management is an important part of the curriculum. Elementary school teachers have lists of daily chores and routinely rotate students through those job assignments. As every parent of young children knows, some of those assignments could be accomplished faster by an adult, but children learn so much when we ask them to share in some of these duties. So why not use technology to help with those chores?

For example, the teacher can have his or her students enter their lunch preferences in a spreadsheet each morning. The teacher learns to use a spreadsheet, teaches students to use it, models organizational skills, shows students how to use technology as a management tool, does the lunch count for the cafeteria, and streamlines classroom bureaucracy. The teacher has to set up the spreadsheet, but student managers can maintain it and save time each day on this routine chore (Figure 2).

Everyone benefits from the process of identifying a task, choosing the appropriate tool to complete it, working with others to gain the knowledge needed to complete it, completing it, and sharing the solution. Let's look at some of the other ways that teachers and students can use the computer to create materials that help manage classroom activities.

Word processing and desktop publishing programs can help with many classroom management activities. For ex-

ample, a classroom newsletter is an easy way for teachers to share their classes' goals and successes with parents (Figure 3). Instead of a weekly newsletter created solely by the teacher, why not have a student-created newsletter? The age level of the students will determine how much prep work the teacher will need to do. A computer connected to a television becomes a white board, allowing the teacher to discuss the newsletter with the whole class, providing guidelines and instruction while students write the text as a group. As the students follow the teacher's model of creating and connecting sentences and paragraphs and correcting grammar, spelling, and punctuation, they interact with each other and get immediate feedback. Students can continue their work on the newsletter at a later time, maybe in pairs or small groups. The guidance given by the teacher to the entire group allows individual students to take ownership of the newsletter and to create a document that follows writing patterns modeled by the teacher.

As younger students begin to read and write and build vocabularies, they need references to assist them; one used by many teachers is the Word Wall. The Word Wall provides a clear and readily available resource for students. Students create these lists of words as they discover them. They can type them into a word processor

and choose different fonts, styles, and colors to make their displays attractive and helpful (Figure 4). Colorful word labels written in another language and, again, created by students can be affixed to items in and out of the classroom.

Draw and paint programs are also basic tools that can help with classroom management. Educators are well aware of the connections between visual stimuli and language acquisition, and, consequently, we provide young children with many media for drawing and painting: crayons, pencils, chalks, paints, and so on. Electronic drawing and painting tools are another medium for students, who, even at ages five and six, display differing talents in each.

Down-to-earth, practical uses of technology can streamline class and school management—giving educators more time to spend with students.

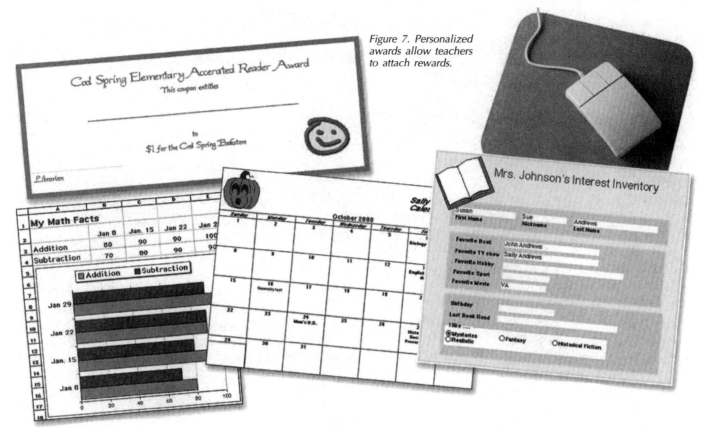

Figure 7. Personalized awards allow teachers to attach rewards.

Figure 8. Students can use technology to track their performance over time.

Figure 9. Class calendars can keep parents informed and students reminded of upcoming projects and events.

Figure 10. Students can share their interests in a class database. Use the database to create reading or project groups.

Each student can draw or paint an individual logo or artwork for his or her storage space in the classroom (Figure 5). Certificates can show students how much their hard work is appreciated. Teachers are discovering that those created by themselves and their students are more valuable than ones they can purchase (Figure 6). Students and teachers can first design a template with the class's logo, to later retrieve and tailor with the individual's name, accomplishment, and an illustrative graphic.

Teachers can create coupons for students (Figure 7). They earn these coupons for successful completion of tasks and trade them for rewards such as additional recess time or privileges. Students and teachers can also create stickers to use as rewards and incentives. Teachers can also create multiple classroom seating charts in a word processing or drawing program to reflect different student groupings.

Spreadsheet programs are natural tools for classroom management. The lunch count spreadsheet described previously is a daily activity in most fourth- and fifth-grade classrooms in Loudoun County.

Math quizzes provide feedback to students as they learn new concepts and facts. Students can take responsibility for their math work by entering their weekly quiz grades into an individual or class spreadsheet. Periodically, teachers and students can select data for each student and create a bar or line graph (Figure 8). This visual representation of the data provides a valuable picture for the student.

A calendar template assists teachers in managing the information to be shared with parents (Figure 9). Parents learn of important dates and assignments through a monthly calendar sent home on paper or published on the school's Web page. Students have also found that a calendar template assists them in tracking their assignments and due dates. Having a calendar that they maintain in a personal folder on a server gives them a management tool

they can access from any computer in the building, and it helps them and their parents take responsibility for submitting their homework and projects on time.

If a teacher has the opportunity to allocate and spend funds for classroom materials (as is the case in many schools), why not bring your students into the process? Give students ownership of their classroom by discussing how much money should be spent on classroom materials for next year: paper, ink cartridges, videotapes, film, transparencies, poster board, software, and so on. The class can create a spreadsheet that lists the needs and the budgeted amount for their "wish list." Wonderful discussions can develop as students consider each purchase and its effect on their ability to make other purchases.

Database programs can also help with classroom management. The beginning of the school year involves collecting information about new students and their families. The student information database provides students with the opportunity to electronically submit this information. At the elementary level, the teacher can quickly discover who knows their addresses and phone numbers as well as who has acquired basic technology skills.

Another way for students to become active learners is by completing an interest inventory database (Figure 10). Teachers and students can then look at class trends or form reading or project groups based on common interests.

Students can quickly learn how to collect, sort, and analyze data generated by a school's election by creating a Voting Booth database. Students can either hand-enter data from a paper-and-pencil election or, taking a page from current U.S. discussion about online voting, they could create a Web page that automatically logs the votes. Students can problem solve issues of one person = one vote" security.

Take the Next Step

Using technology to help manage school and classroom needs is an important way to work smart and, at the same time, begin to integrate technology into your classroom. And having both teachers and students use technology tools for classroom management gives a shared sense of classroom ownership and responsibility, an all-important

step toward building a collaborative classroom in which teachers are not only dispensers of information but also learners working alongside their students. See next month's issue of *L&L* for more of our strategies.

Subject: All academic areas, school information management, classroom management

Audience: Teachers, teacher educators, technology coordinators, library media specialists

Grade Level: K–12 (Ages 5–18)

Technology: Database, spreadsheet, word processing, desktop publishing, draw, and paint programs

Standards: *NETS•T* V. (Read more about the NETS Project at www.iste. org—select Standards Projects.)

Online Discussion: www.iste.org/L&L

Lynn McNally (lmcnally@pen. k12.va. us), a technology resource teacher with Virginia Loudoun County Public Schools, has worked in staff development and tech integration support for the last six years. She is a member of the Board of Directors of the Virginia Society for Technology in Education (VSTE), an ISTE Affiliate. In 1998, she was named an Apple Distinguished Educator. She has presented at state and national conferences; conducted numerous workshops; and received local, state, and national grants. Lynn teaches a graduate class on technology integration at Shenandoah University, has written curriculum for the Discovery Channel's School Page, and recently served as an advisor to America Online's new aol@school.

Cindy Etchison (cetchiso@loudoun. k12.va.us) is a technology resource specialist for Loudoun County (Virginia) Public Schools. She works with 40 technology resource teachers (TRTs) to promote the site-based and district-wide instructional technology program. As a resource specialist, she helps plan and provide training for the TRTs and assists them in helping teachers to teach with technology. Mrs. Etchison has worked as a TRT, computer systems analyst, and teacher of preschool students with special needs.

CONCEPT TO CLASSROOM: WEB-BASED WORKSHOPS FOR TEACHERS

ABSTRACT

Concept to Classroom is a series of free, online workshops developed by Thirteen/WNET New York and Disney Learning Partnership. The series is designed to help teachers explore contemporary issues in education. Such topics as multiple intelligences, constructivism, standards, assessment, and inquiry-based learning are presented along with discussion boards and chat sessions with leading theorists and practitioners in education.

EDITED BY JIM AND TIA DONLEVY

INTRODUCTION

As the pace of educational innovation increases, online professional development opportunities for teachers are essential to help these busy professionals stay current in the field. Recognizing this fact, Thirteen/WNET and the charitable arm of Disney, Disney Learning Partnership, have teamed to produce *Concept to Classroom*. *Concept to Classroom* is a series of online, interactive workshops available to teachers without charge covering a wide range of educational issues, pedagogical approaches and strategies for use in the classroom (www.thirteen.org/wnetschool).

The series includes tutorials, featured experts, online discussion areas and special "live" chat sessions with leading theorists and practitioners in education. Among other session topics, *Concept to Classroom*'s self directed workshops include: "Tapping into Multiple Intelligences," "Constructivism as a Paradigm for Teaching and Learning," "Teaching to Academic Standards," "Assessment, Evaluation, and Curriculum Redesign," and "Why the Net?: An Interactive Educational Tool." Details of these and other workshop sessions are sketched below.

CONCEPT TO CLASSROOM

The following workshops are offered in the *Concept to Classroom* series:

Tapping into Multiple Intelligences

This workshop examines the importance of reaching learners by appealing to their multiple intelligences, according to the principles developed by Howard Gardner. Examples of innovative classroom teaching are included. Through comparisons and discussion, participants learn to develop and adapt their own teaching strategies.

Constructivism as a Paradigm for Teaching and Learning

Collaborative lessons, activities that involve a learner's experience and student-motivated projects contribute to an effective constructivist classroom. Constructivism advocate Jacqueline Grennon-Brooks, associate professor and director of the science education program at the State University of New York at Stony Brook, served as content developer for this workshop. Practical strategies, educational tools and

This material first appeared in the *International Journal of Instructional Media*, Volume 27, Number 2, 2000, pp. 129-131. Reprinted with permission.

resources facilitating constructivist learning are presented.

Teaching to Academic Standards

What are the implications of the new academic standards? This workshop covers critical issues in teaching to the standards and provides guidance on how to make them work in the classroom. Content developers include Marc S. Tucker, president of the National Center on Education and the Economy, and Ruth Mitchell of the Education Trust in Washington, D.C.

Why the Net?: An Interactive Educational Tool

This workshop is for educators who want to investigate what the Internet can do for classroom learning. The tutorial includes Internet resources, evaluation criteria and practical ideas.

Cooperative and Collaborative Learning

Cooperative and collaborative learning are growing in popularity and helping teachers to think differently about structuring student learning. Participants are introduced to common principles including positive interdependence, individual accountability, task and role differentiation and simultaneous interaction.

Assessment, Evaluation, and Curriculum Redesign

How do we know if students are learning and mastering concepts? Education consultant, Heidi Hayes Jacobs, served as content developer for this workshop; it offers effective alternative ways of evaluating student learning.

Inquiry-based Learning

A former teacher and state science director, Joe Exline, developed the content for this workshop on inquiry-based learning. Through discussion and sharing of projects and ideas, participants discover the advantages of inquiry-based learning.

WebQuests

WebQuests were initiated in 1995 by Bernie Dodge at San Diego State University. WebQuests are innovative teaching strategies that use the Internet to help students ask questions, use information effectively and look critically at data.

Making Family and Community Connections

What role do parents, guardians and the community play in education: Joyce L. Epstein, Ph.D., director of the Center on School, Family and Community Partnerships at Johns Hopkins University, developed the content for this workshop, along with experts from the Harvard Family Research Project. The tutorial discusses strategies and provides resources to help teachers bring families and communities into the school environment.

THE *CONCEPT TO CLASSROOM* DESIGN

Each *Concept to Classroom* workshop is divided into four sections: Explanation, Demonstration, Exploration, and Implementation. Each explanation section provides material describing the particular subject under consideration. The demonstration section offers a look at successful implementation in classrooms. The exploration section helps teachers learn about effective strategies to consider and begin implementation; and the implementation section assists with actual lesson plans and additional resources to adapt teaching strategies to specific classrooms.

In addition to the four sections, each tutorial offers opportunities for online discussion. Such discussion helps teachers learn from each other and permits contributions from many different participants. For workshops that are in session, discussions include *Concept to Classroom* facilitators who answer questions, direct participants to more information and provide additional help, as needed.

CONCLUSION

Concept to Classroom is a series of Web-based workshops produced to engage teachers with current ideas and relevant practices important in the field. Each workshop offers teachers expert advice, concrete tools and practical information for implementing effective teaching methodologies in the classroom. Most important, *Concept to Classroom* gives teachers the support they need to bring vital ideas into the curriculum using current technology to enhance student learning. With developments in teaching and learning increasing and the application of technology to the classroom expanding, educational opportunities like *Concept to Classroom* offer stimulating guidance to teachers at all levels.

Direct Reprints Requests to:
Jim and Tia Donlevy
120 Farrington Avenue
Sleepy Hollow, NY 10591–1305
E-Mail: jdonle@aol.com

Unit 4

Unit Selections

Key Points to Consider

❖ Will communication technology such as e-mail, threaded discussion groups, and chat rooms become a major part of teacher education? Why or why not?

❖ Will schools of education focus on structuring telecommunications to create a distributed learning environment for student teachers? Explain your answer.

❖ What will the classroom of the twenty-first century look like? How will it be equipped? What are the benefits of such a classroom to teachers and students?

❖ What effect does the implementation of instructional design and the use of application software have on teacher education programs?

❖ What new opportunities for monitoring, tutoring, and other interactions does online technology bring?

 **Links** **www.dushkin.com/online/**

These sites are annotated on pages 4 and 5.

The goal of teacher education should be to advance all aspects of education, including fundamental research, technology, curriculum, and professional development. However, the most important product derived from teacher education over the past two decades has been the emergence of a vision of what technology has to offer education. Earlier thinking focused on technology as supporting the role and mechanical aspects of learning (drill and practice). The new vision focuses on using technology to support excellence in learning, searching, inferencing, deciding. In this vision, students tackle much harder problems, work on larger-scale and more meaningful projects, have a greater and more reflective responsibility for their own learning, and are able to work in a variety of styles that reflect differences in gender, ethnicity, or simply individual personality. This new vision shows that creative use of technology by skilled teachers offers a promise to restructure education as we know it quickly and effectively. The new vision will ensure that students are afforded classroom or at-a-distance instruction at a pace that suits their learning styles and in a way that gives them a more active role in the learning process. Schools must provide adequate teacher training, at both the preservice and inservice levels, that enables teachers to become fully aware of and skilled in using the vast resources that today's technology offers.

The articles presented in this unit provide evidence that action is being taken to bring the benefits of technology to teachers as well as to children. In the first report, Michael Ruef and Cindy Higgins focus on the World Wide Web in an effort to support teachers in their quest for authoritative resources. They describe the efforts of a panel composed of teachers, family members, researchers, and communication specialists who compiled an annotated list of Web sites providing practical, positively oriented information on challenging behavior.

Next, Dee McGonigle and Renee Eggers identified the typical stages during the instructors' and students' transition into the various aspects of virtual learning. Although this article is geared toward entire courses being offered over the Internet, it can also partially apply to traditional courses that have an Internet component.

Then, Carole Duff describes how the growth of technology brings teachers new opportunities for mentoring through online tutorials, ask-an-expert coaching, and e-mail linking of students with successful professionals in careers of mutual interest. This is especially important to some teachers in Texas who wanted to provide on-the-job experience or guidance to their high school students. They established a telemonitoring program that matched 14 upper-level mathematics and computer-science students with women engineers at Texas Instruments. Later the program was expanded to all four high school grades.

In "Evaluating & Using Web-Based Resources," the authors depict a method for providing guidance to students on how to locate online resources by using a five-step process that includes identification of potential resources, evaluation of appropriate resources, integration into the research paper, citation of the resource, and verification by the instructor. This article provides guidance for teachers who are interested in vastly increasing student access to sources that provide students with a lifelong research skill.

Next, Huann-shyang Lin and Houn-Lin Chiu explore the efficacy of promoting a beginning chemistry teacher's curriculum development and teaching practices through the use of computers. The teacher's teaching practices both before and after the Web site treatment were observed and analyzed. It was found that before the treatment the teacher used the textbook as the only resource of his teaching. After the treatment, the teacher was able to develop suitable curricula for the purpose of increasing student involvement.

The unit concludes with a description of how to use personal digital assistants during the clinical supervision of student teachers. Kent Crippen and David Brooks demonstrate how journalizing can be an important tool to help student teachers reflect on the nature of their student teaching experience. The authors point out how communication of journals to student teacher supervisors is enhanced greatly by using e-mail. They describe how software can be used to enhance journalizing. The software included tools to facilitate writing field notes during in-class observations by the supervisor. E-mail exchange largely has supplanted the need for an electronic journalizing tool. They also identify flexible strategies for using a personal digital assistant (PalmPilot) to facilitate the development of field notes during observations. The notes can then be readily communicated to the student teacher by several means, including e-mail.

Look It Up on the Web

Practical Behavioral Support Information

FOUR WEB CRITERIA
Aesthetics
Navigability
Clarity
Credibility

Michael B. Ruef

Cindy Higgins

What practical resources on student behavior are immediately available to teachers? Increasingly, the World Wide Web (WWW) offers access to information, but finding useful information takes time—a luxury teachers seldom have. Further, the information is only as good as the standards of the Web site publishing it.

In an effort to support teachers in their quest for authoritative resources, a four-person panel—representing teachers, family members, researchers, and communication specialists—has compiled an annotated list of Web sites providing practical, positively oriented information on challenging behavior. All panel members are frequent WWW users and knowledgeable in the area of behavioral support. The family member and teacher panelists support children with challenging behavior. The communications spe-

> **Look for sites with interactive opportunities— live chats, listservs, and on-line discussions.**

cialist and researcher specialize in the area of positive behavior support.

Evaluating Web Sites

Panelists scored a comprehensive list of behavioral Web sites according to the following

- Overall aesthetics (is the Web site inviting?).
- Navigability (is the site easy to negotiate?).
- Clarity (does the site contain clear, usable information?).
- Credibility of content (is the information accurate?).

The 12 Web sites averaging the highest ratings (4 or higher on a 5-point scale) from our panel members fell into two broad classifications: (a) general information on behavior management and (b) positive approaches to behavioral support. For educators or parents wishing to conduct their own Internet search, helpful search engine descriptors including "behavioral support," "positive behavioral support," "challenging/problem behavior,"

From *Teaching Exceptional Children,* March/April 1999, pp. 32-34. © 1999 by The Council for Exceptional Children. Reprinted by permission.

"emotional/behavioral problems," "applied behavior analysis," and "discipline."

General Information on Behavior Management

For general information on behavioral support, the following Web sites offer concise information that you can also use as first-step handouts to parents, teachers, and others interested in behavior.

Guidance and Discipline (http://www.nncc. org/Guidance/guide.disc.page.html). This site, established by the National Network for Child Care, offers over 85 briefs on appropriate behavior, emotions, self-esteem, social skills, and other topics related to behavior. Titles include the following:

- *Five Tips for Guiding Children's Behavior.*
- *What Can I Do About Violence?*
- *Handling Aggression.*
- *Helping Young Children Cope with Anger.*
- *Children Without Friends (a four-part series).*

Though most briefs are geared toward younger children, several titles, such as *The Challenge of Working with Challenging Children,* apply to all ages.

Look for sites that can help parents who have children with disabilities become better informed and effective representatives for their children.

CEC Special Web Focus: Discipline: Behavior Intervention (http://www.cec.sped. org/bk/focus/specfoc.htm). This Special Focus section of The Council for Exceptional Children's (CEC) Web site offers downloadable access to articles on discipline and behavior from the following CEC-related sources:

- The 1998 Special Focus issue on Discipline and Behavior Intervention of *TEACHING Exceptional Children.*

- *CEC Today* articles on behavior (e.g., "Strategies to Meet IDEA '97's Discipline Requirements").
- The *Research Connections in Special Education* issue devoted to schoolwide behavioral management systems.

Safeguarding Your Children (http:www.pta. org/programs/sfgrdtoc.htm). This National PTA and Allstate Foundation-sponsored site provides an annotated list of resources for families, schools, and communities to help plan and implement violence-prevention programs.

Does My Child Have an Emotional or Behavioral Disorder? (http://www.pacer.org/ articles/articles.htm). This article from the PACER Center, which offers programs to help parents who have children with disabilities become better informed and effective representatives for their children, provides guidelines for parents and others for when a

---

Information on the Internet is only as good as the standards of the Web site publishing it.

---

child's behavior becomes challenging. It includes suggestions of what to look for, assessments, influencing factors, and cultural considerations.

Behavior Analysis Internet Resources (http://www.taba.org/publications.htm). Sponsored by the Tennessee Association for Behavior Analysis, this site provides a jumping-off point for a number of behavior-analysis Internet resources, including annotated lists and links to certified behavior-analyst resources, commercial sites, educational institutions, instructional resources, professional organizations, and publications. In addition, this site provides an opportunity for users to participate in live chats on themes relating to behavior analysis.

Responding to Crisis at a School (http:// smhp.psych.ucla.edu/resource.htm). This resource aid packet from the UCLA Center for Mental Health in Schools is one of a variety of downloadable packets/articles available from this site. Also available are valuable links to other government, educational, mental health, and school-based collaborative team sites. In addition, the site provides contact information for consultants

Good Web sites offer concise information that you can use as handouts to parents, teachers, and others interested in behavior.

working on policy issues related to mental health in schools.

Positive Approaches to Behavioral Support

Inclusion: School as a Caring Community (http://www.quasar.ualberta.ca/ddc/incl/ intro.htm#top). This site contains useful information for teachers, including practical comments from elementary, middle, and secondary schoolteachers about behavioral strategies they have used successfully (see "Field Notes" section). It also has a search function and resource section.

LRE for LIFE Project Behavior Full-Text Articles (http://Web.ce.utk.edu/lre/index. htm). Sponsored by the University of Tennessee and the Tennessee Department of Education, this site includes information on positive behavioral support and technical assistance used in Tennessee schools. Teachers and administrators alike will appreciate this site, which includes the following (see "Online Resources and Publications" section):

- Two worksheets (*Behavior Support Plan Recommendations, Functional Assessment Summary*).
- A sample agreement (*Collaboration for Positive Behavioral Support*).
- An in-depth, compact set of implementation guidelines (*Suggested Guidelines for Implementing Positive Behavioral Support Strategies*).

Addressing Student Problem Behavior: An IEP Team's Introduction to Functional Behavioral Assessment and Behavior Intervention Plans (http://www.air~dc.org/ cecp/cecp.htm). Prepared by the Center for Effective Collaboration and Practice: Improving Services for Children and Youth and Behavioral Problems (see "Information Resources"), this 1998 document overviews the 1997 Discipline Amendments to the Individuals with Disabilities Education Act

(IDEA). The document can be downloaded and includes the following topics:

- IDEA Rights and Requirements.
- IEP Team Roles.
- Why a Functional Assessment of Behavior (FAB) Is Necessary.
- Conducting a FAB.
- Alternative Assessment Strategies.
- Behavior Intervention Plans.
- Addressing Skill and Performance Deficits.
- Modifying the Learning Environment.

In addition, the Center offers a collection of on-line resources including articles, e-mail listservs, state resources, and interactive on-line discussions on several topics related to emotional and behavioral problems.

Positive Behavioral Support: A Bibliography for Schools (http://nichcy.org). This bibliography (see "Publications") from the National Information Center for Children and Youth with Disabilities includes materials on many topics: behavior problems related to disability, behavioral assessment, classroom management, conflict resolution, aggressive and disruptive students, communication, discipline, behavioral interventions, multicultural issues, and positive behavioral support. These resources encourage school personnel to

- Look at the student within the larger context of his or her environment at school and beyond.
- Identify what factors influence or trigger challenging behavior.
- Develop a plan for providing the positive behavioral support necessary for the student to behave appropriately at school.

The National Information Center also emphasizes parent involvement in problem-solving and decision making.

Barkley Memorial Center Pareducator Self-Study Program (http://para.unl.edu/ServedDocuments/TrainingIntro.html). Courtesy of the University of Nebraska, this Web site provides paraeducators with an introductory program and includes a unit on behavior management. The unit addresses the following:

- The goals of behavior management.
- Behavior planning.
- Student management strategies promoting positive behavior (e.g., planned ignoring, cue provision, proximity control, humor, effective praise).
- Ethical considerations.

Opening with a pretest, the unit focus is on finding ways to assist and support students in being successful, rather than on controlling misbehavior. It also includes a posttest, further study suggestions, and practicum activities.

Michael B. Ruef (*CEC Chapter #197*), *Director, The Family Connection;* **Cindy Higgins,** *Communications Director, Beach Center on Families and Disability, University of Kansas, Lawrence.*

Address correspondence to Michael B. Ruef, Beach Center on Families and Disability, University of Kansas, Lawrence, KS 66045 (e-mail: mike@dole.Lsi.ukans.edu).

Readers may also wish to visit the Web site developed by the Beach Center on Families and Disability at the University of Kansas: Positive Behavioral Support (http://www.lsi.ukans.edu/beach/pbs/pbs.htm). This site presents an overview of positive behavioral support, research summaries, stories about families who have used positive behavioral support successfully, fact sheets, and resources. This site will also provide links to three new U.S. Department of Education-sponsored Web sites on positive behavioral support currently under construction.

Stages of Virtuality: Instructor and Student

By Dee McGonigle and Renee M. Eggers

The Internet has been a reality for decades for researchers and educators at institutions of higher education. With the development of the Internet, the complexion of higher education has changed. The Internet offers opportunities not available before, and this technology has had a major impact by changing the scope of electronic communication and radically transforming the manner by which our educational coursework and resources can be delivered to our consumers. This Internet offers us the ability to create highly complex virtual learning environments, which are capable of being delivered from local to global educational markets. Additionally, this virtual highly stimulating medium provides us with a tool to distribute our course content and activities anytime and anywhere. Students need only tune in.

As higher education continues to embrace the virtual learning world, students and faculty must adjust to this new medium. The authors have been involved in various aspects of virtual courses before people knew this catch-phrase. This article describes the typical stages identified during the instructors' and students' transition into this new learning frontier, the virtual world. Although this article is geared towards entire courses being offered over the Internet, it can also partially apply to traditional courses that have an Internet component.

Instructor's Stages of Virtuality

For an instructor, there are seven basic stages through which the instructor typically passes when designing and teaching a virtual course. Some stages are more difficult than are others. Yet, as experience in the offering of these courses is accumulated, passing from one stage to another becomes easier. Nevertheless, for the novice virtual course instructor, awareness of the seven stages will at least alert the person as to what to expect before assuming responsibility for a virtual course.

Excited Stage

The instructor begins the journey into virtual course offerings at the "Excited Stage," since the person has an idea about a course that can be offered via the Internet. Once the person gets approval from superiors or the appropriate committee, the instructor, who is soon to be a virtual instructor, excitedly approaches the creation of a new course, or transformation of a traditional course, to provide students with a state-of-the-art way of obtaining education.

Apprehensive Stage

After the Instructor has course approval and advertising of the course is planned, the person soon enters the "Apprehensive Stage." In this stage, thoughts of "I now have to do what I said I would do" keep running through the person's mind. The instructor worries about being able to create the learning environment that was conceptualized. This is the point at which the instructor may feel panicked about the possibility of not creating a "good" course. Instructors often feel that they are "in over their heads" at this point. One instructor told me that she felt as though she was beginning teaching all over again. She went on to say that "This is uncharted water and now I don't know if I want to be out there creating the map."

Questioning Stage

When the time comes to actually start preparing for the virtual course, the instructor soon steps into the "Questioning Stage," and a constant question seems to be "How am I going to get it all together?" Many other questions also surface at this time. These questions tend to revolve around issues such as Web access versus electronic mail (e-mall) access, number and complexity of assignments, meeting university-imposed credit hour requirements, and methods of transforming traditional course materials into ones for a virtual environment. This stage is a critical one in that the questions act as guidelines for the resulting virtual course. Instructors are busy seeking answers. They want to find out "how-to" actually do the work they have now begun. They have moved from apprehension, the worry before action to actually beginning to act. Course development issues continue to surface through development, however, as the instructor begins to navigate these waters, they gain a sense of confidence. One instructor I was assisting told me that, "As I started to do this my legs were shaky and I felt that it was an impossible task to learn everything I needed to know. But, you know as I began to move forward and develop materials and things took shape, it was easier and easier to deal with the 'newness.' The 'newness' was scary at first but then conquering each new hurdle made me grow confident. I began by trying out e-mail and then a conferencing tool—what a hurdle. Hey, I'm on the Web in various formats now and helping others get through."

Determined Stage

Finding, or deciding on, the answers to the questions raised in the previous stage and actually beginning to prepare the course materials moves the instructor into the "Determined Stage." Now, the instructor faces the reality that the course has to be in a condition that it can be taught via the Internet so that it is valuable to the students and enhances the reputation of both the instructor and the university. The instructor becomes focused and is able to begin preparing the course materials that establish the virtual culture for the course. After trying many formats and questioning delivery every inch of the way, the course begins to take shape. The culture is building with every decision or action. Many instructors must be reminded about culture. In our classrooms we have control over the culture in our presence; however, at times, cyberspace eliminates our physical presence. We must guide and facilitate the development of a cultural environment in this new educational medium. This is an area that causes problems for many students and instructors.

Overstimulated Stage

Either during the course-planning phase or at the beginning of the implementation of the course, the instructor soon slides into the "Overstimulated Stage" when the instructor realizes the increased electronic demands from students. There are two major levels in this stage. First, because the course is a virtual course, it makes sense to have the students access related topics that are available on the Internet. Yet, because of the generous, sometimes overwhelming, amounts of Internet information available on certain topics, the instructor becomes overstimulated as to what the instructor specifically wants the students to read and what the instructor wants students to be able to have for enrichment-type references.

The second level of this stage is interaction with students. In a traditional course, the instructor meets face-to-face with the students a scheduled number of times a week, and students also have access to the instructor during the instructor's office hours. In virtual courses, students also need to be able to interact with the instructor.

By using e-mail or some Internet conferencing method, the students have the capability of electronically accessing the instructor 24 hours a day. Since many students enroll in virtual courses because those courses allow for time flexibility, electronic course communication can occur whenever the students decide "to go to class." The global market exacerbates this dilemma when the instructor realizes that some of the course's students are from different states or countries in different time zones. Thus, the instructor has to deal with the problem of how to handle communication when a student's day is just beginning at the same time that the instructor's day is ending. Managing the communicative dilemmas brought on by the energized Internet courses can be overwhelming. Although the seemingly simple answer is communication using e-mail, there are many situations when e-mail is not efficient or sufficient to satisfy communication demands; when that occurs, the instructor has to make a communication decision based on resources available to both the instructor and students. This may even necessitate that the instructor communicate with the student via Internet conferencing tools, telephone, fax, or mail.

Questioning Stage Revisited

Once the virtual course is in full swing, the instructor steps into the "Questioning Stage" again through another door. The instructor then asks, How can this course be better, and is it meeting the students' varied needs?" This is the time when the instructor starts performing formative evaluation. Also, the instructor plans for summative evaluation. Answers to evaluation measures are valuable if the course is to grow and to really meet the educational needs of the students.

Exhausted Stage

When the virtual course ends, the instructor typically advances to the "Exhausted Stage" because the course is over! Duration of the "Exhausted Stage" can continue even when the focus moves to revision of course material and content, based on lessons learned from implementation and evaluations. After moving through the stages initially, the instructor is able to re-enter these stages more confidently and is ready to examine other courses for possible virtualization.

Student's Stages of Virtuality

Instructors are not the only ones who move through a series of stages during a virtual course. Students have their own five stages, and like the instructor, the first time through the stages involved in taking a virtual course is the most difficult. Subsequent progression through the stages as a result of taking additional virtual courses becomes only slightly easier since the student does not have the amount of control in the course that the instructor does.

Confused Stage

Students begin at the "Confused Stage." Many students who are not familiar with taking a Internet-based course, or have not had computer experience, may find themselves enrolled in a virtual course. These students may begin by asking, "How does this work, and how can I do this?" It is definitely confusing to them when they are told about the virtual materials available on the World Wide Web, especially when they ask, "My syllabus is where?" Just being able to understand the concept of how the Internet works, especially when it comes to Websites and links, is somewhat of a major task.

To reduce the amount of negative impact on the students, the instructor must anticipate the needs and concerns of these inexperienced students. That way, when related questions surface, the instructor can provide the students with the information that the students need, and the instructor can be reassuring at the same time.

Students venturing into this virtual world are often met with technical difficulties, "technoproblems," whether they are student-induced or system-induced—they still cause confusion and frustration. One of the system-induced "technoproblems" we had to work through was a new swipe card technology. The idea was to enable the students to swipe their ID cards so they could receive account information such as their initial password for entry into the system or obtain a forgotten password. As with any new procedure, it was difficult reassuring the students that this was really a terrific idea since it expedited new account dissemination and a forgotten password could take as much as three days to recover in the past. When the swipe card did not function properly, it was a little unsettling for the students and another reason to get upset with technology. One student told me that "it did not 'enable' us instead it 'disabled' us." We must help our students recognize that entering an electronic age is not always smooth but rather it mirrors our bumpy lives with their ups and downs. The other main "technoproblem" we had to deal with revolved around our log-on procedure. Our students had to log onto our server using a password and then they had to use another password to get their e-mail and still another password to access selected courses. The students induced their own problems by creating three separate passwords instead of following the suggestion to use one password for all. Therefore, the student would either forget which password was created for which access or they could not remember their passwords at all. We also had combined system-student-induced "technoproblems" when students tried to first set up their access accounts from home. We had to surmount hardware and software interface problems as well as user inexperience on the part of the student trying to connect. At times, the students were not sure that this "virtual stuff," as one student put it, was worth the effort to learn. Instructors become frantic when the technoproblems interfere with their course especially when they have gone to great lengths to make the technology as transparent as possible.

Shock Stage

The students soon try to access the course materials, and after surmounting all of the technical difficulties that they encounter, they enter the "Shock Stage" when they realize they "Got in!" They are accessing the Internet, and the computer commands that they type in are actually carried out! It is a good day when students' access attempts run smoothly and they are able to obtain the Internet-based coursework without a glitch. I have students who will call to tell me they got on and sometimes that necessitates them hanging up their modems and getting off to call me. It is at this phase that the students become more comfortable with the technology barring other technoproblems sending them back through this phase.

Timid Stage

From the "Shock Stage," students progress right to the "Timid Stage" where they are happy to be accessing the Internet and their course materials, but they are tentative about the course materials and how they will manage this new learning experience. At this point, the students may also start experiencing feelings of isolation when they become aware that they don't have a visual contact with other students in this virtual course.

As before, the instructor needs to anticipate this stage. Setting up a listserv or Web site, which includes a Frequently Asked Questions (FAQ) file, and initiating a "get-to-know-your-virtual-classmate" activity may be the answer. There are many activities that have been used for this cultural climate-building exercise. The one that has worked best is having each student create his or her own Web page with a picture (at least) and brief description of themselves. Depending on enrollment, the instructor can create a photo page with a two-sentence descriptor about each student under his or her photo. If you are lucky enough to have a small class, each student must visit all of the Web pages and dialogue with each of the other students. If you use conferencing software, you can create a folder for each student. The students are then directed to note one or two things about each of the other students in the course from their interactions and then place their comments in each student's individual folder. It gives them a sense of "group." Establishing a sense of community among the students is a critical factor.

Frustrated Stage

Since virtual courses rely on computer technology, glitches occur, as they always do. Glitches cause students to quickly move to the "Frustrated Stage." Although the glitches can take various forms, a few of the most prominent ones are discussed here.

One of the biggest problems for students is the seemingly simple task of accessing the Internet. Some students travel to campus to access their materials on the Internet, but there are no computers available for them because it seems they chose a time that everyone else liked. If the students are attempting to access the Internet from home, they cannot get in via modem, or they get disconnected after they get to the Internet. If the students have a lesson to submit or an electronic communication that must be sent, and they cannot do it at a certain time, the student's frustration level increases exponentially.

It is also frustrating to students when the instructor does not respond in what the students perceive to be a timely manner. This is a problem for new instructors because they do not set specific parameters, which are told to the students, to manage the electronic communications (e-communications) necessitated by the virtual course format. Before learning the ropes, the authors experienced the downside of not having time parameters. For example, one student sent e-mail to the instructor at 4:00 a.m.; when the student happened to see the instructor on campus at 9:00 a.m. on the same day, the student expected the instructor to have already read the student's message.

To prevent situations such as this, e-communications must be specifically addressed in the course syllabus as a way to decrease the frustration aspect for the students. Setting e-office hours also helps to ease the students through this stage, especially when it comes to instructor-student communication. E-office hours are any office hours held in any electronic format (e.g., e-mail, video conferences, audio conferences, chat rooms).

As far as frustration caused by not being able to access the Internet, one of the most basic things that the instructor can do is alert the students to the possibility of the problems. The instructor may also want to contact the various computer labs on campus, which have Internet connections, and find out when the busy times are.

Eureka Stage

After all is said and done, students finally reach the "Eureka Stage." The students say, "It's over!" They realize that they have successfully completed a virtual course. It is very rewarding when the majority of students want their remaining coursework to be offered in this format as well. There is also an added benefit to the university: it is able to attract students who need to take a course for professional reasons, but who do not have the time or flexibility to enroll in a traditional university course.

The Internet has opened new territories for pioneering when it comes to university courses. Virtuality is impacting the educational lives of instructors and students. As an instructor, it is important to create exceptional educational climates for students. Instructors must use all of the power of the Internet to develop stimulating learning environments. Students must be willing to enter this new arena and explore its possibilities. Together, instructors and students will build the future of education on the Internet.

Resource List

Note: These sites were active and accessible in October 1997. There are no guarantees that these sites will remain active or continue to contain the information we located at that time.

Interactive Learning Connection-University Space Network Pilot Project. [Online] Available http://www.kcc.ca/project/ library/ ILCpilot/structur.htm. November 5, 1997.

Osberg, K. A Teacher's Guide to Developing Virtual Environments: VRRV Project Support. [Online] Available http://www.hitl. washington.edu/publications/r-97-17/, November 5, 1997

Penn State University. Web Instructional Services Headquarters. [Online] Available http://projects..cac.psu.edu/WISH/, November 5, 1997.

Slippery Rock University. Computing and Technology Resources. [Online] Available http://www.sru.edu/root/tech.htm, November 5, 1997.

Smeaton, A. Developing Online Virtual Lectures for Course Delivery: A Case Study and an Argument In Favour. [Online] Available http://simpr1.compapp.dcu.ie/~asmeaton/pubs/J-Dist-Ed-97-sub. html, November 5, 1997.

University of Durham. Developing a Virtual Community for Student Groupwork. [Online] Available http://www.dur.ac.uk/~dcs1sad/ jtap/, November 5, 1997.

Dr McGonigle is an associate professor of Nursing at Penn State, and vice president, Corporate Training at Care-Advantage® Health Systems.

Dr. Eggers is an assistant professor in the Department of Parks and Recreation/ Environmental Education and Department of Secondary Education/ Foundations of Education at Slippery Rock University, Slippery Rock, Pennsylvania.

Online Mentoring

When Ursuline Academy girls need career advice, guidance about classes, or personal support, they e-mail their mentors—professional women whose knowledge of the "real world" helps the students make informed choices.

Carole Duff

> You mention your struggle between the arts and math and science. I can identify with that. I see no reason that you shouldn't take classes in ceramics and English and still be a reputable mathematician.
>
> —A telementor to student

At least as old as the ancient Greeks, the practice of mentoring creates a sustained relationship between a trusted teacher and a student. Today, in the classroom, on the athletic field, or in internship and shadowing programs, mentoring or coaching is a common instructional tool. The growth of technology brings new opportunities for mentoring; the Internet can offer online tutoring, ask-an-expert coaching and e-mail linking of students with successful professionals in careers of mutual interest. At Ursuline Academy, our telementoring program creates an online environment for communication between Ursuline students and professional women.

The Need for Mentors

Established in 1874, Ursuline Academy of Dallas, Texas, is a private, Catholic, college-preparatory high school for girls. Drawing from a diverse population in the greater Dallas area, students enter Ursuline Academy as 9th graders from a wide variety of feeder schools. Students graduate having experienced a strong, progressive, academic curriculum, including an emphasis on leadership and community service. Over the years, however, we noticed that our students needed encouragement when deciding to take more advanced classes that would prepare them for higher-level professions. We also realized that a college-preparatory curriculum, regardless of the advanced academic content, does not provide much applied, on-the-job experience or guidance.

To address this need, we established a summer internship program with professional women as on-site mentors. These internships provide our students with women role models, a real-world focus, and support.

However, the program is an option for seniors only. In many cases, senior year is too late for students who want direct information about careers and course-work, let alone students who need a little encouragement. And such encouragement often makes all the difference along the road to self-discovery.

Two years ago, Ursuline Academy inaugurated a telementoring pilot program modeled after a National Science Foundation program. We started by matching 14 upper-level math and computer-science students with women engineers at Texas Instruments. By spring 2000, we expanded the pilot to include students from all four high school grades. The students communicate through e-mail with mentors from all around the world an in a wide variety of career areas.

A student is matched with a mentor on the basis of her career interest. Weekly e-mails build a sustained relationship, breaking down the isolation that physical distance usually creates. The technology also creates a mechanism for outreach and collaboration. Students receive personal guidance and encouragement from knowledgeable and successful women who have similar interests.

A Mission

Although we used the National Science Foundation's model, we first constructed goals and objectives centered on our mission statement. The main focus of the Ursuline mission is student-centered learning—supporting and encouraging students in terms of each individual's talents and interests. Another goal is to reach out into the global community and to expose students to wider experiences beyond the classroom.

The motto of Ursuline Academy is *Serviam*—"I will serve." By creating

From *Educational Leadership,* October 2000, pp. 57-61. © 2000 by the Association for Supervision and Curriculum Development. All rights reserved. Reprinted by permission.

an online environment for students to receive personal guidance from practicing professional women, we established a network for those dedicated to community service. As one mentor wrote, "Thanks for introducing me to a wonderful opportunity to give back what I have already taken." Mentors who might otherwise be too busy have the necessary flexibility to participate through e-mail.

Telementors are either alumnae or part of Ursuline's worldwide network of professionals. We use a variety of methods, from contacting those professional women with whom we have established connections to sending a brief recruiting message to alumnae's e-mail addresses. Typically, the message is circulated among alumnae listed in the directory by profession, and we target those in high-interest or under-represented fields for women.

We inform the prospective telementors that we look for practicing, professional women who would be willing to communicate through e-mail once a week with a current Ursuline student. We also tell the mentors that they will be matched with a student who has similar career interests. In addition, we ask all prospective mentors to forward the original recruiting e-mail message to classmates who might be qualified and interested. If the prospective telementor responds with interest to the recruiting message, she receives a mentor application and further information.

Most of the mentor application and orientation process occurs online. At the prospective mentor's request, we send instructions and a one-page application document to fill out and send back to the recruiter. With mentor applications in hand, we start the process of finding a student with similar career interests.

Matching and Orientation

The expansion of the Ursuline telementoring program happened easily because of two factors. First, most of our students are now connected to the Internet either through the school network or at home. Second, we imple-

mented an advisory system, which included interested faculty advisors to monitor students from all four grade levels. Five of us formed a telementoring expansion committee. We offered the opportunity first to our advisees and then to other students who expressed interest in telementoring. All students in the program receive three documents: a letter to parents explaining the telementoring program; the telementoring agreement, including objectives, requirements, and "netiquette" guidelines; and a brief autobiography form. Once the student returns the signed agreement and her autobiography, we match each student with a mentor.

Upon being assigned their mentors, students watch a 15-minute telementoring orientation video, available from Education Development Center's Center for Children and Technology. They then copy the name and e-mail address of their mentor and the school e-mail address of their advisor. All e-mails between students and mentors, whether initiated by students or mentors, are copied to the advisor. Thus, the advisor acts as a fly on the wall, getting better acquainted with the student and responding immediately in case of questions or concerns. For her records, the advisor keeps the copy of the telementoring agreement and the form with the student's and mentor's names and e-mail addresses, but she returns the student's autobiography for the student's first communication with her telementor.

Before the student's first contact, the advisor e-mails the mentor to give her the name of her student so that the mentor can look out for the message. If contact does not happen within the next week, the mentor alerts the advisor so that she can address the problem. Telementors also receive program guideline information, and they agree to communicate with their students once a week and to copy all related e-mails to the students' advisors.

Telementors know that the students will introduce themselves using their autobiographies and are likely to talk about school, outside activities, and

their families—plus ask many questions about career paths, education, and perhaps even family-and career-balancing decisions. We ask mentors to be honest, realistic, positive, and encouraging, and we suggest that they visit the telementoring Web site (www.edc.org /CCT/telementoring/index2.html).

Monitoring Communication and Evaluation

We have found several special advantages to giving students contact with professional women at some point during their high school years. Although the telementoring program is primarily career-focused, younger students tend to write about their adjustments to the demands of high school and the sometimes painful journey during which they discover their interests and talents—making friends; joining clubs and activities; or trying out for cheerleading, plays, or leadership positions. As one student remarked, the program gives her "a person to talk to who went through the same experiences I am going through now."

The mentors support and encourage the students and share their own experiences. "It sounds like you're having a demanding year academically," a mentor related. "I remember the shock of my first year or two of high school. I can't say that it gets easier, but you do learn better how to deal with it." Another telementor wrote,

> As you are just starting your high school years, it would be fairly unusual to know what sort of adult life you wanted to follow. The best thing to do is to take the opportunity to try various things that catch your interest—for example, try out for the play. Remember, you won't be the only one who is not sure of herself. The only thing certain is that you will not get to participate if you do not try. Let me know what you decide to do.

Students also ask about classes they should take, colleges their mentors attended, and their mentors' jobs. Students usually start with general questions but quickly look for more specific information:

- "How did you decide what you wanted to do?"
- How long have you been a pediatrician, and are you happy with your work?"
- "So, as an attorney, do you go to courtrooms or just do legal work? What do you do on a typical day, or is it always different?"
- "What kind of art classes would you suggest? I would like to go into either oil painting or still-life class. Can I practice at home? Is it better to paint from real life or a photograph? Do art colleges require an interview?"
- "How feasible do you think it is for someone to major in a field other than the sciences or biomedical engineering but to still try for medical school?"

The answers are always interesting, but not always what we teachers would have expected or known. One mentor reminded her student, "Medicine uses a lot of math, believe it or not. Some medication dosing is quite intricate, especially for pediatric patients!" Another remembered, "When I was in high school, I liked studying biology and math. I never was a fan of English, either. I wish I had been, though, because of the number of papers that I had to write in grad school."

One student who was interested in engineering received this advice:

Get all the math you can now, but don't ignore speech class or English. After all, you can do the most brilliant work in the world, but if you can't tell people about it, then all your hard work will be for nothing. So work hard on your essays and oral presentations and ask your teachers for feedback on what you do well and how you can do better. By the way, writing was not my strong suit either—keep plugging away at it!

Another mentor urged,

Another thing that is important, and probably helped me get into medical school, is volunteer work. It doesn't have to be in the medical field, but at some point you should volunteer in a hospital. When I did my community service teaching first aid to kids at the Red Cross, it was really fun.

Overwhelmingly, the mentors enjoyed their participation and often commented on the time factor and rewards. One mentor said in her evaluation, "E-mail is fast and convenient for both the student and the professional, which makes it easier to communicate on a regular basis." Flexibility is also important to a busy professional: "I could send off a quick note between tasks or during my lunch hour."

Interestingly, we've discovered that telementors derive a personal satisfaction from their communication with students. "I am grateful to the many mentors I have had along the way," wrote a mentor, "and hoped that I could pass that positive experience on to others." When asked about the strengths of the program, one mentor stated,

I loved being able to connect with a young woman across the country, to hear about her daily activities, and to add a bit of information about what "grown-up" life was like for me. I hoped it opened up her eyes a bit, and it definitely was a breath of fresh air for me. Overall, it was a fun, engaging, and endearing process.

Future Expansion

Next year, we plan to offer this experience to any interested student and advisor. Also, given our growing pool of online experts, we envision a more traditional ask-an-expert program designed for students who need coaching for short-term projects or online tutorials and forums.

Our goal is to meet the students' needs to ask questions to professional women—as our students say, "to find out about future fields I might enter" or "to get in touch with 'the real world' and better understand what is expected out there." As one student stated, "Books or articles never answer everything I want to know, but with a telementor, I can be curious and receive an answer."

Author's note: Susan Bauer (Director of Technology and Academic Dean), Margaret Noullet, Ann Middendorf, Pat Medina, and I were members of the telementoring committee.

Carole Duff is a member of the Social Studies Department and Coordinator of the mentoring program at Ursuline Academy of Dallas, 4900 Walnut Hill Ln., Dallas, TX 75299; cduff@ursuline.pvt.k12.tx.us

Evaluating & Using Web-Based Resources

By Glen Bull, Gina Bull,
Kara Dawson, and Cheryl Mason

Because the World Wide Web is a relatively recent phenomenon, many K–12 teachers are still refining methods for taking advantage of its resources. A recent assignment by one high school English teacher suggests the ambivalence many teachers have about both the promise and the pitfalls of these online resources.

> Select a 20th-century trend and develop an associated thesis. Use references to prove or disprove the thesis. Include at least four references; only one use of the references marked with an asterisk is permitted.
> Books
> Magazines
> Encyclopedias
> *Interviews
> *World Wide Web

In this instance, interviews and the World Wide Web are placed in a different classification from traditional print resources. An interview with an individual who has participated in a 20th-century fad (e.g., the hula hoop) does not undergo the type of editorial review found in a printed article in a book or encyclopedia, so the rationale for limiting use of this resource is apparent.

Web resources are a more difficult case, however. On one hand, many materials on the Web have not undergone any type of editorial review. On the other hand, many potentially valuable resources may only be available on the Web. Placing a limit of one Web citation per student essay is one method of addressing this dilemma.

However, teaching students to appropriately evaluate and integrate Web resources into their research papers will provide a lifelong skill. The number of available Web resources will increase throughout their careers. Many encyclopedias, reference works, and guidebooks are no longer published in printed form. The *Encyclopedia Britannica,* for example, is now available only in an electronic format, either as a CD-ROM or through the Britannica Web site (**www.britannica.com**). The Microsoft encyclopedia, *Encarta,* exists only in electronic form (**www.encarta. msn.com**).

Linton Weeks foretells in a *Washington post* article (Weeks, 2000):

> Within the next five years many types of physical books—travel, science, sports, for example—may disappear altogether.... Erik Engstrom, president of Random House, is one levelheaded publishing executive who entertains this notion. Take his company's popular series, Fodor's travel guides. More and more the travel advice traditionally found in the books will be dispensed on the Internet, he believes. Other types of books with information that changes rapidly will follow....
>
> A mass extinction of many species of physical books may not mean the end of bound-paper volumes as we know them, but it is liable to cause a great shift in the kinds of books or book-like assemblages that publishing companies publish. (p. C01)

At the same time, many resources on the Web that bypass traditional editorial standards may be of suspect value. The Drudge Report (**www.drudgereport. com**), for example, provides access to late-breaking news reports on the Internet—sometimes before they appear in the mainstream press—but in a number of instances, retractions of inaccurate or incorrect information have subsequently appeared.

An instructor can teach students that information from the online *Encyclopedia Britannica* is likely to be reliable and gossip less so. The cases in the middle present more difficulty. There is no easy resolution, but a five-step process may help:

1. Identification of Potential Resources
2. Evaluation of Appropriate Resources
3. Integration into the Research Paper
4. Citation of the Resource
5. Verification by the Instructor

> On one hand, many materials on the Web have not undergone any type of editorial review. On the other hand, many potentially valuable resources may only be available on the Web.

© 2001, ISTE (International Society for Technology in Education), 800.336.5191(U.S. & Canada) or 541.302.3777(Int'l), iste@iste.org, www.iste.org. All rights reserved.

Identification of Resources

Two general methods for locating resources on the Web are readily accessible—(1) mechanical search engines and (2) virtual libraries and directories containing references and resources compiled by human curators. Search engines such as Alta Vista (**www.altavista.com**) employ Web robots (Web bots) to conduct automated searches of the Web to construct databases that form the heart of the search engine. A significant limitation of search engines is that unless they are used intelligently, the search results may be irrelevant. Other services such as Yahoo!® (**www.yahoo.com**) employ human catalogers to compile lists of Web resources and categorize them.

Because these resources did not exist when the majority of current teachers received their training, at present, teachers often find it necessary to develop ad hoc rules for Internet use in their classes. In the future, in part thanks to efforts by ISTE, the National Council for the Accreditation of Teacher Education (1997), and other initiatives (U. S. Department of Education, 2000) designed to integrate technology into teacher education, all teachers will receive training on how to develop effective online resources for their content areas. Until that time, here are some useful guidelines for teachers and their classes.

- Begin with a general search of the Web.
- Use Boolean constraints (e.g., *and*) to narrow the search.

> Two general methods for locating resources on the Web are readily accessible—(1) mechanical search engines and (2) virtual libraries and directories containing references and resources compiled by human curators.

- Restrict the search to noncommercial domains.
- Employ generic authoritative sources.
- Identify discipline-specific resources.

"Important Things to Know Before You Begin Searching the Web," a University of California, Berkeley, library document, provides additional recommendations about searching the Web (**www.lib.berkeley.edu/TeachingLib/Guides/Internet/ThingsToKnow.html**).

General Web Search

Search engines are useful as a starting point for a survey of the Internet. Their chief disadvantage is that search engines can generate far too many references to review, and the relevance and reliability of these resources is often suspect.

Boolean terms such as *and* or *or* can be used to narrow a search. The results can be dramatically different. For example, a search for all the pages containing "Lincoln or dogs" generated a list of approximately three million Web pages in one search. In contrast, a search of all the Web pages containing "Lincoln and dogs" only generated a list of about 10,000 pages. The number of pages generated by the search using *and* eliminated 97% of the references produced by the search using *or.*

Even 10,000 references are still more than anyone could review in a reasonable amount of time. (It would take more than 150 hours to review this many references, or more than four 40-hour weeks, if only five minutes were spent on each reference.) Therefore it may be necessary to reduce the number of references to a smaller number of relevant links by adding further restrictions to the search.

Limiting a search to a specific domain, such as educational servers, can be a useful strategy. The following domains are currently employed on the Internet:

- .com for a commercial company
- .edu for an educational institution
- .gov for a U. S. government organization

> Search engines are useful as a starting point for a survey of the Internet. Their chief disadvantage is that search engines can generate far too many references to review, and the relevance and reliability of these resources is often suspect.

- .mil for a U. S. military organization
- .net for an Internet resource company (such as an Internet Service Provider [ISP])
- .org for nonprofit organizations

Some popular search engines such as Alta Vista® allow students to limit searches to a specific domain. For example, to search for references to "Abraham Lincoln" found within the educational domain, enter the following search term on the Alta Vista server:

+domain:edu+"Abraham Lincoln"

The University of Virginia's library has developed, "How to Search Alta Vista," an online document that offers other recommendations for that particular search engine (**www.lib.virginia.edu/education/altavista.htm**).

Generic Authoritative Sources

It is not the Web per se that makes sources suspect or unreliable—it is editorial review versus lack of editorial review. As a first-order generalization, printed media often undergo a greater degree of editorial review than materials posted on the Web, but that is not always the case. For example, the vanity press allows authors to pay for publication of works that bypass any type of editorial review and that otherwise might not see the light of day. Similarly, information in publications such as *The National Enquirer's* stories of alien abductions seem to be reviewed primarily for potential libel rather than accuracy of sources.

Once teachers understand this, they can allow their students to make unlimited use of authoritative sources such as the *Encyclopedia Britannica* (**www.britannica.com**) or the *Washington Post* (**www.washingtonpost.com**). Sources of this kind undergo the same level of editorial review and rigor regardless of whether they appear in print or in an electronic format. Helping students to understand this and differentiate sources of information is an improvement over a blanket restriction on use of Web sources or variants of this policy such as restricting use to one Web citation per paper.

Both public television and commercial news networks may be useful sources of authoritative information about current affairs. These include sources such as PBS (**www.pbs.org**), CNN (**www.cnn.com**), and MSNBC (**www.msnbc.com**).

A number of virtual libraries can help identify reliable sources on the Web, many of them affiliated with universities and educational institutions. For example, the University of Michigan has established the Internet Public Library (www.ipl.org) staffed by reference librarians who can identify resources. Similarly, librarians at UC Berkeley have developed the Librarians' Index to the Internet (**www.lii.org**), an annotated subject directory of several thousand Internet resources selected and evaluated by librarians for their usefulness to users of public libraries.

Discipline-Specific Resources

Students engaged in research in specific content areas also will need guidance on specific resources in each content area. Although librarians can assist, it ultimately becomes the responsibility of teachers to be familiar with resources in their content areas.

Although specific resources differ from discipline to discipline, teachers in each content area can employ some general strategies to identify reliable resources in their respective discipline. A useful starting point is the profes-

sional association for a specific content area (e.g., the National Council of Social Studies [**www.ncss.org**], the National Council of Teachers of Mathematics [**www.nctm.org**], National Science Teachers Association [**www.nsta.org**], and the National Council for Teachers of English [**www.ncte.org**]). For example, the NCSS Web site declares: "Site Search: from Assessment to Zuni, we'll help find information on the subjects you teach. Use our site search engine."

Sometimes these sites also provide assistance with subjects of topical interest—the NCSS Web site also promises: "Election 2000—Our list of election-related Internet resources can help you teach the citizens of tomorrow about today's democratic process."

> **It is not the Web per se that makes sources suspect or unreliable—it is editorial review versus lack of editorial review.**

Many university sites have developed resources specific to particular disciplines. For example, the Virginia Center for Digital History (VCDH, **www.vcdh.virginia.edu**) provides access to the nation's most-visited Civil War site. The best of these sites also provide supplementary materials specifically interpreting use of these resources in a K–12 context. The VCDH site, for example, provides access to K–12 resources at **www.vcdh.virginia.edu/teaching/intro.html**.

Other digital resource centers developed by university faculty members at academic institutions are listed in "Exemplary Digital Resource Centers."

Evaluation of Resources

Once teachers have identified Web resources, it is important to teach students how to evaluate their potential reliability and accuracy. As more and more information is posted on the Web, this will increasingly become an important life skill. Evaluation methods

include (1) Authority, (2) Domain, and (3) Internal and External Consistency.

Authority. A good starting point in evaluation of any resource is the authoritativeness of the citation. This can be further resolved into two components—institutional authority and individual authority. Institutional authority speaks for itself—some institutions, such as The New York Times (**www.nyt.com**), Consumer Reports (**www.consumerreports.org**), and major research laboratories at academic institutions, have well-established reputations. Materials from these sites can be relied upon with a fair degree of confidence.

University course materials, now widely available on the Web, bear particular scrutiny. In this instance, it is important to closely examine the credentials of the instructor. For example, is the faculty member a recognized authority in his or her field or a graduate student who is just embarking upon a career? In many cases, undergraduate students are now posting materials and papers for course assignments on the Web. It is important to recognize the potentially reduced reliability of such resources, unless they are affiliated with an institution site, such as a university research center, that vouches for their accuracy.

Domain. The domain name can be a useful secondary gauge of reliability. Information in the commercial domain (.com) can be presumed to incorporate a bias of some type. Sites that offer free postings by individuals, such as Geocities (**www.geocities.com**), bear a special burden of proof. Not only do the individuals who post information on such sites generally lack credentials in specific information domains, it is also a common practice to secure and then abandon Web sites of this kind. As a result, it is often difficult to even make an accurate attribution of authorship, much less to evaluate whether the author possesses appropriate professional credentials. That is not to say that information on such sites is always inaccurate, but such information should be viewed critically prior to incorporation into a research paper.

Internal and external consistency. Science and mathematics instructors teach students to evaluate whether a mathematical result is reasonable. The specific digits are not important if an answer appears to be off by an order of magnitude. This method can be extended to other areas of inquiry. A document should first be evaluated for internal consistency. Are there contradictions within the document itself? If it is internally consistent, the student can next assess whether it is in agreement with other sources, particularly authoritative resources. The following Web resources may be useful to students and teachers.

- How to Critically Analyze Information Sources: **www.library.cornell. edu/okuref/research/skill26.htm**
- Evaluating the Quality of Internet Information Sources: **http://itech1. coe.uga.edu/faculty/gwilkinson/ Webeval.html**
- The Web—Teaching Zack to Think: **www.anovember.com/articles/zack. html**
- Tips for Evaluating a World Wide Web Search: **www.uflib.ufl.edu/hss/ref/tips.html**

William of Occam was a philosopher who taught at the University of Oxford in the middle centuries. He is best known today for a guideline, known as "Occam's Razor," that suggests that the simplest explanation is often the most likely one: "If two theories explain the facts equally well, then the simpler theory is to be preferred." This medieval rule of thumb is equally useful today in evaluating Web resources.

Integration and Citation

Once a resource has been identified and judged acceptable for use in a paper, it is necessary to teach students how to appropriately incorporate these resources into the paper. It has always been possible for students to recopy

work, then present it as their own, but the mechanical difficulty of retyping or rewriting material placed some limits on this practice. It is now possible to copy entire works from a Web browser window to a word processing window in a matter of seconds.

This can serve as both a research aid and a practice that blurs the line between student work and external authorship. In its most extreme form, this might be deemed plagiarism, but often the practice stems from lack of understanding of academic practice and scholarship.

> Once a resource has been identified and judged acceptable for use in a paper, it is necessary to teach students how to appropriately incorporate these resources into the paper.

We recommend that students begin by creating a bookmark folder within the Web browser. As students identify potentially useful Web sites, they can store their addresses in a bookmark folder for that topic. Students can create subfolders to develop a preliminary outline of the topic. Depending on which Web browser students are using, they can create bookmark folders in slightly different ways. Each browser provides mechanisms to save the bookmark folder onto a floppy disk so students can transport their bookmarks from computer to computer as they work on their papers. (For more on bookmark managers, see *Learning & Leading with Technology, 28*(3), pp. 46–49, 57.)

As the outline of the paper begins to emerge, it can be re-created as a parallel outline in a word processing file. We recommend creating a resource file for each paper. Students can then copy original sources from

the Web and place the information within appropriate subcategories of the word processing outline. It is extremely important to include the source of each site that is cited as this occurs.

The resource file can then be used as an information repository employed to facilitate the development of the initial draft of the paper. Whether these sources are paraphrased or quoted verbatim, it is important to include citations that provide academic credit to the source and allow the readers to visit the Web site to evaluate the original themselves. Web resources can be referenced in a number of ways. Two of the more common are in the Modern Langauge Association (MLA, **www. mla.org/style/sources.htm**) style and the American Psychological Association (APA, **www.apa.org/journals/ Webref.html**) style. Find a general guide on citation of Web resources at How to Cite Internet Resources: **www.library.unt.edu/genref/ internet_citations.htm.**

Verification

It will be increasingly important for K–12 teachers to provide guidance to students on appropriate uses of Internet information resources. One of the more effective ways of providing this guidance is for teachers to spot-check selected references within papers. There are several ways this can be done easily.

The student can turn in the bookmark file used to write the paper on a floppy disk along with the paper. Most word processing software, such as Microsoft® Word, now includes an "Insert Hyperlink" feature that makes it possible to provide a direct Web link within the word processing file itself. This allows the teacher to simply click on a selected citation within a paper to access the Web site.

This allows the teacher to examine selected citations and provide the student with appropriate feedback. In many cases, the teacher may have extensive professional knowledge or a context for evaluating resources that

Exemplary Academic Resources

The resources listed below are representative of exemplary digital resources developed at universities and other academic institutions. Often university faculty who have developed exemplary resources for their classes are more than willing to share with K–12 teachers. Teachers who identify exemplary Web resources may find it useful to call or e-mail the faculty member who developed the Web site to discuss ways of adapting the materials for K–12 use. In some cases, the faculty member may be willing to discuss ways of repurposing scholarly materials.

Virginia Center for Digital History:
   http://jefferson.village.virginia.edu/vcdh

The Lewis H. Beck Center for Electronic Collections & Services:
   http://chaucer.library.emory.edu

Center for Electronic Texts in the Humanities:
   www.ceth.rutgers.edu

Center for History and New Media:
   http://chnm.gmu.edu

Center for International Earth Sciences Information Network:
   www.ciesin.org

Digital Media Center:
   www.lib.virginia.edu/dmc

Documenting the American South:
   http://metalab.unc.edu/docsouth

Electronic Text Center at the University of Virginia:
   http://etext.lib.virginia.edu

The Geospatial and Statistical Data Center:
   http://fisher.lib.virginia.edu

Institute for Advanced Technology in the Humanities:
   http://jefferson.village.virginia.edu

Perseus Digital Library:
   www.perseus.tufts.edu

Schoenberg Center for Electronic Text and Image:
   www.library.upenn.edu/etext

will provide guidance and assistance to the student. Because the Web is ephemeral and ever-changing, a certain percentage of Web sites will be obsolete or inaccessible even before the instructor reviews the paper, but the fact that a citation is transient provides a useful clue regarding its reliability.

Summary

For better or worse, the world is changing as both academic institutions and commercial firms transfer more and more information to the Web. This provides greater access to original sources that otherwise might not be available to K–12 students and at the same time provides vastly increased access to sources of information that have not undergone traditional editorial review or evaluation.

Rather than restricting use of resources, guidance in their appropriate use provides students with an important lifelong skill. This involves a five-step process that includes:

1. identification of potential resources,
2. evaluation of appropriate resources,
3. integration into the research paper,
4. citation of the resource, and
5. verification by the instructor.

Although the Web provides ready access to a greater range of information sources—many of which have not been subject to editorial review—than in the past, it also makes it easier for teachers to directly view the citations upon which papers have been based. This introduces changes in the ways in which papers are written as well as changes in the way in which instructors evaluate student work.

Visit **teach.virginia.edu/go/mining** for links to resources listed in this column.

References

National Council for the Accreditation of Teacher Education. (1997). *Technology and the new professional teacher: Preparing for the 21st century classroom.* Washington, DC:L National Council for Accreditation of Teacher Education.
U. S. Department of Education. (2000). *Preparing tomorrow's teachers to use technology* [Online]. Available: www.ed.gov/teachtech/.
Weeks, L. (2000, April 24). The end. *Washington Post,* p. C01.

Glen Bull (GlenBull@virginia.edu) is a professor of instructional technology in the Curry School of Education at the University of Virginia. Contact Glen at Curry School of Education, University of Virginia, Charlottesville VA 22903.

Gina Bull (GinaBull@virginia.edu) is a computer systems engineer in the Information Technology and Communication (ITC) organization at the University of Virginia. Reach Gina at Information Technology and Communications, University of Virginia, Charlottesville VA 22903.

Kara Dawson (dawson@coe.ufl.edu) is an assistant professor of instructional technology at the University of Florida.

Cheryl Mason (clmason@virginia.edu) is an assistant professor of social studies in the Curry School of Education at the University of Virginia. Reach Cheryl at Curry School of Education, University of Virginia, Charlottesville VA 22903.

Using Computers to Support a Beginning Teacher's Professional Development

This study explored the efficacy of promoting a beginning chemistry teacher's curriculum development and teaching practices through the use of computers. Using pictorial analogies, historical cases of science, and discrepant events in a web site designed by the researchers as curricular samples, the beginning teacher was asked to develop similar curriculum for his own teaching. After taking the researchers' advice into account and making adjustments, the beginning teacher implemented the curriculum in his classroom teaching and shared his experience with the researchers by e-mail communications. The teacher's teaching practices both before and after the web site treatment were observed and analyzed. It was found that before the treatment the teacher used the textbook as the only resource of his teaching. Extra curriculum was rarely seen, there were not many student-teacher interactions, and analogies or examples used in his explanation of abstract concepts were not preorganized. On the other hand, after the treatment, the teacher was able to develop suitable curricula by himself for the purpose of increasing student involvement. He also explained the applications of chemical concepts in daily lives and his analogies and demonstrations were well organized. Although the beginning teacher was able to develop curricula after the treatment, many aspects of his teaching can be improved, especially in the areas of student-teacher interaction and the implementation of students activities in science teaching.
KEY WORDS: Computers; curriculum; science teaching.

Huann-shyang Lin[1] and Houn-Lin Chiu[1]

INTRODUCTION

Science teachers' professional development has long been a major concern of the science education community. Science educators and teachers are interested in how expert science teachers and beginning teachers perform differently. If there is a gap, or some stages exist between the two groups of science teachers' performance, what can be done to bridge the gap or help the beginners get through the stages? Many studies have been done which are related to the above questions. For instance, Tobin and Fraser (1990) investigated 20 exemplary teachers' performance and found that these teachers used a variety of strategies to facilitate student engagement, increase student understanding of science, encourage student participation in learning activities, and maintain a favorable classroom learning environment. In contrast to Tobin and Fraser's (1990) investigation of exemplary teachers, Brickhouse and Bodner (1992) described how beginning teachers struggle to resolve constraints and difficulties by devising survival strategies rather than designing thoughtful instruction.

It can be found from the above literature that the professional development of a science teacher is a complex issue that includes many aspects of ability ranging from classroom management to curriculum design and instructional strategy. Knowing the complexity of the professional development of teachers, this study simply focuses on the investigation of the development of a beginning teacher's ability in curriculum design. We believed in Parke and Coble's (1997) conclusion that curriculum development can become a

From *Journal of Science Education and Technology*, Vol. 39, No. 4, 2000, p. 367. © 2000 by Plenum Publishing Corporation. Reprinted by permission.

vehicle for professional development and school reform. The two researchers concluded that if a training program provides teachers the opportunities of collaborating with colleagues and examining and reflecting on research expertise in the pursuit of improved practice, it could effectively enhance a teacher's ability to design curriculum. In fact, this type of innovative curriculum program is dependent on the active participation of teachers. Without teachers' involvement in curriculum reform, educational reform is unlikely to succeed. In other words, the ability to design curriculum is critical both in a teacher's professional development and in educational reforms.

Despite most preservice training programs that introduce the theory and practice of curriculum design, beginning teachers tend to rely heavily on textbooks or officially approved curriculum materials (Brickhouse and Bodner, 1992; Lantz and Kass, 1987; Powell, 1997). Self-designed curricula are rarely seen in beginning teachers' teaching. This is not because that they do not have the knowledge of curriculum design, but because they lack the ability to apply the knowledge in their own teaching situations. As Schwartz (1997) pointed out, to simply broaden learners' knowledge without enhancing their ability of linking pieces of knowledge in appropriate ways is not enough. Science teachers and educators should help learners construct deep or even creative understandings. Based on Schwartz, with "creative understanding" in mind, the learner would be able to link pieces of knowledge in "multiple alternative ways." This argument is consistent with the theory of the learning cycle (Karplus, 1980). Proponents of the learning cycle assert that an application phase is needed to provide learners opportunities for applying newly learned concepts or knowledge in various situations. Although beginning teachers have learned theories regarding curriculum development, limited opportunities were provided for them to link theories and practices.

Linn and Muilenbury (1996) pointed out that educators were challenged to design instruction that creates a lifelong habit of learning. If participants of preservice and in-service programs are regarded as learners too, then science educators would be encouraged to help science teachers become lifelong learners. In fact, if science teachers can continue to reflect, revise, and reevaluate their own teaching, the quality of teaching could be improved through this type of dynamic process. Although it is believed that institutional support systems are important for beginning teachers' professional development (Goodman, 1987), the question is, what resources and support can science teachers get from teacher training institutes?

We believe that the computer can play a role in communicating with science educators and those beginning teachers trained by them. With the use of web

sites beginning teachers can plan, discuss, and reflect on their own curriculum. Science educators can send away their suggestions and support instantly whenever there is a need.

Linn (1992) also recommended that computers be incorporated as a learning partner in science education reform. If computers are used wisely they can lead to effective learning. On the other hand, the use of computers for presenting electronic texts could reinforce students as memorizers of science facts. Only if students are challenged to interpret or reflect on the information that is displayed can a productive partnership emerge. With this recommendation in mind, we were curious about the effectiveness of using computers in beginning science teachers' professional development, especially in teachers' curriculum design ability.

METHODOLOGY

Sample

A student teacher and 42 eleventh graders were participants in the study. The student teacher finished a 4-year preservice chemistry teacher's training program with an average grade point. He was chosen from a group of 30 student teachers because of his willingness to participate, computer ability, and accessibility of Internet linkage at school and home. The 42 students were from a typical school located in the suburb of a big city. In this school, students were from families representing a broad range of socioeconomic backgrounds.

Instrument

The following materials were included in the web site constructed by the investigators.

1. Pictorial analogies of density, pressure, heat, temperature, and heat capacity. These analogies have been confirmed as effective tools of promoting students' conceptual understanding (Lin *et al.*, 1996).
2. Historic cases of science in atom, molecule, atomic weight, mole, and phlogiston theory. These supplemental teaching materials were developed and used successfully in high school (Lin, 1998).
3. Discrepant events and chemical demonstrations that mostly used in the investigators' teaching methods class.
4. Subject matter knowledge questions raised by former student teachers during the past six years while the investigators were supervising them.

The above materials were used as suggestive curricular samples for the student teacher to design similar curricula.

Procedure

In the pretreatment stage, which is also the middle of the first semester, the student teacher's classroom teachings of a whole chapter were observed and audio taped. Following each observation, the student teacher was interviewed to understand more about his beliefs and reasons for his practices. In addition, students were randomly selected and interviewed on their perceptions of each classroom teaching.

In the treatment stage, the student teacher was asked to review the content of the web site. After discussing his comments about the sample curricula, he was requested to design similar curricula for his own teaching to promote student interest in and understanding of the specified content knowledge. All the discussions and communications were conducted via e-mail. Prior to the implementation of these curricula the investigators of the study, who are also responsible for supervising student teachers, criticized the inappropriate parts of the curricula and made suggestions for possible adjustments. The student teacher then reevaluated and conducted the curricula in his classroom. The teaching practices of this stage were observed and audio taped. Similarly, the student teacher and randomly selected students were interviewed after each class period throughout the teaching of the whole chapter.

FINDINGS

Pretreatment Teaching Practices

The teaching performance of the student teacher in the pre-treatment stage can be best described by the following three statements.

Relying Heavily on the Official Textbook

Extra curriculum was rarely seen. Although the student teacher emphasized the importance of motivating student interest, promoting conceptual understanding, and providing opportunities for relating subject matter knowledge to daily life, his classroom teaching was dominated by lecturing and presenting mathematical calculations of examples listed in the textbook. For instance, while explaining weight percentage concentration, he introduced the formula, explained the meaning of solute and solvent, and executed the calculation to find how many grams of sodium chloride were needed to prepare a 3% NaCl solution. Strategies of motivating student interest or relating subject matter knowledge to daily life were not seen in the pretreatment stage.

Focus on One-Way Lecturing

Very few teacher-student or student-student interactions happened. As mentioned, a typical 50-minute pe-

riod of the student teacher's classroom is dominated by lecturing textbook content. More specifically, it is one-way lecturing. Although sometimes he has tried to interact with students by asking questions, he neither provided wait time, nor did he successfully use questioning skills. For example, when teaching molarity, the only question he raised was "if 1 liter = 1000 c c, then 100 c c = how many liters?" Because there was no student answering this convergent question immediately, the student teacher wrote the answer on the blackboard. This was the only attempt of creating student-teacher interaction. Unfortunately, it did not result in fruitful response.

Using Analogies Inappropriately to Explain Chemical Concepts

Although the student teacher used analogies in his explanation of chemical concepts, he neither organized the analogies in advance, nor did he match the relationship between target concepts and analogies as recommended by Harrison and Treagust (1993). For example, to explain the chemical reaction of $CH_4 + Cl_2$ {arrow}$CH_3Cl + HCl$, he explained as follows:

> The molecule of CH_4 consists of one big carbon atom in the center and four small hydrogen atoms around it. The chlorine atom has to collide with the CH_4 molecule to make the reaction happen. It's like that a husband and wife have to sleep together. Otherwise, there is no chance for them to have a baby.

In the following explanation of the relationship between concentration of reactants and reaction rate, he continued to say:

> In order to create a chemical reaction, chlorine molecules must collide with methane molecules. There are two possibilities of the collision. The first one is that the chlorine molecule goes through the space between the hydrogen atoms, which are located around the big carbon atom of the methane molecule. The second possibility is to collide with the hydrogen atoms directly. Only the first type of collision can result for a chemical reaction to happen. Consequently, it depends on the probability of a type one collision. How can the probability be increased? You can increase the number of chlorine and methane molecules. In other words, you can increase the concentrations (of the reactants). It's like playing basketball. When you are struggling with low shooting accuracy, one way of promoting your score would be taking more shots, like Michael Jordan did recently. This is like that, you add more particles (molecules or reactions) in a container to increase the probability of effective collision.

The treatment is using the web site resource and e-mail communication to support the student teacher's ability of curriculum development.

After knowing that the student teacher used the teaching strategy of analogy without providing complete explanation of the relationship between an analogy and the target concept, we suggested the student teacher design his analogy teaching in advance and explain it carefully. The web site pictorial analogies were strongly recommended as examples and their teaching strategies were discussed via e-mail.

When the student teacher was asked what was the most difficult issue in his 4 months of teaching, he raised the issue of student interest and involvement. He asked for help and suggestions to teach the chapters on "Chemical Elements and the Periodical Table" and "Inorganic Compounds and Inorganic Chemical Industry." His major concern focused on the descriptive nature of the two chapters and the low interest levels of students. After several e-mail discussions, the following strategies were chosen by the student teacher: (1) relating chemical elements and compounds with daily life; (2) using history of science to introduce how a theory or scientific knowledge was developed and accepted by scientists; and (3) integrating discrepant events or chemical demonstrations into classroom instructions.

Posttreatment Teaching Practices

Initially, before the treatment, the student teacher perceived that the teaching of "Inorganic Compounds and Inorganic Industry" would be boring. However, with the well-organized and preplanned curricula resulting from the stimulation of the web site examples, his teaching of the whole chapter and the following chapter has come up with a feeling of satisfaction instead of frustration. The following descriptions illustrate how he managed the teaching.

Applying a Variety of Examples to Motivate Students' Interest

To motivate student interest and help them make sense of scientific knowledge, the student teacher planned a series of ordinary examples in advance to explain related extraordinary chemical concepts. For instance, in the explanation of the property of carbon monoxide, he indicated that the poisonous gas was the main reason of many accidents mentioned as the top news of social issues at the time. He stated:

> Recently, newspapers and televisions frequently reported that a couple of people drove their car into a motel's garage and pulled down the door. They forget to turn off the engine. They walked into the upstairs room which is under the same roof as the garage. Since the gasoline keeps burning without having enough oxygen, the poisonous gas carbon monoxide was produced and filled the closed room. These people were killed silently. Why would that happen? Because carbon monoxide is very poisonous but doesn't have a strong smell. It can be hazardous when the air contains more than 10 ppm of carbon monoxide. That is the reason why its called the silent killer.

In the illustration of heavy metal pollution, the textbook described "mercury, lead, and cadmium as

heavy metals. When they are accumulated in a human body to a certain amount, they will cause neural diseases."

The student teacher provided additional information to explain how the heavy metals entered the human body:

> It's not a good habit to read the newspaper while you are eating food, because there is a high potential of rubbing the ink of the newspaper with your hand and mixing it with the food, especially when the ink is not totally dry. You might ingest a lot of lead into your body.

The student teacher continued to indicate local problems to pollution:

> There are a couple of factories located along the two sides of the river near our school. Some factories may produce a certain kind of heavy metal and discharge it with the water into the river. The heavy metal could be accumulated in fishes' bodies and transmitted to human bodies. Additional river pollution problems in our community include the discharge of household detergents.
> Phosphates such as sodium tripoly phosphate ($Na_5P_3O_{10}$) are always contained in detergents. These substances are super nutrients for the algaes and other small plants that grow on the surface of lakes and streams. A steady supply of phosphates can cover the surface of the water and prevent atmospheric oxygen from reaching the marine life below the surface. Eventually, it brings detrimental results of death to aquatic animals.

Adapting the Strategy of Demonstrations to Encourage Student Involvement

The student teacher realized that one-way lecturing did not work very well for him to motivate student interest. After reviewing the discrepant events and demonstrations in the web site, he discussed some of his ideas with us and evolved a couple of interesting demonstrations. For example, the "greenhouse effect" demonstration (Golden and Sneider, 1989) was recommended by the investigators and adopted by the student teacher. The students in his classroom expressed their interest of this activity while they were interviewed. In the following demonstrations, the students were actively involved in predicting possible outcomes, explaining their ideas, and discussing the principles of the events. The student teacher was satisfied with the implementation of this teaching strategy.

In explaining the explosive nature of hydrogen gas, the student teacher collected H_2 in a small plastic bottle from the electrolysis H_2O. An ignition gun was inserted through a stopper and the stopper inserted into the bottle (Fig. 1). Although the students were able to predict the explosion of the hydrogen gas when sparks were created by the ignition gun, they were all surprised that the plastic bottle can be shot

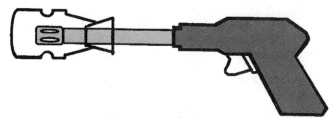

Fig. 1. The ignition gun used for demonstration.

such a long distance from the gun. The demonstration soon became a popular game for the students. The student teacher then explained the safety reason why helium has been used for filling balloons instead of hydrogen, despite the fact that the density of H_2 is smaller than He. Finally, 1 mL of alcohol was put in the plastic bottle to replace the H_2 gas. The liquid state of alcohol took 2 minutes to evaporate. A similar explosion was heard and observed. The students were then asked to compare the similarities and differences of the alcohol demonstration with the principle of a gasoline engine.

In explaining the nature of a supersaturated solution, the student teacher prepared 100 mL of CH_3COONa supersaturated solution in an Erlenmeyer flask. The students were asked to predict, observe, and explain what would happen and why it happened when one grain of solid CH_3COONa was added to the solution. The students were all amazed by the spectacular crystallization process of the supersaturated solution and the heat that evolved from the process. They enjoyed and discussed the mysterious outcome of the demonstration.

Planning Analogies in Advance and Providing Complete Explanations

In addition to the above demonstration, the student followed the sample analogies displayed in the web site and created his own analogy for teaching the greenhouse effect. He drew pictures on the black board and explained as follows:

> The carbon dioxide discharged from cars and factories will accumulate and spread around the atmosphere. You can imagine that the layer of the carbon dioxide that surrounds the earth has many tiny holes. The particles of the sunlight are smaller than these holes and pass the hole freely. After the particles of sunlight are absorbed by the earth, they become heat energy. You can imagine the heat energy as bigger balls than the sunlight particles and the holes. Consequently, the heat energy is trapped around the earth's surface. This is the main reason why the temperature of the earth surface is becoming higher annually. In this analogy, the sunlight particles with short wave length are likened as small balls; the heat energy around the earth with long wavelength is analogized as big balls. Although the real sizes of the small and big balls are much smaller than the pictures I draw, the paths of action are similar to the analogy. We are going to explain the properties of light and heat latter.

DISCUSSION AND IMPLICATIONS IN SCIENCE EDUCATION

It seems that the student teacher in this study changed his teaching strategy from one-way lecturing to a multi-activity strategy of using demonstrations and explaining chemical concepts by analogies. In addition, his teaching activities were all preoriginated through the reference of the sample curricula posted on the web site. Apparently, during the posttreatment teaching, he depended much less on the textbook than during the time of pretreatment. In other words, his ability to design alternative curricula has been greatly improved through the use of computers. Yager (1992) indicated that in the 1980s, 90% of all science teachers were using a textbook page by page in excess of 90% of the time. The case study of Brickhouse and Bodner (1992) also found that the science teacher in this study, like many beginning teachers, relied heavily on the textbook to meet the daily demands of teaching. This study has the same finding in the pretreatment investigation. However, during the posttreatment stage, it appeared that the textbook only served as one part of the student teacher's teaching resources, no longer as the only resource. Based on Yager's (1992) conclusion, one of the most important requirements for success in educational reform would be that science teachers willingly abandon standard textbooks and professionally use new teaching approaches and materials. If Yager's argument is correct, then the strategy of this study can be served as an alternative for science educators to meet the requirement, in which sample curricula are provided in a web site as references and starting points of inspiration for science teachers. Additionally, opportunities are provided for them to review and modify the new approaches and materials they created in their own classrooms. Computer technology could be used effectively in promoting a teacher's ability of designing alternative curricula which in turn, can make a difference in a teacher's teaching practices. All the results together extend support to Linn's (1992) argument of incorporating computers as learning partners in science education reform.

Although the student teacher in this study has made significant progress on developing curricula, there is enormous space for him to improve his teaching practices. For example, from the classroom observations, it was found that the questioning skills recommended by Trowbridge and Bybee (1986) and Carin and Sund (1989) were not properly used to promote student-teacher or student-student interactions. In addition, the wait time proposed by Rowe (1987) to promote meaningful answers was not implemented. Further research can investigate how these teaching practice can be improved.

ACKNOWLEDGMENTS

This study was made possible by the financial support from the National Science Council (NSC 86–2515–S–017–006), Taiwan, Republic of China.

References

Brickhouse, N., and Bodner, G. M. (1992). The Beginning science teacher: Classroom narratives of convictions and constraints. *Journal of Research in Science Teaching* 29: 471–485.

Carin, A. A., and Sund, R. B. (1989). *Teaching Modern Science,* Merrill, Columbus.

Golden, R., and Snieder, C. (1989). The greenhouse effect in a vial. *The Science Teacher* 57: 57–59.

Goodman, J. (1987). *Key factors in becoming (or not becoming) an empowered elementary school teacher: A preliminary study of selected novices.* Paper presented at the annual meeting of the American Educational Research Association, Washington, DC.

Harrison, A. G., and Treagust, D. F. (1993). Teaching with analogies: A case study in grade 10 optics. *Journal of Research in Science Teaching* 30: 1291–1307.

Karplus, R (1980). Two-year community college chemistry: Joules. An Application of Piaget's theory of cognitive development in teaching chemistry. The learning cycle. *Journal of Chemical Education* 57: 135–136.

Kumar, D., and Wilson, C. L. (1997). Computer technology, science education, and students with learning disabilities. *Journal of Science Education and Technology* 6: 155–160.

Lantz, D., and Kass, H. (1987). Chemistry Teachers' Functional Paradigms. *Science Education* 71: 117–134.

Lin, H. (1998). The effectiveness of teaching chemistry through the history of science. *Journal of Chemical Education* 75: 1326–1330.

Lin, H., Shiau, B., and Lawrenz, F. (1996). The effectiveness of teaching science with pictorial analogies. *Research in Science Education* 26: 495–511.

Linn, M. C. (1992). Science education reform: Building on the research base. *Journal of Research in Science Teaching* 29: 821–840.

Linn, M. C., and Muilenbury, L. (1996). Greeting lifelong science learners: What models form a firm foundation? *Educational Researcher* 25: 18–24.

Parke, H. M., and Coble, C. R. (1997). Teachers designing curriculum as professional development: A Model for transformational science teacher. *Journal of Research in Science Teaching* 34: 772–789.

Powell, R. (1997). Teaching alike: A cross-case analysis of first-career and second-career beginning teachers' instruction coverage. *Teaching and Teacher Education* 13: 341–356.

Rowe, M. B. (1987). Wait time: Slowing down may be a way of speeding up. *American Educator* 11: 38–47.

Schwartz, J. L. (1997). What Happened to the Voice of the Author. *Journal of Science Education and Technology* 6: 83–90.

Tobin, K., and Fraser, B. J. (1990). What does it mean to be an exemplary science teacher?. *Journal of Research in Science Teaching* 27: 3–25.

Trowbridge, L. W., and Bybee, R. W. (1986). Becoming a Secondary School Science Teacher. Merrill, Columbus.

Yager, R. E. (1992). Viewpoint: What we did not learn from the 60s about science curriculum reform. *Journal of Research in Science Teaching* 29: 905–910.

Department of Chemistry, National Kaohsiung Normal University, 116 Hoping, 1st Road, Kaohsiung 802 Taiwan. e-mail: t1666@nknucc.nknu.edu.tw

Using Personal Digital Assistants in Clinical Supervision of Student Teachers

Journaling is an important tool to help student teachers reflect on the nature of the student teaching experience. The communication of journals to student teacher supervisors is enhanced greatly by using e-mail. Previously we described software that can be used to enhance journaling. This software included tools to facilitate writing field notes during in-class observations by the supervisor. E-mail exchange largely has supplanted the need for an electronic journaling tool. Here we describe flexible strategies using a personal digital assistant (PalmPilot) to facilitate the development of field notes during observations. These notes are then readily communicated to the student teacher by several means including e-mail.

KEY WORDS: Journaling; supervision; student teachers; observation.

Kent J. Crippen,[1,2] and David W. Brooks[1]

The March 22, 1999, draft of the NCATE 2000 Standards (National Council for Accreditation of Teacher Education) includes "Standard 3, Field Experiences and Clinical Practice" (Education, 1999). From the related rubrics provided within that document: "Candidates observe and are observed by others; engage in group discussion and reflection on practice with faculty and other candidates. . . ."

Systematic electronic journaling is an established practice for fostering a positive mentor relationship between student teachers and university supervisors. A variety of electronic tools have emerged to enhance journaling activities. E-mail is the mainstay of the electronic "relationship" between mentor and student, and has been shown to increase computer proficiency for student teachers (Wepner and Seminoff, 1997; Wepner, 1997). Electronic journaling serves as a forum for discussing teaching, and it keeps university supervisors more in touch with student teachers and allows them to have a greater impact on their classroom experience (Wepner, 1997).

It is our policy to have students write daily journals describing their student teaching experience, and to transmit them twice weekly to the supervisor. In practice, most student teachers communicate more often than this, sometimes more than once per day when special circumstances arise. Electronic journaling for student teachers

has been found to increase the reflective nature of student teachers, increase their rapport with university supervisors, and increase their proficiency with working with computers (Casey, 1994). Practices related to computer-mediated communication between supervisors and student teachers have been reviewed elsewhere (van Gorp, 1998).

In addition to e-mail, computer software tools such as *Student Journal* have been described to facilitate journaling (Anders, 1994). This software included tools to facilitate in-classroom observations. The observer (supervisor) takes a portable computer into the classroom to make observations, and subsequently passes this information back to the student teacher either by e-mail or with the exchange of a floppy disk. Kuralt (1987), a middle school principal, uses a laptop computer in clinical supervision and suggests that observations are more objective and allows the teacher to add input into the evaluation, making supervision a "joint venture." Central to the issue of journaling is the documentation and subsequent discussion of the classroom experience where the student teacher is in command and the university supervisor is serving in an observational capacity.

The purpose of this paper is to describe the use of a palm device, or personal digital assistant, by the university supervisor during the observation of the student

From *Journal of Science Education and Technology*, Vol. 39, No. 3, 2000, pp. 207-211. © 2000 by Plenum Publishing Corporation. Reprinted by permission.

teacher to aid in documenting the lesson and providing an electronic transcript to foster journaling.

THE PALMPILOT DEVICE

Personal digital devices such as the IBM Workpad, Casio Cassiopeia, or 3Com PalmPilot, are very handy and effective for recording in-classroom notes. The advantages of using such devices include their size, connectivity, and cost. The 3Com PalmPilot device includes numerous productivity tools useful to essentially all professionals. Recently, *Learner Profile*, a software system for recording in-class student behaviors, has been adapted for the PalmPilot (Sunburst Technology, 1999).

Using the built-in features of the PalmPilot to assist the process of recording classroom observations has proven to be straightforward. By entering one special character followed a pair of letters or numbers in the PalmPilot, a time-stamped phrase is recorded in the device's memory that elaborates classroom observations. Portions of a sample-recorded transcript are shown in Fig. 1.

Any transcript thus created at the teaching site is available for discussion with the student teacher immediately after the observation is completed. Upon returning to a computer equipped with a cradle, it is a straightforward matter for the supervisor to e-mail the transcript to the student teacher.

ENCODING THE PALMPILOT

The PalmPilot uses a form of handwriting recognition based on *Graffiti* symbols whereby text is entered by making small motions of the scribing device (stylus) on the bottom of the screen. This is not quite the same as recognition of conventional English handwriting.

Each Graffiti symbol is formed in a distinctive and very unique manner. The Graffiti penmanship is well described in print materials and charts that come with the PalmPilot. The PalmPilot uses an insertion point, a flashing line, similar to those used in most computer word processing programs. Letters, numbers, or punctuation written in Graffiti at the bottom of the screen in one of two areas designed expressly for that purpose are inserted as if typed at the insertion point. After a small amount of practice, entries can be made quite quickly. A screen-based keyboard also is available that permits entering letters by touching the keyboard symbols with the stylus.

The power of the PalmPilot for classroom observations lies in the creation of shortcuts. A shortcut is like a scrapbook or a typing macro. We advocate the creation of shortcuts for adding frequently typed text. Most of our shortcuts are annotated to the *time stamp* that is built into the PalmPilot. The time stamp, when activated, replaces the text of the shortcut with the current system

time for the device in hour:minute/am:pm format. To include the time in any string of text, the user scribes a loop symbol followed by the letters **t** and **s**. For a moment these three characters appear on the PalmPilot screen, but they are replaced very quickly by the current time. Detailed instructions for encoding are available at the authors' Web site (Crippen and Brooks, 1999).

A NEW DIAGNOSTIC TOOL

Scripting in clinical supervision is considered a valuable tool in working with student teachers and includes such methods as "Script Taping," advocated by Hunter (1983) and the Interaction Analysis schemes proposed by Flanders (1970) and Medley (1972). Each of these methods could be successfully applied to the PalmPilot device.

The Interaction Analysis scheme developed by Flanders (1970) and used extensively in analysis of classroom behaviors about 25 years ago involved encoding times every 3 seconds. For the purposes of generating useful transcripts that include information for stimulating discussions with student teachers, we have found nearest minute recordings to be very satisfactory. A sophisticated, flexible tool for classroom observations still is available as Macintosh freeware for persons needing such software (Brooks, 1999).

Because our particular situation involves working with student teachers in science areas, we encode with two different sets of codes. We use one set of codes when the student teacher is working with the entire group and a different set when s/he works with small groups or individuals in laboratory or related settings. So, for one set of codes we begin using numbers 01 to 15, and for the other 31 to 45. The supervisor can create whatever text codes seem appropriate for his or her particular situation.

Upon review of the literature, it can be noted that our time coding scheme could be adapted to a number of schemes for evaluating student teachers, which include the cooperative education environment (Furtwengler, 1992; Johnson *et al.*, 1998; Shapiro and Sheehan, 1986; Tuckman, 1976). On occasion we have created codes to note positive or negative behaviors of just one or two

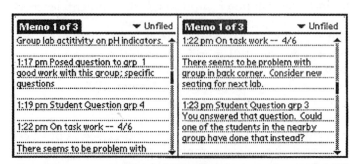

Fig. 1. Screen capture from PalmPilot showing transcript created with the aid of ShortCuts as described herein.

students in the class being observed. When the student teacher repeatedly uses a word, term, or phrase, or engages in some enhancing or disenhancing behavior, a shortcut is created to log each such event. For a given observation, the record becomes a sort of score card logging the occurrence of these behaviors.

Using the numbers 21 through 27 as labels, there are several ShortCuts we have developed that have proven to be very practical. These are illustrated in Table I.

If you adopt this system, you may create whichever codes suit your needs. Remember that student teachers have much on their minds—too much detail can be added when discussing transcripts with them.

Table I. Sample ShortCut Encodings

21	Date, Label, Supervisor Name
22	Student Teacher
23	Cooperating Teacher
24	School
25	Course
26	Time Stamp followed by 'Lesson Begins'
27	Time Stamp followed by 'Lesson Ends.'

CONCLUSIONS

The use of journaling with student teachers can be greatly enhanced by documenting their lessons electronically using a PalmPilot or other personal digital assistant. In doing so, discussion of the lesson transcript can occur shortly after the session on site. The supervisor can easily e-mail the transcript to the student teacher at a later time in an electronic exchange. If the student teacher also uses a PalmPilot device, it is possible to use the built-in infrared data transfer system to "beam" the transcript to the student.

PalmPilot devices are much less obtrusive than laptops, but are still noticed in classrooms. The back-lighting feature of the PalmPilot is essential and handy for rooms darkened for use with a video or overhead projection device.

We have come far in our work in support of student teacher journaling, considering that our journey began with hardbound journals. We then went to a series of computer tools that emphasized exchange of floppy disks. We now use tools that emphasize Internet-based communications. As noted already, the frequency with which we communicate with student teachers has risen significantly using the Internet and tools such as the PalmPilot. Communications are now 5 to 10 times more frequent than a decade ago with non-Internet systems. The PalmPilot is an especially effective professional tool for student teacher supervisors to use in connection with visitations and observations.

REFERENCES

Anders, D., and Brooks, D. W. (1994). Electronic journal writing for student teachers. *Journal of Computing in Teacher Education* 10: 6–11.

Brooks, D. W. (1999). *UNL Observer Project Software*. Available at http://dwb.unl.edu/Software/UNLObserver/UNL Observer.html [1999, 10/19].

Casey, J. M. (1994). TeacherNet: Student teachers travel the information highway. *Journal of Computing in Teacher Education* 11: 8–11.

Crippen, K. J., and Brooks, D. W. (1999, 1/17/1999). *Setting up a Palm-Pilot PDA to Supervise Science Student Teachers* [Web page]. Available at http://dwb.unl.edu./Software/PalmPilot/supervise.html [1999, 7/17].

Education, N. C. f. A. o. T. (1999). *NCATE 2000 Standards*, [PDF Document]. National Council for Accreditation of Teacher Education. Available at http://www.ncate.org/specfoc/2000stds.pdf [1999, 6/19].

Flanders, N. A. (1970). *Analyzing Teaching Behavior*, Addison- Wesley, Reading, Massachusetts.

Furtwengler, C. B. (1992). How to observe cooperative learning classrooms. *Educational Leadership* 49: 59–62.

Hunter, M. (1983). Script Taping: An Essential Supervisory Tool. *Educational Leadership* 41: 43.

Johnson, B., Borleske, B., Gleason, S., Bailey, B., and Scantlebury, K. (1998). Structured observation. *Science Teacher* 65: 56–49.

Kuralt, R. C. (1987). The computer as a supervisory tool. *Educational Leadership* 44: 71–72.

Medley, D. M. (1972). *Supervisor Use of Observation Systems*. Paper presented at the Supervision of Instruction Symposium, Garfield Heights, OH.

Shapiro, P. P., and Sheehan, A. T. (1986). The supervision of student teachers: A new diagnostic tool. *Journal of Teacher Education* 37: 35–39.

Sunburst Technology (1999). *Learner Profile To Go*. Sunburst Technology. Available at http://thunderbox.nysunburst.com/cgi-bin/catdetail?product.title=Learner+Profil [1999, 10/7].

Tuckman, B. W. (1976). The Tuckman Teacher Feedback Form (TTFF). *Journal of Educational Measurement* 13: 233–237.

van Gorp, M. J. (1998). Computer mediated communication in preservice teacher education: Surveying research, identifying problems, and considering needs. *Journal of Computing in Teacher Education* 14: 8–14.

Wepner, S. B., and Seminoff, N. E. (1997). Electronic connections through teacher education triads. *Journal at Computing in Teacher Education* 13: 11–19.

Wepner, S. B. (1997). You can never run out of stamps: Electronic communication in field experiences. *Journal of Educational Computing Research* 16: 251–268.

Notes
1. Department of Curriculum and Instruction, University of Nebraska–Lincoln.
2. To whom correspondence should be addressed at Department of Curriculum and Instruction, University of Nebraska—Lincoln, Lincoln, Nebraska 68588-0355. e-mail: Kcrippen2@unl.edu

Unit 5

Unit Selections

Key Points to Consider

❖ You are asked to develop and maintain a staff development program involving computer technology and to train teachers in a new software program to use in the classroom. How would you go about it? On what does a successful program depend?

❖ Can we create virtual classrooms with interactive Internet multimedia? What are the problems involved in implementing such technology? Can virtual classrooms provide instruction that is as good as today's classroom instruction? Discuss.

❖ What instructional factors should teachers consider when selecting multimedia? When selecting multimedia that are appropriate for students with learning disabilities?

 **Links**

www.dushkin.com/online/

These sites are annotated on pages 4 and 5.

Multimedia is important to education because of its potential to improve the quality of classroom and distance learning. It can pull together text and pictures, as well as audio and moving video in any combination to provide a richer environment that will engage all of the senses. It offers a new means of communicating, an easier way to illustrate difficult concepts, and a way to entice the learner into becoming actively involved in collecting and manipulating information anytime and anywhere.

Because of the nature of multimedia systems, it is easy to provide a number of choices to the learner. This capability enables designers and developers to build systems that fit the requirements of interactive, problem-solving systems. Such systems are called multimedia inference engines. The learner can access information in a variety of media forms in order to build inference models to solve problems based on inferences assembled from the knowledge base. The computer can assess the learner's data and decide whether the learner has collected an adequate sample and if the conclusion reached is justified. Such systems will allow learners to develop their problem-solving skills. Without multimedia, instructional problem-solving systems would not be feasible, nor would we be able to enrich the problem-solving facilities within schools at a fraction of the cost of physical laboratories. Such applications of multimedia provide a cost-benefit ratio that is quite favorable, and return-on-investment analysis is one of the side benefits provided by this powerful technology.

The articles in this unit review some of the issues emerging from the widespread interest in designing, developing, implementing, and publishing multimedia titles. In the lead article, Michael Ruffini guides teachers in developing multimedia projects using a systems approach, based on instructional design principles. Ruffini focuses on analyzing the learners, selecting the topic, writing objectives, defining the project type, designing text, cards, and buttons, exploring hyperlink navigation, and evaluating multimedia projects.

In the next essay, Barbara Becker presents an overview of the goals of the MindWorks program for science curriculum development. The project hopes to address student motivation, student understanding of the structure and workings of the physical world, and students' and teachers' ideas about the process and culture of scientific activity. The author also discusses the progress of pilot implementation and evaluation.

"Designing Instructional Technology From an Emotional Perspective" presents strategies for making instructional technology more emotionally sound. The authors discuss how fear, envy, anger, sympathy, and pleasure can be experienced during a learning situation. They also describe 20 general instructional strategies than can be used to decrease negative emotions and increase positive emotions. For all of these strategies they describe different features of instructional technology that can help educators integrate these strategies into regular instruction.

The following article, "Multimedia or Not to Multimedia?" presents instructional factors that teachers should consider when selecting multimedia materials that are appropriate for students with learning disabilities. Specific programs and Web sites that use design features effectively are discussed, and problematic features in multimedia software packages are described, along with strategies that make appropriate accommodations.

In the final article, Juhani Tuovinen describes the nature of multimedia interactions in distance education and synthesizes approaches based on distance education theory, cognition research, and multimedia development. The author provides a composite framework for discussion of multimedia and multimodal interactions in distance education context. These interactions take place between the instructor, students, and content. This framework can be used to establish clear relationships among the existing interaction literature for classifying interactions in distance education instructional design and as a basis for further research.

Multimedia

Do It Step-by-Step

A Systematic Approach to Designing Multimedia Projects

Multimedia software programs are interactive, are student-centered, and motivate students to engage in higher-order thinking. A step-by-step approach to project design can result in effective multimedia projects. This article guides teachers in developing multimedia projects using a systems approach.

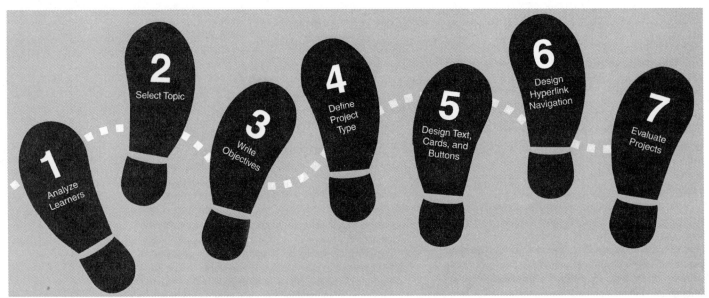

Figure 1.

By Michael F. Ruffini

It has been my experience in teaching multimedia authoring to undergraduate students and teachers that a model is essential in guiding the project design process. In Figure 1, the design elements are arranged sequentially. The internet is to convey an order of steps necessary to ensure a comprehensive and high-quality product.

Using a model prevents frustration and makes efficient and productive use of time in creating projects from start to finish.

Multimedia authoring software (e.g., HyperStudio®) is very popular in today's classrooms. Multimedia and similar authoring programs are based on three fundamental characteristics:

1. students have nonlinear access to information instead of predetermined sequences to follow,
2. students make real-time decisions on what information to access, and
3. students can use multiple information formats other than just text, such as graphics, animation, video, and sound (Yang & Moore, 1996).

© 2000, ISTE (International Society for Technology in Education), 800.336.5191 (U.S. & Canada) or 541.302.3777 (Int'l), iste@iste.org, www.iste.org. All rights reserved.

Systems Approach

Instructional design (ID) is the systematic planning of instruction. Employing ID principles in creating a multimedia project can help ensure a high-quality product that meets the needs of specific learners. The steps outlined here can be used by teachers in designing projects to present to students or by students in designing their own hypermedia projects. The systems approach can be integrated into both traditional and constructivist learning environments. In a traditional classroom, the teacher may use a multimedia project to teach a particular subject, or students may work individually on an assigned project. In a constructivist classroom, the teacher may have three or four students work together to develop a multimedia project on a specific subject.

The ID process for developing a multimedia project includes:

1. analyzing learners
2. selecting a topic
3. writing objectives
4. defining project type
5. designing text, cards, and buttons
6. designing hyperlink navigation
7. evaluating the project

Analyzing Learners

The first step in multimedia project design is to consider the learner. Identifying general characteristics of your

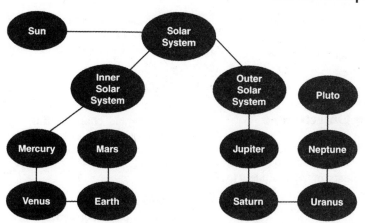

Figure 2. A concept web created with Inspiration® can be used to organize cards and stacks.

learners will help you select proper objectives, vocabulary, and content for the project. Before moving to the next step, ask yourself the following questions:

8. What are the ages and reading and grade levels of students creating or using the program?
9. What if any experiences do they have using HyperStudio or creating a project with it?

Selecting the Topic

The project topic should be selected as for any other research topic, by choosing one correlated to the curriculum. After selecting a topic, construct a concept map or web either on paper or with concept-mapping software (e.g., Inspiration®). Concept maps or-

ganize content and illustrate its interrelationships (Figure 2). Project designers can then use this information to develop cards and stacks.

Designers also can use concept maps to outline the scope and sequence of a particular topic. The main topics generated from their outlines can then be used for home page buttons. The following is an example of a scope and sequence outline from Figure 2.

The Solar System

A. Sun
B. Inner Planets
   1. Mercury
   2. Venus
   3. Earth
   4. Mars
C. Outer Planets
   5. Jupiter

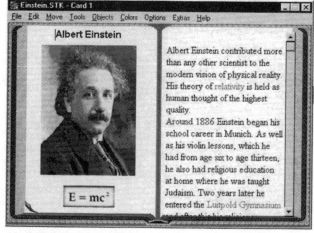

Figure 3. Hyperbook on the biography of Albert Einstein.

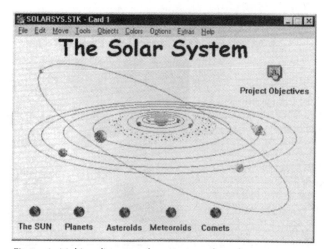

Figure 4. Multimedia research project on the solar system.

6. Saturn
7. Uranus
8. Neptune
9. Pluto

Writing Objectives

The third step is writing clear, well-stated objectives. Objectives are precise statements of what students will learn as a result of creating and using the project. Objectives provide a framework enabling the project designer to select and organize the instructional content and evaluate a project. Write objectives in behavioral terms, including an action verb, a subject content reference, and an optimal level of achievement or degree of performance. Objectives should correlate to content standards developed by the academic department, school district, or state. The following is an example of objectives from a fourth-grade solar system unit correlated to Delaware science standard 4 (Delaware Department of Education, 1995):

Delaware Science Standard Four (Earth in Space).
Earth's system is part of the solar system that exists within a vast universe. Earth's motion and position relative to the sun and the moon are unique among planets of the solar system, allowing diverse forms of life to be supported on Earth. Students will learn that even though the distributions and types of materials differ from planet to planet, the chemical composition of materials is identical and the same laws of science apply across the universe.

Objective 1. The student will observe and record the apparent path of the sun and chart the times and directions of sunrise and sunset over a 30-day period.

Objective 2. The student will be able to construct a simple model to explain how the earth's position relative to the sun's determines the length of daylight.

Objective 3. The student will be able to develop a multimedia project that demonstrates the tilt of Earth in relation to the sun and use it to explain seasons at different locations on Earth.

Before moving on to the next step in the process, ask yourself the following questions:

1. Is the topic correlated to the curriculum?
2. Is the content organized using a concept map or web?
3. What is the objective of my project?
4. What type of project format will best communicate my content?

Defining Project Type

Four basic types of interactive projects are possible: Hyperbook, Research Report, Tour, and Oral presentation. To determine the best type for your topic, review your objectives and intended audience and decide whether the project will be presented for a class or individual setting.

Interactive Hyperbook Project. Designers create an electronic book in which each card appears to be a page. The pages can include multiple information formats other than just text (graphics, hyperlinks, animation, video, and sound). The Hyperbook format is good for biographies, short stories, picture books, and creative writing projects (Figure 3).

Interactive Research Report. This is very much like any traditional research report, except it uses multimedia elements to present research (Figure 4). This format is the most common and can be used for all types of research topics.

Interactive Class Presentation. Designers use a multimedia project to present information with question-and-answer feedback. The presentation requires a video projector (Figure 5).

Interactive Tour. This is just what the name implies: a tour of places,

Figure 5. Interactive project presentation on dinosaurs.

Figure 6. Interactive tour.

times, or events. An interactive tour presents information by linking pictures and locations (Figure 6). Examples of interactive tours include a famous place (e.g., museum), an historical tour of a time period (e.g., Jurassic), or a location (e.g., the human body).

Designing Text, Title Card, & Buttons

Visual design of text, cards, and buttons is critical for effective communication. Text design includes font, style, size, and color. The following considerations are general design guidelines for creating text, cards, buttons, and graphics.

Fonts fall into several broad categories, the two most common being *serif* and *sans serif*. Serif fonts (e.g., Times New Roman, Garamond) have beginning or finishing strokes on each letter (Figure 7). Sans serifs (e.g., Arial, Helvetica) have no strokes (Figure 8). Sans serif fonts are best suited for titles, headers, and labels because they are easily recognized and understood. Serif fonts are more suited for body text because they are easier to read for extended time periods than sans serif fonts. As a general rule, use no more than two different typefaces and colors (e.g., Times New Roman for body text, Verdana for headings). Use bold for titles, bold or plain for body. Shadow and Outline are too difficult to read.

Balance of Text on Card refers to the way authoring software uses cards and stacks to develop a project. Each screen of information is called a *card*. A group of related cards is called a *stack*. When placing text on cards, it is important to balance text and graphics. Although you can choose a scrolling text object, be careful not to place so much text on one card that the reader has to keep scrolling and scrolling to read it all. Readers get bored quickly when they have to scroll through too much information on one card. Try to write in a succinct manner and fit the amount of

Figure 7. Serif fonts should be used for body text.

Figure 8. Sans serif fonts should be used for titles.

text that can be viewed without scrolling in the text object box.

The *Title Card* is the most important card in any multimedia project. The title card is an index of the subject content and provides the links to other cards and stacks (see Figure 6). It functions much like a table of contents. The title card should include:

- Project Title
- Author Name
- Project Subject
- Project Objective(s)
- Graphics
- Navigation buttons

Before moving on to the next step in the ID process, ask the following questions:

1. Are the fonts and style readable?
2. Is there too much text on the card?
3. Are the color combinations harmonious?
4. Do the graphics communicate the main idea of the particular card?
5. Is the card visually balanced?

Designing Hyperlink Navigation

Navigation through a multimedia project refers to the order or path the designer uses to connect cards and stacks. These connections are called

hyperlinks or, more commonly, links. The links connect cards sequentially or nonsequentially. Three navigation structures are available to show the interrelationships of the project's content: linear, hierarchical, and network.

Linear navigation is easy. Information is arranged in alphabetical or chronological order. However, this navigation design does not take full advantage of hyperlinks, which can link information to any other piece of related information (Figure 9).

Hierarchical organization allows navigation through information in a family tree type of sequence (Figure 10).

A *network organization* allows navigation through information based on the interrelationships between cards. The complexity of a network structure depends on how many interrelationships between cards and stacks exist (Figure 11).

Multimedia projects are built around these three structural themes. The title or home card is designed based on the structure and sequence of the content information. In designing multimedia projects, the subject content is commonly organized in a hierarchical sequence. The complexity of content organization and network structure is based on the subject matter, learner characteristics, and project objectives (Yang & Moore, 1996). Before moving on to the next step of the design process, ask the following questions:

1. Which navigation structure is best suited for my content?
2. Is the content organized into subtopics (this can help with complex interrelationships)?

Evaluating Multimedia Projects

Multimedia project assessment is based on criteria that reflect the project's quality. Because a multimedia project is outcome-based, one of the best assessment tools is a rubric. A rubric should contain project tasks and a grading scale.

The rubric should be holistic, be criterion-referenced, and indicate how

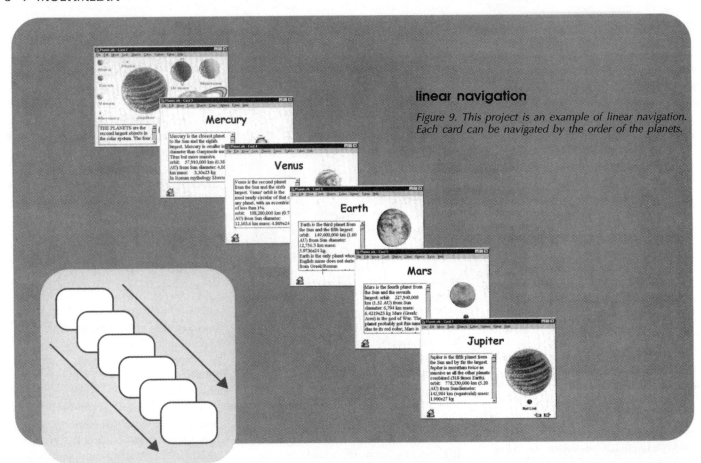

linear navigation

Figure 9. This project is an example of linear navigation. Each card can be navigated by the order of the planets.

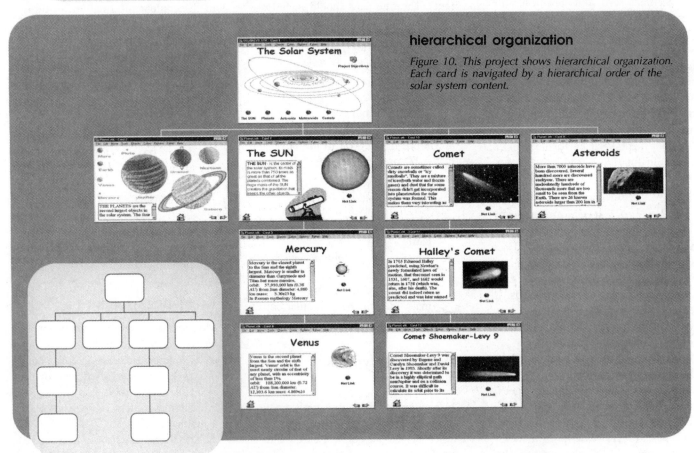

hierarchical organization

Figure 10. This project shows hierarchical organization. Each card is navigated by a hierarchical order of the solar system content.

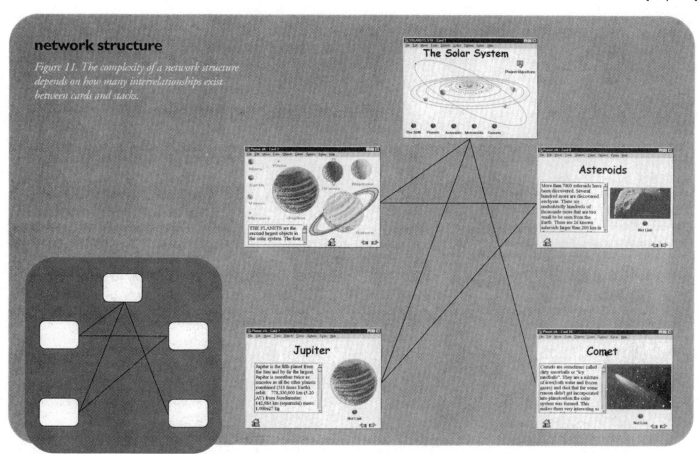

network structure

Figure 11. The complexity of a network structure depends on how many interrelationships exist between cards and stacks.

Multimedia Project Evaluation Rubric

Planning	Project followed Multimedia Project Model steps	1	2	3	4	5
	Storyboard was scripted on index cards	1	2	3	4	5
Mechanics	Correct spelling, punctuation, and grammar	1	2	3	4	5
	Buttons go to correct cards and links	1	2	3	4	5
	Buttons on each card link to home card	1	2	3	4	5
Design	Home card is appropriately designed	1	2	3	4	5
	Graphics correlate to topic	1	2	3	4	5
	Colors and background are harmonious	1	2	3	4	5
	Titles and text are easy to read	1	2	3	4	5
Visual Effects	Transitions used on links	1	2	3	4	5
Internet Links	Three or more Internet links	1	2	3	4	5

An **iste** copy-me page.

"Do It Step-by-Step: A Systematic Approach to Designing Multimedia Projects" by Michael F. Ruffini
Learning & Leading with Technology, Feb. 2000, vol. 27, no. 5.
© 2000, ISTE (the International Society for Technology in Education),
800.336.5191 or 541.302.3777, cust_svc@iste.org, www.iste.org.
Freely reproducible for classroom use.

well the student successfully designed the project according to specific criteria. The criteria will vary according to the level of project difficulty.

Tasks. Authentic assessment of a project is contingent on the development of specific tasks that produce a high quality project. The tasks should reflect the level of difficulty and indicators of mastery of project objectives. To determine the difficulty of the project tasks, you have to review steps one (Analyzing Learners), two (Selecting Topic), and three (Writing Objectives) of the design process. However, basic tasks should include:

- Planning
- Mechanics
- Design
- Visual Effects
- Internet Use

Grading Scale. The final step in constructing a project rubric is to create a grading scale that will adequately reflect student performance. Once the task expectations of the project have been determined, the instructor needs to specify levels of performance for each task, calculate, and then convert the scale to a numerical or letter grade scale. One of the most common ways of indicating project proficiency levels is to use a 1–5 ranking of lowest to highest, 1 = poor, 2 = fair, 3 = good, 4 = very good, 5 = outstanding (see the copy-me). A letter grade can be based on the total number of points, for example A = 55–50, B = 49–44, C = 43–33, D = 32–22, and an F = 21–below.

Conclusion

Systematic planning can help teachers efficiently design high-quality and effective multimedia projects. The approach provided in this article moves users through a process that begins with analyzing the audience and ends with evaluation. Try it the next time your students design a multimedia project.

Resources

HyperStudio is available from Roger Wagner Publishing, El Cajon, CA; 800.545.7677; hypersrudio@ education.com; www.hyperstudio.com.

Inspiration is available from Inspiration Software, Inc., 7412 SW Beaverton Hillsdale Hwy., Ste. 102, Portland, OR 97225–2167; 800.877.4292 or 503.297.3004, fax 503.297.4676; www.inspiration.com.

References

Delaware Department of Education. (1995). *State of Delaware science curriculum framework* [Online document]. Dover, DE: Author. Available: wwwdoe.srate.de.us/Srandards/Science/ science_toc.hrml.

Yang, C., & Moore, D. M. (1996). Designing hypermedia systems for instruction. Journal of Educational Technology Systems, 24(1), 3–30.

Michael F Ruffini (mruffini@ brandywine.net) is an assistant profrssor of lnstructional Technology at Delaware State University. He teaches both undergraduate and graduate courses in Web page design and development. He holds an EdD from Widener University. In addition, he is an adjunct IT faculty member at Penn State Great Valley and Web training consultant for school districts and businesses. He can be reached at 236 E. Evergreen Street, West Grove, PA 19390; 610.869.2631.

Subject: Multimedia authoring using systematic planning

Grade Level: Preservice and inservice teachers of all grades

Technology: HyperStudio® (Roger Wagner Publishing, Inc.), Inspiration® (Inspiration Software, Inc.)

Standards: *State of Delaware Science Standard 4.* (Read more about the Delaware science curriculum at www.doe.state.de.us/Standards/Science/science_toc.html.)

Copy-me page: page 12

Online: www.iste.org/L&L

MindWorks: Making Scientific Concepts Come Alive

ABSTRACT. The Southwest Regional Laboratory, through major funding from the National Science Foundation (ESI-9450235), has developed a series of eight instructional modules for use in common secondary school physical science that address three central goals of U. S. science literacy education: (1) to motivate students who have previously shown little interest in science; (2) to accomplish deep change in students' internalized conceptions of the structure and workings of the physical world; and (3) to build greater understanding, in both teachers and students, of the process and culture of scientific activity.

Beginning with a discussion of the conceptual scaffolding that undergirds the project's pedagogical approach, the paper presents an overview of MindWorks' goals, the materials that have been developed to achieve these goals, and the progress of the pilot implementation and project evaluation.

BARBARA J. BECKER

INTRODUCTION

Acquainting young people today with contemporary scientific understanding of structure and process in the natural world is a daunting task—there is so much that can be taught, and really so very little time. Educators are faced with critical choices in terms of the content they present and the method by which they present it in order to maximize their opportunities to influence, in a positive way, the world views being built by their students.

For kids, learning about the world is a 24 hour a day operation—it's what they do for a living. And formal instruction in science—the way science educators like to think that students acquire their knowledge of the world—is only a few hours a week, at best. That's not really a problem for kids. They are able to locate the bricks and mortar with which to construct their own nearly indestructible views on how the world works from a wide range of readily available sources: parents, friends, the media, in addition to personal observation and experiment. By early adolescence, most students have a pretty good idea what scientists are like, what they do, and why it is that they believe the things they do.

This is not to say that we are privy to our students' private beliefs about the structure and function of the natural world. For one thing, students are adept at learning to say what they know we want to hear. For another, we have a hard time learning to palpate productively for signs of cognitive dissonance. Patterns which order our thought space have become so familiar that we forget they are constructs of the human intellect deemed convenient, efficient, and useful for organizing the information we gather daily. We have become desensitized to our own deeply ingrained systems of belief.

How can we learn to confront the boundaries that delimit the realm of our personal and professional thought space? How can we learn to ask our own questions within a new and unfamiliar context? How can we then help students recognize the existence of alternatives to their private beliefs about the world and give them useful means by which to examine them?

Exposing students to the social construction of scientific knowledge through historical episodes that emphasize the intellectual struggle involved in developing key physical science concepts will help them articulate their own theories about the world and recognize a need to change the form and structure of these theories.

We have chosen to use the history of science as a vehicle toward that end, considering the literature's admonition to draw upon relevant incidents from the history of science as a heuristic device to anticipate and address alternative conceptions in science across the grade levels.

"SCIENCE FOR ALL"

In the United States, the call to make its students first in science and mathematics by the year 2000 has shifted the national perspective on the role of secondary science education away from the post-Sputnik emphasis on the need to train a new generation of scientists and engineers toward the challenge of raising the science literacy of ALL students. The American

Association for the Advancement of Science's (AAAS) K–12 science reform goals, as stated in *Science for All Americans* (1990), encourage curricula that include important historical perspectives, understanding of the designed world, and common themes like models, systems, and scale.

The new *National Science Education Standards* have been developed to both guide and assess this improvement process. Integral to these new standards—and the numerous curriculum frameworks that have been developed in recent years (e.g., Biological Science Curriculum Study & Social Science Education Consortium 1992; California Department of Education 1990; Hickman et al. 1987)—is the principle that effective science content instruction must be deftly woven into a rich and meaningful social context.

Historical examples provide an ideal setting for accomplishing this integration of content, context, and method. Issues of stability and change, scale and structure, and systems and interactions can readily be explored as part and parcel of the social construction of scientific knowledge, giving students and teachers a greater appreciation for the rhetorical and often opportunistic character of scientific investigation that is commonly hidden from public view.

It has been argued that to trace the social progression of scientific/technical ideas over time during science instruction may have sound cognitive as well as affective results (Wandersee 1992; White 1995). Elaboration and organization assist learners in retaining complex information (Gagné 1977). The use of elaboration in the form of episodes and story lines is supported in studies of language acquisition (Schank and Abelson 1977). Much as with content-specific knowledge, language is acquired most effectively when introduced and reiterated in a meaningful context (Krashen 1982). Approaching scientific inquiry in the context of history may then be an effective means of increasing scientific literacy and not just the rote memorization of facts and formulas. We have chosen to test this by using historical video vignettes involving role playing, and by related activities derived from video vignettes.

CONCEPTUAL CHANGE

It has been 30 years since the last large-scale efforts to produce and use a systematic sequence of history-based science lesson plans and units. The *Project Physics Course*—the most renowned of these curricula—aimed to meet the diverse needs and interests of those students identified as traditionally alienated from the world of science and technology. Its developers hoped to increase enrollment in high school physics (Holton 1978). In many ways, they succeeded. Students who took the course found it satisfying, diverse, historical, philosophical, humanitarian, and social. They not only felt they had developed a good understanding of basic physics concepts, but they found the historical approach to be interesting and the text enjoyable to read as well (Welch 1973; Ahlgren and Walberg 1973).

Unfortunately, *Project Physics* missed much of its intended audience. The students exposed to it were predominantly advanced students who already planned to take physics. If a broader cross-section of the student population is to be reached, learning modules need to be developed that incorporate history of science, not for existing physics classes, but for the general physical science course taken by most noncollege bound or nonscience-oriented students during the last years in middle/junior high school or the first years of high school.

Since the development of *Project Physics,* and the nearly contemporaneous *History of Science Cases* developed by Leopold Klopfer (Klopfer 1969; Klopfer and Cooley 1963, 1961), research on alternative conception has pointed to an important new focus for science education researchers—conceptual change (Wandersee et al. 1994). As a result, we have improved our understanding of the mechanics of conceptual change. We have learned that children, like scientists, can tolerate a wide range of observations that do not match their expectations, or that even directly conflict with them, without abandoning their own system of beliefs about the natural world (Clement 1983; Driver and Easley 1978; McCloskey 1983). It is important, therefore, for students to identify and verbalize their *a priori* beliefs about natural phenomena.

While some may claim that the history of science previously included in science instruction was quasi-history, pseudo-history, or simplified history, Matthews (1992, p. 21) advises that a simplified history of science in a science lesson that illuminates the subject matter while not caricaturing the history is certainly not heresy. Indeed, traditional approaches—even laboratory experiences that support textbook presentations of theories—do not guarantee students will alter their convictions concerning how things "ought" to work. In contrast, a history-grounded approach to presenting scientific concepts has the potential of doing precisely that. Strike and Posner remind their readers that "what is crucial is for teachers [or here, historical characters] to function as models of rational inquirers and for them to exhibit the practices and values of inquiry in their teaching" (1992, p. 171). They speak of initiating the young to the social nature of scientific knowledge via a mix of observation and discourse. That is just what we are endeavoring to do in this curriculum project—with our ultimate goal being conceptual change toward important scientific/technical concepts and principles. Exposing students to the social construction of scientific knowledge through historical episodes that emphasize the intellectual struggle involved in developing key physical science concepts will help them articulate their own theories about the world and recognize a need to change the form and structure of these theories.

PROJECT DEVELOPMENT

In June 1993, the Southwest Regional Laboratory (SWRL) embarked on a project to develop science curriculum materials that would answer these needs. After gaining the support of local school districts and teachers, institutions of higher learning, and an experienced educational television producer, SWRL submitted an ambitious proposal to the National Science Foundation (NSF). In October 1994, the NSF awarded SWRL nearly $1.2 million to conduct the 3-year curriculum development project, "Making Scientific Concepts Come Alive."

The decision was made early on to build the project around the production of a set of eight professionally produced, 10–15 minute video dramatizations. Previous efforts to incorporate history in science instruction relied almost exclusively on reading materials, supplemented by the relatively limited audiovisual aids available 30 years ago. The power of videos to motivate students is widely recognized (Russell and Curtin 1993). Recent technological advances in video production coupled with the increased affordability of equipment to make sophisticated audiovisual materials accessible to students further supported our decision to make the videos central to our materials development project.

Historical episodes were selected both for their attention to basic physical science concepts commonly treated in introductory physical science courses and for their inherent dramatic character—raising social, philosophical, and/or political issues that will interest adolescents. Though the episodes deal with Western advances in science, five of the eight videos feature the scientific investigations of women, or of persons of color. Los Angeles' public television station, KCET, was selected to produce the videos because of its proximity to SWRL; its familiarity with, and access to, resources that would strengthen the historical and artistic integrity of the product; the quality of its past work; and its expressed concern for promoting educational excellence.

Beginning in October 1994, SWRL and KCET began converting the concept outlines for each video into scripts. Budgetary constraints limited the structure of the planned dramatizations to those that could be effectively portrayed using only two adult characters, could be filmed in local venues, and that had limited production element requirements. Original script concepts were modified or replaced to conform to these constraints. The video series was named "MindWorks."

The script development for the eight videos took approximately six months. During that time, feedback was gathered from historians of science, engineers, physicists, teachers and students to ensure that the episodes contained good science and good history packaged in a format that not only appealed to students, but enhanced their understanding of the process of science as well. It was particularly helpful to project staff to have had the opportunity to gather input from members of the Advisory Board in November 1994, when script development was still in its early stages. Advisors have included such notable advocates of the use of history in science teaching as Leo Klopfer from the University of Pittsburgh, Jim Wandersee from Louisiana State University, Jim Ellis and Don Maxwell from Biological Sciences Curriculum Study, and Rick Duschl from Vanderbilt University.

Feedback from a group of junior high school students who were shown a videotaped reading of a script developed for the statics unit (based on George W. Ferris' plans for construction of his famous observation wheel for the 1983 World's Fair in Chicago), bolstered our assumption that students can be motivated to learn through historical vignettes. These students—all low socio-economic status, many with limited English proficiency, and several with learning disabilities—were drawn into the story of George Ferris and his design for the giant wheel. The students were interested in the steps taken by Ferris and his assistant to overcome the challenging physical constraints imposed by Ferris's vision of a 250 foot tension wheel capable of carrying over a thousand passengers. But they were most intrigued by the need for Ferris to convince investors to fund his colossal project. They grasped the complexity of the task Ferris had undertaken. They followed the process by which he accomplished it. And they appreciated the scientific and technological expertise required to make such a vision a reality.

Actual production of the eight videos took a little over a month, beginning at the end of March 1995. The post-production phase, originally scheduled for completion in mid-June, was not completed until mid-September. However, participating teachers and SWRL staff were able to plan the units around the roughcut of each video during the written materials development workshop held at SWRL in July and August 1995.

CURRICULUM MATERIALS DEVELOPMENT

A 10-minute video can provide only a limited view into the social and intellectual setting of the scientific enterprise. It can initiate, but not resolve, the personal confrontation with conflicting ideas necessary to produce significant changes in students' conceptual understanding. Though the videos form the centerpiece for each module, the teachers are the project's vital link to the ultimate goal of improving science literacy and increasing motivation to explore the physical sciences for students who have shown little interest in science. Modules designed from a teacher's perspective have increased probability of becoming integral parts of the curriculum, weaving in an historical perspective and an awareness of the culture and process of scientific inquiry.

Drawing upon the experience, enthusiasm and creativity of effective teachers was the key to enhancing the existing curriculum for students who were otherwise unlikely to pursue further coursework in the physical sciences. A team of seven expert teachers, assisted by project staff and one advisory board member devised activities and guides for each of the eight modules (SWRL, 1996). Teachers were recruited by recommendations from district supervisors and from the science education department at a nearby university. All of the teachers had advanced degrees and had worked successfully with very diverse groups of students. The team included veteran and relatively new teachers. Several teachers had previous experience writing curriculum. Others had experience in science and industry or as teachers at the community college level. Flexibility and a willingness to try non-traditional approaches to physical science instruction were important traits. Permission to pilot selected units was obtained at each teacher's school site.

Because of the importance of the unit planning and the intense pressure of developing original materials in a short period of time, every effort was made to support the work done by the teachers. Project staff assembled resources for the teachers to use. Workspace, computers and Internet connections were provided to the teachers at SWRL. Most importantly, teachers were given a great deal of autonomy in preparing the units.

Teachers and staff worked in pairs to design the units. Wherever possible, teachers were able to select the units they would develop and pilot. Four units were completed during each of two, two-week time blocks. After completing the first two-week unit, the pairs rotated to work on a new module during the second two weeks.

A principal feature of the project's curriculum is the inclusion of original historical documents and summaries of biographic and historical information in a variety of hands-on, cooperative or competitive group and dramatic activities. An extensive collection of historical and biographical materials was gathered in advance by SWRL staff for teachers to use in constructing curriculum units, lesson plans and student activities. Taking the story line in the video as a point of departure, teachers developed a range of activities that include creative and reflective writing, classroom simulations, debates, and discussions that immerse the learners in the work of scientists and inventors.

Great care has been taken to conform to the best practices available for including learners of varying abilities by relating activities as closely as possible to real-life situations. Where appropriate, activities have been modified in order to maximize participation in the module activities. In addition to the rich comprehensible input provided by the historical vignettes, the accompanying activities come with clear and concise directions for the students and teachers. Activities follow a logical sequence of concept development and relate as closely as possible to real-life situations.

Through authentic assessment tasks, students will demonstrate mastery of real-life skills. Students will be observed on individual and group tasks that include both quantitative and qualitative problem-solving activities. In this way, all students are likely to experience success and challenge.

During the 1995/96 academic year, each module underwent a careful and thorough field-testing process. Teachers who developed the modules piloted their own designs to fine tune the teacher and student materials. Formative evaluation of the freshly revised materials was conducted by a team from Rockman, et al. in classrooms in the San Francisco Bay area. The classrooms used represented socio-economically, ethnically, and linguistically diverse student populations.

This small-scale pilot demonstrated that embedding science learning in a historical context successfully conveys the creative and very human character of scientific explanation—its tentative, probabilistic, and serendipitous nature. By integrating well-chosen historic episodes into traditional content-centered science units, the *MindWorks* modules have helped teachers establish a classroom atmosphere that stimulates productive discussion and nurtures student's critical thinking about the meaning of scientific activity—e.g., the design of measuring instruments, individual observational interpretation, measurement error, and the often ignored rhetorical challenge faced by scientific investigators in the aftermath of discovery. Classroom use of *MindWorks* materials has thus far shown that basing science instruction on historic episodes can open up opportunities for students to identify their own untutored beliefs about the workings of the natural world, to examine them critically in the light of considered historical debate, and to confront these beliefs in a way that results in positive, long-lasting conceptual change.

LARGE-SCALE PILOT

In April 1996, teachers were recruited from Los Angeles and Orange counties to participate in a large-scale field test of the *MindWorks* materials during the 1996/97 academic year. Our goal was to recruit 50 teachers: 25 to receive two weeks of training prior to piloting the materials; 25 to pilot the materials without any previous training. Over a hundred teachers responded to our announcement. Of these, 46 have been selected to participate in the pilot. These individuals have been randomly assigned to a pilot group: 23 participated in the training session held at SWRL July 8–18, 1996; 23 will be given copies of all *MindWorks* materials. A group of 50 introductory physical science teachers is being recruited from Los Angeles and Orange counties to serve as controls in the study.

Four of the original seven teachers/developers assisted project staff during the training session. Each day of the eight-day training was devoted to one unit. Included in each day's activities were discussions of rationale for the selection and development of the unit's structure and content, historical background, basic science content, and pedagogy. Teachers were assigned to small groups. To increase social cohesion in the training group as a whole, teachers were reassigned to new groups every two days.

Care was taken in the selection of training activities. Time was extremely limited, so activities were chosen that best model active group collaboration, creative design and problem solving, and use of the unit's historical materials. The principal aims of the training were to motivate and engage the teachers, build up confidence in their personal ability to implement the materials, generate a bond of support with each other and SWRL staff, and provide guidance for planning their overall instructional program during the upcoming year.

It was anticipated that time and, perhaps considerable, energy would be spent during the training defending the expenditure of precious science instruction time on what could be construed as extraneous topics. This did not turn out to be the case. The teachers quickly and eagerly bought into the rationale behind the development of the *MindWorks* materials. One teacher commented, while constructing her telegraph, that while electricity and magnetism did not seem to agree with her, she was encouraged to master it because she wanted to be able to teach her students about all the "railroad stuff" in the historical materials.

The 1996/97 piloting effort will be closely monitored throughout the school year by the summative evaluation team and project staff. Students will be assessed on their basic science achievement, knowledge of the scientific enterprise, and attitudes toward science.

To measure science achievement, a pre- and post-assessment instrument is being developed for administration to students of teachers in all three study groups. The instrument is being designed by Michael Martinez from the University of California, Irvine, and will assess students' basic understanding of science content and process, as well as probe for fundamental misconceptions.

To measure students' knowledge of the scientific enterprise, they will be assigned a few select open-ended tasks near the end of the school year. These tasks will assess students' ability to analyze and interpret evidence, their appreciation of the creative role of argument and uncertainty in the development of scientific thinking, and their personal views of scientists and the methods of scientific investigation.

Students from all study groups will be surveyed concerning their attitudes about science both at the beginning of the school year and at the end. Assuming an average class size of 30 students, we will have gathered information on approximately 3,000 students by the conclusion of the 1996/97 academic year.

By refining our materials and methods over the next year, a polished product will be ready for publication and dissemination at the conclusion of the project.

REFERENCE

Ahlgren, A. & Walberg, H. J.: 1973, 'Changing Attitudes Toward Science Among Adolescents', *Nature* **245**, 187–190.

American Association for the Advancement of Science: 1990, *Science for All Americans,* Oxford University Press, New York.

Becker, B. J., Younger-Flores, K. & Wandersee, J. H.: 1995, 'MindWorks: Making Scientific Concepts Come Alive', in F. Finley, D. Allchin, D. Rhees & S. Fifield (eds.), *Proceedings of the Third International History, Philosophy, and Science Teaching,* Vol. 1. The University of Minnesota, Minneapolis, MN, 115–125.

Becker, B. J.: 1992, 'Incorporating Primary Source Material in Secondary and College Science Curricula', in K. Hills (ed.), *Proceedings of the Second International Conference on the History and Philosophy of Science and Science Teaching,* Vol. 1. The Mathematics, Science, Technology, and Teacher Education Group, Kingston, ON, 69–76.

Biological Science Curriculum Study & Social Science Education Consortium: 1992, *Teaching About the History and Nature of Science and Technology: A Curriculum Framework.* Colorado Springs, CO.

California Department of Education: 1990, *Science Framework for California Public Schools: Kindergarten Through Grade Twelve.* Sacramento.

Clement, J.: 1983, 'A Conceptual Model Discussed by Galileo and Used Intuitively by Physics Students', in D. Gentner & A. Stevens (eds.), *Mental Models,* Lawrence Erlbaum, Hillsdale, NJ, 325–340.

Driver, R. & Easley, J.: 1978, 'Pupils and Paradigms: A Review of Literature Related to Concept Development in Adolescent Science Students', *Studies in Science Education* **5**, 61–84.

Gagné, Robert: 1977, *The Conditions of Learning,* Holt, Rinehart, and Winston, New York.

Hickman, F. M., Patrick, J. J. & Bybee, R. W.: 1987, *Science/Technology/Society: A Framework for Curriculum Reform in Secondary School Science and Social Studies.* Social Science Education Consortium, Boulder, CO.

Holton, G.: 1978, 'On the Educational Philosophy of the Project Physics Course', in G. Holton (ed.), *The Scientific Imagination: Case Studies.* Cambridge University Press, Cambridge, MA.

Klopfer, L. E. & Cooley, W. W.: 1963, 'The History of Science Cases for High Schools in the Development of Student Understanding of Science and Scientists', *Journal of Research in Science Teaching* **1**, 33–47.

Klopfer, L. E. & Cooley, W. W.: 1961, *The Use of Case Histories in the Development of Student Understanding of Science and Scientists,* Harvard University Press, Cambridge, MA.

Klopfer, L. E.: 1969, 'The Teaching of Science and History of Science', *Journal of Research in Science Teaching* **6**, 87–95.

Krashen, Stephen: 1982, *Principles and Practice in Second Language Acquisition,* Pergamon, Oxford.

Matthews, M. R.: 1992, 'History Philosophy, and Science Teaching: The Present Rapprochement', *Science & Education* **1**(1), 11–47.

McAleese, R. (ed.): 1978, *Perspectives on Academic Gaming and Simulation 3: Training and Professional Education,* Kogan Page, London.

McCloskey, M.: 1983, 'Intuitive Physics', *Scientific American* **248**, 122–130.

National Research Council: 1996, *National Science Education Standards.* National Academy Press, Washington, D. C.

Russell, A. & Curtin, T. R.: 1993, *Study of School Uses of Television and Video: 1990–1991 School Year,* Corporation for Public Broadcasting, Washington, D. C.

Schank, R. & Abelson, R.: 1977, *Scripts, Plans, Goals and Understanding,* Lawrence Erlbaum, Hillsdale, NJ.

Southwest Regional Laboratory: 1996, *MindWorks,* Los Alamitos, CA.

Strike, K. A. & Posner, G. J.: 1992, 'A Revisionist Theory of Conceptual Change', in R. A. Duschl and R. H. Hamilton (eds.), *Philosophy of Science, Cognitive Psychology, and Educational Theory and Practice,* SUNY Press, Albany, 147–176.

Wandersee, J. H.: 1992, 'The Historicality of Cognition: Implications for Science Education Research', *Journal of Research in Science Teaching* **29**(4), 423–434.

Wandersee, James H., Mintzes, Joel J. & Novak, Joseph D.: 1994, 'Research on Alternative Conceptions in Science', in Dorothy Gabel (ed.), *Handbook of Research on Science Teaching and Learning,* Macmillan, New York, 177–210.

Welch, W. W.: 1973, 'Review of the Research and Evaluation Program of Harvard Project Physics', *Journal of Research in Science Teaching* **10**(4), 365–378.

White, Richard T.: 1995, 'Thoughts for Ph.D. Research', *Subject Matter and Conceptual Change Newsletter* **23**, 5.

Southwest Regional Laboratory, 4665 Lampson Avenue, Los Angeles, CA 90720, USA

Designing Instructional Technology from an Emotional Perspective

Abstract *This article discusses an aspect of systematic instructional design that has received relatively little attention so far: strategies for making instructional technology more emotionally sound. Within the framework presented here, a set of prescriptive propositions is deduced from a review of concepts, theories, and empirical findings in the research on emotion. Five major dimensions of emotions are identified: (1) fear, which arises in response to a situation judged to be threatening; (2) envy, which comes from the desire to either get or not lose something; (3) anger, which comes in response to being hindered in reaching a goal; (4) sympathy, which is experienced in response to people in need of help; and (5) pleasure, which is experienced when mastering a situation. We describe 20 general instructional strategies that can be used to decrease negative emotions (fear, envy, and anger) and increase positive emotions (sympathy and pleasure). For all instructional strategies, we describe different features of instructional technology that can help educators integrate these strategies into regular instruction. (Keywords: computer-assisted instruction, emotions, FEASP approach, feelings, instructional design, Web-based education.)*

Hermann Astleitner
University of Salzburg

Detlev Leutner
Erfurt University of Education

Despite the importance of emotions in daily life, for decades the focus in instructional design and technology was on the learner's cognitive and motivational processes (Reigeluth, 1997). Human emotions have not received adequate attention, not even in the latest comprehensive reviews of instructional psychology and design closely related to instructional technology (e.g., Liebowitz, 1999; Tennyson, Schott, Seel, & Dijkstra, 1997). One reason for this situation might be that practitioners in the field of instructional technology do not call for knowledge and skills in emotional design of instruction. Many designers believe that the emotional education of students is the duty of parents or peers rather than computers, which are *cold* technologies without any emotions and will never be successful in this intimate area of human life.

Instructional designers may also have neglected emotions because they may interfere with the achievement of important cognitive or motivational objectives (Hannafin & Peck, 1988; Keller & Suzuki, 1988). A new approach in the field of emotion and instruction that tried to overcome these shortcomings of traditional instruction and instructional design is *self-science* based on the concept of emotional intelligence (Stone-McCown & McCormick, 1999). But, courses and projects within the self-science approach need instructors with high emotional and even psychotherapeutical competencies that cannot be delivered by computers. Practitioners in the field of instructional technology agree that computers cannot understand emotions or represent them in a human manner, not even within artificial intelligence models of emotions (Pfeiffer, 1988). Recent research projects at the Massachusetts Institute of Technology (MIT) question these assumptions (MIT Media Lab, Affective Computing Research Group, 1999). However, MIT's Affective Computing Research Group uses high-level research methods and technologies that will not be available to schools in the near future, like many of the products of the "intelligent tutoring" research area. Although this kind of

Reprinted with permission from *Journal of Research on Computing in Education*, Vol. 32 No. 4, © 2000, ISTE (International Society for Technology in Education), 800-336-5191 (U.S.& Canada) or 541-302-3777 (Int'l), iste@iste.org, www.iste.org. All rights reserved.

research holds out great hopes for the future, actual instructional technology should concentrate on more practical methods of emotional soundness.

None of the existing instructional design approaches comprehensively answer the question of how instructional technology should be designed to educate students and even young children in an emotionally sound manner. We will try to answer this question within a framework of emotional design reflecting actual and practical possibilities in instructional technology.

TYPES OF EMOTIONS AND THEIR RELEVANCE FOR THE DESIGN OF INSTRUCTIONAL TECHNOLOGY

Emotionally sound instruction consists of instructional strategies to increase positive and decrease negative emotions when using instructional technology. The term *instructional technology* often refers to all current methods of computer-based delivery of instruction, for example, traditional computer-assisted instruction, multimedia-based learning, Web-based (distance) education, and cognitive or collaborative tools (Jonassen, 1996a). The approach presented here is a systematic set of prescriptive propositions obtained from deductively and inductively established relationships between concepts, theories, and empirical research in emotion, learning, and instruction. Prescriptive propositions point out how instructional technology should be designed to get the desired emotional outcomes from the students.

According to our design approach, the instructional designer must understand and use five basic categories of emotional conditions to produce emotionally sound instructional technology. These emotions were selected within a theory-based procedure and comprehensively described (Astleitner, 2000) *Fear* is a negative feeling arising from subjectively judging a situation to be threatening or dangerous. *Envy* is a negative feeling resulting from the desire to either get something that others possess or not lose something one already possesses. *Anger* is a negative feeling coming from being hindered in reaching a desired goal and being forced to an additional action. *Sympathy* is a positive feeling referring to an experience of feelings and orientations of other people who are in the need of help. *Pleasure* is a positive feeling based on mastering a situation with a deep devotion to an action.

According to the Fear-Envy-Anger-Sympathy-Pleasure (FEASP) approach for designing emotionally sound instruction (Figure 1), the instructional designer must analyze emotional problems before and during instruction. Fear, envy, and anger should be reduced during instruction, and sympathy and pleasure should be increased. Based on the observed problems, emo-

tional strategies must be designed and implemented into instructional technology. Then the consequences of the strategy must be evaluated. Each of the following five components of the FEASP approach is a category that subsumes several microconcepts or microtheories of emotion. Each category describes a general emotional condition that the instructional designer must match with suitable instructional strategies.

Fear: Concepts and Instructional Strategies

Theoretical approaches for reducing fear in instruction come from many areas of research—behaviorist learning theories, learned helplessness theory, attribution theory, or self-efficacy theory. One common element appears in all these approaches: the probability of failure represents a major factor in the development of test anxiety. If students expect to fail an important examination, they react with fear. From this circumstance, the first instructional strategy is deduced— *F1: Ensure success in learning.* Realizing this strategy means using all instructional variables closely related to the reduction of cognitive and motivational problem behavior during the use of instructional technology. These variables concern, for example, the availability of learning support (feedback, overviews, advance organizers, self-checking exercises, continuing goal orientation, etc.), pace of instruction, reduction of task difficulties, and others that are traditionally in the focus of cognitive and motivational design of hypermedia or Web-based instruction (e.g., McCormack & Jones, 1998).

But even addressing all of these variables cannot guarantee success. In a theoretical model concerning the reduction of test anxiety, Strittmatter (1993) postulated that when students experience failure in learning, they need to understand that mistakes can be corrected and serve as a valuable chance to learn. This leads to the second instructional strategy—*F2: Accept mistakes as opportunities for learning.* When using instructional technology, mistakes are often highlighted by special sounds, graphics, animations, or error statistics. Mistakes must be pointed out to improve learning, but they should not become the sensations of learning (according to the principle of "bad news is good news"). Without special audiovisual effects and without error statistics, mistakes have more chance of becoming a positive emotional part of learning with instructional technology. Audiovisual effects are especially meaningful when they are related to critical features or steps of solving a given problem. They are of little relevance, however, for successful and anxiety-free learning when they only indicate success or failure after a task has been finished. Error statistics should be replaced by success ratios—that is, the computation of successful problem-solving behavior in relation to all attempts for solving given tasks. Usually, the learner's

Figure 1. *Overview of emotional design strategies in CAI.*

	Emotional Strategies	Instructional Technology Features
Fear Reduction	F1 Ensure success in learning.	Cognitive learning design
	F2 Accept mistakes as opportunities for learning.	Q&A, success statistics
	F3 Create a relaxed situation.	Training delivered through multimedia
	F4 Be critical, but sustain a positive perspective.	Cognitive tools (semantic networking)
Envy Reduction	E1 Encourage comparisons with autobiographical and criterion reference standards instead of social standards.	Student progress tracking, using target lists
	E2 Use consistent and transparent methods of evaluating and grading.	Programmed fact-based evaluation and feedback
	E3 Inspire a sense of authenticity and openness.	Personal information board
	E4 Avoid unequal distribution of privileges among students.	Rule-based granting of privileges
Anger Reduction	A1 Stimulate the control of anger.	Anger buttons
	A2 Show flexible views of things.	Linked information
	A3 Let anger be expressed constructively.	Anger help option
	A4 Do not show or accept any form of violence.	Nonviolent action: motivational design
Sympathy Increase	S1 Intensify relationships.	Synchronous and asynchronous communication tools
	S2 Install sensitive interactions.	On-/Offline trainings for empathic communication
	S3 Establish cooperative learning structures.	Collaborative learning tools
	S4 Implement peer helping programs.	Social networks on the Web
Pleasure Increase	P1 Enhance well-being.	User-friendly interface design
	P2 Establish open learning opportunities.	Virtual classrooms
	P3 Use humor.	Story-/comic-/cartoon-production systems
	P Install play-like activities.	Instructional computer games

competence increases during instruction, thus not all tasks worked on from the outset of instruction should be taken into account when reporting success ratios to the learner. The success should be calculated by considering, for example, the five most recent tasks. These will represent a more valid estimate of the learner's current level of competence (Leutner, 1992).

Help in emotionally coping with mistakes during learning can also come from lists of questions and answers (Q&As). These lists should be available to all students during instruction, and students should be advised to use this list when they experience insecurities in learning. Each mistake can be formulated as a question; the answer can be a hint to help others avoid the mistake. Students should contribute to this list when they make mistakes. By doing this, they learn from their mistakes and constructively help themselves and others avoid making the same mistakes in the future.

Another central line of theory and research in the field of text-anxiety reduction comes from relaxation training (e.g., Hammer, 1996). Such training offers students lifelong tools for maintaining calm or preventing overreactions to fearful situations. Relaxation training can easily be integrated into instruction to help students learn to relax at almost any time. This brings us to our third instructional strategy—*F3: Create a relaxed situation*. Relaxation methods can easily be offered in instructional technology through audio texts or videos easily played on standard multimedia computers. Such spoken texts or videos are available on commercially distributed CD-ROMs, often combined with relaxing music or with highly standardized classical relaxation methods. Using headphones makes it easy, even during instruction, to avoid disturbing other students.

According to Földy and Ringel (1993), a cognitive overload with negative information (e.g., bad news in the media) may result in a fear of failure, in qualms of conscience, and finally in a general fear of life. Educators can prevent this general fear of life by teaching students to critically evaluate information during instruction. Critical thinking helps in reducing redundant and irrelevant information. It also gives students opportunities to cope with highly complex and therefore fear-provoking situations. From these assumptions, we formulate a fourth strategy for reducing fear in instruction—*F4: Be critical, but sustain a positive perspective*. Jonassen (1996b) found that computers are efficient tools for teaching critical thinking. Cognitive tools (e.g., semantic networking tools, databases, spreadsheets, microworlds, etc.), in particular, may facilitate critical thinking, because they help students sort out the hierarchy and logical flow of ideas. Any instructional technology activity in which students are asked to identify main points, search for cause and effect, find patterns and relationships, rank ideas, develop time lines, build taxonomies or categorization schemes, make comparisons, or examine pros and cons is an exercise in critical thinking. Such activities must be supported by the teacher or other students, and students should use suitable learning strategies; as a rule, computers are not able to think critically, but they can offer tools to assist in the acquisition of critical-thinking skills.

Envy: Concepts and Instructional Strategies

The most typical feature of envy is that it depends on self-evaluations and comparisons with others on attributes one considers important. When people feel envy, they lack something important to them, and this lack is shown by social comparisons. In instructional contexts, educators can avoid envy between students by avoiding or downplaying comparisons of students' performances with those of their peers or members of other social groups. Performance evaluations should be based not on social standards but on autobiographical and criterion-referenced standards (Rheinberg & Krug, 1993). This conclusion informs our first strategy for reducing envy in instruction—*E1: Encourage comparisons using autobiographical and criterion-referenced standards instead of social standards*.

An *autobiographical standard* is defined by the student's own past performance—for example, "Since last week, your performance in this area of mathematics has much improved." Within instructional technology, autobiographical comparisons can easily be accomplished by recording individual achievements during learning using the evaluation options often found in available software. The learner periodically gets learning feedback consisting of, for example, data about the past performance in the form of a table with percentages or a graphical display showing the curve of successfully solved tasks in relation to all tasks presented during a given period.

A *criterion-referenced standard* is defined by introducing teaching or instructional objectives—for example, "You have reached 80% of our standards in arithmetic." Criterion-referenced standards can be included in regular feedback as, for example, optimal achievement levels indicating a certain percentage of tasks that must be solved successfully to meet a given teaching objective. Another way of using criterion-referenced standards requires a task analysis in which all steps for fulfilling a given task are listed. Criterion-based feedback should show the learner which steps of the given list have been achieved successfully. This method of presenting criterion-referenced standards is more helpful than presenting percentages because of its close connection to explicit learning steps. Practitioners in the field of instructional technology, however, must be aware that this method is much more time consuming than the first.

A further rich tradition of research work suggests that envy appears when the envied person's advantage is undeserved, especially when the advantaged person is similar in most other characteristics. This sense of injustice may result from psychological balance forces prescribing that similar people ought to have similar fortunes (Parrot, 1991). In instruction, teachers can prevent this source of envy by treating all students equally, particularly during assessment. This conclusion leads to our next instructional strategy—*E2: Use consistent and transparent methods of evaluation and grading*. The computer is an ideal medium in which to be consistent. Computers can be programmed to orient on facts they receive from individual learning achievements. According to these achievements and to given evaluation standards (e.g., number of successfully solved tasks required for a certain grade), the computer will always present the same evaluation and grading results. The computer will not be influenced by personal attributes of the learner or other relevant persons. Computers also allow high transparency: learners can recall evaluation standards and personal progress at any point during the learning process using the evaluation components of educational software.

Another method of reducing envy comes from research on communicative responses to jealousy and from uncertainty reduction theory. Jealousy follows a loss or a threat to self-esteem or to the quality of a close (romantic) relationship. Uncertainty can be reduced through the use of communication and information-gathering techniques about social relationships and about taking or receiving different kinds of possessions (Guerrero & Andersen, 1998). When envy occurs, social relationships and conditions of possessions are uncertain, particularly the future of the relationships and the legal or social quality of possessions. On the basis of this conclusion, we formulate our next instructional strategy—*E3: Inspire a sense of authenticity and openness.* Within instructional technology, it would be easy to implement and present messages such as, "Be honest," or, "Be open," on the screen during the learning process. But it is doubtful whether such messages would have positive effects on the learners. Another probably more effective way would be to establish a "personal information board" on which students and teachers present messages and news about their family backgrounds, hobbies, school successes and failures, hopes and fears, and so on. Such an information board can be implemented as a Web page or as part of an electronic mailbox with restricted access. Before implementing and presenting such information, however, students and teachers should work together and discuss the degree of openness and authenticity discoverable within the contents of the personal information board.

According to Whiting's envy theory (as cited in Herkner, 1993), envious people identify themselves mainly with people who get more attention or acknowledgements than others. Envy generally appears when some people have more privileges than others. In instructional contexts, envy can be avoided when no students have more privileges than other students. This ideal informs our next instructional strategy—*E4: Avoid unequal distribution of privileges among students.* As with strategy E2, the computer is a good medium to install an objective way of distributing privileges among students. Computers do not react subjectively; rather they collect facts (e.g., achievement, learning time, etc.) and act accordingly. Within instructional technology, instructional strategies can be programmed based on rules about such privileges and

the granting of them—for example, if the percentage of successfully solved tasks is less than 50, then allow an additional 10 minutes for learning.

Anger: Concepts and Instructional Strategies

The literature contains many theoretical explanations of anger and aggression, and the treatment of anger and aggression is equally multifaceted (Boekaerts, 1993). The most wide spread cognitive behavior and social cognitive strategies conceptualize anger in general as consequences of reinforcement and punishment contingencies, of one's problem-solving capabilities, or of the development of interpersonal understanding. One important common assumption of all these approaches is that in instructional and other settings anger can and should be controlled so as not to spread and accumulate. This conclusion leads to our first strategy to reduce anger during instruction—*A1: Stimulate the control of anger.* Anger control when using instructional technology can be stimulated by, for example, an *anger button.* The anger button should always be available on screen, and students should be instructed to press it when they experience anger. After pressing the button, self-instructional substrategies for controlling anger, especially anger reminders and reducers, can be presented.

Anger and aggression are also modulated by higher-order cognitions, such as expectations, assessments of outcomes, or attributions. People who see the cause of problems as reflecting global or stable dimensions more likely engage in anger reactions than people who do not generalize from negative events to broader issues. People who are more flexible in their thinking and behavior experience fewer negative feelings (like anger) than people who are more rigid (e.g., Schmuck, 1996). This finding leads us to deduce the next instructional strategy—*A2: Show flexible views of things.* In instructional technology contexts, flexible views can generally be induced when information is linked with other information in information networks, as it is usually given in hypertexts or in the Web. Students go different ways through information networks, so the information in a node is seen differently according to the earlier visited nodes. For example, the information in a node concerning silicon is different for people who have visited earlier nodes concerning biology (where silicon is an important trace element) than for people who have visited earlier nodes concerning geology (where silicon is a mineral-building compound). In this way, the same concept can be viewed in different contexts, which should make students' thinking more flexible.

Anger cannot be avoided even if it is controlled or reduced by flexible thinking. Sometimes anger has to be expressed, which can lead to positive effects. For example, anger expression can help extricate one from accumulated negative emotions. Communications energized by anger can help underscore one's beliefs or attitudes making them hard to miss. Tangney et al. (1996) described two main ways of expressing anger: *destructive* and *constructive*. It is the constructive way that helps people deal successfully with an event that provokes a negative emotional response; the destructive way, however, leads to hostility and maladjustment. This conclusion led us to formulate another instructional strategy—*A3: Allow anger to be expressed constructively.* Averill (1993) presented major rules regarding the constructive expression of anger that can be used in instructional settings.

1. Students have the right to show anger in the case of intentional wrongdoing or unintended mistakes, particularly if wrongdoing or mistakes can be corrected.
2. Students should direct anger at persons or objects that are responsible for their anger and should not displace anger to innocent third parties.
3. The goal of the anger reaction should be to correct the situation, restore fairness, prevent the instigation from happening again, and avoid intimidating others.
4. The reaction to anger should be in proportion to the instigation.
5. The reaction to anger should closely follow the provoking event.
6. The expression of anger should entail resolution and follow-through when necessary.

Constructive anger coping within instructional technology contexts means that students are instructed by computers to express their anger in a more or less standardized instructional procedure. This procedure could be based on the rules from Averill (1993), and it should help students think explicitly about their anger, its releasing factors, and its consequences. The triggering of this procedure can be linked to the previously mentioned anger button. The anger button could lead students to a list of options, including one called, for example, Anger Help, which could lead users through an instructional procedure. Of course, this procedure cannot replace human interaction in teaching successful anger coping skills, but it can inject a rational element into a highly emotional situation.

As part of a general theory of anger and emotional aggression, Berkowitz (1993) describes another important anger-provoking aspect: behaviors consistent with prototypes of angry responses are themselves important in eliciting angry responses. These prototypical responses represent different forms of violence and should be avoided as a means to reduce anger. Such forms of violence can often be found in daily instruction, but should not be shown and accepted by students and teachers—*A4: Do not show or accept any form of violence.* In the context of instructional technology, any form of violence in animations, video sequences, written or spoken texts, and other multimedia elements should be avoided. Many educational software products follow this principle, but outside school, students are familiar with computer games that contain many forms of violence. Violence often means highly motivating "action" to students; therefore, nonviolent teaching software might be boring for students. To prevent this phenomenon, instructional technology should motivate students without violence. As mentioned previously, Keller and Suzuki (1988) elaborated many instructional strategies to engage students in action without elements of violence (e.g., the use of novel, surprising, incongruous, or uncertain events in instruction).

Sympathy: Concepts and Instructional Strategies

Fear, envy, and anger represent—according to the FEASP approach—important negative feelings that should be avoided or reduced during instruction. Sympathy is a positive feeling concerning the liking and the support of other people and should be increased during instruction. A first step to achieve higher overall sympathy in [the] classroom is *S1: Intensify relationships.* New information technologies offer many tools for simplifying communication and therefore for intensifying human relationships within instructional technology contexts. Communication tools can be asynchronous or synchronous. Asynchronous tools include e-mail, listservs, and newsgroups. Synchronous tools include chat, Internet Relay Chat (IRC), multiuser dungeons or domains (MUDs), and Internet phone. Communication tools should be available for all students in school and at home.

Intensifying relationships between students and teachers represents a first step for all partners to become more familiar with each other. A second necessary step in establishing sympathy is to increase *empathy.* Empathy is the matching of emotional states, and it is highly correlated with the feeling of sympathy and offering support to others. In respect to empathy, Barbee and Cunningham (1995) presented a comprehensive theory of sensitive interaction systems. Barbee and Cunningham's work informs our next instructional strategy—*S2: Install sensitive interactions.* First, students and teachers should show *direct* support-seeking behavior instead of *indirect* support-seeking behavior. Second, students and teachers should show emotional adaptive reactions. Third, sympathy will arise most probably under certain context conditions that should be dealt with and clarified during instruction.

- The problem is viewed as an important crisis.
- The cause of the problem is externally given.

- The problem does not make the supporter feel personally threatened.
- The problem seems to have a controllable solution.

Finally, sympathy will increase when attachment between students and teachers is secure. *Secure* means that interacting persons have a positive view of oneself and others. Insecure attachments (having a negative view of oneself and of others) should be avoided. Computers are very limited in their sensitiveness in interaction with humans (MIT Media Lab, Affective Computing Research Group, 1999). But instructional technology can be used to instruct students how to interact sensitively according to the approach of Barbee and Cunningham. A self-directed hypermedia program *based on methods of* teaching knowledge about emotions can fulfill this task. For example, Pajama Sam (1999, for reducing fear of darkness) or The Lie (1999, for inspiring openness and avoiding not telling the truth) are commercially available programs in this field that help teach emotional knowledge (see Shapiro, 1997).

After student interactions have become sensitive, a further step must be taken to strengthen sympathy—*S3: Establish cooperative learning structures*—which were found to make students feel sympathy and care about one another regardless of individual differences (Marr, 1997). Within instructional technology contexts, collaborative learning tools can be used to establish cooperative learning structures. Software tools, such as groupware or integrated classroom management tools, or general functionalities of computers, such as application sharing, file exchange, and whiteboards, enable knowledge and resources to be shared, of knowledge and resources promoting active and interactive learning from multiple perspectives. With so-called workflow management systems, the planning of common work is organized. Low-level authoring tools allow students to put their work in workspaces where other students can use and extend it (Pea, 1994). Also, the Web is used for many different group activities, such as team competitions, panel discussions, symposia, debates, team concept webs, picture making exercises, or buzz groups.

The final step in getting sympathy into instruction is implementing peer helping programs. Within such programs, students are not only cooperating with each other, but are helpers throughout the school in a role of caring support for peers—*S4: Implement peer helping programs.* Peer helping programs turn schools into caring communities in which sympathy is a central part. Harasim (1993) pointed out that computer networks form social spaces and virtual communities if their technical capabilities are used in a purposive manner based on a desire or need to solve a social problem. Grant and Grobman (1998), in their Internet handbook for social workers, present social support structures available on the Web, including social support institutions, social funding possibilities, self-help associations, online individual and group counseling, connecting different social offers to social packages, giving legal and other advice in social questions, and connecting people with similar disabilities.

Pleasure: Concepts and Instructional Strategies

One of the most desirable emotions is pleasure. Closely related to the concept of pleasure is *well-being,* a global moderate feeling of pleasantness in one's life over time. Thus, to enhance pleasure, *P1: Enhance well-being.* Hosen (1990) presented several substrategies that may promote subjective well-being during instruction. Computers are able to engage people in intrinsically satisfying activities (e.g., playing games or programming software), to perform learning outcome averaging, or to increase skills. In this way, computers are a good medium to enhance well-being in a broad sense. When interacting with computers, a user-friendly environment facilitates well-being. Such an environment offers hardware, software, connection speed, user settings, and so on in a way that allows learners to easily and efficiently use the learning system. The environment is based on certain interface-design principles, such as providing structural cues, clearly identifying selectable areas, indicating selections and progress made, offering help systems, keeping pages short, and labeling links appropriately.

Pleasure also comes from having freedom and control over important aspects of a situation. For example, reading a novel is a pleasant activity because it gives the reader the impression that he or she can freely wander in a fantasy land. Students also like learning within Web-based environments because they can freely explore information bases, discover relationships for themselves, or transform and organize information in ways compatible with their own needs. This conclusion leads to our next instructional strategy—*P2: Establish open learning opportunities.* Open learning in respect to instructional technology means establishing *virtual classrooms* based on *distance learning* (Astleitner & Sindler, 1999). Distance learning takes place when (1) teacher and students are separated by physical distance and (2) technology, sometimes in combination with face-to-face communication, is used to bridge the gap. If new information technologies, such as the Web, e-mail, and videoconferencing, are applied, then virtual classrooms emerge. Within virtual classrooms, content, course planning, and course organization are presented and performance evaluations are completed using Web pages. Feedback is delivered by e-mail. Teachers are content facilitators more than content providers. And collaborations are based on synchronous and asynchronous interactions.

People who feel pleasure are often exhilarated. The most reliable elicitor of exhilaration is humor—*P3: Use humor.* Software can include humorous elements

(Shapiro, 1997). For example, some programs allow students to use certain design elements (e.g., scenes, persons, and objects) to build their own funny worlds. With other programs, students are able to generate comic books that include daily life scenes from a humorous point of view. Students can, for example, select any of a dozen heroes and implement different speaking and thinking balloons. Also, programs give students the opportunity to build cartoons without any special assistance. Facial expressions, gestures, or language can, for example, be selected for depicting different characters and their moods. Many such products can easily be implemented using instructional technology such that humorous elements become an integral part of any educational context.

One of the most pleasant activities in human life is play. To enhance pleasure during instruction—*P4: Install play-like activities.* Many instructional computer games include play-like activities (Kinikoglu & Yadav, 1995). There are hundreds of simulations, microworlds, role-plays, and adventure games on the market that allow a teacher to find suitable games for different subject areas or teaching goals. Well-designed instructional computer games are balanced: they affect pleasure with motivational design features, and they enhance learning with cognitive design features.

CONCLUSIONS AND DISCUSSIONS

Within the FEASP approach of emotional design, 20 general instructional strategies for making instructional technology emotionally sound are proposed (see Figure 1). The framework has—in addition to its prescriptive character for practical use—heuristic and predictive functions. It can help instructional designers and teachers identify emotional problems during the use of instructional technology. And it can guide empirical research and practitioners in diagnosing and treating educational defects in practice. Of course, the proposed strategies do not work with students who suffer from severe emotional problems such as depression, eating disorders, drug abuse, and hyperactivity. In these cases, school psychologists, social workers, or other mental health personnel must help teachers and parents.

Despite many open questions concerning indication, efficiency, usability, and other characteristics, the framework presented in this article should motivate instructional technology designers to consider emotional processes on a larger scale. Within the FEASP approach, many concepts, microtheories, and empirical results of emotional research were reviewed, categorized, and transformed for the practical field of instructional technology. Of course, by such a transformation some specific information from research is lost, but much information for practice may be gained.

Contributors

Hermann Astleitner is an associate professor of education and specializes in research on educational technology and emotional education. Detlev Leutner is a professor of instructional psychology with emphasis on research methods, psychological assessment, and instructional systems design. (Address: Hermann Astleitner, Institut für Erziehungswissenschaft, Universität Salzburg, Akademiestrasse 26, A–5020 Salzburg, Austria, Hermann.Astleitner@sbg.ac.at.)

References

Astleitner, H., & Sindler, A. (1999). *Pädagogische grundlagen virtueller ausbildung* [Pedagogical foundation of virtual education]. Wien, Austria: Universitätsverlag.

Astleitner, H. (2000). Designing emotionally sound instruction: The FEASP approach. *Instructional Science, 28,* 169–198.

Averill, J. R. (1993). Illusions of anger. In R. B. Felson & J. T. Tedeschi (Eds.), *Aggression and violence. Social interactionist perspectives* (pp. 171–193). Washington, DC: American Psychological Association.

Barbee, A. P. & Cunningham, M. R. (1995). An experimental approach to social support communications. Interactive coping in close relationships. *Communication Yearbook, 18,* 381–413.

Berkowtitz, L. (1993). Towards a general theory of anger and emotional aggression. Implications of the cognitive-neoassociationistic perspective for the analysis of anger and other emotions. In R. W. Wyer & T. K. Srull (Eds.), *Perspectives on anger and emotion* (vol. 6, pp. 1–46). Hillsdale, NJ: Erlbaum.

Boekaerts, M. (1993). Anger in relation to school learning. *Learning and Instruction, 3,* 269–280.

Földy, R., & Ringel, E. (1993). *Machen uns die medien krank? Depression durch überinformation* [Do the media make us feel ill? Depression from over-information]. München, Germany: Universitas.

Grant, G. B., & Grobman, L. M. (1998). *The social worker's internet handbook.* Harrisburg, PA: White Hat Communications.

Guerrero, L. K. & Andersen, P.A. (1998). Jealousy experience and expression in romantic relationships. In P.A. Andersen & L. K. Guerrero (Eds.), *Handbook of communication and emotion* (pp. 155–188). San Diego, CA: Academic Press.

Hammer, S. E. (1996). The effects of guided imagery through music on state and trait anxiety. *Journal of Music Therapy, 33,* 47–70.

Hannafin, M. J. & Peck, K. L. (1988). *The design, development, and evaluation of instructional software.* New York: MacMillan.

Harasim, L. M. (1993). Networlds. Networks as a social space. In L. M. Harasim (Ed.)., *Global networks. Computers and international communication* (pp. 15–34). Cambridge, MA: MIT Press.

Herkner, W. (1993). *Sozialpsychologie* [Social psychology]. Bern, Switzerland: Hans Huber.

Hosen, R. (1990). Strategies for enhancing psychological well-being. *Psychology: A Journal of Human Behavior, 27,* 20–29.

Jonassen, D. H. (Ed.). (1996a). *Handbook of research for educational communications and technology.* New York: Macmillan.

Jonassen, D. H. (1996b). *Computers in the classroom. Mindtools for critical thinking.* Englewood Cliffs: Prentice-Hall.

Keller, J. M., & Suzuki, K. (1988). Use of the ARCS motivation model in courseware design. In D. H. Jonassen (Ed.), *Instructional designs for microcomputer courseware* (pp. 401–434). Hillsdale, NJ: Erlbaum.

Kinikoglu, Y. T. & Yadav, S. B. (1995, August). *Determination of the features of instructional computer games.* Paper presented at the meeting of the American Association for Information Systems, Pittsburgh, PA.

Leutner, D. (1992). Das Testlängendilemma in der lernprozeß–begleitenden Wissensdiagnostik [The test-length dilemma of assessing knowledge during learning]. *Zeitschrift für Pädagogische Psychologie* [Journal of Educational Psychology], *6,* 233–238.

The lie [Computer software]. (1995). Torrance, CA: Davidson & Associates Inc.

Liebowitz, J. (Ed.). (1999). *Knowledge management handbook.* Boca Raton, FL: CRC Press.

Marr, M. B. (1997). Cooperative learning. A brief review. *Reading & Writing Quarterly: Overcoming Learning Difficulties, 13(1),* 7–20.

Massachusetts Institute of Technology Media Lab, Affective Computing Research Group. (1999). *Affective computing.* [Online document]. Cambridge, MA: Author. Available: www.media.mit.edu/affect.

McCormack, C., & Jones, D. (1998). *Building a Web-based education system.* New York: Wiley.

Pajama Sam [Computer software]. (1999). Woodinville, MA: Humongous Entertainment.

Parrot, W. G. (1991). The emotional experiences of envy and jealousy. In P. Salovey (Ed.), *The psychology of jealousy and envy* (pp. 3–30). New York: Guilford.

Pea, R. D. (1994). Seeing what we build together. Distributed multimedia learning environments for transformative communications. *The Journal of the Learning Sciences, 3,* 285–299.

Pfeiffer, R. (1988). Artificial intelligence models of emotion. In V. Hamilton, G. H. Bower, & N. H. Frijda (Eds.), *Cognitive perspectives on emotion and motivation* (pp. 287–320). Amsterdam: Kluwer.

Reigeluth, C. M. (1997). Instructional theory, practitioner needs, and new directions. Some reflections. *Educational Technology, 37,* 42–47.

Rheinberg, F., & Krug, S. (1993). *Motivationsförderung im schulalltag* [Enhancing motivation in daily school]. Göttingen, Germany: Hogrefe.

Schmuck, P. (1996). *Die flexibilität menschlichen verhaltens* [The flexibility of human behavior]. Frankfurt/M., Germany: Lang.

Shapiro, L. E. (1997). *How to raise a child with a high EQ.* New York: Harper Collins.

Stone-McCown, K., & McCormick, A. H. (1999). Self-science: Emotional intelligence for children. In C. M. Reigeluth (Ed.), *Instructional-design theories and models. A new paradigm of instructional theory* (pp. 537–561). Mahwah, NJ: Erlbaum.

Strittmatter, P. (1993). *Schulangstreduktion* [Reduction of school-related fear]. Neuwied, Germany: Luchterhand.

Tangney, J. P., Barlow, D. H., Wagner, P. E., Marschall, D. E., Borenstein, J. K., Sanftner, J., Mohr, T., & Gramzow, R. (1996). Assessing individual differences in constructive versus destructive responses to anger across the lifespan. *Journal of Personality and Social Psychology, 70,* 780–796.

Tennyson, R. D., Schott, F., Seel, N. M., & Dijkstra, S. (Eds.). (1997). *Instructional design. International perspectives* (vol. 1). Mahwah, NJ: Erlbaum.

MULTIMEDIA
or Not to
MULTIMEDIA?

That Is the Question for Students with Learning Disabilities

Cheryl A. Wissick

J. Emmett Gardner

What kid or kid at heart would not be attracted to titles like these? *The Ecotourist Game, Ahupua'a Adventure,* and other intriguing programs are all *multimedia* learning materials (see box, "What Is Multimedia Instruction?"), and they are being used in many classrooms today. What do we know about the reliability and validity of such programs in the education of our children? Are they just attention-getting devices? Do they have any real educational purpose—and do they garner results in the form of student success—particularly for students with learning disabilities?

This article presents instructional factors that teachers should consider when selecting multimedia materials appropriate for students with learning disabilities. Here, we ex-

plore what we know about effective instruction for students with learning disabilities and relate this knowledge to multimedia design features. We also discuss specific programs and Web sites that use design features effectively to enhance student learning. Finally, we describe some problematic features in multimedia software packages and suggest strategies that make appropriate accommodations.

Multimedia Supports Effective Instructional Strategies

Ideally, instructional principles determine teachers' selection of methods or materials

Instructional multimedia can help with the following instructional principles: overlearning and automaticity, mastery learning, direct instruction, cooperative learning, mnemonics and memorization skills, reading comprehension, written composition, and study skills.

to use for instruction. In the context of computerized instruction, Vockell and Mihail (1993) have illustrated the importance of using instructional principles to shape teaching methods. These researchers described instructional principles that special educators frequently used and suggested guidelines and methodologies for aligning computer instruction with those principles.

For example, Vockell and Mihail (1993) examined the following instructional princi-

From *Teaching Exceptional Children,* March/April 2000, pp. 34-43. © 2000 by The Council for Exceptional Children. Reprinted by permission.

ples: overlearning and automaticity, mastery learning, direct instruction, cooperative learning, mnemonics and memorization skills, reading comprehension, written composition, and study skills. Each of these principles suggests specific instructional strategies that teachers often use effectively with students with learning disabilities (see also Deshler, Ellis, & Lenz, 1996; Mastropieri & Scruggs, 1994). In this article, we examine Vockell and Mihail's list of principles with one addition: "situated cognition." Table 1 summarizes these instructional principles and lists multimedia programs that employ each principle.

Instructional Principles and Multimedia Selection

When selecting a multimedia program, teachers should focus on an instructional principle and examine how a particular program implements that principle. For example, teachers often instruct students with learning disabilities on basic skills by developing automaticity.

Basic Skills and Automaticity

Multimedia programs can enable teachers to create a context for meaningful learning that includes basic skill development (Cognition and Technology Group at Vanderbilt, 1993). Multimedia technology incorporates auditory and visual instructions and feedback to the learner. Older computerized drill-and-practice programs provided students with opportunities for overlearning but frequently were nothing more than computerized worksheets or flash cards. Newer programs can be more interesting and effective when they feature voice-input and allow students opportunities to compare their oral answers with the answers of the computer.

Mastery Learning

The strategy of mastery learning promotes high levels of learning by all students. This strategy may be difficult to implement with students with learning disabilities in the general education classroom because of the diversity of learning styles and the different rate of skill acquisition. Traditional computer-based instruction can assist by providing students with academic difficulties opportunities for mastery through automaticity and overlearning and offering students who learn faster than the rest of the class chances to extend their study (Vockell & Mihail, 1993).

What is Multimedia Instruction?

The term *multimedia* has come to represent a computer-based environment that utilizes multiple media (e.g., graphics, motion video, text, and sound) to deliver instruction (Poole, 1997). The current proliferation of computer programs, CD-ROMs and Web-based activities that provide swift access to multimedia seems to offer unlimited possibilities for both teachers and students to experience novel, exciting, and creative learning environments. Special educators seeking to design curricula that incorporate technology-based learning activities for students with learning disabilities seem quick to attribute increased motivation and academic outcomes to software using multimedia aspects. Are these newfound opportunities and instantaneous access to multimedia beneficial to all students with learning disabilities?

Are We Doing It Right? Despite good intentions, teachers may be doing a disservice to students when they assume that the "bells and whistles" of multimedia applications are beneficial for all learners. Considering the diverse learner characteristics of students with learning disabilities, special education teachers may be making a serious mistake if they base software decisions principally on whether a program uses multimedia or not.

Although excellent multimedia activities are available for all areas of the curriculum, teachers are challenged to select materials that are both content related and accommodating of individual students needs. For example, what should a teacher do when research on learner control and computer-based learning suggests that less advanced learners profit from program control (Larsen, 1995). In contrast to these research findings, many multimedia programs and Web sites allow students total control. Educational software often uses video game features, such as auditory and visual embellishment, but this can be distracting and counterproductive to learning for some students (Okolo, 1993).

Let's Do Our Homework. Teachers of students with learning disabilities need to guard against choosing multimedia programs that may actually deflect learning, be overwhelming, or be frustrating to the less able learner. More important, when considering the features of multimedia, teachers need to base their choices on a solid theoretical framework for instruction (Larsen, 1995).

Higher-Order Thinking Skills

Multimedia programs can help students practice basic facts and then transfer the focus from basic skills to the development of higher-order thinking skills. The development of these more complex skills is especially important for students with learning disabilities. To have sufficient time to pursue higher-order thinking skills, teachers frequently spend time training their students with learning disabilities mnemonic strategies and memorization skills. Multimedia may offer memorable metaphors and visual models for building context clues and memory skills.

Direct Instruction

Direct instruction incorporates rapid pacing, frequent feedback, active student engagement, explicit examples, and a cumulative review of skills (Engelmann & Carnine, 1982). Multimedia can give teachers tools for demonstrating many explicit examples and can provide students numerous possibilities for interaction. Multimedia programs that incorporate direct instruction strategies give teachers ways to enhance whole-class instruction. Although research supports the use of direct instruction for students with learn-

ing disabilities, other researchers have criticized this approach as focusing too narrowly on discrete skills without promoting global skills for problem-solving and reasoning (Cognition and Technology Group at Vanderbilt, 1991).

Problem-Solving Skills

Multimedia can provide teachers with tools to go beyond direct instruction to provide generative learning environments in which students have a chance for an apprenticeship and learn how to solve the type of multistep problems that occur in real life. Multimedia can embed basic skill practice within realistic situations, enabling teachers to improve their instruction by giving students with learning disabilities functional life skills.

Cooperative Learning Groups

Teachers establish cooperative groups as an instructional strategy to help students develop two other life skills: social learning and group problem-solving. Many multimedia programs foster cooperative learning. Tom Snyder Productions develops multimedia programs that provide each student or

Table 1. Multimedia Programs and Web Site That Complement Instructional Principles

Instructional Principles	Implementation with Multimedia	
	Multimedia Context	**Programs and Web Sites**
Automaticity and Overlearning	Provides a context for application of basic facts, anchors instruction in visual context, uses auditory feedback.	Spell It Deluxe, Davidson (Grades 1–5) Simon Sounds it Out, Don Johnston (Grades K–4) Simon Spells, Don Johnston (Grades K–4) Supersonic Phonics, Curriculum Associates (Grades 1–12) Wild World of Words Challenge, Web Page
Mastery Learning	Arranges instruction so that all students learn objectives to mastery	Net Frog: Web Page (high school) WebQuests, Matrix of Examples, Web Page
Mnemonics	Uses visual and auditory stimuli to assist the memorization and retention of important information and skills.	Curious Creatures, Curriculum Associates (Grades 2–8) BioSci, Videodiscovery (Grades 3–12) A World Alive, St. Louis Zoo (all grades) Inspiration, Inspiration Software (Grades 3–12)
Direct Instruction	Structures educational environment with specific objectives, rapid pacing, frequent feedback, and opportunities to answer.	Mastering Series Systems Impact (Grades 5–12) Windows on Science, Optical Data (Grades 1–8) Windows on Math, Optical Data (Grades 1–8) Earobics, Cognitive Concepts (Grades K–6)
Situated Cognition	Provides situations from which students can generate their own questions within authentic situations.	Adventures of Jasper Woodbury, Optical Data (Grades 4–8) Science Sleuths, Videodiscovery (Grades 3–9) The Real Scoop on Tobacco, WebQuest
Cooperative Learning	Provides students opportunities to work together to solve problems and assist one another in learning new information.	Decisions, Decisions, Tom Snyder (Grades 5–10) Choices, Choices, Tom Snyder (Grades K–6) Cultural Debates, Tom Snyder (Grades 6–12) Great Solar System and Ocean Rescue (Grades 5–8)
Writing Instruction	Incorporates visual and auditory prompts to assist with creating writing.	Write OutLoud & Co.: Writer, Don Johnston (Grades K–12) Imagination Express, Edmark (Grades 2–8) Student Writing Center, Learning Company (Grades 5–12) Storybook Weaver, Learning Company (Grades 1–6) Postcards, Curriculum Associates (Grades 5–8) The Read to Write Project, Web Page
Reading Comprehension	Presents text with visual and auditory clues to enhance comprehension.	Living Books, Broderbund (Grades K–3) Little Planet, Little Planet Software (Grades K–3) Start-to-Finish Books, Don Johnston (Grades 5–8) Rainbow, Curriculum Associates (Grades 1–3) Online story, Web Page
Study Skills	Encourages student research, provides models for management and searching of data.	TrackStar, Web Page Yahooligans, Web Directory & Search Engine The Traveling Tutor from the Alphabet Superhighway, Web Inspiration, Inspiration Software (Grades 3–12) My First Amazing Incredible Dictionary, DK (Grades K–4) Multimedia Encyclopedias

Multimedia technology incorporates auditory and visual instructions and feedback to the learner.

groups of students with a role and specific tasks to accomplish in that role. In contrast, the *Adventures of Jasper Woodbury* Series creates a context for cooperative learning by allowing students to define their own subproblems and create their own roles in the solution (Cognition and Technology Group at Vanderbilt, 1993). The concept of a WebQuest, developed by Bernie Dodge (1995), allows students opportunities for both situated cognition and cooperative learning using Web resources. Exemplary WebQuests provide students contexts and roles through which they explore certain situations using real sources on the Web. The WebQuest matrix of examples provides teachers with activities for a variety of content area and a range of grade levels (http://edweb.sdsu.edu/webquest/webquest. html).

Language Arts Skills

Teachers can foster reading comprehension, written composition, and study skills in cooperative groups and with a variety of programs. Teachers can provide students with an annotated hierarchy of instructions for research on the Web, thereby creating a scaffold for learning. Teachers can also develop Instructional tracks or scaffolds using Track-Star (http://scrtec.org/track). TrackStar is a free, online resource that allows one to create Web-based lessons without knowing how to use HTML, the programming language behind Web pages. Filamentality (http://www.kn.pacbell.com/wired/fil), another free, online resource, provides teachers with tools to create their own WebQuests or guided treasure hunts.

Other Content Areas

Teachers should choose multimedia programs or Web sites that focus on specific content areas and offer features such as the ability to view and review video, record and hear speech, and view visually annotated definitions of vocabulary. Developments in assistive technology permit students to read any text from a Web page. Word-prediction programs assist students by suggesting possible words that might come next in their writing. All these special features allow stu-

dents with learning disabilities to work collaboratively or independently and participate in meaningful dialogue with other students in their class.

After selecting multimedia programs that implement particular instructional techniques, teachers must carefully evaluate the specific design characteristics of those programs. Multimedia can offer effective alternatives for students with learning disabilities to acquire content knowledge, as long as teachers recognize that some instructional design techniques may assist some learners and frustrate or confuse others.

Accommodation Strategies When Using Multimedia

In a review of research on learning with media, Kozma (1991) reported that capabilities of a particular medium interact with the ways learners process information; therefore creating different learning outcomes. For example, some multimedia programs use hypertext and links that may actually intensify some of the problems encountered by students with learning disabilities. Despite the possible benefits hypertext and links offer in accessing help options or providing guides for navigation, the fact that students have to click through multiple links/levels searching for desired information may be cognitively confusing and frustrating. Students will not take advantage of help options or use navigation guides if they require more personal processing energy than they can evoke. Some students may ignore instructional feedback if obtaining that feedback takes too much time. Others may focus on fancy feedback for their personal amusement only and may not learn through it.

Another example illustrating how learners process information relative to types of instructional software can be found in recommendations made by Kenworthy (1993). Kenworthy suggested that when using software with poor readers, teachers should evaluate new and updated programs to ensure that they include appropriate audio and visual aids, careful use of text, and simple computer navigation. Teachers should also pay close attention to the use of graphics in both still-photo and motion video and to the navigation used in the programs. Similarly, Larsen (1995) mentioned learner control, motivation, feedback type, graphics, and screen designs as theoretical considerations in the selection of quality-designed technology. When making instructional decisions for using multimedia with students with learning disabilities, simply knowing how multimedia implements effective instructional strategies is not sufficient.

Multimedia software usually has multiple features, some of which may be favorable and others that could be detrimental to stu-

WebQuest allows students opportunities for both situated cognition and cooperative learning using Web resources.

dent learning. Table 2 lists several of the common features of multimedia, notes difficulties that students with learning disabilities might encounter with each feature, and suggests ideas for mediating the problems. The following discussion focuses on three factors often associated with multimedia software that may be problematic for students with learning disabilities, proposing accommodation strategies to help compensate for (a) factors of learner control and feedback, (b) the presentation of graphics and navigation options, and (c) encouragement of active involvement. For easy reference, Tables 3 and 4, respectively, list the Web sites and software programs cited in this section.

Learner Control and Feedback

Learner control represents the learner's ability to select, regulate, or control certain aspects of the learning experience. Typical software features permit learners to progress through instruction at their own pace, to set difficulty levels, to access help menus or acquire feedback when desired, and to enable or disable sounds and graphics. The amount of learner control actually used depends on student ability and the goals of the assignment (Locatis, Letourneau, & Banvard, 1990).

Research has indicated that students with more prior knowledge and higher ability can achieve higher scores and work faster with programs allowing learner control than can students with lower ability and less prior knowledge (Gay, 1986; Morrison, Ross, & Baldwin, 1992). McGrath's (1992) work with college students indicated that high-ability students took more time but viewed fewer screens and had fewer misconceptions than did low-ability students. The lower-ability students acted confused and viewed more screens without purpose, indicating that they could not make choices regarding their control. Apparently, the higher-ability students spent time making thoughtful decisions regarding the screens they viewed and gaining important information from those screens. Morrison et al., studying children in fourth and fifth grade, also found that students with higher ability could use learner-control options better than lower-ability students. In addition, they found that students could

TrackStar is a free, online resource that allows one to create Web-based lessons without knowing how to use HTML.

choose the context for learning without affecting their achievement.

Although none of the preceding studies was conducted with students with learning disabilities, the results provide insights for structuring multimedia environments. Students without prior knowledge, such as students with learning disabilities, will need to be guided by the teacher or the multimedia program or be given only small amounts of learner control until they reach a level of proficiency at which they can access the learner-control options (Hooper & Hannafin, 1988a; Kinzie, Sullivan & Berdel, 1988). Teachers can use TrackStar (http://scrtec.org/track) to guide learning by providing specific directions for researching individual Web pages.

Within programs, feedback is used to provide reinforcement or information conducive to learning (Flemming, 1987). Even students who are familiar with the content and select to use learner control should be provided guidance and appropriate feedback (Hooper & Hannafin, 1988b). Consider a multimedia educational game designed to teach through automaticity. Students with learning disabilities may be distracted by bonus feedback that provides no academic information, or they may be bored with the recurrence of the same feedback. Feedback can be as simple as giving students the results or as complicated as the process for arriving at the correct answer. The Watershed Game (http://www1.umn.edu/bellmuse/mnideals/watershed/watershed.html) is a good example of online instruction that provides academic feedback for each answer, giving students additional information about the content.

Navigation, Nonlinear Access, and Exploration

We might define the nonlinear nature of multimedia as the ability to move from any place within a document without having to go in a linear manner page by page or in a particular direction as directed by the author. This design feature of nonlinearity has the potential to increase learning by providing numerous choices for exploration and mak-

ing the learner an active participant. The ability to point and click icons reduces keyboarding demands and frees the learner to interact with the program and access information in a nonlinear fashion—in a manner that is consistent with human learning and memory (Dede, 1987). Nonlinear features allow students to move between topics according to their interests, not according to a developer's predetermined order. Using Microsoft Dangerous Creatures (1994) or Oceans (1995), students can access photographs, text, and movies on animals of their choice. They can move around the program using selected guides, locating animals alphabetically, and choosing animals by species or geographical region. This open arrangement of multimedia and hypermedia environments can create problems with some learners. Learners can get lost during exploration and are unaware of their exact position in the learning environment (Mory, 1996). Therefore, for some students with learning disabilities, the benefits of this freedom may also have some navigational costs. For example, Hasselbring (1992) found that students who are less advanced in text comprehension did not explore as much as their more advanced counterparts. If teachers can provide students with learning disabilities structured instructional cues within the multimedia environment and select programs that have aural feedback for text, then the students have the possibility to explore successfully.

Word-prediction programs assist students by suggesting possible words that might come next in their writing.

Multimedia programs incorporate different formats to assist learners in navigating the links or connections within the program. Special icons and metaphors, such as highways, globes, books, and planets, provide references for locating information in the program. The Dinosaur Exhibit from Hawaii (http://www.hcc.hawaii.edu/hccinfo/dinos/dinos.2.html) features clear navigation buttons at the bottom of each Web page.

Salomon (1988) suggested that, when students explore and move or link from one idea to another, they are prompted to think beyond the content to the way the specific ideas are connected. Unfortunately, students with learning disabilities frequently lack the ability to see patterns and form relationships

between ideas. Teachers need to foster students' ability to see patterns in multimedia programs and Web programs.

McLellan (1992) encouraged the use of the story format in multimedia programs to help reduce the cognitive load in creating the links and problems with navigating. The story format, McLellan suggested, would be familiar to students and offer opportunities to explore, make predictions, and problem-solve. Multimedia programs that feature story format include: *Adventures of Jasper Woodbury* (1992), *Living Books,* (1991–1996), *Let's Go Read* (1997), *Science Sleuths* (1995), and the *Rainforest Research* (1996). Web sites with story formats support a variety of content areas: *Ahupua'a Adventure* (http://tqju-nior. advanced.org/3502/), *Survive, a Tiger Adventure* (http://www.5tigers.org/ habitats/al.htm), *The Ecotourism Game* (http://www.eduweb.com/ecotourism/eco1.html), *The Real Scoop on Tobacco* (http://www.itdc.sbcss.k12.ca.us/curriculum/tobacco.html), and *A. Pintura: Art Detective* (http://www.eduweb.com/pintura/index.html).

Encouragement of Active Involvement

Successful learning environments have active, attentive, and involved students (Ormrod, 1995, Stipek, 1998). Sometimes people assume that because multimedia environments contain enticing multiple media, students in those environments will be actively involved in the learning process. That is not necessarily the case. Multimedia instruction for students with learning disabilities must take into account many student learning characteristics. For example, students with learning disabilities, in addition to being deficient in content knowledge, typically function as field dependent or passive learners.

Burwell (1991) found that students who were field dependent or who tended to accept information at face value benefited more from multimedia instruction than did students who were field independent. Apparently the multimedia programs in Burwell's study did not intimidate the field-dependent students, but rather fostered a spirit of exploration. This is one example of the suggestion that multimedia features seem conducive to the learning styles of students with learning disabilities.

Some students with learning disabilities, however, are passive learners. In a study with active and passive learners, Lee and Lehman (1993) reported that active learners achieved better, spent more time on task, and demonstrated a higher frequency of selecting elaborated instruction. In contrast, passive learners needed structured instructional cues to outperform their counterparts.

In multimedia software, students with learning disabilities need programs that are

---

Table 2. Intervention/Accommodation Ideas Matched to Multimedia Instructional Features

Features of Multimedia	Potential Challenges of Students with Learning Disabilities	Intervention/Accommodation Ideas
Models the structure of human learning	Students have memory and attention difficulties, learning patterns are not consistent	Provide advance organizers and activate prior knowledge.
Increases learner control	Students typically do not take advantage of guides or help features provided under learner control.	Choose programs that have guided tours before allowing learner control. Review options for assistance and encourage use of those help features.
Encourages exploration	Students have problems with navigation. They make unnecessary moves without gaining additional information or remembering where they are.	Provide students with lesson objectives before using program. Provide the context for exploration or allow students to state their own objectives for the exploration.
Fosters the creation of individual relationships	Students do not remain focused to gain worthwhile information and do not discover important relationships.	Provide examples and not-examples of concepts using a variety of sources with and without the technology. Encourage students to review the video or source to check their ideas.
Encourages active involvement	Students are passive learners.	Seek out programs that are engaging and focus on student interests as well as the curriculum objectives. Provide instructional scaffolds to maintain involvement.
Provides numerous choices for navigation	Students use their cognitive processes to focus on the options for navigation instead of the content.	Provide concrete models for navigation that can be attached or placed near the computer. Challenge students to draw a map or diagram of the various paths in the program.
Uses icons and metaphors to aid navigation	Students are not able to understand the metaphors or think abstractly to relate metaphors to program navigation.	Review and discuss organization first, provide additional examples related to the navigation metaphor.
Allows for levels of different prior knowledge	Students have gaps in prior knowledge.	Use as independent activity only after direct teaching.
Enables users to see a subtask as part of the whole	Students have problems forming relationships and seeing patterns.	Provide closure activities to discuss patterns and relationships noticed by the students. Have students keep journals of their observations.
Allows users to adapt materials to their own learning style.	Students do not have the metacognitive skills to be aware of what is needed to perform the task.	Present options to the student and have them suggest the best approach for their work. Have students review different aspects of the program and decide what assists their learning.

In multimedia, learners interact with the program and access information in a nonlinear fashion—in a manner that is consistent with human learning and memory.

engaging, that focus on student interests as well as the curriculum objectives, and that provide instructional scaffolds to maintain involvement. Multimedia instruction should be supplemented with activity sheets, study guides, journals, and other concrete examples from nontechnology sources to help the passive learner maintain involvement. When encouraging students to use the World Wide Web, teachers can facilitate engagement with tools or planning designs that help impose structure. Resources such as TrackStar or the design principles associated with WebQuests provide excellent tools that enable teachers to create online Web-based activities. These activities provide engaging multimedia

learning environments for students with learning disabilities.

Final Thoughts

Multimedia allows for different levels of prior knowledge, encourages exploration, enables students to see a subtask as part of the whole task, and permits students to adapt materials to their own learning styles (Stanton & Baber, 1992). These aspects of multimedia may, at times, be in direct conflict with some of the learning characteristics of students with learning disabilities. Students

Table 3. Sample Web Sites

Name of Web Sites	URL Address	Author/Publisher
A. Pintura: Art Detective	http://www.eduweb.com/pintura/index.html	Eduweb: Educational Web Adventures
Ahupua'a Adventure	http://tqjunior.advanced.org/3502/	ThinkQuest and ThinkQuest Junior Challenge
Dinosaur Exhibit from Hawaii	http://www.hcc.hawaii.edu/hccinfo/dinos/dinos.l.html	Honolulu Community College
Ecotourism Game	http://www.eduweb.com/ecotourism/eco1.html	Educational Web Adventures
Filamentality	http://www.kn.pacbell.com/wired/fil	Pacific Bell: Knowledge Network Explorer
Net Frog	http://curry.edschool.Virginia./EDU/go/frog/	University of Virginia, Curry School of Education, Kinzie & Strauss
Read to Write Project	http://www.rialto.k12.ca.us/curriculum/ReadtoWRite/ReadtoWite/Rial	Unified School District, California
Real Scoop on Tobacco	http://www.itdc.sbcss.k12.ca.us/curriculum/tobacco.html	Educational Media & Technology, San Bernardino County Schools, CA
Tiger Adventures: 5 Interactive Adventures	http://www.5tigers.org/adventur.htm	The Tiger Information Center
TrackStar	http://www.scrtec.org/track/	South Central Regional Technology Education Consortium (SCR*TEC)
Traveling Tutor	http://www.ash.udel.edu/ash/tutor/tutorframe.html	Alphabet Superhighway: A Knowledge Resource for Schools of the 21st Century
Watershed Game	http://www1.umn.edu/bellmuse/mnideals/watershed/watershed.html	Bell Live! at the University of Minnesota
WebQuests Matrix of Examples	http://edweb.sdsu.edu/webquest/matrix.html	Webquest San Diego State University, Concept developed by Bernie Dodge
Wild World of Words Challenge	http://www.ash.udel.edu/ash/challenge/challengeframe.html	Aphabet SuperHighway
Yahooligans	http://www.yahooligan.com	Yahoo! Inc.

with learning disabilities can have one or a combination of difficulties in the area of active learning; short- and long-memory; attention; following directions; cognitive processing; language; academic achievement in reading, math, spelling, and written language; and self-esteem (Mercer, 1991). Teachers need to consider the specific strengths and weaknesses of their students and how each student's learning abilities might interact with specific characteristics of multimedia.

Although multimedia can provide realistic situations using full-motion video and clear graphics, the teacher still needs to act as the mediator for instruction. Students without prior knowledge of concepts or prerequisite reading or math skills, as well as those who are passive learners, will need additional structure and scaffolds when accessing multimedia programs. Teachers *can* guide this learning and also provide or offer their students exciting multimedia contexts in which they can explore and learn without considerable hindrance.

References

Burwell, L. B. (1991). The interaction of learning styles with learner control treatments in an interactive videodisc lesson. *Educational Technology, 31*(3), 37–43.

Cognition and Technology Group at Vanderbilt University. (1991). Technology and the design of generative learning environments. *Educational Technology, 31*(5), 34–40.

Cognition and Technology Group at Vanderbilt University. (1993). Integrated media: Toward a theoretical framework for utilizing their potential. *Journal of Special Education Technology, 12,* 71–85.

Dede, C. (1987). Empowering environments, hypermedia, and microworlds. *The Computing Teacher, 15*(3), 15–25.

Deshler, D. D., Ellis, E. S., & Lenz, B. K. (1996). *Teaching adolescents with learning disabilities: Strategies and methods* (2nd ed.), Denver, CO: Love.*

Dodge, B. (1995). Some thoughts about WebQuests. The WebQuest Page [online]. Available: http://edweb.sdsu.edu/courses/edtec596/about_webquests.html (20 Dec 1999).

Engelmann, S., & Carnine, D. (1982). *Theory of instruction.* New York: Irvington.

Flemming, M. L. (1987). Displays and communication. In R. M. Gagne, (Ed.), *Instruction technology: Foundations.* Hillsdale, NJ: Lawrence Erlbaum.*

Gay, G. (1986). Interaction of learner control and prior understanding in computer-assisted video instruction. *Journal of Educational Psychology, 78,* 225–227.

Hasselbring, T. S. (1992, June). *Interactive multimedia applications for special education.* Paper presented at the National Educational Computer Conference, Dallas, TX.

Hooper, S., & Hannafin, M. J. (1988a). Cooperative CBI: The effects of heterogeneous versus homogenous grouping on the learning of progressively complex concepts. *Journal of Educational Computing Research, 4,* 413–424.

Hooper, S., & Hannafin, M. J. (1988b). Learning the ROPES of instructional design: Guidelines for emerging interactive technologies. *Journal of Educational Computing Research, 4,* 413–424.

Kenworthy, N. W. (1993). When Johnny can't read: Multimedia design strategies to accom-

Table 4. Software References

Publisher	Web Address	Software, CD-Roms, and Laserdiscs
Curriculum Associates North Billerica, MA	http://www.curriculumassociates.com/	Curious Creatures Postcards Rainbow SuperSonic Phonics
Don Johnston Volo, IL	http://www.donjohnston.com	Co: Writer Earobics by Cognitive Concepts Simon Sounds it Out by Hasselbring & Goin Simon Spells by Hasselbring & Goin Start-to-Finish Books Write OutLoud
Edmark Redmond, WA	http://www.edmark.com	Imagination Express Let's Go Read
Inspiration Software, Inc.	http://www.inspiration.com	Inspiration
Dorling Kindersley	http://www.dorlingkindersley.com	My First Amazing Incredible Dictionary
Knowledge Adventure Torrence, CA	http://www.knowledgeadventure.com/home/	Spell It Deluxe
Lawrence Erlbaum Mahwah, NJ	http://www.erlbaum.com/jasper.htm	Adventures of Jasper Woodbury by Cognition and Technology Group at Vanderbilt University
Learning Company Cambridge, MA	http://www.learningco.com/	Living Books by Broderbund Storybook Weaver
Broderbund Cambridge, MA	http://www.broderbund.com/	Stellaluna
Little Planet Publishing Nashville, TN	http://www.littleplanet.com/index2.htm	Little Planet Series
Microsoft Corporation Redmond, WA	http://www.microsoft.com/catalog/	Dangerous Creatures Oceans
Optical Data School Media Atlanta, GA	http://www.opticaldata.com/main.html	Windows on Science Windows on Math
Systems Impact, Inc. Washington, DC	http://www.systemsimpact.com/	Mastering Series
Tom Snyder Watertown, MA	http://www.tomsnyder.com/	Choices, Choices Decisions, Decisions The Great Ocean Rescue The Great Solar System Rescue The Rainforest Researchers
Videodiscovery Seattle, WA	http://www.videodiscovery.com/	BioSci Science Sleuths
Voyager Seattle, WA	http://www.voyager.learntech.com/	A World Alive

modate poor readers. *Journal of Instructional Delivery Systems, 7,* 27–30.

Kinzie, M. B., Sullivan, H. J., & Berdel, R. L. (1988). Learner control and achievement in science computer-assisted instruction. *Journal of Educational Psychology, 80,* 299–303.

Kozma, R. B. (1991). Learning with media. *Review of Educational Research, 61,* 179–211.

Larsen, S. (1995). What is "quality" in the use of technology for children with learning disabili-

ties? *Learning Disability Quarterly, 18*(2), 118–130.

Lee, Y. B., & Lehman, J. D. (1993). Instructional cueing in hypermedia: A study of active and passive learners. *Journal of Educational Multimedia and Hypermedia, 2,* 25–37.

Locatis, C., Letourneau, G., & Banvard, R. (1990). Hypermedia and instruction. *Educational Technology Research and Development, 37*(4), 65–77.

Mastropieri, M. A., & Scruggs, T. E. (1994). *Effective instruction for special education* (2nd ed.). Austin, TX: PRO:ED.*

McGrath, D. (1992). Hypertext, CAI, paper, or software control: Do learners benefit from choices? *Journal of Research on Computing in Education, 24,* 513–532.

McLellan, H. (1992). Hyper stories: Some guidelines for instructional designers. *Journal of Research on Computing in Education, 25,* 28–49.

Software and Publishers

Cannon, J. (1996) *Stellaluna* [Computer software]. Cambridge, MA: Broderbund and The Learning Company.

Cognition and Technology Group at Vanderbilt University (1992). *Adventures of Jasper Woodbury* [Computer software]. Mahwah, NJ: Lawrence Erlbaum.

BioSci [Computer software]. (1991). Seattle, WA: Videodiscovery.

Choices, Choices [Computer software]. (1988). Watertown, MA: Tom Snyder.

Co:Writer [Computer software]. (1992–1995). Volo, IL: Don Johnston.

Curious Creatures [Computer software]. (1996). North Billerica, MA: Curriculum Associates.

Dangerous Creatures [Computer software]. (1994). Redmond, WA: Microsoft Corporation.

Decisions, Decisions [Computer software]. (1992). Watertown, MA: Tom Synder.

Cognitive Concepts (1998). Earobics [Computer software]. Volo, IL: Don Johnston.

Great Ocean Rescue [Computer software]. (1992). Watertown, MA: Tom Snyder.

Great Solar System Rescue [Computer software]. (1991) Watertown, MA: Tom Snyder.

Imagination Express [Computer software]. (1996). Redmond, WA: Edmark Corporation.

Inspiration [Computer software]. (1997). Portland, OR: Inspiration Software, Inc.

Let's Go Read [Computer software]. (1997). Redmond, WA: Edmark Corporation.

Little Planet Series [Computer software]. (1996). Nashville, TN: Little Planet Publishing.

Living Books by Broderbund [Computer software]. (1991–1996). Cambridge, MA: Learning Company.

Mastering Series: Core Concepts in Math and Science. [Computer software]. (1986). Washington, DC: Systems Impact, Inc.

My First Amazing Incredible Dictionary [Computer software]. (1994). New York: Dorling Kindersley.

Oceans [Computer software]. (1995). Redmond, WA: Microsoft Corporation.

Postcards [Computer software]. (1995). North Billerica, MA: Curriculum Associates.

Rainbow [Computer software]. (1996). North Billerica, MA: Curriculum Associates.

Rainforest Researchers [Computer software]. (1996). Watertown, MA: Tom Snyder.

Science Sleuths [Computer software]. (1995). Seattle, WA: Videodiscovery.

Simon Sounds it Out [Computer software]. (1996). Volo, IL: Don Johnston.

Simon Spells [Computer software] (1997). Volo, IL: Don Johnston.

Spell It Deluxe [Computer software]. (1996). Torrence, CA: Knowledge Adventure.

Start-to-Finish Books [Computer software]. (1998). Volo, IL: Don Johnston.

Storybook Weaver [Computer software]. (1994). Cambridge, MA: Learning Company.

St. Louis Zoo (1992). A World Alive [Computer software]. Seattle, WA: Voyager, Co.

SuperSonic Phonics [Computer software]. (1995). North Billerica, MA: Curriculum Associates.

Windows on Science [Computer software]. (1989). Atlanta, GA: Optical Data School Media.

Windows on Math [Computer software]. (1997). Atlanta, GA: Optical Data School Media.

Write: OutLoud [Computer software]. (1999). Volo, IL: Don Johnston.

Mercer, C. D. (1991). *Students with learning disabilities.* New York: Macmillan.*

Morrison, G. R., Ross, S. M., & Baldwin, W. (1992). Learner control of context and instructional support in learning and elementary school mathematics. *Educational Technology Research and Development, 40,* 5–13.

Mory, E. H. (1996). Feedback research. In D. Johassen (Ed.), *Educational communications and technology* (pp. 919–956). New York: Macmillan.*

Okolo, C. M. (1993). Computers and individuals with mild disabilities. In J. Lindsey (Ed.), *Computers and exceptional individuals* (2nd ed.) (pp. 111–142). Austin, TX: PRO-ED.*

Ormrod, J. E. (1995). *Human learning.* Englewood Cliffs, NJ: Prentice-Hall.*

Poole, B. J. (1997). *Education for an information age.* New York: McGraw-Hill.*

Salomon, G. (1988). A1 in reverse: Computer tools that turn cognitive. *Journal of Educational Computing Research, 4,* 123–134.

Stanton, N., & Baber, C. (1992). An investigation of styles and strategies in self-directed learning. *Journal of Educational Multimedia and Hypermedia, 1,* 147–167.

Stipek, D. J. (1998). *Motivation to learn: From theory to practice* (3rd ed.). Boston: Allyn & Bacon.*

Vockell, E. L., & Mihail, T. (1993). Behind computerized instruction for students with exceptionalities. *TEACHING Exceptional Children, 25*(3), 38–43.

BooksNow

To order books marked by an asterisk (*), please call 24 hrs/365 days: 1–800–BOOKS–NOW (266–5766) or (801) 261–1187; or visit them on the Web at http://www.BooksNow.com/TeachingExceptional.htm. Use VISA, M/C, or AMEX or send check or money order + $4.95 S&H ($2.50 each add'l item) to: BooksNow, Inc., Suite 220, 348 East 6400 South, Salt Lake City, UT 84107.

Cheryl A. Wissick *CEC Chapter #165), Associate Professor, Programs in Special Education, College of Education, University of South Carolina, Columbia.* **J. Emmett Gardner,** *Associate Professor, Department of Educational Psychology, College of Education, The University of Oklahoma, Norman.*

Address correspondence to Cheryl A. Wissick, College of Education, 235 D Wardlaw, University of South Carolina, Columbia, SC 29212 (e-mail: cwissick@sc.edu).

TEACHING Exceptional Children, *Vol. 32, No. 4, pp. 34–43.*

Copyright 2000 CEC.

Multimedia Distance Education Interactions

Abstract

The nature of multimedia interactions in distance education discussions has been approached from many different perspectives. This article attempts to synthesize approaches based on distance education theory, cognition research and multimedia development. As a result a composite framework for discussion of multimedia and multimodal interactions in distance education context is proposed, which is based on interactions between the instructor, students and content. This framework should be useful for establishing clearer relationships among the existing interaction literature, for classifying interactions in distance education instructional design, and as a basis for further research.

Juhani E. Tuovinen, *Churchill, Victoria, Australia*

Introduction

The importance of multimedia and the value of interaction in distance education are commonly accepted. However, both of these concepts and the relationships between them are not always as clear, or as fully elaborated as we may assume. In this article these issues are examined on the basis of distance education theory and educational cognition theory. Four main interactions in distance education will be discussed, mainly based on Moore's conceptualization (Moore, 1989; Moore and Kearsley, 1996). Each of these interactions will then be elaborated in terms of the communications media involved and the educational implications of recent cognition research. The resulting interaction framework for distance education provides a useful basis for discussion of distance education technologies, techniques and instructional design. It helps to map out issues requiring further research, and should point out the relationships between existing research and its implications for distance education practice and theory.

The Moore distance education interaction model

We shall begin with the model of distance education interactions proposed by Moore (1989; with Kearsley, 1996). He distinguished three main types of interactions in distance education. They are *learner–content* interaction, *learner–instructor* interaction and *learner–learner* interaction. He argued that articulating and defining these interactions would help to dispel some of the misunderstandings that had arisen in the debates about educational media.

His three interactions model will be used in this paper, although Soo and Bonk (1998) added to this *learner–self* interaction, where they highlighted the importance of the learner's reflections on the content, the 'self-talk', in distance learning. This was treated as an essential aspect of the learner–content interaction process by Moore (1989). In this discussion we will treat the learner–self interaction as part of the learner–content interaction as Moore did in the original formulation of these ideas.

Learner–content interaction

Learner–content interaction is without doubt one of the most fundamental interactions in any educational situations. The intellectual engagement of the learners with material which changes their understanding, attitudes, etc. is basic to all educational processes (Moore, 1989).

One-way presentation technologies

We could classify the content presentation distance education media and communications technologies available for this engagement using the media/technology categories developed in a discussion of online learning (Tuovinen, 1999). The nine categories are text-only, graphics, video, virtual reality, sound, and combinations of sound with the other elements. Each of the categories in the sequence: 'text → graphics → video → virtual reality' can contain the previous means of communication in the sequence, e.g. in a picture (graphics) text may in-

From *Educational Media International*, March 2000, pp. 16-24. © 2000 by Routledge Publishing. Reprinted by permission.

corporated, and a video may convey still pictures and text. Thus as we progress to the media on the right we move to richer dimensions of educational communication and engagement.

The explicit separation of the sound category may appear trivial at first but recent cognitive research indicates it is very important to consider the added contribution sound makes to the educational engagement between a learner and the content. If we consider the structure of the human cognitive architecture it becomes clear that we have a very small capacity for conscious processing in our central thinking space, usually called the working memory (Baddeley, 1990; Logie, 1996; Miller, 1956). However, the working memory is thought to consist of separate processing spaces for visual and auditory information (Baddeley, 1992), which means we have a greater capacity for problem solving and learning if the information is presented in these two modes rather than in either mode alone (Mousavi, et al., 1995; Tindall-Ford et al., 1997). Thus we have evidence to support the use of multimedia, i.e. educational multimodal presentation.

The experiments on multimodal presentation of information indicate that the best benefit is gained when the information to be learned is complex, i.e. has high element interactivity (Sweller and Chandler, 1994), and when the two modalities present different aspects of the learning content. When material from different sources needs to be integrated mentally in a given cognitive task, such as from a picture and text or verbal explanation, the research indicates that a combined graphic-auditory presentation is better than the graphic-textual version (Mousavi et al., 1995; Tindall-Ford et al., 1997). This result is best understood in terms of the dual parallel processing capabilities of the human working memory, where the single modal graphics-text presentation overloads the single visual working memory loop. In contrast the graphic-verbal separate modal presentation engages both the visual and auditory processing components of the working memory and enables the learner to deal with more information.

Thus we have solid evidence to indicate importance of multimodal or multimedia presentations of learning–content to students in the distance education learner–content interactions if the material to be learned is complex. On the other hand, educational cognition research suggests that if the material is simple, i.e. has low element interactivity, then presenting it in multimedia form, especially if exactly the *same* information is presented both verbally and in text or graphics, may make learning more difficult due to the redundancy effect (Bobis *et al.*, 1993; Chandler and Sweller, 1991).

2-way learner-content interaction via interactive multimedia

In all of the above interactions between the learner and the content, the interaction is assumed to be one-way, i.e. the content is presented to the learners for their consumption, without the learners affecting the content as they internalize it (see figure 1). However, the promise of interactive multimedia has always been an active engagement of the learner with the learning environment. We shall consider how this may be achieved from the perspective of an educational multimedia designer.

Seven (plus one) levels of multimedia interaction

Sims (1994) argued that a multimedia designer may structure educational software to provide the learner seven levels of interaction. The designer may confine the software user to passive interactivity where they can simply influence movement through a single sequence of presentations. At the second level the learner may work through a hierarchy of choices in navigating through presentation screens, and at the third level the operator can update information in the programme. The fourth level consists of construct interactivity where the user manipulates objects to achieve a goal. At the fifth level the learner participates in a simulated operation of an environment. At the sixth level of free interactivity, the operator is provided a hyperlinked source of information, which can be traversed at will. Finally at the seventh level, the learners are able to work in a meaningful, job-related context. They experience a microworld of the actual operational environment they seek to master.

A further level of interaction may be added to this list. In many educational situations the benefits of involving students in creating multimedia as part of their learning is recognized (Blumstengel and Kassanke, 1998; Dunlap, 1998). This constructive activity goes beyond the seven levels suggested by Sims, where the students act to design the multimedia. Thus eight levels of learner engagement with multimedia content are possible, these levels are summarized in table 1.

Are there any empirical guidelines to help choose the level of interactivity desired for given content and students? Some initial pointers may be gleaned from research into discovery learning and the use of computers in schools. Research on discovery learning in a computer environment indicates that if the learning content is demanding, i.e. has high element interactivity, unless the students have good domain schema they will not benefit as much from free exploration as from more structured study, such as practice with worked examples (Tuovinen and Sweller, 1999). However, the same study also indicates that once the students have adequate schema in the domain, an exploration approach is at least as good, and may even be better, than a more structured approach, indicating the benefits of increasing student control of learning and 'fading' of tutorial support as they master particular content area (Cox and Cumming, 1990).

Another study found that the benefits gained from students constructing educational multimedia (level 8 activity) was related to their skills with the authoring environment (Wallace and Tuovinen, 1992). Thus if the students are expected to benefit from constructing educational multimedia, as suggested at the eighth level of interaction above, they will need to be familiar with the software authoring environment and processes (Blumstengel and Kassanke, 1998).

Schwier's (1993) taxonomy of multimedia interactions also recognizes the highly structured multimedia learning environments, like the worked examples practice discussed previously. He would call it a *prescriptive* environment. He also identifies

Table 1 *Eight levels of 2-way interaction with multimedia*

Level	Learner–multimedia interaction
1	Passive, 2-way flow control
2	Choices from a hierarchy
3	Information update control
4	Construction with components
5	Participation in simulation
6	Navigation of hyperlinked information
7	Operation in a microworld
8	Multimedia creation

a *democratic* learning environment, where the students are proactive, very similar to levels six and eight identified in table 2. Although he discusses the relative merits of these environments for different students and course aims, he does not appear to explicitly recognize the need for students to move from the prescriptive to the democratic environments as they progress. He also describes a third multimedia learning environment, a *cybernetic* environment, where mutual adaptive interactions occur between the learning system and the learner. This might be equivalent to the seventh level of interaction in table 1. However, an important feature of this environment is the availability of various forms of hints and assistance from the learning system. Such learning systems may use artificial intelligence to monitor and assist the students and perhaps interface with the students via virtual reality. Thus the key aspects of Schwier's taxonomy appear to be covered in table 1 and the discussion of the various media in figure 2 deals with some of his media dimensions.

Instructor–learner interaction

The second of Moore's interaction categories focuses on the instructor–learner interaction. Research indicates this dimension is vitally important for distance students without onsite teacher support (Braggett *et al.*, 1995; Brown, 1996; Stephenson, 1997–98). The communication between the instructor and the learner may employ any combination of the nine media/technology categories shown in figure 2 but is by definition two-way in nature, rather than one-way. Thus whether the student and the tutor exchange messages via mail, email, phone, voicemail, or participate in audiographic sessions, videoconferences, or even in real-time virtual reality activities, they are engaged in an interchange of information in two directions.

Some instructor–learner exchanges are *synchronous* and others *asynchronous* in nature. All the learner–content interactions are synchronous, but in many of the instructor–learner engagements time delays add a further complicating dimension. Usually the longer the time delay, the less effective the feedback, as shown in the exchange of distance education materials (Biner *et al.*, 1997) and feedback on assignments

(Roberts, 1996). So it appears the asynchronous mode is less desirable, but the possible time delays in many types of tutor-student meeting systems—even with the most modern technologies, such as email exchanges, online newsgroup discussions, etc.—may have some real advantages. When complex issues are discussed, for example, the participants need time to thoroughly digest new information and formulate considered replies. Thus both asynchronous and synchronous tutor-learner sessions need to be considered in planning total distance education programmes, as well as the characteristics of the media to be utilized.

In the choice of the instructor–learner interaction mechanisms the evidence from the multimodal research discussed in the first part of this paper needs to be considered. Katz (1999), for example, found that video-conferencing was a more effective and acceptable method of learning from an instructor at a distant site than interactive internet or audiographic communication. It appears that the combined visual and auditory aspects of the lecturer's performance, i.e. the social and the instructional interactions listed in table 2 (Gilbert and Moore, 1998), were conveyed most effectively by the videoconferencing system. The broad thrust of the Katz study may be predicted on the basis of Mousavi *et al.* (1995) and Tindall-Ford *et al.* (1997) results discussed earlier.

Learner–learner interaction

Moore's third interaction dimension, learner–learner communication, is recognized as an important factor for students' suc-

Table 2 *Social and instructional interactions in educational sessions (Gilbert and Moore, 1998)*

Social interactions	Instructional interactions
Body language	Communication of content
Greetings, socializing	Setting objectives
Exchanging personal information	Questioning
Scheduling	Answering
Logistics	Exchanging information
Class management	Pacing
	Sequencing
	Branching
	Adapting
	Evaluating
	Individualizing
	Handling responses
	Confirmation of learning
	Controlling navigation
	Elaboration

cess in distance education (Benson and Rye, 1996; McGill *et al.*, 1997). There is a vast literature on group and collaborative learning outside the distance education context (Webb and Palinscar, 1996), which may be used as a basis for the development of learner–learner interactions, as well as the emerging literature on this issue in the distance education context (Chiappini *et al.*, 1999; Freeman and Capper, 1998; Milter and Stinson, 1999; Ribbons and Hornblower, 1998; Spector *et al.*, 1999). Essentially the importance of this mode of interaction needs to be acknowledged in educational planning for distance education to ensure appropriate learner–learner collaborative activities are explicitly organized for the situations where such learning is beneficial (Bourdeau and Bates, 1997; Burke *et al.*, 1997; Coombs and Smith, 1998; Luetkehans and Nailey, 1999; May, 1993; Webb and Palinscar, 1996).

All the media/technologies available for the learner–content and instructor–learner interaction may also be used for learner–learner interaction. These interaction systems would mostly be two-way in nature but may be either synchronous or asynchronous. The same considerations of immediacy benefits and the competing need for adequate time for deep consideration of complex issues apply as in the instructor–learner interaction. In fact, often the instructor–learner and the learner–learner interaction mechanisms are the same. At major Australian distance education universities (such as Charles Stuart University and Monash University) internet forums or discussion groups (newsgroups) are routinely available for use in all distance education subjects for combined instructor–learner and learner–learner communications.

Burke *et al.* argue that in learner–learner interaction both cognitive and social interaction aspects are important. Thus rather than simply focusing on the capability of the interaction facility to communicate cognitive content, its capacity to emotionally support students is also important. If we take this issue seriously, then we may begin to question the value of only providing shared staff–student discussion areas, such as web forums or staff-led videoconferences, because the students often feel inhibited from discussing real concerns and obtaining the affective support they need. Pearson (1999), for example, found that allowing students to participate anonymously in computer conferences increased their participation significantly and added value and quality to their communications. Similarly the students in Freeman and Capper (1998) study benefited from anonymous web-based role play.

The value of multimodal interaction, already noted in the above two interaction contexts, needs to be kept in mind for learner–learner communications. In fact, in the development of interactive multimedia for distance education, the need for learner–learner (and/or instructor–learner) interaction can be satisfied by incorporating distance collaborative communications learning activities among students into the content itself, as well as employing multiple modal communications. For example, it is quite feasible to develop interactive distance education software at any of the seven levels suggested by Sims (1994) and add to it links to text-only (Feldmann-Pempe *et al.*, 1999), sound-only (Kötter *et al.*, 1999), text and graphics, graphics and sound (Steeples and Goodyear, 1999), desktop

videoconferencing (Trentin and Benigno, 1997), or virtual reality (Jackson *et al.*, 1999) collaborative online communication and online computer supported collaborative work (CSCW) environments. Such software could be supplied on CD-ROMs or on a Web server and would allow students to collaborate in learner–learner communications sessions, either in real time or asynchronously, via networked computers. An example of this approach is the 'DreamTeam' synchronous CSCW Web environment where the presentation and collaboration functions are closely integrated (Roth and Unger, 1998).

Instructor—content interaction

Moore's (1989; with Kearsley, 1996) model of three types of distance education interactions has provided a useful framework for the above discussion. However, from an instructor's point of view the conventional deadlines of distance education often bar the inclusion of relevant up to date time-changing information. If lecturers are used to being able to change the lecture content up to the last minute, they often feel constrained by the long lead times required for the preparation of printed, audio-visual or computer-based distance education materials. Some new technologies, such as the internet and voicemail, may be used to overcome these irritations. In fact these technologies provide a new dimension in distance education instructor-content interaction.

The first way that distance education content may be made more timely for the students is by careful separation of the web-content or voicemail presentations into two parts: invariant content; and changing content.

The content which does not vary during the course needs to be provided to the web-designer or prepared for voicemail delivery in good time, just as the printed distance education notes and readings must be provided for the distance education departments in adequate time for typing, printing, collation and timely dispatch to students. In contrast, the second type of content may be altered by the lecturer as new information becomes available. The possibility and shape of the varying content and the mechanisms for its inclusion need to be planned at the time of the invariant material preparation. Thus lecturers may have the chance of adding web hotlinks to new relevant material while the course is in progress, or provide voicemail comments on new developments in the course.

An even better method of allowing the lecturer to change the web content before and during the course is to present the instructional web materials via a web database (McNaught *et al.*, 1998), such as the TopClass Web classroom building system (McCormack and Jones, 1998). In this case there are also the stable and variable aspects of web learning content. When a database is used to contain the learning content to be delivered to the students via the web, then the shape and structure of the database must be carefully designed before the course begins. However, once the database structure—including the student and instructor interfaces—have been designed then the rest of the content control and maintenance may be handed to the instructors. They can add the content at the pace that best

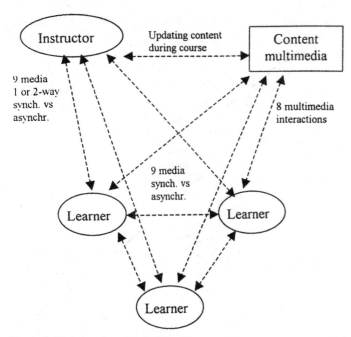

Figure 1 *Distance education four interaction models*

suits their students' learning needs and allows the staff to include up to date information.

If the staff can interact with the content during the course the learning material can be more timely or include motivating current information not available at the beginning of the course. The material may also be adapted to suit expressed student needs, perhaps indicated by feedback from the students via discussion forums, etc. (Pearson, 1999). As well as responding to the expressed student needs by changing the learning content dynamically, the instructor-learner interactions may be modified. So the students may be assisted in more than one way, thereby probably suiting a greater range of student learning styles and coping better with individual differences.

Total interaction model

Taking a holistic view of the distance education interactions we develop a single model which may be represented. This model suggests the following implications for instructional design in distance education:

1. In planning a distance education programme all the four interaction aspects must be addressed. This model may form the basis of an instructional design checklist.
2. The means for interaction may include nine forms of media/technologies, which may be synchronous or asynchronous and 1- or 2-way in nature.
3. The more demanding and complex the content, the more beneficial the multimodal interaction in content presentation, instructor–student interaction and learner–learner interaction.
4. The learner interaction with multimedia content may be at eight different levels.

5. Optimal learning activities depend on the students' prior knowledge. For students with minimal background more structured learning activities are required.
6. Multimedia may be designed to incorporate learner–learner and/or instructor–learner interactions via the internet using multiple modalities and either synchronous or asynchronous communications.

Many aspects raised in this paper have not yet been thoroughly researched, and so some of the conclusions and recommendations can only be tentative. For example, the educational benefits of the instructor–content interaction during the course have not been thoroughly researched. The implications of multimodal methods of instructor–learner and learner–learner interactions have not been comprehensively studied in realistic distance education contexts. What are the comparative benefits and disadvantages of synchronous and asynchronous instructor–learner and learner–learner interactions? What are the optimal ways of including instructor–learner and learner–learner interactive activities in distance education multimedia? Questions such as these are demand answers. The intention of this paper is to provide ideas for action, both in distance course and multimedia development and for research into educational interactions.

References

Baddeley, A (1990) *Human memory. Theory and practice,* Lawrence Erlbaum, Hillsdale, NJ.

Baddeley, A (1992) Working memory, *SCIENCE,* 255, 556–559.

Benson, R and Rye, O (1996) Visual reports by video: an evaluation, *Distance Education,* 17, 117–131.

Biner, P, Barone, N, Welsh, K and Dean, R (1997) Relative academic performance and its relation to facet and overall satisfaction with interactive telecourses, *Distance Education,* 18, 318–326.

Blumstengel, A and Kassanke, 5 (1998) A hypermedia learning environment by students for students, paper presented at the EDMEDIA & ED-TELECOM 98, Freiburg, Germany.

Bobis, J, Sweller, J and Cooper, M (1993) Cognitive load effects in primary-school geometry task, *Learning & Instruction,* 3, 1–21.

Bourdeau, J and Bates, A (1997) Instructional design for distance learning. In S Dijkstra, NM Seel, F Schott and RD Tennyson (eds) *Instructional Design: International Perspectives,* Lawrence Erlbaum, Mahwah, NJ, 369–397

Braggett, E, Retallick, J, Tuovinen, JE and Wallace, A (1995) *Distance Education Project NATCAP. Report on the establishment of Telematics delivery systems in one priority cluster area in NSW. 1993–94,* Charles Stuart University, Wagga Wagga.

Brown, KM (1996) The role of internal and external factors in the discontinuation of off-campus students, *Distance Education,* 17, 44–71.

Burke, C, Lundin, R and Daunt, C (1997) Pushing the boundaries of interaction in videoconferencing a dialogical approach, *Distance Education,* 18, 350–361.

Chandler, P and Sweller, J (1991) Cognitive load theory and the format of instruction, *Cognition and Instruction,* 8, 293–332.

Chiappini, G, Chiccariello, A and Gibelli, C (1999) Collaborative teacher training through telematics, paper presented at the Communication and Networking in Education: Learning in a Networked Society, Aulanko, Finland.

Coombs, SJ and Smith, ID (1998) Designing a self-organized conversational learning environment, *Educational Technology,* 38, 17–28.

Cox, R and Cumming, G (1990) The role of exploration-based learning in the development of expertise, paper presented at the Computers in Education, WCCE9O, Sydney.

Dunlap, JC (1998) Encouraging lifelong learning with learner-constructed Web-based performance support systems, paper presented at the EDMEDIA & ED-TELECOM 1998, Freiburg, Germany.

Feldmann-Pempe, B, Mittrach, S and Schlageter, G (1999) Internet-based seminars at the Virtual University: a breakthrough in open and distance education, paper presented at the ED-MEDIA 1999, Seattle, Washington.

Freeman, MA and Capper, JM (1998) An anonymous asynchronous web-based role play, paper presented at the ASCILITE'98, Wollongong.

Gilbert, L and Moore, DR (1998) Building interactivity into web courses: tools for social and instructional interaction, *Educational Technology*, 38, 29–35.

Jackson, RL, Taylor, W and Winn, W (1999) Peer collaboration and virtual environments: a preliminary investigation of multi-paticipant virtual reality applied in science education, paper presented at the ED-MEDIA 1999, Seattle, Washington.

Katz, YJ (1999) The comparative suitability of three ICT distance learning methodologies for college level instruction, paper presented at Communications and Networking in Education: Learning in a Networked Society, Hämeenlinna, Finland.

Kötter, M, Rodine, C and Shield, L (1999) Voice conferencing on the internet: creating richer on-line communities for distance learning, paper presented at the ED-MEDIA 1999, Seattle, Washington.

Logie, RH (1996) The seven ages of working memory. In JTE Richardson, RW Engle, L Hasher, RH Logie, ER Stoltzfus and RT Zacks (eds) *Working Memory and Human Cognition*, Oxford University Press, Oxford, 31–65.

Luetkehans, L and Nailey, ML (1999) Facilitating virtual learning teams in online learning environments, paper presented at the ED-MEDIA 1999, Seattle, Washington.

May, S (1993) Collaborative learning: more is not necessarily better, *The American Journal of Distance Education*, 7, 39–50

McCormack, C and Jones, D (1998) *Building a Web-based Education System*, John Wiley, New York.

McGill, TJ, Volet, SE and Hobbs, VJ (1997) Studying computer programming externally: who succeeds? *Distance Education*, 18, 2, 236-256.

McNaught, C, Whithear, K, Browning, G, Hart, G, and Prescott,J (1998) The best of both worlds: redeveloping a multimedia project for the Web, paper presented at the EDMEDIA & ED-TELECOM 98, Freiburg, Germany.

Miller, GA (1956) The magical number, seven, plus or minus two: some limits on our capacity for processing information, *Psychological Review*, 63, 81–97.

Milter, RG and Stinson, JE (1999) Electronic collaborative learning architecture: spanning time and distance in professional development, paper presented at the ED-MEDIA 1999, Seattle, Washington.

Moore, MG (1989) Editorial: three types of interaction, *The American Journal of Distance Education*, 3, 1–6.

Moore, MG and Kearsley, G (1996) *Distance Education: A Systems View*, Belmont: Wadsworth.

Mousavi, S, Low, R and Sweller, J (1995) Reducing cognitive load by mixing auditory and visual presentation modes, *Journal of Educational Psychology*, 87, 319–334.

Pearson, J (1999) Lurking, anonymity and participation in computer conferencing: data from a case study on an initial teacher education course, paper presented at the Communications and networking in education: Learning in a networked society, Aulanko, Hämeenlinna, Finland.

Ribbons, RM and Hornblower, BFP (1998) Virtual collaboration: using email to provide flexible learning and support environments, paper presented at the ASCILITE'98, Wollongong.

Roberts, D (1996) Feedback on assignments, *Distance Education*, 17, 95–116.

Roth, J and Unger, C (1998) 'DreamTeam'—a synchronous CSCW environment for distance education, paper presented at the EDMEDIA & ED-TELECOM 98, Freiburg, Germany.

Schwier, RA (1993) Learning environments and interaction for emerging technologies: implications for learner control and practice, *Canadian Journal of Educational Communications*, 22, 163–176.

Sims, R (1994) Seven levels of interactivity: Implications for the development of multimedia education and training, paper presented at the APITITE 94, Asia Pacific Information Technology in Training and Education Conference and Exhibition, 28 June–2 July 1994, Brisbane, Australia.

Soo, KS and Bonk, CJ (1998) Interaction: what does it mean in online distance education?, paper presented at the EDMEDIA & ED-TELECOM 98, Freiburg, Germany.

Spector, JM, Wasson, B and Davidsen, PI(1999) Designing collaborative distance learning environments for complex domains, paper presented at the ED-MEDIA 1999, Seattle, Washington.

Steeples, C and Goodyear, P (1999) *Enabling professional learning in distributed communities of practice: descriptors for multimedia objects*, paper presented at the ED-MEDIA 1999, Seattle, Washington.

Stephenson, S D (1997–98) Distance mentoring, *Journal of Educational Technology Systems*, 26, 181–186.

Sweller, J and Chandler, P (1994) Why some material is difficult to learn, *Cognition and Instruction*, 12, 185–233.

Tindall-Ford, S, Chandler, P and Sweller, J (1997) When two sensory modes are better than one, *Journal of Experimental Psychology: Applied*, 3, 25 7–287.

Trentin, G and Benigno, V (1997) Multimedia conferencing in education: methodological and organizational considerations, *Educational Technology*, 37, 32–39.

Tuovinen, JE (1999) Research framework and implications for online multimedia education practice based on cognition research, paper presented at the Communications and Networking in Education: Learning in a Networked Society, Aulanko, Hämeenlinna, Finland.

Tuovinen, JE and Sweller, J (1999) A comparison of cognitive load associated with discovery learning and worked examples, *Journal of Educational Psychology*, 91, 334–341.

Wallace, A and Tuovinen, JE (1992) Linking computers to curriculum: a re-think of logistics, paper presented at the ACEC'92 Computing the Clever Country? Proceedings of Australian Computers in Education Conference, Melbourne.

Webb, NM and Palinscar, AS (1996) Group processes in the classroom. In DC Berliner and RC Calfee (eds) *Handbook of Educational Psychology*, Macmillan, New York, 841–873.

Biographical note

Juhani Tuovinen, is currently the Senior Research Fellow in Interactive Multimedia at Monash University's Centre for Learning and Teaching Support and the Director of the Centre for Multimedia and Hypermedia Research. Previously he was a secondary teacher, then lecturer in education at Charles Stuart University, working in both on campus and off campus modes. Research interests are in pedagogy and technology of distance and flexible learning.

Address for correspondence

Juhani E. Tuovinen, Centre for Learning and Teaching Support, Monash University, Churchill, Victoria, 3842 Australia; e-mail: juhani.tuovinen@celts.monash.edu.au

Unit 6

Key Points to Consider

❖ Describe how a "technology-enhanced learning environment" could stimulate classrom activity.

❖ Where do you stand on the intellectual property rights issue? Should learning materials distributed over the Internet be free?

❖ Katy Kelly writes in "False Promise" that some educators, doctors, and child development experts believe that early computer use may diminish creativity, imagination, motivation, and attention spans. Do you agree or disagree? Defend your answer.

 **Links** **www.dushkin.com/online/**

These sites are annotated on pages 4 and 5.

Some of the problems with integrating technology into education are receding due to the spread of technology in our society. During the years 1995 through 2000, the computer moved into the classroom as a mainstream teaching tool. More than 70 percent of college and university professors claim to use computers as part of their instructional activity. In addition, the computer has become widespread enough to become a basic need similar to automobiles, telephones, and television. In 2001, there is one computer for every four students. Today, educators show excited interest in interactive computer-based multimedia applications and the World Wide Web. The computer has become a reference and communications vehicle for the majority of teachers and students. We are raising the level of computer-based instruction from skill-based and procedure-oriented applications to inquiry-based and decision-oriented levels through the use of teacher/technology-centered learning teams. These teams use the communication and reference tools of the Internet along with multimedia-simulated lab and field study modules to spark interest, improve performance, and change attitudes.

Although the immediate future looks very bright, questions remain. In spite of all the progress that has been made, there are schools that are technology poor. In addition, there is an inequity of women in the information technology field. Many educators and child development experts and doctors are speaking out against early computer use and television for providing too much screen time. Administrators are concerned with how to measure the productivity factor that technology-based education may provide. Policymakers wonder how to get educators to form consortiums in order to assess joint educational facilities and thus increase the usage of the facilities while decreasing the per unit cost of delivery. Intellectual property rights remains a thorny question and teachers wonder how technology can best be used with existing programs in a distance-learning environment. Finally, the public is concerned about the return on investment that will be realized from the new technologies in the home and classroom.

The articles in this unit shed some light on the promises and areas of concern. In the first article, "Guerrilla Technology," Royal Van Horn provides advice on what to do about schools that are technology poor. Van Horn spells out how to change the situation with almost no money. The writer suggests that teachers go on a scavenger hunt to find important equipment that is unused. Often the least obvious places conceal lots of useful stuff. The article provides real examples of where to look and what you might find.

Next, Deborah Radcliff focuses on the inequity of women in the information technology field. The writer points out that some female IT professionals are spearheading grassroots mentoring. She claims that educational organizations are working to reverse the trend and entice more women into

technical jobs. Several programs that focus on this problem are identified and described.

Then, Katy Kelly sounds an alarm by declaring that a growing number of educators, child development experts, and doctors are beginning to speak out against early computer use, especially when coupled with regular television watching. Too much "screen time" at a young age may actually undermine the development of the critical skills that kids need to become successful. In addition, they see a possibility of diminishing creativity, imagination, motivation, attention spans, and the desire to persevere. Rosemary Skeele and James Daly state the case for teacher education institutions to experiment with the effective application of computer technology for teaching and learning in their own campus practice. They describe how the Seaton Hall faculty has made a commitment to the greater integration of technology into instruction, and are at the forefront of this movement. They are trying to articulate a wider vision for technology, making it as essential a tool as the chalkboard.

Finally, in "Who Owns the Courses?" Sally Johnstone makes a case for ignoring intellectual property rights when distributing learning materials over the Internet. The author provides an example of an institution that has already done so. Her point is that the person who creates the material owns the rights, but those who help produce it have already been paid for doing so, and thus require no further compensation.

Guerrilla Technology

By Royal Van Horn

THIS column is dedicated to Leslie, Leonore, Talitha, and all the other teachers who are toughing it out in poor schools with underprivileged kids and awful technology. Leslie and Leonore teach in inner-city elementary schools; Talitha teaches in an inner-city high school. After one of my evening classes, we all spent a few hours discussing their schools, their students, the technology they have or don't have, and lots of other things. These are three very bright, high-achieving professionals who could quickly climb anyone's corporate ladder, earn two to three times their current salaries, and succeed at just about anything they set their minds to. Yet they continue to teach under poor conditions, and the paycheck isn't the reason. They continue to teach because they are able to touch the lives of a few kids every year and really make a difference.

I came away from that evening's discussion pretty depressed. So depressed that I had to drive around my neighborhood for a while just to collect my thoughts. I finally decided that, while I couldn't fix their schools or their students, I darn well ought to be able to give them some decent advice on what to do about their poor technology. After a lot of thought, the only advice I could come up with was: sometimes you just have to take matters into your own hands! Hence the title of this column.

In many of my past columns I've talked about high-tech projects that cost upwards of $1.6 million dollars. I don't apologize for these columns; kids are worth whatever it takes. Furthermore, if you're building a new school for 1,000 students, you need to "future proof" it as best you can. You can either pay now or pay later. In this column I want to consider "how to make a difference" with almost no money.

The first tactic in the art of guerrilla technology is to *find all the hidden technology.* Whenever I am asked to help a school do anything with technology, the first thing I do is get a master key and look in all the locked cabinets, closets, storerooms, unused offices, and custodial areas. (Hint: custodians always have master keys.) I have never gone on this kind of scavenger hunt without finding important equipment that is unused. Here are a few examples of the things I've uncovered in my searches.

In an elementary school storeroom, I found 10 unused Macintosh LC III computers and monitors, complete with networking cable, that used to be part of a Jostens computer lab. The computers were deemed useless because they didn't have hard disk drives. I found reconditioned disk drives for these computers at $80 apiece and quickly made them usable. It did take a whole bottle of glass cleaner to get the grime off the outsides.

In a cabinet inside a high school science department's 100-seat mini-auditorium, I once found an IBM model 80 server, complete with Novel Netware 3.1 software. The out-of-sight, out-of-mind server was even connected to a Sony three-gun projector mounted on the ceiling of the auditorium. Since the server didn't have any usable software installed on it and since no one knew how to run it, no one was using either it or the gorgeous three-gun projector in the ceiling. Teachers had been dragging into the auditorium an audiovisual cart with a 21-inch television set and a VCR so they could show videos to their classes while the projector went unused! Anyone could have had the server for the asking.

Often the least obvious places conceal lots of neat stuff. In a storage closet that housed the intercom system in one elementary school, I found a brand-new (in the original box) Pioneer five-disc audio CD changer. I suspect that the original specifications for the intercom system called for the device but that no one at the school wanted to use the CD player for the intended purpose of providing background music throughout the school.

Scrounging around behind the curtains of another school's auditorium stage, I once found two wireless FM microphones, a mic mixer, two or three mic stands and mics, and a miniature audio system. This whole system was used every year or two when the school

From *Phi Delta Kappan,* February 1999, pp. 476-478. © 1999 by Phi Delta Kappan. Reprinted by permission.

board held a meeting in the building. We quickly put it to work to form the audio system for the school's makeshift television studio that we were assembling. All we had to do was buy new batteries for the wireless mics.

In the storeroom of a middle school library, I once found a brand-new, unused, 42-inch Hitachi rear-projection television monitor and six new computers. On questioning the librarian about this gear, I learned that the television had been ordered for Title I reading instruction, but that the school had lost its funding for the program. The unused computers had been purchased to allow students to access the school's automated library system, but there were no network connections in the media center for these computers. These didn't seem like very good excuses for leaving such neat stuff in the storeroom.

The second tactic in the art of guerrilla technology has to do with a simple fact that schools *have many special budgets that are often used to buy technology*. Budgets for such programs as Title I, English as a second language, career education, vocational education, library "maintenance of effort," the parent/teacher organization, and the school foundation, as well as special funds for "high-cost science equipment" might be available. "Maintenance of effort" funds are an interesting example. These dollars are usually given to librarians to replace old and worn-out books and to add to the collection. But these same dollars can be used to buy such media as filmstrips (or videodiscs and CD-ROMs) and such equipment as filmstrip projectors (or computers). This is why we now call our libraries "media centers"! Moreover, most media center directors usually have a system in place that allows teachers to request that certain books or other items be purchased during the next budget cycle. Most teachers never make any such requests!

The third tactic of those engaged in a war of guerrilla technology is to *help other people spend their money and do the paperwork for them*. The second part is especially important because you want to make it as easy as possible for someone to buy you something!

Because of all the press given to the data from TIMSS (the Third International Math and Science Study), a lot of special funding is now available to reform science and math education at all levels. Even if you're an elementary teacher who rarely teaches science, you might want to start—especially if you can do it with computers, CD-ROM discs, and so on. Get a copy of the

NCTM (National Council for Teachers of Mathematics) and the NSTA (National Science Teachers Association) standards and build your proposals for funding using the standards that relate to a "hands-on" or laboratory approach. Just make sure yours is a high-tech, hands-on lab.

I recently supervised a middle school science intern and so had to make four or five visits to observe his teaching. We usually met in an office/storeroom that was filled with glassware, pan balances, and sundry pieces of lab equipment. As we were conferring, I noticed a shelf filled with large, colorful, but very dusty boxes labeled "Windows on Science." As it turned out, the science department had been given several complete sets of Optical Data Corporation's "Windows on Science" laser videodiscs. There was even an unopened box with a new disc player in it. I believe the money for the discs came from some special "high-cost science" budget that someone had to spend in a hurry at the end of some budget cycle. Sadly, the discs had not been used, and anyone could probably have borrowed them.

The fourth tactic of the art of guerrilla technology is *if you can't scrounge it up locally, go elsewhere*. The first place to look for free computers is at universities and technology-savvy businesses such as large national banks. My university, for example, is now listing as surplus anything less than 90-MHz Pentium processors or Power Macs. We have already put on the surplus list a good number of Power Mac 6100s that were complete with the video digitizers that make them capable multimedia machines. University people often hate to do the paperwork needed to render old equipment obsolete, so the old computers just get stacked in closets, storerooms, or warehouses. You'll need to find a helpful professor or technician who is willing to look for the stuff and do the paperwork, or you'll have to talk to the property-control person or director of purchasing. You might even have to go directly to the university president. Just get your principal to make an appointment with the university president. Most presidents would not refuse an appointment requested by a school principal, and most presidents can twitch their noses and get the surplus equipment sent your way!

I want to state emphatically that teachers and students deserve better than hand-me-down technology, but sometimes you just have to make do. Besides, it's a challenge. Depending on

what part of the country you're from, you'll need a lot of Yankee ingenuity or redneck know-how. But let's suppose you do manage to scrounge up some old computers. When you go to pick them up, ask for all the old disks, CDs, and manuals too. And try to get twice as many machines as you need so you can swap parts around and make at least half of them work. My experience has been that a computer's mouse is the first thing to wear out, so get as many "mice" as you can. You may even end up buying a few at about $50 each. And don't forget to ask about old printers as well.

When you do get some hand-me-down computers, remember the fifth tactic of a guerrilla technology campaign: *almost any computer can be made useful with an old operating system and an old word processor*. To this day, I carry a double density (800-K) diskette with DOS 3.3 and WordStar in my briefcase. This single disk will make almost any old PC boot and launch a very usable, albeit character-based, word processor. Incidentally, I don't recommend that you fool around with Windows on old PCs unless you can get at least a 66-MHz machine with ample RAM. I would just turn old slow Windows machines into fast DOS machines. For really old Macs, like Classics, you'll need something like Mac System 6.7, and I recommend MacWrite. Even machines without hard drives are very usable with such software. On not so old Macs, like those in the LC series, I recommend you first try Mac OS 7.6, although on some you'll have to drop back to version 7.1. The principle is simple: old machines can't run new software, but lots of the old software works great. You just have to have it or find it.

If you really want to be a revolutionary, you might try the following, the sixth tactic of the art of guerrilla technology: *regardless of what they say, put it on your computer or their server anyway*. (This tactic could endanger your job, but I do it all the time. My son got caught doing this once and had to take a forced leave from work for a day and a half as punishment. He went surfing.) Furthermore, this tactic works only if you thoroughly understand the directory structure of your computer's operating system. By the way, I'm not suggesting that you use pirated software. The point here is that many districts and schools have lots of fussy rules, such as "Don't put any software on your classroom computers." I guess the computers really are *theirs*, not yours. But the trouble is that the software they install for you is often not the software you or your students need. If you want to take matters into your own hands, here's how I do it.

First, nearly all CD-ROM-based educational software requires that you install at least parts of it on your computer's hard drive—precisely what you are forbidden to do. But the software usually lets you decide where to put it on your hard drive. If you don't tell the install program where to put the software, a Windows machine will usually put it in the "programs directory"; a Mac will usually make a new folder and install it there. No problem here—just know and remember where the installer puts the program so that you can delete it later if someone gets nosy. Another trick is to make your own directory or folder and call it whatever you want. Then install the software to your own little directory or folder, which you can dump in a hurry. If you want to be really sneaky, hide your own directory or file folder.

On Macs, a good hiding place is the "Extensions (disabled)" folder inside the System Folder. On a Windows PC, a good hiding place is a directory inside another directory, labeled something like DRVR3D8. Better yet, get a good hacker or techie to do all this for you. Just remember, always do a custom install, and never let an install program put anything important in your system folder/directory. This is especially important on Macs, since the software often puts an old version of QuickTime in the Extensions Folder. I suspect that more than 95% of all software can be installed without doing any harm whatsoever to a computer. Of course, you might want to have a back-up plan—or the phone number of a smart techie who can fix any problems you cause.

Maybe I should label this column "editorial opinion." I suspect I'll get fan mail from teachers who can use a suggestion or two, but I'll probably get hate mail from lead computer teachers and heads of district MIS departments. At the very least, this column might cause people to discuss the meaning of personal computers. I take the term personal not to mean "small in size," but to mean "mine" or "yours." Good luck, all you guerrillas, and have a fall-back position and a retreat strategy planned!

ROYAL VAN HORN is a professor of education at the University of North Florida, Jacksonville (e-mail: rvanhorn @unf.edu).

Champions of Women in Technology

Despite huge increases in the number of students heading into IT degree programs, the percentage of women opting for IT careers is dropping fast. A few women are doing something about it.

Abstract:

The percentage of technical jobs held by women reportedly hangs at a static 28%, even as the number of women in the workforce approaches 50%. Corporations need to clean up their advertising imagery to better portray females in technical fields. And they need to listen to the myriad reports on gender differences and embrace diversity of thinking in the workplace. Some female IT professionals are spearheading grassroots mentoring and educational organizations to reverse that trend and entice more women into technical jobs. Lenore Blum, founder of the first computer science program at the all-women Mills College, will soon organize the multitude of fragmented women's outreach programs at Carnegie Mellon University in Pittsburgh into a pipeline program. At the primary school level, Anne Redelfs, associate director at the National partnership for Advanced Computational Infrastructure (NPACI), is working to change the way teachers treat girls. The NPACI's outreach workshops teach educators proven ways to make technology and science more attractive to girls and minorities.

By DEBORAH RADCLIFF

When Shelley Hayes, fresh computer science degree in hand, landed her first IT job, she wound up answering phones. That's where the company's owner thought women belonged.

But Hayes paid attention to those callers—mostly resellers in need of an entirely new software line—which she soon developed behind the owner's back. "By the time the owner knew about it, orders were coming in for the new products. He set the issue [of keeping females in clerical jobs] aside because we were already making money on the products, and I was six months ahead on the technology," says Hayes, now a systems architect at Xerox Corp. in Stamford, Conn.

That was 15 years ago. Although women have made many advances in the workplace since then, things haven't changed all that much for women working in the information technology field. In fact, the percentage of technical jobs held by women reportedly hangs at a static 28%, even as the number of women in the workforce approaches 50%, according to the U.S. Bureau of Labor Statistics. Despite the fact that enrollments are dramatically on the increase for computer science degrees, the percentage of women seeking such degrees is dropping fast.

According to the National Science Foundation, the number of bachelor degrees in computer science awarded to females was 40% in 1984, says Anita Borg, founding director of the Institute for Women in Technology (IWT) and a member of the research staff at Xerox's Palo Alto Research Center in California. That number has dropped to 27.5%, according to the U.S. Department of Education's most recent survey of 1996 graduates.

Borg asserts that companies are acutely aware of that growing gender gap in their IT departments. But most businesses still unwittingly perpetuate the problem. Corporations need to clean up their advertising imagery to better portray females in technical fields, she charges. And they need to listen to the myriad reports on gender differences and embrace diversity of thinking in the workplace.

Borg isn't holding her breath waiting for such changes to take place, however. She and others like her are spearheading grassroots mentoring and educational organizations to reverse that trend and entice more women into technical jobs. In so doing, they're taking on educators from the primary to postgraduate levels. And they're tackling stagnant corporate mentalities to make technology itself more female-friendly.

LEADING THE WAY

One such woman is Lenore Blum, an educator, author and research scientist who founded the first computer science program at the all-women Mills College in Oakland, Calif., in the 1970s. Soon, she will organize the multitude of fragmented women's outreach programs at Carnegie Mellon University in Pittsburgh into a pipeline program. She says she hopes the program will serve as a national model for other universities to follow.

In fact, when Blum moves to the university this summer, she will join her husband and son, both professors in the computer science department at Carnegie Mellon.

"A few years ago, women couldn't get jobs in the departments where their husbands worked," Blum says. "This shows a change of attitude is already taking place."

INCLUSIVE METHODS

At the primary school level, Anne Redelfs, associate director at the National Partnership for Advanced Computational Infrastructure (NPACI), under the auspices of the San Diego Supercomputer Center, is working to change the way teachers treat girls. The NPACI's outreach workshops teach educators proven ways to make technology and science more attractive to girls and minorities.

If you're looking for inspiration at the corporate level, you're likely to run into Borg, who, with the help of Sun Microsystems Inc. in Mountain View, Calif., is developing Web technologies to unite women's technical and scientific professional organizations.

She also has strong words for technology developers: "We're at a time when women are beginning to use technology in a very significant way. Companies that can really understand and build for this market have tremendous opportunities. I don't think they can do that with a nearly all-male engineering workforce."

STARTING EARLY

Even the Girl Scouts recognize the importance of early mentoring. The Girl Scouts of America offers proficiency badges in technology and the Internet for Brownie, Junior and Senior levels.

In fact, one former Girl Scout, 18-year-old Pheonix Maa, achieved her Golden Award for building three Web sites for Girl Scout chapters. Maa is now a first-year computer science student at Rensselaer Polytechnic Institute in Troy, N.Y. There, she's working with a mentor, also a former Girl Scout, on another undergraduate Web project.

"A lot of people have ideas, but they don't know where to begin. They need direction. The Girl Scouts certainly helped me get started," Maa says.

As obvious (and as stereotypical) as it may sound, the real problem, Borg says, is that females and males are just so different. And most educators and work environments still cater to males, she adds.

For example, boys are more aggressive in the classroom, Borg says, adding, "Boys elbow girls off machines." That practice, she says, is carried over to the workplace, where men are given a "can-do" pat on the back, while women are often held back.

In addition, women's contribution to technology is woefully underrepresented in the classroom and technical field at large, Borg says.

"A young cousin of mine taking a [University of California at Berkeley] computer course was really upset that the professor had shown this highly acclaimed video, Triumph of the Nerds. It leaves out any role women have ever had in computing," says Borg, who was recognized this month as one of the top 25 women on the Web by the San Francisco-based forum Women on the Web. "The women in this class get the message that they have to be different or strange to get into this field."

The NPACI strives to reverse such presumptions before young women reach college. Working with its sister partnership, the National Computational Science Alliance, the program concentrates on faculty education, partnerships with educational and mentoring programs and student mentoring programs such as science camps and career development. Those efforts have resulted in a 63% retention rate at undergraduate schools and 97% at the graduate level, according to Redelfs.

"Girls who participated in after-school technology programs years ago are now attending Stanford, MIT and U.C. Berkeley," Redelfs says. "They return each year to speak in the same after-school programs that got them started."

KEEPING THE FAITH

Workplace discrimination hasn't gone away. Dory Kim, technical recruiter at West Valley Technology in Sunnyvale, Calif., still hears veiled favoritism from a handful of male clients. "They'll say stuff like, 'This is definitely a men's shop,' or 'Find me someone who can lift over 100 pounds,' " she explains.

Many, such as Sharon McVeigh Pettigrew, would rather leave than fight. "I think more women in technology like me are opting out," says Pettigrew, principal at Call Center Group in San Mateo, Calif. "They're moving into small business and managerial positions because they can see there's more opportunity to control their own destiny."

Indeed, of the 40 women in attendance at a December meeting of the San Francisco chapter of Women in Technology International, only four were actual technologists. The remainder worked in product marketing, management, public relations and recruiting.

Enter Borg, who was raised by women working in male-dominated fields. She even has an Amelia Earhart-like snapshot of her aunt, a World War II pilot, posted on her bulletin board. Borg wants to see more women involved in the development of technology from the get-go.

That's a good idea. Women perceive and use technology differently from men, according to a white paper by three computer science faculty members at Carnegie Mellon, in which 29 male and 20 female computer science students were interviewed. According to the report, males said they use computers as the ultimate toys, whereas females consider computers tools, such as teaching instruments, to perform service "in a larger world."

In the IWT's second brainstorming session late last year, Borg mixed nontechnical women with technical women to hash out some uses for technology. "They came up with very unique ideas, from family calendaring and communications to plumbing sensors," she says.

Through its collaborative Web development project with Sun, the IWT will rebuild the technology behind Borg's 12-year-old Systers.org virtual community to extend the community to all technical and scientific women's support and mentoring groups. It also will serve as a virtual product development center, where female technologists can build on the ideas generated from the IWT's focus groups.

"I want all of these folks connected. We're all doing too much reinventing of the wheel," Borg says. "The Internet enables us to share the ideas we have without having to create another hierarchy. We hope that these two projects will come together and create a structure of continued involvement."

WAIT IT OUT

Although it will take time for the goals of these women and others like them to make a lasting impact, it's still a very good time for women to enter the IT field. Most employers are happy to hire women, especially now that there's a shortage of technical hires. In fact, many of Fortune 500 companies now cosponsor technical women's groups.

And nowadays, those famous "people skills" traditionally associated with women are in high demand, says Vivian Victor, application development manager at Ernst & Young LLP.

"It's not enough to develop programs anymore," she says. "We need to focus more on our client's business needs. Women's understanding of people and integration of concepts are needed more today than ever."

Read the Book

DOES JANE COMPUTE? BY ROBERTA FURGER gives simple solutions for evenly distributing computer access between boys and girls. Recommended by Anita Borg, founding director of the Institute for Women in Technology.

Radcliff is a freelance writer in northern California. She can be contacted at DeRad@aol.com.

False Promise

Parking your child in front of the computer may seem like a good idea, but think again

BY KATY KELLY

Perched in his mother's lap, Jonathan Foldi taps on the keyboard. "*Car* starts with the letter *C*," says the pleasant computer-synthesized voice as a red roadster zips around the screen, and Jonathan stares, transfixed, ignoring the toy trucks, plastic balls, and rocking horse that cover the hardwood floors of his suburban Maryland home. His mouth open in wonder, Jonathan pecks another letter, and another. At the age of 13 months, he's already familiar with JumpStart Toddlers and several other computer games, all designed for kids under 2. Wire racks set up beside him hold more than 20 others, the collection of his 4-year-old brother, Matthew.

This is the face of childhood, circa 2000: Parents have been told that it's their responsibility to prepare children for a multi-tasking, technology-driven future, so they "JumpStart" their babies, leave 6-year-olds in the care of Carmen Sandiego, and tutor third graders on the finer points of PowerPoint presentations. Believing that starting earlier is starting better, they invest in "lapware" and special keyboards designed to withstand drool and tiny fists, and they stick children who aren't even forming sentences yet in front of computer screens. The idea: Buy the computer and the software, and the brain will grow. Without an early start, parents fear, their kids will fall so far behind they'll never catch up.

But a growing number of educators, child development experts, and doctors are beginning to speak out against early computer use, especially when coupled with regular television watching. Too much "screen time" at a young age, they say, may actually undermine the development of the critical skills that kids need to become successful, diminishing creativity and imagination, motivation, attention spans, and the desire to persevere.

Last week, some experts—including Mary Pipher, author of *Reviving Ophelia;* Harvard professor of psychiatry Alvin Poussaint; and noted child and adolescent psychiatrist Marilyn Benoit—went even further, putting their names to a petition calling for "an immediate moratorium on the further introduction of computers in early childhood and elementary education" until it can be determined what effect they have on young children. "The only way to do that is to slow down, look at the research and evaluate," says Pipher.

Early action. Keep kids *away* from computers? It seems to fly in the face of everything the 21st-century cyber-ready parent is told to believe. A recent Kaiser Family Foundation study showed that on a typical day, 26 percent of 2- to 7-year-olds spent time on the computer, averaging 40 minutes. Matthew Foldi's parents started him playing on the computer at 8 months—partly as an alternative to the bland baby babble on *Teletubbies* but also, says his mother, Bonnie Glick, because "we spend so much time on the computer at work that it's important for kids to know this is part of the real world."

"Parents have been sold a bill of goods about how valuable these experiences are," says Frank Wilson, a neurologist and the author of *The Hand: How Its Use Shapes the Brain, Language, and Human Culture.* Wilson and other skeptics say that as a nation we leapt without looking, launching a grand experiment without doing any serious long-term studies on the possible developmental, behavioral, or physical effects early computer use has on kids. "Many of the answers won't play out for five, 10, or 20 years," says Michael Rich, coauthor of an American Academy of Pediatrics position paper that calls for some limits on screen time.

That's certainly the opinion of the Alliance for Childhood, a child-advocacy group that last week released the report "Fool's Gold: A Critical Look at Computers in Childhood," in which they say that computers can potentially damage the health and intellectual and social development of young children. Challenging many of the claims about computers' ability to motivate the young, the report asserts: "Children need stronger personal bonds with caring adults. Yet powerful technologies are distracting children and adults from each other."

The reaction to the report and petition was heated and mixed. Educators who have worked for almost a decade to update classroom technology were outraged. "If we don't bring the institution of schooling into the 21st century," says Cheryl Williams, director of the education technology program at the National School Boards Association in Alexandria, Va., "then the institution of schools will become irrelevant." At the same time, some teachers are reporting shrinking attention spans and decreasing motivation, while many child-development specialists say they see kids who have withdrawn socially, passing up friends in favor of computer games. "For certain types of learning," says educational psychologist Jane Healy, author of *Failure to Connect: How Computers Affect Our Children's Minds—for Better and Worse,* "certain mental habits such as motivation, perseverance, concentration, and certainly reading and language skills, everything we know suggests that this technology may do more harm than good."

From *U.S. News & World Report,* September 25, 2000, pp. 48-52, 54-55. © 2000 by U.S. News & World Report. Reprinted by permission. Visit us at our Web site at www.usnews.com for additional information.

IN THE EARLY YEARS, CHILDREN BEGIN to learn many of the skills that will carry them through the rest of their lives: language and socialization, the ability to organize their thoughts, and the concept of cause and effect. They learn to find solutions, to be creative, to imagine, to self-motivate, and to respond to failure by trying again. They develop and refine small and large motor skills, depth perception, and hand-eye coordination. They are beginning to understand how they fit into a larger world and gain a sense of competence and a basic self-esteem.

How do they learn so much? Through experience, experimentation, and observation: tasting, smelling, hearing, touching. It is the real-life lessons—the climbing over and scooting under, putting one cup inside another, and chasing Cheerios around the kitchen floor—that teach a child how the world and his body work. Pushing a computer key to make an animated monkey dance does not have the same effect. "Two-dimension play is not as good as three-dimension play," says Kathy Hirsh-Pasek, director of the Infant Language Laboratory at Temple University in Philadelphia. "For young children, seeing circles and squares is not as good as manipulating circles and squares."

A chief criticism is the quality of software. Healy, for one, believes much of the educational software marketed to parents is "drill and practice, thinly disguised as some sort of game." Math programs that teach a child to memorize but fail to let the child explore and understand the concept are missing the point. And "having them blast letters out of the sky is not the way to teach kids reading and reflection," says Bob McCannon of the New Mexico Media Literacy Project. Reading, he says, involves "concentration, attention span, enjoyment of detail, and some level of inspiration. . . . To this date we haven't seen any soft-ware that accelerates that, and there is a tremendous amount of software that detracts from that." Further, computer learning is often by rote, and "children tend to lose that kind of knowledge," says Claire Lerner, a child development specialist with Zero to Three, a nonprofit group that promotes healthy development in the early years. For example, rather than using a computer program to teach a toddler about proportion, she recommends finding a way to describe it in daily life. "Talking about big shirts and small shirts while you do the laundry is much more meaningful and long lasting."

Virtual tiaras. Then there is the importance of imagination in encouraging creativity. A child can pop in a CD-ROM and pop up a princess, her wardrobe, and the crown jewels, but it would be far better for the child to pretend to be a princess herself. "She has to grab a pink pillowcase and make a skirt," says Healy, with a kitchen chair for her castle and the floor for a moat. Even though princess jobs are hard to get in the real world, playacting teaches kids to problem solve and thus prepares them for their future. "The people who have re-

---

TEENAGE YEARS

Logging on young, and paying later

Adam Hathcock has been hooked on computers since 1989, when he first laid eyes on his family's new Intel 286 at the age of 7. He spent hours playing Pitfall and pecking out book reports; later on, he got his own PC and spent even more time online, rarely leaving his CD-ROM-cluttered room, except to go to school.

For a shy kid like Adam, the computer was a godsend. It allowed him to overcome his awkwardness and hang out with virtual pals, and the fact that he was the tech whiz in his family built confidence. But the 18-year-old now recognizes that it caused some problems, too. "It gave me a reason why I didn't have to go out," says the Auburn, Ala., native, noting that he never had many real-world friends. He also stopped playing sports and slacked off in school. Sometimes, he'd play computer games like Doom for so long that he'd stop blinking, but he'd keep going anyway, tears streaming down his face. All along, his parents urged him to go outside, to spend more time with family and peers, but Adam's teen rebellion was to keep logging on.

Today's teenagers are the first generation to use computers nearly all their lives. But while benefits like easier access to information and freer communication far outweigh the disadvantages in most cases, researchers are increasingly concerned about some potentially harmful effects on teens.

Lone rangers. A controversial 1998 study at Carnegie Mellon University found that teenage computer users showed signs of increased loneliness and isolation. While adolescents are seemingly always talking with peers online, these can be weak social ties, says Harvey Waxman, principal investigator of the Project on the Internet and Human Behavior at Harvard Medical School. "Young people can come to feel very lonesome if all their connections are on the Net," he says. Often, those who are struggling with other problems log on as a means of escape. Take Andrea Kelton, 16, who suffers from social anxiety disorder. She turns to the comforts of all-night Web surfing, searching for guitar tabs and working on her personal sites until dawn. "I try to replace people with the computer," she says.

In addition, while teenage rebellion is nothing new, the Internet can be a breeding ground for bad behavior. "There is something about the impersonal and anonymous nature of the Web that makes it easier to say things and do things you wouldn't do if it was a face-to-face encounter," says Elizabeth Kiss, director of the Kenan Institute for Ethics at Duke University, noting that this seems particularly true for adolescents. For some, there's a different set of rules online, which allows cheating—kids downloading plagiarized term papers, for example—and the seemingly constant spate of teen hackers who terroize various organizations.

Still, while Adam Hathcock admits that computers have had some adverse effects on his life, he's not about to give them up. "They're going to provide a job and lots of money if I do it right," he says. However, the Auburn University freshman *is* making a concerted effort to be more social these days. He has joined the school's computer gaming club, for starters, and now meets dozens of other guys in a campus lab twice a week to play games like Quake 3 and Starsiege: Tribes together. "This way," he explains excitedly, "you can yell in someone's face when you beat'em."

—*Carolyn Kleiner*

warding jobs are going to be the people who have ideas," says Healy.

But there is some good software out there, if you know where to find it (see box Ready, Set, Shop). "Modern software can provide very, very rich environments for learning," says Susan Haugland, a Denver-based early childhood education professor. Children exposed to high-quality developmental software showed significant gains in intelligence, nonverbal communication skills, long-term memory, and self-esteem, according to a nine-month study of 4- and 5-year-olds she conducted while at Southeast Missouri State University in 1992. The children who were exposed only to drill-and-practice software, however, showed a 50 percent drop in creativity.

BACK IN 1994, WHEN PRESIDENT CLINTON vowed to connect every school to the information superhighway, fulfilling that pledge seemed like a distant and costly dream. Only about 1 in 3 schools, and just 3 percent of classrooms, were wired to the Internet. But by 1999, according to the National Center for Education Statistics, 95 percent of schools—and 63 percent of all classrooms—had Internet access.

Bringing computers into the schools has, without a doubt, served many students well, particularly lower-income or geographically isolated kids and learning-disabled students. Word processors, for instance, can help kids who struggle with handwriting or translating thoughts into prose organize their work and compose stories. Certain kinds of software can help dyslexics learn to associate letters with their corresponding sounds, while other "assistive technologies" can enlarge words for sight-impaired students or respond to voice instructions.

So it's not surprising that many in the education field were dismayed by the Fool's Gold report and the petition asking that schools hold off on buying new equipment. "I cannot conceive of why we'd want to take computers out of their hands," says Linda Roberts, the director of the Office of Educational Technology at the U.S. Department of Education, who has spent years trying to get computers into classrooms. Like blackboards or fingerpaint, she says, the computer "is just one of many tools" that help children develop everything from critical-thinking skills to problem solving.

The key is to use the technology well. For some schools, this means waiting until a child has mastered reading and writing. At Forest Bluff Montessori in Lake Bluff, Ill., kids can start on keyboarding when they are 9, but aren't introduced to the Internet until the age of 12. Other schools start earlier, but take a thought-out approach. "We don't do drill and practice here," says Betty Carle, a computer teacher at Dows Lane Elementary School in Irvington, N.Y., which last year embarked on an ambitious program to enhance the curriculum with computers and a high-speed Internet connection. Instead, students work in pairs on class-related "Web quests," making books and creating PowerPoint presentations. This fall, third graders are learning to classify things and creating graphic "personality inventories." And, says Carle, Dows Lane teachers don't just plop students down in front of the computer and disappear. She also disputes the notion that computers create unsocial loners or phlegmatic students, she says. "If a kid is passive, he will be passive no matter where. I have a niece who would sit and read all day." And no one thinks that is an antisocial activity. Then again, muses Carle, "sometimes it's the way the child is raised."

Her point hits home. In school, after all, few kids get to spend all that much time in front of the screen. But a child who gets 20 minutes of computer time each week at school may get 20 hours at home. Parents who would limit TV watching often encourage cybergame playing. And they're often driving the excesses in school: Even at the preschool level, some parents insist on having a computer in the classroom, says Silvia Dubovoy, a San Diego psychologist who trains Montessori teachers working with 3- to 6-year-olds. "They are very concerned about their children being able to go to Harvard."

Anne Alpert, director of the Side by Side Community School in Norwalk, Conn., says she can tell from afar which of the younger students are home-computer nuts and which spend their off time goofing around with friends. The computer users "are reticent," she says, less inclined to take the small risks that build competence and creativity and more likely to have trouble negotiating the politics of the playground. The computer-free kids, who spend hours doing old-fashioned things like playing dress-up and Crazy Eights and reading books, are social and outgoing, curious, and work well in groups.

There may be physical ramifications as well, though the evidence is mixed. The American Optometric Association says that computers can exacerbate conditions like nearsightedness, but the American Academy of Ophthalmology says no evidence has been found of damage and that eye strain is a normal reaction to prolonged close-up work. Still, some in the field, like pediatric optometrist Pia Hoenig, are concerned. In practice since 1973, Hoenig says that in the late '90s she noticed a "significant increase" in kids with weak focusing skills. "We used to see [these] problems just in children doing an incredible amount of reading," says Hoenig, a professor and chief of the binocular-vision clinic at the University of California-Berkeley. "The increase has been exponential . . . with the rise of computers in homes." In years past she found these problems among heavy readers who read chapter books before the fourth grade. "Now, I'm seeing them around second grade. . . for computer-related problems."

And, since computer workstations are rarely designed for kids, there are longstanding concerns—and, again, no consensus—about the effects on young wrists, arms, and backs. Cornell professor of ergonomics Alan Hedge says that today's ergonomic habits could have a lasting effect. "We know these injuries typically take five to 10 years to develop," he says. There really hasn't been enough time to see what the consequences are going to be. Laptops are particularly likely to cause problems, he says. But with children as with adults, prevention is pretty easy. "It's not one size fits all," he says.

SEVENTH GRADER ANDREW BENWARE is an A student "with the occasional B plus or A minus" at Ralph Waldo Emerson Junior High in Davis, Calif. Andrew is also perfectly comfortable on the computer—even though his parents waited until last year to buy one. "When Andrew was younger [we felt] it was important for him to learn to rely on his imagination . . . to play, to have tangible contact with things," says Jana Tuton, his mother. "Our idea was to make life so boring that reading . . . would look good," she says, laughing.

Instead of using it as a doorstop

OK, so you've bought the computer for your kid. Good luck! The market is loaded with rubbish, and you can't necessarily rely on best-sellers, retail displays, or following what schools use. At least 75 percent of children's "education" software shouldn't go home at any price, says Susan Haugland, a Denver-based early childhood education professor.

How do you find the gems? A good program should be "open-ended," encouraging children to be actors and not reactors. Avoid programs that stoope to drilling—rote single-answer questions—dolled up with bouncy graphics, bells, and buzzers. Modern PCs with CD-ROMS and speedy chips have meant better software, but also "edutainment" bordering on video game banality.

Log on. The Web offers some answers. One of the better software checklists is on Haugland's Web site (*www.childrenandcomputers.com*). She likes software from Edmark, including the "Thinkin' Things" series, and the "I Spy" series from Scholastic New Media. She's critical of the best-selling Reader Rabbit series from the Learning Company and the popular JumpStart titles from Knowledge Adventure.

Of course, the experts don't all agree. Some versions of those titles, including Reader Rabbit's first-and second-grade software, earned a "very good" mark from *Children's Software Revue.* The company behind the publication rates thousands of titles at *www.childrenssoftware.com*, which also links to other review sources. Favorites include Math Blaster Ages 7–8 from Knowledge Adventure and Music Ace 2 from Harmonic Vision.

One catch: Some of the best-rated programs are hard to find. But almost all vendors sell their wares over the Internet—if you don't mind first doing a little homework yourself.

—David LaGesse

Offline. So Andrew spent much of his childhood swimming, riding bikes and scooters, and staging what his mother calls "elaborate dramas" with his friends. Not that he didn't miss the machine: "He pointed out that he was the only kid in the neighborhood who didn't have a computer," says Tuton. ("I know a second grader with a computer in his *room,*" says Andrew.) But now that there's a PC in the house, is Andrew a devoted user? No. "I think it gets boring after a while," he says. "I have more interesting things to do."

The bloom is off for the Foldis, too. For a while, they were impressed with the way their older boy, Matthew, learned hand-eye coordination and language on the " 'puter." At age 3, he knew how to say "Eustreptospondylus" from playing Dinosaur Adventure 3D. By then, though, he was spending as much as three hours a day on the computer. When his parents wanted to use a program to work on their finances, Matthew would ask how many minutes they really needed. Eventually, after he showed little interest in an easel and paint set he got for his birthday, they restricted Matthew to one hour on the computer a day. (Younger brother Jonathan gets 10 minutes.)

TV over PC? Experts disagree over when the ideal time is to introduce children to computers. "I am very reluctant to have any child under the age of 7 spending any time on a computer, certainly not alone," says Healy. "He probably is better off watching TV" with a parent. Douglas Sloan, professor of history and education emeritus at Teachers College, Columbia University, favors postponing computer use "until kids develop conceptual abilities, at around the sixth grade at the earliest." But Tufts psychologist David Elkind believes kids can begin limited, supervised fooling around on the computer after their third birthday.

What's crucial is that parents be involved. "Too much of the time we think the computer is supposed to do it all, and we don't really appreciate how important the people are," says Massachusetts Institute of Technology Prof. Sherry Turkle, a clinical psychologist and author of *The Second Self: Computers and the Human Spirit.* "It's the computer plus the human environment around the computer that matters." A child who is left alone to use the software and doesn't understand it will have a shallow experience. Look for balance, she urges: "You want to be sure your children are comfortable in the complex, messy shades-of-gray world of people and in the clean, black-and-white world of machines."

When kids do log on, they may do best to start by using the machine as a simple word processor, rather than playing with fancy software. "At 7, children love to write stories on computers," says Healy. The American Association of Pediatrics and other experts also advise against putting a computer in the child's bedroom, preferring a room that gets a lot of family traffic, such as the den or kitchen.

And it's important to feed the body, not just the mind: "If we want to capitalize on what evolution has given us, we don't want to make them sit in a chair and stare at moving pictures," says neurologist Frank Wilson. "What we want is to get them outside to play."

With Mary Lord and David L. Marcus

Symbiosis: University/School Partnerships

ABSTRACT—"Rather than wait to see what tomorrow's classrooms will be like, teacher education institutions must experiment with the effective application of computer technology for teaching and learning in their own campus practice" (NCATE 1997, 1). Seton Hall faculty have made a commitment to the greater integration of technology into instruction. We are at the forefront of this movement. We are trying to articulate a wider vision for technology, making it as essential a tool as the chalkboard. Partnerships allow us to share our vision more broadly with practicing teachers and the public. We are excited.

by Rosemary W. Skeele, James K. Daly

Seton Hall is very fortunate to have some of the most current tools, techniques, and training available for use in our teaching. As the number one wired catholic institution of higher education in the United States and sixteenth out of all colleges in the country (Bernstein 1999), much planning and effort has taken place to achieve this status. Seton Hall has made mistakes and has had successes, although many issues remain unresolved, with technology and in other areas.

Technology and Pedagogy

At Seton Hall we have allowed technology to change the way we live, communicate, and learn. Our charge as teachers is to adapt to these changes—to adopt methods and strategies that exploit this change in our lifestyle, culture, and learning.

In the College of Education and Human Services we believe that in our profession the areas affected by this technology revolution include: the new role of the teacher as a team leader and a learner; the use of new teaching methods; the need to explain the cultural mores and ethics associated with new technologies, and the need to bring technology to all economic and social groups in society. Take a closer look at these changes and how they affect learning.

New Role for Teachers

A pedagogical change is the new role of the teacher. As teachers, we have the opportunity to promote transformation and become members of a community of learners that encompasses both students and teachers. We are all learning together. It is important to encourage students to become independent learners and information managers. We can't memorize everything we need to know to be successful. We have to know how to locate information as we need it. The Internet is the largest source of information in the world today.

Originally published in conference proceedings from "Consortia Building and Industry Support for Implementing Instuctional Technology in Schools," July 1999. Reproduced with the permission of Learning Technology Institute, 50 Culpepper St., Warrenton, VA 20186.

Many students have this resource available at home where its use is growing by dramatic leaps. Teachers must be prepared to model technology use within the curriculum.

New Teaching Methods

Computer-based technologies have opened new paths for us to communicate with our students and for our students to communicate with each other. What we are doing at the college level is already trickling down into lower schools. We communicate with our students and sometimes their parents via email. They are in contact with us 24 hours a day. They submit their homework assignments via email. Between classes, we present topics for discussion on Learning Space, a software package that allows everyone in the class to view and respond to each other's comments as well as allowing the teacher to make comments. Students are required to stay electronically in touch with each other every day. Sometimes we hold entire classes electronically. We present the material, give assignments, and invite discussion—all from our remote computers.

Technology and Popular Culture

Educators at all levels have the responsibility to introduce the social, cultural, legal, and ethical implications of computing. Students must learn their rights and responsibilities, as well as the cultural mores of communicating electronically. They should know the ramifications of computing within the contexts of a larger society, and today that larger society is the world. The discipline of computing has been shaped by worldwide scientific, legal, political, and cultural trends.

The computing culture contains myths and misunderstandings that lead to the misuse of the technology. Turkle explains, "For every step forward in the instrumental use of a technology (what the technology can do for us), there are subjective effects. The technology changes us as people, changes our relationships, and our sense of ourselves" (1995, 232). Educators cannot solve all the problems of computer crime, guarantee that our students will behave ethically, or ensure that they will always be conscious of the inherent differences between cyberspace and real life. We can contribute to their awareness of the problems, open their eyes to these behaviors, and

hope that as members of society they will perpetuate the basic legal and ethical practices that enhance our quality of life.

Technological Equity

We need to bring technology use to all economic and social groups in our society because of its importance in our National Information Infrastructure. The telephone has been our main source of communication for almost 100 years in the United States. Telephones, poles, and lines made up our communications infrastructure. Today we are rapidly moving toward replacing the phone system with the Internet or a parallel network. Speedier, safer, wired and wireless transmission through network service providers, access by keyboard or voice or devices too numerous to mention, and audio, video, and interactive capabilities for communicating will come with this new medium.

Technology-proficient teachers are needed to close the so-called digital divide that separates schools in high- and low-income communities. To have a true communications infrastructure, everyone in the United States must know how to use the Internet and have access, whether public or private, to computer systems. Schools are seen as an integral part of the plan to establish this new infrastructure. Government funds for technology are available to school districts whose clientele can't afford to buy the equipment, training, and connections to be part of this infrastructure.

Partnerships

"Successful partnerships are characterized by an exchange of ideas, knowledge, and resources." (Danzberger et al. 1996) The partnerships in which we have participated arose from a variety of activities. A common link, however, seems to be our proximity or physical closeness to each other, although we do have a partner in Nova Scotia. The common goal of the partnerships has been to deliver services to students and faculty to improve education. Our partnerships have been among schools, service agencies, businesses, and professional organizations. Some are funded partnerships, required by the funding agencies; others have been developed through student intern placements, professional relationships, and serendipity.

School Needs

We are told that today only 15% of all classroom teachers across the United States have the skills to integrate technology into their classrooms effectively. We glibly say "The kids will show the teacher how to turn it on," but getting "it" turned on is different from using the technology effectively in the classroom. The current demand to use technology in the curriculum often intimidates many teachers. They adopt a rationale for avoiding its use. It's too impersonal, or technology prevents human interaction, they say. It's too dangerous or too risky for a teacher to use. I often hear that it wastes too much time or you can't cover the required material with technology. It's great for ___ (pick any subject), but there's nothing you can do with it in a ___ (pick another subject) class. Teachers need training to overcome this resistance before technology can be used effectively in the classroom. Teachers often misuse technology. They have not been taught that it is another pedagogy to be learned and incorporated where appropriate.

University Needs

University professors usually have very few experiences in a real teaching environment. Other than student teacher placements, which Smith and Auger (1986) refer to as "marriages of convenience," they rarely develop close working relationships with classroom teachers. Teaching methods have undergone vast changes. New paradigms must be created that allow and encourage new models for training teachers. Dror tells us that despite the research completed by Sirotnik and Goodlad (1988) or Schwartz (1990), school-university partnerships still require a theoretical basis. The theoretical foundation is missing because the field suffers from a lack of research. Practitioners and university faculty must discover ways to communicate, build relationships, and become active partners. More inquiry must be made about the links between the practical and theoretical aspects of school/university collaboration (Dror 1997).

Technology-Based Partnerships

Through a variety of technology-based partnerships we are able to communicate the valuable knowledge and skills that we have developed and reap benefits for our students and faculty in return. As part of its mission, the College of Education and Human Services at Seton Hall University helps both public and private schools in a variety of ways to implement technology. We have developed user policies for school districts, trained teachers, helped set up laptop lending programs, designed technology-based curriculum, partnered for grants, and more. In return we have gained experience, discovered internship programs for our students, shaped more marketable students, encountered sources for publication, and achieved our college and university objectives.

Encouraging teachers and preservice teachers to discover new ways to enhance their instruction through technology can be a challenge for university professors. Partnerships have provided motivation, technical training, collegial support, funding, shared staff and resources, friendship, and synergy. Karwin states that to be successful, partnerships must have three key ingredients—"intellectual content, joint conduct, and synergistic outcomes (Karwin 1992, xxii)." When two or more groups work together and the results are greater than the singular achievements, we have created synergistic effects. This term more fully describes the collaborative endeavors we have developed. Our partners guide us and assist us to create change in activities both inside and outside the classroom. We will describe in detail several successful partnership projects with K–12 schools.

City of Orange Public Schools

In 1996, President Clinton states that it was his goal to make every American child technologically literate by the year 2000. "What we are trying to do in the White House is to work in partnership with everybody in America . . . to see that by the year 2000 every classroom . . . in the entire United States is hooked up to the Information Superhighway, that all our children have access to computers . . . , and all of our teachers have [this] kind of training and support" (Clinton 1996). Among the federal initiatives to accomplish this objective were Technology Literacy Challenge grants. Many school districts applied for these monies to improve the quality of education for their students. Goals 2000 grants required school districts to include a university partner in their plans. Seven districts requested our assistance and four received funding enabling us to form four diverse partnerships with school districts in New Jersey. Funding varied greatly and we played a variety of roles for these schools. One of the funded districts was the City of Orange because it is classified as having special needs. They combined a number of resources and produced a well-planned and innovative program to implement technology throughout the district. Technology would be incorporated into all areas of the curriculum, not taught as a separate subject. A technology-rich environment for teachers would be created in Orange.

The plan was developed by an experienced administrator in the district and is a model for medium size urban school districts. The goal was to make an entire district—teachers, administrators, students, and some parents - computer literate. The plan included:

- the purchase of laptop computers for all teachers, administrators, and selected students in the district;
- 32 hours of computer training for every teacher, administrator, paraprofessional, and clerical worker;
- a computer lab for every school in the district;
- a computer in every classroom in the district;
- Internet access for every school;
- email for every teacher;
- summer technology camps for the students;
- 12 hours of computer training for interested parents;
- Saturday technology programs for students;
- ongoing professional development for teachers using technology.

The plan was funded, and the district contacted its partner university for advice and assistance. Our philosophy at the university is that technology is a technique like collaboration or critical thinking that is used to enhance the learning process. We treat it as a necessary pedagogy. Students must know how to find information quickly and easily. Teachers must know how to find resources. At the college we were able to help develop the plan.

District User Policy. Writing a comprehensive user policy seemed daunting to the district. A bare-bones policy had been submitted with the grant, but a more comprehensive policy was needed. Attention to the different groups that would be using hardware and networks was essential. Student guidelines would vary from those of the district employees. Parental permission would be needed for Internet access. University faculty researched a variety of policies and found one available for purchase at a very low cost that could be modified to meet the district's needs. It incorporated the areas the district wanted to include, and discussed many others. This project became manageable using a well-developed template.

CyberCamp. A creative summer program for students was designed by the district's Director of Special Projects. Students could attend two-week sessions that combined the learning of computing and Internet skills with traditional subjects like math, reading, and writing. A variety of thematic sessions with topics ranging from baseball to travel would be offered. Help from the university was needed to plan the curriculum, train the CyberCamp faculty, and to monitor the progress of the project. Designing curriculum for elementary and middle school students was a real-life experience for college faculty who have the theoretical framework and skills, but are rarely enlisted to collaborate with teachers to design curriculum. This opened a door for new relationships. University faculty had experience designing computing course sequences, so they organized the content, catalogued pedagogy appropriate for teaching technology, and coordinated training and projects for the CyberCamp instructors.

Technology Training. "Technology's successful adoption in the classroom is unlikely without effective training" (Johnson 1999). This was the easy part, or so we thought. We train hundreds of students to use computers and software every semester. With many adjuncts in our employ, we had a ready staff to commence training teachers, administrators, and staff in the district. We developed a list of skills that combined learning the basics of Microsoft Office and the Internet with techniques, lessons, projects, and materials for integrating technology into instruction. Every training session brought modifications to accommodate our audience. We now faced a mature, professional, adult professional audience, a group that didn't play computer games or visit arcades, a group that didn't need the computer to do well in their other classes. This was a group that felt successful doing things without a computer. This was a challenging group. It was very important that what they learned was logically linked to classroom practice. The information technology programs are located in the College of Education. This unique location enabled us to meet both the technology and instructional design needs of the practitioners. During the training we were able to move seamlessly from software skills to pedagogy to designing lessons to meet the needs of this district.

Outcomes. The school district and the college faculty spent many hours together over the past two years completing the activities described above. Making connections between university faculty in colleges of education and classroom teachers positively affected both groups. Many of the traditional barriers that arose between university faculty and practitioners disappeared when they were engaged in joint projects with outcomes that benefitted both. The practitioners had the advantage of having trainers with skills in both instructional design and technology—trainers familiar with K–12 schools, curriculum, and school culture. The university faculty dispelled the notion that drill and practice is what kids in disadvantaged areas need. They demonstrated activities for using software tools for complex reasoning and problem-solving. Practitioners were encouraged to use these tools to engage in challenging projects in their classrooms and to go beyond drills.

The university faculty enjoyed the monetary incentives for training the teachers and the opportunity to gain first-hand experience in a school district. The partnership added experiences that aid the communication process. Classroom teachers are a valuable resource. Their recommendations positively affected curriculum content at the teacher training institution. The collaboration also provided the dividend of securing professional development opportunities for student interns.

Mount Vernon Middle School

Over the past three years an informal partnership was developed with the Mount Vernon School in Newark, New Jersey. Culturally diverse, the students represent over thirty-five language groups. Now under state control, the Newark public schools have suffered from years of academic and financial neglect. High staff absenteeism, high incidence of student failure, and high occurrence of drop-outs, combined with poorly maintained schools and inadequate supplies have produced serious consequences.

Creating a Partnership. Our first experience in the Mt. Vernon School was to support their peer mediation initiatives. Later, while supervising student interns, we began to build a relationship with a teacher who was seeking to improve her curriculum and methods for teaching social studies. By the end of the year we were in agreement that building a partnership could be beneficial both for her and her students and for us and our students. The next summer we met to identify partnership objectives for each institution based on our individual needs. The practitioner needed assistance to identify content material most important to the success of her students. She requested new ideas and motivating activities for her students. She felt they would also benefit from increased contact with university students. We needed an on-going opportunity to see social education presented in an urban setting, and our students, armed with research and theory from the university classroom, wanted opportunities to design lessons and units for real students. During the first year, the university students helped the classroom teacher design and teach lessons at the school and developed a collaborative working relationship. There was no technology available at the school, other than the teacher's laptop computer. At the end of the year, the eighth graders were invited to the Seton Hall campus to learn how to do web-based research. This was coordinated with a social studies project.

In debriefing the experience at the end of the semester, both groups of students highly rated the experience. The classroom teacher said her eighth-grade students enjoyed working with and learning from university students. They stated they would like even more contact with them. Faculty and students agreed that a regularly scheduled experience with organized activities would be advantageous.

Introducing Technology. Over the second summer we met with the teacher at Mt. Vernon to frame the next year's experience. We agreed to:

- increase the use of technology to better meet the needs of students from both schools with college students designing materials and lessons;
- create computer-based lessons for the teacher including PowerPoint presentations;
- and seek grant funding for the partnership.

We wanted to make technology a major component of the partnership which was difficult, but not impossible, with no equipment at the school. The university students had access to computers and the practitioner had a laptop. To encourage discussion between the university students, the professor, and the practitioner, email was used to communicate. A Lotus Notes discussion group was set up for the preservice teachers and the professor. They shared problems, lesson plans, and resources.

The university students designed the first presentations package used at the school. They carried a projector from the university to the school, the teacher hung a sheet on the wall as a screen, and the interns began the first in a series of mediated presentations. Other teachers in the school often came to learn from the student teachers. They were impressed by the content and quality of the presentations. The eighth graders evaluated the lessons, indicated they were stimulating and informative, and requested additional lessons from the student teachers.

Reflections on the Experience. By the end of the semester, the university students had begun reflecting on the experience for their portfolios. They saw the value of partnering university students with technology skills and practitioners who wanted assistance in designing lessons and materials using technology. The lack of equipment and training at the Mt. Vernon School created unique challenges, but even in previous field experiences where the technology and support existed, the university students observed that practitioners often lacked the time or the skills to design multimedia lessons. Partnerships where university students bring technological skills while gaining from the expertise of practitioners in working with school students were perceived as very valuable.

In their reflections, the university students wrote of their surprise at the lack of technology in the classrooms throughout the school, and of the potential that it presented to revive student interest and learning in the social studies. They valued the discussion group as a tool for communicating ideas and concerns as they arose throughout the semester, and were pleased with the quality and quantity of advice and resources they were able to provide for one another. Previously existing stereotypes of urban schools were eradicated by the reality of working with students anxious to learn, and particularly enthusiastic about using technology.

The world of the pre-collegiate school is slow to change. Among other circumstances, teacher isolation within the institution as it currently exists makes change difficult (Britzman, 1991). How will increased use of technology influence this phenomenon? While technology has integrated virtually all other areas of our culture, schools are interestingly resistant. The need to integrate technology and new pedagogical practices that enhance the new technologies could be met to a significant extent by utilizing the skills of the college preservice teacher candidate and teacher training faculty. The college student entering a school classroom can bring strong technology skills, an awareness of research and new pedagogy, as well as enthusiasm and a desire to succeed. The same student benefits from the experience, guidance, and ideas gathered while working with school practitioners and their students. In this type of partnership, the teacher training faculty has the opportunity to become a vital part of the world of practice in the K–12 setting where their students are involved in student teaching and field experiences.

Educational Technology Training Center

The Essex County Educational Technology Training Center (ETTC) is a partnership between Seton Hall's College of Education and Human Services and the local South Orange—Maplewood School District. The ETTC provides technology training and professional development opportunities for the 23 public school districts in the county. The ETTC is funded by the federal government through a grant administered by the state. The university/school partnership was mandated by the grant. Faculty and administrators from the college are on the advisory board for the Essex County ETTC. This partnership is a model for resource sharing.

We participate in many cooperative ventures with the ETTC. We have jointly sponsored conferences. Faculty and students offer workshops. The ETTC employed a student from the College of Education to develop its web page which was linked to the university web site. Students in the course called Integrating Technology and Education research web sites that are useful for teachers. They critique the sites which are then hyperlinked to the ETTC home page. They check the sites periodically to keep links current. Students in education courses develop technology-based lesson plans and activities that are distributed to practicing teachers at workshops. The college provides televised distance-learning courses for teachers through the ETTC.

Center for Law-Related Education

The New Jersey Law-Related Education Center (NJLREC) is a grant funded partnership between the College of Education and Human Services and the National Law-Related Education Network. Each state has one LRC that provides training and technical support for K–12 teachers enabling them to integrate law-related education into existing curriculum. The NJLREC/SHU partnership assists faculty to: affiliate with K–12 teachers, administrators, and students; identify research opportunities; situate student teachers; discover employment opportunities; collaborate with motivated, cutting-edge practitioners; and achieve recognition for providing high-quality professional development.

Three grant funded projects—Bias Free Youth Program, Conflict Resolution in US History, and The Supreme Court Institute—are projects of the NJLREC. These special programs include partnerships with schools throughout the state to train teachers about social and ethical issues that arise in the curriculum. They provide an electronic arena for dialogue, reflection, and sharing. The university provides participants in these programs with access to online discussion groups, web-based document repositories, and maintains these sites. The electronic link provides a collegial forum for interaction between individuals who have worked together and share common goals and interests. The document repository is open to the public and contains lesson and unit plans designed by participants. These special projects help the college to fulfill its mission to promote ethical educational practices.

MediaSpark

One of our partnerships is a university/business/school collaboration. A Seton Hall alumnus is a representative of a company in Nova Scotia that develops software that allows schools to safely and easily use the Internet. He believed that we could help each other through a partnership. Specialists at the company critique our students' web-based lessons. Lesson plans that are acceptable are published by the company on their web site. The company believes that well-developed resources related to curriculum here in the United States will make their products more marketable. Their knowledge of resources that work well on the Internet has been invaluable. The opportunity to publish has been an incentive for our students to develop good products. The company also makes a contribution to the university when they use one of our students' plans. Indirectly, we help teachers all over the globe to use the Internet effectively in their classrooms.

Conclusions

Colleges that prepare teachers have a greater responsibility than ever before to work with K–12 schools (Boyer 1994). Describing education as a seamless web, Boyer states that all levels of schooling are inextricably intertwined. Often, this involvement is not examined or utilized for the benefit of students and teachers at all levels. Working together, universities and schools can identify and build on common needs and shared strengths. The promise that such collaboration holds can best be achieved through partnerships between schools and universities. Higher education faculty have a need to better understand the nature of schooling, and the experience and skill to lead a reflective examination of the impact technology has on those institutions.

How can those in higher education begin to build partnerships? Expanding on existing models can be valuable. One form of partnership, born of necessity more than thoughtful reflection, is student teaching. College and university students work with practitioners, with the systematic involvement of a university supervisor. University students can be more actively involved in projects and activities centered around field experiences that meet the needs of the teacher training institution as well as providing support and resources for practitioners and their students.

Moving beyond partnerships limited to student teaching, the key to building stronger and richer collaboration requires that there be a potential value to those involved (Hechinger 1994). This means that goal setting must be mutual, with agreed on priorities and procedures. The role and impact of expanding technology use in the schools provides an excellent rationale for building partnerships. As new technologies become available in schools, increased needs arise for teacher training. Partnerships can meet this need. Collaboration permits identification of individual needs, agreed-upon objectives, and a collegial setting in which partners freely share their expertise while learning from one another.

Technology can easily transform the manner in which such partnerships take place (Lasaga 1994). Email and discussion groups provide continuous communication. Ideas and plans can be shared and critiqued quickly. College students can provide ideas and information to assist school students with research assignments and homework. Technology can also be the focus of that transformation. The college student becomes a change agent for the school (Marcovitz 1997) while still a student. The college student can provide direct support, design and implement technology based projects, and provide a source of information on the nature and uses of technology in the classroom.

The research culture of university faculty can be used to help partnership members reflect systematically on what they are doing, why they are doing it, and how it is changing them, their students, and their institutions. Recognizing change as it occurs assists participants to revisit goals and objectives, and to consider new possibilities as circumstances change. The areas for investigation seem unlimited, and could easily focus on the very nature of schooling, the outcomes a democratic society needs and expects, and how we can adequately measure what our efforts have produced.

Marc Liebman, a superintendent of schools who brought millions of dollars worth of services to his school district through a variety of partnerships, states that "Partnerships need three things to succeed: tenacity, a clear sense of what you want, and luck (Creating . . . 1997)." Partnerships are two-way. Groups that are willing to work together, set clear objectives, and share resources, responsibility, knowledge, and technology have the opportunity to grow. Through partnerships you build vision, teamwork, a solid understanding of your options, and a well-developed plan. Collaboration is a link to training, equipment, connectivity, and the future. Invest in yourselves and your students by seeking a link to current technology funding initiatives. Exploit the positive aspects of each partner in the collaboration.

References

Bernstein, R. (1999). America's 100 most wired colleges. *Yahoo! Internet Life*. 5(5).

Boyer, E. (1994). Summer. New directions for collaboration [21 paragraphs]. *On Common Ground* [on-line serial], (2). Available: http://www.cis.yale.edu/ynhti/pubs/A15

Britzman, D. (1991). *Practice makes practice: A critical study of learning to teach*. Albany, New York: State University of New York Press.

Clinton, W. J. (1996). *Remarks by the President in education technology discussion with students, teachers and business leaders*, 15 February, at Christopher Columbus School, Union City, NJ. [On-line] Available: http://www.bergen.org/AAAST/Prez/transcript.html

Creating successful partnerships: Marc Liebman. (1997). *Technology and Learning*. Dayton: Miller Freeman Inc. [On-line] Full text from: ProQuest File. Available: http://proquest.umi.com/

Danzberger, J., C. Bodinger-deUriarte, and M. Clark. (1996). *A guide to promising practices in educational partnerships*. Washington, D. C.: U. S. Department of Education.

Dror, Y. (1997). *Systematic partnership of university level schools of teacher training for improvement and Change in the field*. Westminister Studies in Education. Abingdon: Carfax Publishing Company. [On-line] Full text from: ProQuest File. Available: http://proquest.umi.com/

Hechinger, F. (1994, Summer). About partnership: Breaching walls of academia [15 paragraphs]. *On Common Ground* [on-line serial], (2). Available: http://www.cis.yale.edu/ynhti/pubs/A15

Johnson, D. (1999). Nothing ventured, nothing gained. *Childhood Education*. 75 (3): 161–166.

Karwin, T. J., Ed., (1992). *Beyond the handshakes: An examination of university-school collaboration*. Long Beach, CA: California Academic Partnership Program.

Lasaga, A. C. (1994, Summer). Collaboration and technology [9 paragraphs]. *On Common Ground* [on-line serial], (2). Available: http://www.cis.yale.edu/ynhti/pubs/A15

Marcovitz, D. M. Technology and change in schools: The roles of student teachers [54 paragraphs], *Preservice Teacher Education* [on-line]. Available: http://www.coe.uh.edu/insite/elec_pub/HTML1997/to_pt.htm

National Council for the Accreditation of Teacher Education (NCATE). (1997). *Technology and the new professional teacher: Preparing for the 21st Century classroom*. Washington, DC: NCATE.

Schwartz, H. S. (Ed.). (1990). *Collaboration: Building common agenda*. Washington, DC: Clearinghouse on Teacher Education and American Association of Colleges for Teacher Education.

Sirotnik, K. A. and J. I. Goodlad. (1988). *School-University partnerships in action: Concepts, cases and concerns*. New York: Teachers College Press.

Smith, D. and K. Auger. (1986). Conflict or cooperation? Keys to success in partnerships in teacher education. *Action in Teacher Education*: 1–9.

Turkle, S. (1995). *Life on the screen: Identity in the age of the Internet*. New York: Simon & Schuster.

Rosemary Weiss Skeele is an associate professor in the Educational Studies Department, College of Education and Human Services at Seton Hall University, South Orange, NJ. Her phone number and email address are: 973–275–2120 and skeelero@shu.edu. Dr. Skeele directs the Graduate Program in Instructional Design & Technology; Graduate Program in Educational Media; Computing Certificate Programs; and computing courses. She teaches graduate technology and research courses and enjoys the creative process involved with developing instruction. In the past she has directed the Media Center and Continuing Professional Education for the College of Education and Human Services. Dr. Skeele has degrees from Jersey City State University, the University of Wisconsin at Menomonie and New York University.

James K. Daly is an associate professor in the Educational Studies Department, at Seton Hall University, South Orange, NJ. His phone number and email address are: 973–275–2726 and dalyjame@shu.edu. Dr. Daly instructs graduate and undergraduate students in the elementary and secondary education programs. He is the associate director of the New Jersey Center for Law-Related Education. He teaches social education and educational psychology courses. In the past he taught social studies at High Bridge Middle School for 16 years. Dr. Daly has degrees from West Virginia University and Rutgers University.

Who Owns the Courses?

Sally M. Johnstone

An issue getting too much attention these days is that of intellectual property rights. Some faculty members seem so concerned about who owns the material they put together in an electronic course that they are paralyzed and unable or unwilling to create materials for electronic distribution. Instead they spend their time arguing with university and college administrators over protective issues that will probably never matter anyway. Unless the electronic course is exceedingly well developed, packaged, and supported by a team of people with different skills, most of what a faculty member will create for a single course will have value only within his or her particular course. It seems unlikely that the average faculty member will ever become a dot-com millionaire by being an online entrepreneur.

There are some issues involving electronic course production over which faculty should have complete control, such as the length of time course material is relevant. However, not to contribute to the creation of electronic resources just because the faculty member does not have full control over how they are used seems like a sad situation.

We could argue that all the team members involved in creating and supporting a good electronic course could have as much right as the faculty member to claim ownership of intellectual property. After all, one of them may have created some superb graphics or animation to illustrate a difficult-to-learn concept. Another may have devised a student discussion scheme including logistics to handle multiple time zones and published it as part of the course package. Are these intellectual endeavors any less worthy of control by the individual who developed them?

It quickly reaches a point of absurdity if we assume every member of a team has complete control of the use of his or her team efforts. Textbook publishers use a model that seems to work. The publisher of the product owns it. The production team members (including the writer of the material) are paid for their work and may give up some of that pay to gamble on a successful sale and receive a royalty. Otherwise, they receive a fee for their contributions to the team.

Not all faculties are concerned about the issue of intellectual property rights. Recently, the faculty at MIT announced they would put courses up on the Web in an open courseware arrangement, inviting anyone anywhere to use their work. While no one would suggest that having the course materials is equivalent to taking a course from MIT, it does open up the content of a wide range of disciplines. This content may end up having multiple uses. It is not impossible for other universities to use it by adding their own support systems. Some company may choose to repackage it and market its version of it. But the best uses will be created by those who would not otherwise have access to this type of material.

At an international conference a few days before the MIT announcement, a gentleman from an African university asked me when U.S. universities would start making electronic courses and programs available at an affordable price. I responded with an explanation of the funding realities at American public universities and the priorities given to serving the needs of the states that supported them. I suggested that he not hold his breath waiting for low-cost courses from American universities. I have never been happier to be proven wrong.

As founding director of the Western Cooperative for Educational Telecommunications (WCET) at the Western Interstate Commission for Higher Education (WICHE), Sally Johnstone serves as a resource on higher education technology issues. She also serves on the Board of the American Association of Higher Education, the U.S. Open University's Board of Governors, and the Advisory Panel for the Consortium for the Advancement of Private Higher Education. Sjohnstone@wiche.edu

Unit Selections

Key Points to Consider

❖ What do you believe is the future of the use of the Internet within the educative process? What effect will it have on education in the twenty-first century?

❖ What is the role of telecomputing in the classroom, the library, the administration, or the home?

❖ What effect will hand-held technology have on educational programs and institutions?

 **Links**   **www.dushkin.com/online/**

These sites are annotated on pages 4 and 5.

The history of humankind has been tied closely to the tools of each age and the conditions shaped by these tools. During the last decade of the last century, the global implementation of Internet tools has turned the global village produced by television into a global mindset by enabling us to collectively process information. This collective processing is done by making each one of us an integral part of the processing. In this way we preserve our individuality, which is maintained while we enjoy the benefits of collective thinking. The Internet may be the most important tool since the development of the printing press. It enables us to develop an international point of view without leaving our desktop.

However, there is cause for caution. The torrential hype that has surrounded the Internet and the World Wide Web has created expectations high above its current capabilities. We are not at the moment where multiple gigabit connections are available to the masses. This may happen in the future, but if we focus on what the Internet is now, there is much to be excited about.

The articles in this section address several issues about the Internet and other networks, including the need to build critical skills that enable students to benefit from using the Web as a ready reference tool.

In the first article, "Internet 2 and the Next Generation Internet: A Realistic Assessment," Cecilia Preston describes new developments, such as Internet 2 and the Next Generation Internet (NGI) initiative, as well as other potential advances in high-performance applications that these new electronic resources will create. The article relates these developments to the evolution of the Internet, and looks ahead to their likely impact beyond the higher education and research communities.

Next, in "Intelligent Campus Buildings for the Information Age," Jack Coloz predicts that a well-designed electronic infrastructure will provide the educational and operational components of intelligent campus buildings, leading to a more effective, less costly educational experience.

Then Glen Bull, Gina Bull, and Steve Whitaker claim in the article "Web Clippings" that the solution to enhancing students' access to computers and online resources may soon rest in the palms of their hands. These mobile devices can readily access and retrieve Internet-based information. The authors believe this offers a wide range of possibilities for both educational and administrative uses in the classroom.

In the following article, "Avaricious and Envious: Confessions of a Computer-Literate Educator," R. W. Burniske asks the question, "Is there more to a computer than technical skill and is computer literacy more than a neutral term?" The author also ponders the paradox of whether hunger for computer literacy can invite computer dependency or whether computer literacy is an absolute necessity for life in the twenty-first century. When writers are processing words they also must "feel" the words.

Finally, in "Wireless Andrew," Michael Fickes describes how the use of the Internet and laptops helps Carnegie Mellon University students carry out sophisticated research anywhere on campus. The author also provides a description of how the university became a wireless community.

The Internet and Computer Networks

Internet 2 and the Next Generation Internet:

A Realistic Assessment

by Cecilia M. Preston
Preston and Lynch

Clearly, the Internet is now firmly established as the major commercial and consumer pathway to electronic information resources for both historical database providers such as Dialog or LEXIS-NEXIS and for the plethora of new and old content from government and private sources flowing onto the World Wide Web. And all of the Net-and Web-born electronic resources come to the users under a bewildering range of constantly-shifting economic models. Every searcher today uses the Internet routinely as a way to reach traditional sources and as a tool to search for information from the new sources. The Internet is no longer merely a place for researchers to communicate, exchange data, and obtain access to supercomputers, as was the case in its early days. It has become an integral part of the corporate and consumer mainstream.

We have begun to hear about new developments, such as Internet 2 and the Next Generation Internet (NGI) initiative, and about a new generation of advanced, high-per-formance applications these new developments will empower. This article will try to describe these developments and their context, to relate them to the evolution of the current Internet, and to provide some sense of their likely impact beyond the higher education and research communities.

The Context for Internet 2 and the NGI Initiative

Today's commercial Internet in the United States is completing a transition from a largely government-supported system designed to serve research, higher education, and federal agency missions to a public networking infrastructure serving businesses and consumers. The federal government's role was largely eliminated in the mid-1990s when the National Science Foundation phased out NSFNET. In recent months, the last of certain support functions having to do with the management of network numbers, the domain name system, and related activities has gone to the private sec-

tor or to non-governmentally supported, not-for-profit international organizations. While the issues involved in such transfers are very important, they have little to do with the day-today user of the Internet. The private corporations that currently offer Internet services have a massive program of capital investment, capacity expansion, consolidation, and service refinement underway that will likely continue for some years to come. Basically, the corporate sector faces the basic issues of keeping up with growing demand for connectivity, capacity, and service quality, and doing so while making a profit. Appropriately, corporate Internet providers have focused on the near-term needs of the business and consumer marketplaces.

Major Internet Service Providers (ISPs), such as Worldcom/MCI and Sprint, have made massive capacity expansions in Internet backbone systems. In the last few years the backbones have moved from DS3 (45 MB/second) speeds to OC–3 (155 MB/second), OC–12 (622 MB/sec-

From *SEARCHER: The Magazine for Database Professionals*, January 1999, pp. 66-70. © 1999 by Information Today, Inc.
Reprinted by permission.

ond), and above. But we must keep this growth in capacity in perspective: Huge and ever-growing numbers of users share these backbones. Still, the connections available to large corporate or research campuses have increased in speed significantly, and connections at OC–3 or above have become more commonplace. Networking speeds seen by consumers or small businesses have changed little, with the tremendous problem remaining of "last-mile" network capacity for organizations that cannot justify investments of hundreds of thousands or millions of dollars a year for high-speed connectivity. This last-mile performance bottleneck still fundamentally shapes the design and deployment of most of the applications that run on the Internet, since it defines what most end users can and cannot reasonably do.

Most end users today work with analog modems running at speeds of less that 56K/second; a few end users, and many small businesses, reach the Net through similar dial-up lines or through marginally faster technologies, such as ISDN or slow-speed frame relay. Despite the promises of new technologies that will relieve the last-mile bottleneck, such as cable TV-based connectivity, direct broadcast satellite, or digital subscriber line (DSL) schemes, the actual rollout of high-speed, low-cost connectivity is moving relatively slowly. It will be a number of years before the typical user of the Net can use advanced, bandwidth-intensive services. Note also that as a rule, a different set of companies from the traditional ISPs has the job of solving the last mile bottleneck—cable TV companies, local telephone companies, utility companies, and other new-to-the-Net players. The capital requirements and scales of these businesses differ greatly from that of the traditional ISPs offering dial-up access to consumers and leased line connectivity to large organizations.

Only the relatively small number of users at universities, research or-ganizations, and large corporations have access to the Net at higher speeds—most typically only about 10 MB/second Ethernet. Interestingly, we already see some new applications in development in these communities, such as some universities where every dorm room now connects at Ethernet speeds (so called "Ethernet to the pillow"). Transfer of a large amount of text, as well as the (not always legal) distribution of music in digital form, will require such bandwidth.

For the next few years, then, the emphasis in the commercial ISP world, and in the applications developed to run over the commercial offerings, will probably work around the realities of market demand and available connectivity. The research and higher education sectors, however, eagerly want to begin exploring a new generation of advanced network applications that involve orders of magnitude more end-to-end bandwidth than the current network can provide, or likely can provide in the near future. They also want to explore applications that require new network services beyond the best-efforts packet delivery offered by today's networks.

This is the strategic context within which the Internet 2 and NGI programs have developed.

Before going into detail about these programs, let me make three additional points to correct some misapprehensions. It is a mistake to think of Internet 2 and NGI as responses to market failures—rather they are a strategy to support advanced applications development (and supporting infrastructure technology development) not yet viable in the commercial marketplace. The results of these efforts will feed into the evolution of the commercial In-ternet and the applications that it supports. The existing ISPs as well as the networking and information technology providers are major participants in, and generous underwriters of, the advanced networking initiatives.

It is also an error to think of the advanced networking efforts as programs to create a new separate set of networks for an elite group of organizations that will then disconnect from participation in the current commercial Internet. Rather, these

"It is a **mistake to think** of Internet 2 and NGI as responses to market failures. . . "

supplementary networks will function as protected testbeds within the fabric of the existing Internet for advanced applications development. The organizations participating in Internet 2 and NGI will continue to have a major presence on the existing Internet. Indeed, only minimal commercial traffic will likely go over the experimental networks. Internet 2 and NGI participants will still need the commercial networks for e-mail, electronic commerce, access to databases, and all of the rest of the activities that they perform today.

Finally, remember that the Internet is a global phenomenon, not a U.S. national network. This article addresses only U.S. developments. Other nations, including Canada and the European Community members, also have major high-performance networking initiatives in various stages of development. The public and private sector roles in networking vary from one nation to another and shifts take place at different rates than in the U.S. Also, with leadership from the U.S. National Science Foundation, some international efforts have begun to link the emerging high performance networks. [For details on these developments, check http://www.startap.net.]

Internet 2: A Higher Education Initiative

In 1996 a group of about 35 universities joined together to build a "better faster" Net. By 1997 they had formed UCAID, the University Corporation for Advanced Internet Development, to provide administration and other support for the Internet 2 project [http://www.internet2.edu]. This project now has 120 members of both university and private sector sponsors.

The major goals set out for the Internet 2 on the UCAID Web page include the following:

- "Creating and sustaining a leading edge network capability for the national research community. . . . the frequent congestion of [the network's] commercial replacement have deprived many faculty of the network capability needed to support world class research."
- "Directing network development efforts to enable a new generation of applications to fully exploit the capabilities of broadband networks, media integration, interactivity, real time collaboration. . . . This work is essential if new priorities within higher education for support of national research objectives, distance education, lifelong learning, and related efforts are to be fulfilled."
- "Rapid transfer of new network services and application to all levels of educational use and to the broader Internet community; both nationally and internationally."

UCAID is building a mesh of high-performance connectivity among the participating organizations called Internet 2. Internet 2 involves a multi-tiered strategy with regional groupings of institutions establishing what they call "gigaPoPs" or gigabit point of presence (regional networks of connection points designed to tie together the high-speed Internet 2

and other types of networks). These work somewhat similarly to the regional networks established in the mid-1980s to aggregate clusters of organizations for connection to national backbone services. The installation of about 10 gigaPoPs in various regions around the country set the stage for all participating universities to have a stable Internet 2 connection by the first quarter of 1999.

Several high-speed networks will interconnect the gigaPoPs to support research in advanced applications. These include the NSF-sponsored vBNS network, running ATM (asynchronous transfer mode) service at 622 MB/second, with typical connectivity to each gigaPoP (or in some cases directly to participating institutions) at OC–3 or OC–12 speeds. In addition, the very high-speed Abilene network will serve as an additional backbone for Internet 2; this will run Internet Protocol connections over Sonnet, another high-speed network, at speeds of OC–12 and higher, using fiber provided by Quest and switches and routers from Nortel and Cisco.

UCAID is supported by member dues and by corporate contributions. Dues run around $50,000 a year. But besides the dues needed to support the central UCAID organization, participating organizations, in order to exploit the new capabilities of Internet 2, must make massive investments in upgrading campus networking infrastructures. This will require financing by institutional funds or by grant support.

The UCAID Internet 2 effort focuses sharply on advanced application rather than simply infrastructure improvement. UCAID employs a team of "middleware" developers and network engineers to facilitate these efforts for participants. Here are some of the goals for the Internet 2 project:

- The ability of researchers to collaborate in conducting experiments.
- "Virtual Proximity" to deliver education and other services such as telemedicine and remote monitoring of the environment.
- Quality of Service (QoS) to guarantee the service level required by an application. For example, a video stream requires a stable continuous path, whereas e-mail works reliably with the current routing infrastructure.
- Promote experimentation with new communications technologies.
- The development of standards to insure interoperability.
- Technology transfer to the rest of the Internet community.
- Monitoring the impact of the new technologies and applications on the higher education and Internet communities.

The Next Generation Internet (NGI) Program

Unlike Internet 2, which one can view as a network (or set of networks) and related technologies developed by a university consortium, NGI [http://www.ngi.gov] is a coordinated federal funding strategy that works through an array of existing federal agencies, such as NSF and ARPA (Advanced Research Projects Agency) to support advanced networking. In many ways, one can look upon NGI as a logical successor and complement to the older High Performance Computing and Communications (HPCC) program.

President Clinton announced NGI during the fall of 1996. The program went into place in 1997 and became a high enough priority to receive mention in the 1998 State of the Union address.

Established as a five-year program with budgeting of roughly $100 million per year, NGI essentially gets funded by Congress year by year. Nor should one consider all that $100 million as "new money"; instead, it represents money that the federal agencies earmark for NGI

"Clearly, **NGI and Internet 2** have a highly synergistic relationship and share many **common goals and objectives."**

activities with some of it certainly involving new money. The vast majority of this money will be spent in grants to the research and higher education communities for the development of advanced networking applications and infrastructure, and for research on key networking issues such as security, scalability, reliability, and network management.

There are three goals set out in the Administration's initiative:

- Connect the universities and national research labs with networks that are 100–1,000 times faster than the current Net.
- Experiment with new technologies, especially those that support real-time video, as well as those providing "testbeds" for related experiments.
- Develop new applications for health care, national security, distance education, energy, biomedical research, environmental research, and manufacturing engineering.

The White House National Science and Technology Council's Committee on Technology, Subcommittee on Computing, Information and Communication (CIC) R&D, Large Scale Networking Working Group oversees the NGI Implementation Team coordinating the work of the initiative.

Clearly, NGI and Internet 2 have a highly synergistic relationship and share many common goals and objectives. The goals of NGI stretch rather broader than those of Internet 2, including a direct research agenda, attention to the needs of federal agencies and national laboratories, and to applications such as national security that go beyond the

interests of the higher education community. Certainly, much of the work on Internet 2 applications and some support for infrastructure will get funding through NGI dollars via agency-based funding programs.

Recently, some have called for a major expansion in funding for advanced networking and information technology research. [See the interim report from the Presidential Committee on Information Technology at http://www.hpcc.gov/ac/interim/.] It is unclear how these proposals will fare in the political process of competing for funds, however.

The New Networks: Not Just Bandwidth, but Enhanced Services

Networks currently under development to support advance applications research via Internet 2 and NGI will certainly operate much faster than today's networks—with backbones likely reaching operating speeds of gbits/second. More importantly, with an appropriate combination of local infrastructure and long-haul backbones, this network will permit reasonably large numbers of hosts to sustain traffic rates of tens to hundreds of millions of bits per second for applications. They will also offer new network services such as Quality of Service (QoS) and multicasting, which will be important in supporting advanced applications.

As technologies, both multicasting and QoS today lie somewhere between research and large-scale, deployable engineering. In a few cases, individual ISPs on the commercial Internet have begun to offer some of these services. Both engineering and business problems pose

barriers to making these technologies widely available on the Internet as Internet-level services. One of the key goals of Internet 2 and NGI is to gain more experience with these technologies on an operational basis and to explore their interaction with application requirements.

Very briefly, QoS involves schemes by which some applications can take priority on the network, as well as ways in which the applications can request and receive guarantees of network performance (data rates, loss rates, packet delivery delays, etc). Those interested in the technical details can consult the book by Paul Ferguson & Geoff Huston, *Quality of Service: Delivering QoS on the Internet and in Corporate Networks* [John Wiley & Sons, New York, 1998, ISBN 0–471–24358–2]. QoS will be vital in supporting time-sensitive activities such as tele-immersion, video and audio interactions for scientific collaboration or distance education, control of instrumentation and telemetry capture, and the like. Clearly, QoS also implies the need for management schemes to determine who may obtain "premium" services and on what basis, as well as the technology to actually deliver the service.

Multicasting is important for the support of multimedia information distribution and a variety of advanced applications involving interactions among groups of sites, rather than only two endpoints. It involves a network capability that allows a network host to transmit packets destined for a group of hosts rather than a single target computer. The routers in the network take the responsibility for duplicating the packet as required to get it economically to all of its destinations. In an application where a machine transmits a video signal to a large number of receivers, the availability of multicasting can result in a massive reduction in network traffic loads.

As well as new network services, the new system will need new software infrastructure (sometimes termed "middleware") to support advanced applications—functions such as authentication and authorization, object naming, synchronization, and the like. While these are not considered direct Internet 2 or NGI issues, since they don't rely on the high bandwidth or new network services that the experimental networks will offer, applications developers will still need the new software developments to offer ubiquitous service. Since the experimental networks will connect relatively small and homogeneous communities (in comparison to the commercial Internet), it should be possible to deploy these software services in support of applications much more rapidly, and then, as one gains experience, extend them gradually to the broader commercial network. Certainly the design and development of such services very much form a part of the NGI and Internet 2 focus on facilitating advanced applications.

The New Applications

We have just begun to understand the shape of the new applications. Clearly, they will include a degree of interactivity so far in advance of today's applications as to represent a truly qualitative shift—shared collaborative tele-immersion environments, for example. Distributed simulations will become commonplace. The way large databases are treated is likely to change: For example, large-scale data mining, involving massive movements of database contents across the Net, will become an active area of experimentation in the new research nets. Further, the new environment will place video, audio, computer-generated graphics, geospatial data, and high-resolution images on a much more equal footing with traditional textual content—creating enormous problems about how to store, index, retrieve, browse, and manage this new content. The coupling of the research networks with new developments in

low-cost sensor and video capture technologies should constitute a particularly powerful combination.

Visually striking applications will likely get the most press attention and publicity, since the environment lends itself well to supporting them and they are easy to illustrate. But one should recognize that beyond these applications we will probably see some fundamental reconsideration of assumptions about how to manage data and computational resources and also considerable renewed attention on the issues involved in organizing and providing access to multimedia content. A less obvious consequence will probably include considerable evolution in thinking about authoring and reading practices for genres of multimedia works, as they become more useable within the research community.

It is difficult to generalize about applications at this early stage: Many will develop in response to the specific needs and interests of various research communities. The Internet 2 site [http://www.internet2.edu] contains descriptions of a number of the projects currently underway. Another excellent source for a view of how the next generation of networking may reshape scientific computation is *The GRID: Blueprint of a New Computing Infrastructure*, edited by Ian Foster and Carl Kesselman [Morgan Kaufmann Publishers, San Francisco, 1999 ISBN 1–55860–475–8].

Conclusions

For those not directly involved in the development and use of the advanced applications hosted on Internet 2 and other research networks, what do these developments promise?

1. The technologies developed here will, in probably a three to five year time frame, migrate to the commercial Internet. Migration will come in a gradual and piecemeal

process. Some technologies may move faster than others.

2. The advanced networks will provide the first serious testbed for massive libraries of digital multimedia. This content will then begin to shift to the broader commercial and consumer marketplaces, as the last mile bandwidth crunch eases. Almost everything about this kind of content, from an information management and retrieval perspective, is poorly explored. Lots of work is needed there.

3. Data mining may begin to occur in a serious way outside of individual organizations mining organizational resource databases. Sholom M. Weiss and Nitin Indurkhya in *Predictive Data Mining: A Practical Guide* (Morgan Kaufman, San Francisco, 1998 1–55860–403–0) define data mining as "the search for valuable information in large volumes of data. It is a cooperative effort of humans and computers. Humans design databases, describe problems, and set goals. Computers sift through data, looking for patterns that match these goals." Imagine the implications of "public" data mining and of repositories and tools set up for this on the life of the professional searcher.

4. Research networks will mainly focus on scientific, research, and education applications. Just as we saw a huge development of commercial and consumer applications in the World Wide Web as that technology moved out of the research labs and into the mainstream, we will see a similar flourishing of commercial and consumer applications as the underlying technologies of Internet 2 and NGI migrate to the commercial networks.

Acknowledgments: My continuing gratitude to Cliff Lynch for getting me into this area and his continuing contribution to my understanding of these technologies.

Intelligent Campus Buildings for the Information Age

By Jack Caloz

Three "Information Age" trends have colleges and universities scrambling to take a hard look at the flexibility of their campus infrastructure systems: rapid-fire changes in technology, particularly information technology; increased demand for flexible, technology-focused teaching spaces; and increased systems' interconnectivity.

Today's campuses are becoming heavily reliant on infrastructure technology and systems. Student and faculty require access to campus information systems, computerized databases, and research tools from almost anywhere on campus—dormitory, lecture hall, cafeteria, lab bench, the commons, or library—and from remote, off-campus locations. Today's wired generation and the future wireless generation will make demands on campus infrastructure, particularly information technology infrastructure, that are unprecedented.

Rapid-Fire Technology Change

To maximize today's significant investment in telecommunications technology and infrastructure support, colleges and universities must focus campus-wide, rather than cobble together a building-by-building or school-by-school system. Campus facility managers and information services (IS) department heads must also develop an intelligent campus infrastructure that will accommodate today's Information Age systems as well as new, rapidly emerging technologies. Yet, how can colleges and universities avoid investing millions in infrastructure systems that become obsolete almost as quickly as they are installed?

The crucial factor is to develop a flexible, expandable, and adaptable campus backbone—one maintained and expanded to accommodate growing institutional aspirations, while supporting the legacy systems needs of ongoing operations. Today, technology initiatives are woven throughout the goals of al-

most every institution, from campus networking plans to distance learning hubs, multi-modal presentations, teleconferencing centers, and computer-assisted experimentation, to name a few. Without a solid, flexible backbone, these initiatives will fail.

We need to pave today's electronic highways for tomorrow's development. The adage "Build it and they will come" is as true today as it was in the days of the ARPANET. The Internet has shown the previously unimaginable leverage achievable on an information highway on a global scale. Entire industries have emerged that are dwarfing our traditional ones. We cannot afford to choke the lifeblood of our educational institutions. To backbone infrastructure is the information highway to future opportunities for the students, faculty, and the institution.

Technology Master Planning

Picking the right backbone involves a technology master planning effort that focuses on an iterative solution as opposed to an ultimate solution. With the speed of technological change accelerating, your plan needs to be reviewed annually in context of the institution's goals and objectives and the technology that supports those goals and objectives. With goals and objectives defined, the foundation of your technology infrastructure—the backbone—then can be accurately assessed.

With microprocessor speed doubling every 18 months since the mid-1970s, a healthy diet of fiber is recommended. Insight into where the backbone is going is based on working with the next generation of IP (Internet protocol) service providers and Web hosting/co-location firms. While single-mode fiber is still king of the long-haul, high-bandwidth market, there is significant shift in the intermediate range. Distance and bandwidth continue to be the drivers in this mar-

From *Facilities Manager*, May/June 2000, pp. 25-28. © 2000 by the APPA: Association of Higher Education Facilities Officers.

ket. Gigabit Ethernet is stretching the bandwidth and distance limitations of the standard 62.5-micron fiber. We have seen a material shift in the market from 62.5-micron to 50-micron fiber for those applications where gigabit Ethernet is required or expected.

Copper is still king of the last 90 meters, although specialty requirements are still prevalent and wireless is growing rapidly. While not in the volumes of the past, copper is a backbone dietary must, if not for the building systems and legacy systems, at least enough for dial tone to call the service provider when the fiber lights go dim.

Wiring is a Key

Making a wrong choice in wiring will have far-reaching implications for future expansion and adaptation. The days of ad-hoc cabling systems are numbered. The increasing demands that high-speed telecommunications systems place on cabling require a highly structured system. The proper design of physical telecommunications infrastructure elements—today's critical "fourth utility"—is a key in assuring optimal network system performance.

In contrast, when various brands of layer-upon-layer of wiring is pulled, connected, disconnected, and reconnected in response to changing technology, it doesn't take long for wiring to become a tangled and confusing mess.

Cabling systems have traditionally been deployed in such a way that the system is not a system at all. The infrastructure becomes a conglomeration of vendor-specific components with little or no interconnectivity. Just as other building utilities must provide high quality service, telecommunications systems must be capable of providing performance, interoperability of systems, and efficiency of administration. Consistent standards-based solutions and careful attention to the associated support systems are essential in assuring many years of information exchange.

Existing and new buildings must give careful consideration to cabling performance, pathways and spaces, power provisions, and the infrastructure's relationship to system performance. Network downtime is often attributable to problems with the cabling media, either at termination points or along the cable length. Add to that the associated administrative time required to track down the problem and costs rapidly rise.

Problems can occur anywhere along the cabling system. Poorly sited or cramped closets, inadequate installation, pathways that do not provide needed support and protection, equipment and termination spaces not properly planned, or power provisions that cannot support the loads incurred, all can lead to system breakdowns.

One reason for a structured cabling system is technology is rapidly catching up to cable performance.

Until recently, performance issues were not as important in many networks because cabling systems were typically designed for transmission speeds beyond the information exchange capabilities of electronic equipment. This is changing rapidly as more aggressive standards emerge and the price of associated high-speed network technology improves. Thus the capabilities of cabling infrastructure will be fully realized.

Standards-Based Systems

Manufacturers have also recognized the advantage of allowing universal interface with recognized structured cabling systems. Thus a standards-based structured cabling system will provide connectivity for voice, data, video, fire alarm, security, and building management systems.

With the best available cabling media in place, attention must be given to interconnecting hardware. This component is as critical as the cable when serving high-performance networks. Universal connecting hardware provides a common interface for building systems and allows efficient management of moves, changes, and additions. Connecting hardware is a very hot industry topic, with a focus on assuring cable segments and connections achieve the same signal performance.

A common misconception is that the infrastructure is temporary and does not warrant the expense required to be "standards compliant." The reality is that the infrastructure often is in place for 15 years or more and congested closet spaces invariably lead to administrative problems due to difficulty in cable termination and identification. Twisted-pair telephone infrastructures, for example, have been in place in many facilities for half a century and are still supported. If technicians do not have adequate working space to terminate, the physical connection may be compromised. The sheer magnitude of cable routed to an undersized closet results in a situation where locating a problem becomes impossible.

Pedagogical Changes

The second trend affects how teaching spaces are designed. Learning environments must be flexible, able to accommodate multi-modal presentations and group learning, as well as the traditional pedagogical system of text-based lectures and testing—all within a single space. As a result, barriers that in the past typically separated lecture halls, classrooms, seminar rooms, and student gathering and study areas are quickly coming down. The goal of the Information Age campus design is to provide more intimate surroundings suitable for a variety of teaching methods for increasingly smaller groups of students.

These multiple-use spaces will require a creative and collaborative application of a media mix consisting of copper fiber and, yes, wireless. As means, methods, and approaches change to meet the future challenges of today's teachers, the support infrastructure needs to be there to facilitate the process. Significant interaction between the end users and the designers needs to occur to assure that the tools of the future are not precluded. Audiovisual support for teachers and state-of-the-art connectivity for students is a must. Today's students need to be prepared for the technological work environment they will enter. They will need to be adept at the use of today's tools and the school has to provide that experience. These challenges are economically achievable or at least not precluded when the collaborative efforts of the designer and users are combined to support the aspirations of the institution and the needs of its students and faculty.

Various room shapes and teaching styles notwithstanding, technology is fast becoming the central element in equipping classrooms and student gathering areas. Yet, since a space's design will far exceed the technology's useful life it is essential that good planning principles be applied to the infrastructure used within the space. For instance, a supporting system we have looked at many times but that has always fallen short of the viability mark was wireless LANs (local area networks).

Until recently the price/performance functionality was just not there. They were too expensive per point and performance was less than adequate for anything but the least demanding of applications. It has always been less expensive to cable than to go wireless. While that is still true for most applications, the latest 10 + mps product offerings appear robust enough for prime time. The applications in non-traditional spaces such as student gathering areas, historical renovations, and exterior areas, are making wireless LANs a part of the viable solution mix for today's campus. They are not ready for the engineering or graphical arts labs yet, but will be providing an additional tool for the right media mix formula to facilitate the intelligent campus for the Information Age.

Systems Interconnectivity

The third trend is the increased interconnectivity of systems. This means that in the future flexibility is enhanced as building automation systems (temperature control, lighting control, closed-circuit TV, intrusion detection, and access control) and educational automation systems (voice, data, video distribution, Internet access) all migrate to a common platform. This migration, with the right infrastructure system, ultimately will allow the plug-and-play approach to all educational systems in the future. Incorporating wireless, personal communications devices, which increasingly will enter the educational universe, will also be a major consideration.

This is an area where we can see some cost relief instead of more capital expense just to keep pace. The improving economics of electronic infrastructure, with its potential exponential increases in productivity, is only now becoming a reality. We see it in the stock markets as Wall Street rewards the "dot-coms," and on the campuses as we begin to leverage the migration to a common platform and the true sharing of infrastructure and data among systems.

A well-designed electronic infrastructure will provide the educational and operational requirements over the same wires and fibers. They will share data and combine the data from diverse systems to generate information. The information gathered from the campus systems will provide a new, more effective, and less costly educational experience, enriching students, faculty, and the institution simultaneously. New amenities for students will produce additional revenue sources for the institution and expanded opportunities for the faculty. A new paradigm is being created where the pie increases for all at the same time that your campus is Information Age-ready.

Jack Caloz is principal, information technology systems group, at Einhorn Yaffee Prescott Architecture & Engineering, P. C., New York, New York. He can be reached at jcaloz@eypae.com.

Web Clippings

The solution to enhancing your students' access to computers and online resources may soon rest in the palms of their hands.

By Glen Bull, Gina Bull, and Steve Whitaker

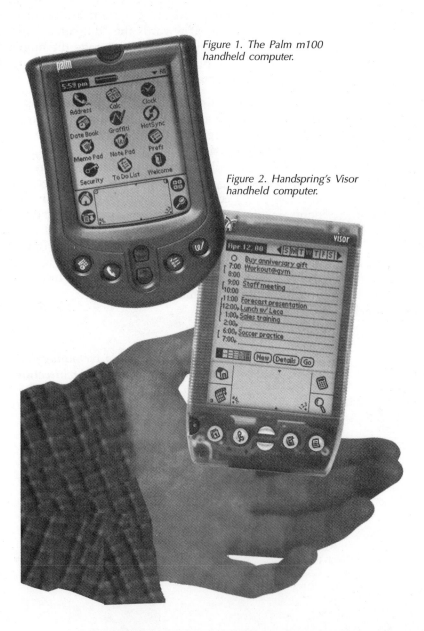

Figure 1. The Palm m100 handheld computer.

Figure 2. Handspring's Visor handheld computer.

Sometimes it is possible to see the glint of the future over the horizon. A new generation of portable handheld computers that fit in the palm of the hand may represent a future in which there is a computer in each student's pocket.

Despite a quarter century of progress in educational technology, today's K–12 students have limited access to computers in schools. There are few truly "personal" computers in public schools—only institutional machines shared by many students. The average student's access to school computers is typically measured in minutes per week. Teachers report that limited access to computers is one of the most significant barriers that many classes face.

Meanwhile, the price of handheld computers has been dropping rapidly. Both Palm (Figure 1) and Handspring (Figure 2) now offer handheld computers for less than $150. More advanced models offer features such as color and wireless Internet connectivity at additional cost. As prices continue to drop, it soon will be possible to equip an entire class for the price of two or three PCs, allowing each student access to his or her own personal, pocket-sized computer at any time. The affordable cost—less than most printers—makes this an ideal time for teachers to begin exploring educational uses of handheld comput-

© 2001, ISTE (International Society for Technology in Education), 800.336.5191 (U.S. & Canada) or 541.302.3777 (Int'l), iste@iste.org, www.iste.org. All rights reserved.

ers. By the time schools begin equipping entire classrooms, teachers in those classrooms will have a good sense of the educational capabilities of these devices and will be comfortable using them.

Handheld computers also have a great potential for mining the Internet. They are designed to be linked to the Internet through a desktop computer. Wireless modems such as OmniSky are also available as accessories, but their use involves a monthly service fee that makes them better suited for business applications than school use. When the hand held computer is dropped into a cradle connected to the desktop computer or connected through an infrared link, information from the Internet is transferred to it. If you are a teacher or administrator who is exploring the use of a handheld computer, or if you are about to acquire one, what are some of the educational possibilities?

Web Clippings

Handheld computers can be used to clip Web sites, or parts of sites, just as a pair of scissors is used to clip articles from newspapers or magazines. *Web clippings* is a phrase that has been adopted to describe information transferred from the Internet to the handheld computer in this manner. Many services can be used to secure Web clippings. AvantGo's free mobile Internet service is one of the more popular.

The newest Palm model, the m100, is sold with the AvantGo software pre-installed. (If you have another model, a handheld that uses Microsoft Pocket-PC, or even a wireless Web phone, you can download the software at no charge at AvantGo's Web site.) To clip a Web site from the Internet, specify the address of the Web site, the depth of links that should be transferred, and the maximum amount of information (in KB) that should be transferred (Figure 3).

AvantGo also offers the choice of including or omitting images. Though handheld computers can display images, they are better suited for display

of text except in the case of sites developed for mobile devices.

Web Channels

AvantGo offers a number of Web services designed specifically for mobile devices such as handheld computers. The AvantGo service checks selected Web sites (termed "Web channels" in its nomenclature) and updates the handheld computer to reflect the most recent information from that site. Web channels currently offered directly from the AvantGo Web site include the front page of *The New York Times* and other news services from around the world (BBC, *The Economist, USA Today,* etc.). A class equipped with handheld computers could compare headlines around the world in current events or civics class.

The technology offers forecasts from The Weather Channel, connections to Web portals (Yahoo!), science and technology information (*Wired* News, ZDNet, *PC World*), and a host of other services. Some of the services offered are interactive; for example, MapQuest (Figure 4) allows users to enter a location on the handheld computer once this channel has been added. Students could access maps of

the local area as they follow a planning commission session or even use a global positioning satellite (GPS) module in an interdisciplinary class integrating science, mathematics, and government.

The LearnLots Web channel offers online tutorials. When a tutorial (ranging from general computing to business and finance) is checked on the Palm, the information is transferred to the handheld computer the next time it is synchronized. The Hi-Ce Educator channel invites users to access "inquiry-driven, technology pervasive middle/high school science curricula from the University of Michigan."

In addition to existing channels, the AvantGo service allows users to create their own Web channels, which entails entering a Web address and a corresponding name. This can be used to transfer existing Web sites to the handheld computer or to access Web sites developed specifically with handheld devices in mind.

Classroom Applications

A classroom in which every student has a handheld computer would offer a number of options and opportunities. A class Web channel, for exam-

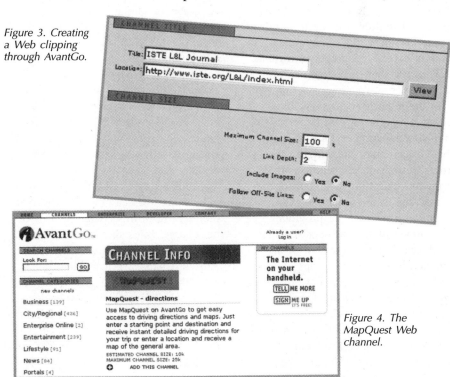

Figure 3. Creating a Web clipping through AvantGo.

Figure 4. The MapQuest Web channel.

ple, would allow the teacher to provide students with a class calendar offering schedules and assignments. Students could access this calendar anywhere, anytime, and the teacher could update it almost immediately when necessary.

A typical classroom scene today consists of a teacher writing information on the chalkboard while students copy it. Students in these classes become human recording machines, concentrating more on the documentation of a lesson than the lesson itself. A class fully equipped with mobile computing devices would allow teachers to post study guides and outlines using the class Web channel, saving time for inquiry-driven discussion.

A lightweight handheld device weighing several ounces can contain the equivalent of several thousand pages, making it feasible to include examples and resources that go beyond the information that schools now distribute. It is also possible to include interactive forms that might allow students to complete a self-test once they have reviewed the materials.

Pupils in science classes could use their computers to record information and observations during experiments and post the results to a common database, which would tally the statistics. The data could even come from other regions of the world, allowing students in diverse geographical regions to work together on a common project.

In the majority of today's classrooms, a significant cost is associated with dissemination of information. This cost is either measured in the time required for teachers to copy information onto the blackboard or the cost of duplicating materials. Once the initial investment of providing each student with a personal computing device is made, the cost of disseminating information drops markedly. Several states have already provided graphing calculators for each mathematics student, demonstrating the feasibility of providing each student with a portable handheld device. For instance, three years ago the Virginia Legislature allocated funds to

provide every high school student with a graphing calculator. And in Iowa, the state Board of Education established a plan with the same goal in mind, just as many school districts in other states have done. Acquisition of general purpose devices that incorporate graphing calculator software as well as other applications is the next logical step.

Devices equipped with document readers would allow teachers to distribute almost any reading material electronically. Infrared printers could allow documents to be transmitted to the printer through an infrared link.

Because handheld computers are also general-purpose computing devices, they could be used in a variety of other ways. For example, the next generation of graphing calculators is now being translated into software programs that will run on handheld computers. As a result, when new enhancements and refinements are made, students will be able to acquire them through a software upgrade, rather than by replacing the hardware. The current generation of handheld devices also incorporates text editors that can be used for notes and outlines. Notes can be entered with a stylus on the screen of the handheld computer or through a folding portable keyboard that can be acquired as a peripheral. Probes and sensors are available for the current generation of handheld computers for use in science class. Administrative applications are also available; Handango offers several. Teachers can, for instance, use grade-book programs that can also be synchronized with a database on a desktop computer.

Modern-day electronic libraries provide access to many classic works of literature in downloadable form without charge. Sites such as Memoware offer works by Charles Dickens, Jane Austen, Chaucer, Edgar Allan Poe, and other authors in formats designed for handheld computers. Other documents such as the U.S. Constitution, the Declaration of Independence, and the Bill of Rights are also readily available in this format (www.memowave.com).

Acquiring a Handheld Computer

Currently, two types of handheld computers dominate the market. Devices that use the Palm OS (operating system) constitute approximately three-fourths of all handheld computers. Devices with this operating system are sold by Palm and by Handspring, which makes the Visor. The Microsoft PocketPC (formerly Windows CE) represents the other market force in this arena. Devices with the MS PocketPC operating system are sold by companies such as Hewlett-Packard, Casio, and Compaq.

The two operating systems represent differing design philosophies. The majority of the Palm PC models are small, compact, and have monochrome screens that can run for several months on two penlight batteries. The entry-level models can be purchased for $150. Color is a desirable feature but comes at the cost of a higher price and shorter battery life.

Most PocketPC computers have color screens but consequently have a battery life that is measured in hours rather than months. They are designed as multimedia machines that can also play MP3 songs and short digital movies, and they can be acquired for about $500. Because more handheld computers currently use the Palm OS, a greater range of applications has been developed for this market. This could change if Microsoft is successful in increasing its market share in the future.

If you purchase either a Palm/Visor or a PocketPC, you will find a wide range of software available on the Web. Because handheld computers were designed in the age of the Internet, most programs are distributed this way rather than through traditional outlets such as bricks-and-mortar stores. Many applications are available in freeware and shareware versions as well as in commercial formats.

The Gadgeteer is a useful starting point for information about Palm and PocketPC hardware and software as well as a host of other personal digital assistants (such as the Newton, the Franklin, the REX PC, the Psion, and others). *PalmPower Magazine* provides information and reviews of Palm-based applications. Extensive, downloadable software libraries can be found at Handango, PalmPilotWare, and ZDNet.

The Future of Classroom Computing

The future of classroom computing is one in which every student has his or her own personal computer. The dropping price of handheld computers will make this both affordable and inevitable. The difference between access to an institutional computer a few minutes per week and access to a portable personal computer 24 hours a day, seven days a week, will result in a qualitative shift in the types of educational options that will be possible.

The form factor of handheld computers may change as the price of LCD screens drops. A handheld computer with a screen the size of a paperback book, similar to the electronic book readers now available on the market, might be better suited to school use. Wireless technologies such as Bluetooth will make it economical to connect handheld computers to the local area network without cables or hardwired connections. In this school of the future, students will have access to any reference work at any time throughout the school day. As this transition occurs, the focus may shift from rote memorization to the ability to identify, access, and evaluate information.

Summary

The high cost of desktop computers is a significant barrier limiting student access to computers in schools. One promising solution is a classroom in which every student has a handheld computer. These mobile devices can readily access and retrieve Internet-based information. With this capability, handheld computers offer a wide range of possibilities for both educational and administrative uses in the classroom. Teachers could readily track student information and could quickly create resources available to all students. Students themselves could access these resources almost instantly, and they could use their handheld computers for academic endeavors ranging from simple notetaking to cross-country collaborative projects.

The ancient Greeks were concerned that widespread use of writing would result in deterioration of the ability to memorize classic works, as readers would be able to retrieve information in letter-perfect form by picking up a book. They were correct—the world did change as a result of spreading literacy. Invention of the printing press by Gutenburg made these works affordable, further reducing reliance on memorized information. A future in which everyone has continuous access to information through mobile personal computing devices may also change the world in as yet unforeseen ways.

Resources

AvantGo, Inc., software and services: www.avantgo.com.

Bluetooth: www.bluetooth.com.

The Gadgeteer: www.the-gadgeteer.com.

Handango: www.handango.com.

Handspring's Visor: www.handspring.com.

Memoware: www.memoware.com.

OmniSky modems: www.omnisky.com.

Palm's m100: www.palm.com.

PalmPilot Ware: www.palmpilotware.com.

PalmPower Magazine: wwwpalmpower.com.

ZDNet: www.zdnet.com.

Glen Bull (GlenBull@ virginia.edu) is a professor of instructional technology in the Curry School of Education at the University of Virginia. Contact Glen at Curry School of Education, University of Virginia, Charlottesville VA 22903.

Gina Bull (GinaBull@ virginia.edu) is a computer systems engineer in the Information Technology and Communication (ITC) organization at the University of Virginia. Contact Gina at University of Virginia. ITC-Astronomy Building, PO Box 400324, Charlottesville, VA 22904-4324.

Steve Whitaker (whitaker@virginia. edu) is a graduate instructor in the instructional technology program in the Curry School of Education. Contact Steve at Curry School of Education, University of Virginia, Charlottesville VA 22903.

Subject: Handheld computing

Audience: Teachers, teacher educators, technology coordinators, library/media specialists

Standards: *NETS•S* 1, 3–3. *NETS•T* II–III. (Read more about the NETS Project at www.iste.org—select Standards Projects.)

Avaricious and Envious

Confessions of a Computer-Literate Educator

How did educators come to rely on networked computers and find themselves sitting before iridescent screens with their hands pecking at keyboards like blind chickens? Why have we submitted to this form of bondage? Perhaps a backward glance at one initiation story—Mr. Burniske's—will suggest an answer to this riddle, while helping computer-literate educators envision the future.

BY R. W. BURNISKE

IT WAS TIME to stop when the garbage can bulged. That's what I thought one evening a decade ago, as I restored the files on my computer's hard disk. Sometimes I wonder why I didn't hold myself to that vow, which would've spared me the nuisance of hardware and software upgrades, not to mention the anxiety—baseless, as it turned out—of Y2K.

Ironically, it is often because of such complications, not in spite of them, that we find ourselves thinking about educational technology. This may explain why, despite surviving millennial madness and Y2K locusts, I still cling to the memory of that dreadful rite of passage 10 years ago. I can't shake it—or the suspicion that we're suffering a serious delusion if we think our technological problems vanished the moment we stepped across the threshold of the 21st century.

It seems appropriate, therefore, to ask a few critical questions before memories of the 20th century fade. We might begin with this one: How did educators come to rely on networked computers and find themselves sitting before iridescent screens with their hands pecking at keyboards like blind chickens? Why have we submitted to this form of bondage? Perhaps a backward glance at one initiation story will suggest an answer to this riddle, while helping computer-literate educators envision the future.

In the beginning there was the Word.

Microsoft Word 1.0, that is. Like millions of other classroom practitioners, I didn't know the difference between an operating system and a software application, a modem and a mouse, when I purchased my first personal computer. Nor did I plan on giving such distinctions much thought or squandering

From *Phi Delta Kappan*, March 2001, pp. 524-527, by R. W. Burniske, author of "Literacy in the Cyberage" (Skylight 2000) and coauthor of "Breaking Down the Digital Walls" (Suny 2000). Reprinted by permission of Phi Delta Kappan and the author.

time fretting over a hard disk that served me without incident for three years. I had quickly grown accustomed to its operating system and the software applications I acquired along the way. Consequently, I expected to use the computer as a glorified typewriter, tapping perhaps 10% of its potential. This upsets computer jocks, I know, because they're always straining to discover new uses for the machine, but as a writer and teacher I was more interested in tapping my brain's potential. I preferred thinking about my destinations—including short stories, course syllabi, student assignments, and personal letters—rather than the vehicle. The less visible the vehicle, I thought, the less chance there was for it to distract me from my purpose.

Unfortunately, the "bomb icon," indicating a serious system error had occurred, shattered the illusion of an invisible medium. I could no longer "look through" this medium and focus on my work; the time had come to "look at" it as well. What I had formerly shoved to the background had suddenly jumped to the foreground. I didn't like this. I didn't appreciate the way this writing tool interfered with my reading and writing, calling attention to itself at a time when I wanted to think about other matters. It was there to serve me, I thought, not to be a nuisance. Why wouldn't it just leave me alone and let me do what I wanted? Beneath the frustration and the misdirected anger, however, lurked a subtle truth that I couldn't deny: while I had been working on that computer, it had also been "working on" me.

This forced a personal admission, as well as a hard look at the computer's influence. Like many computer novices, I had allowed my hands and mind to reach outward, groping for that which the logo at the base of the computer subtly recalled. The logo, a multicolored apple, sat there while I opened and closed files, concentrating on my destination rather than the vehicle that helped me get there. The logo sat there still, a dull reminder of another forager, while I dug out the manuals, committing myself to a weekend of computer "nerd work" that promised more intimacy with this vehicle than I had desired. That was the moment I realized there was far more to computers than just technical skills. There was something much more profound, indeed. For the first time, I realized that computer literacy was not a neutral term. Rather, it was a highly charged concept, brimming with connotations that one couldn't possibly anticipate or comprehend prior to the acquisition of that lit-

eracy. It was also the first time, though definitely not the last, that I wondered if my hunger for computer literacy had invited a debilitating computer dependency.

There was a time when I would've scoffed at such concerns. Twenty years ago I was an undergraduate at the University of North Carolina. At that time, computers could be operated only by means of language like Fortran and Basic, and only a person with a surfeit of time or antisocial tendencies could afford to play with them. I typed all my academic papers and many an article for the university newspaper on an electric Smith Corona, boosting sales of correction fluid with each endeavor. It wasn't until I neared the end of my college career, in the early Eighties, that I first heard of *word processors.* The very term recalled contraptions featured in old sci-fi movies, the kind that absorbed a human being at one end and produced an android through a tube at the other. How could people "process" words? I wondered. How could anyone get used to writing on a machine like that, which naturally detached one from the words themselves? "A writer needs to *feel* the words," I said, sounding like both a precious undergraduate and a neo-Luddite. Little did I know what the future had in store for me.

My bout with system failure occurred because I, in my prodigious ignorance, had somehow installed several system folders on my computer's hard disk. There was a system folder in the word-processing package. There was another on the hard drive setup. Still more accompanied a few software applications that I had copied from diskettes. Unfortunately, all those systems had confused not only the operator of the computer but the computer itself. Unbeknownst to me, my computer had suffered an identity crisis for quite some time. When I ran it through a test, the hard disk failed and asked that I "reinitialize" it. I spoke enough computerese to know that "reinitialize" was a bad word, at least when applied to a hard disk that contained three years of files. So I re-read the manuals and called my computer-literate friends, but no manual or friend would contradict the machine's message: reinitialize.

One year after college I accepted a job at a New England boarding school. It had recently invested in a large mainframe computer system, with terminals networked throughout the campus. This is how the Digital Decword system, now defunct, became an integral part of my initiation into the "depraved new world" of technology (as a young humanities teacher, I felt obliged to make such remarks). Students and faculty members were issued private accounts and passwords. This made computer work seem like membership in a holy order; participants recited secret passwords like monks carrying out rituals at morning vespers. The only drawback to a mainframe system, I was told, is that you can't take your data with you. I didn't mind, though. All I wanted was to use the machine like a typewriter to see if it helped or hindered the writing process. At least, that's all I wanted initially.

It didn't take long to see the advantages of this arrangement or to forestall the disadvantages. The machine encouraged me to edit; rearranging prose felt less tedious, more playful. Like everyone, I learned to save material through ugly trials, losing an hour's effort when an electrical storm shut down the system. From the mainframe I moved on to personal computers that the school considered purchasing, including an Apple IIe and IBM clones like Eagle and Leading Edge. Within a few years I wanted a computer of my own, especially as I pondered a departure for work overseas. It took months of research before I settled on a Macintosh Plus, equipped with the wonders of a graphical interface. "It has a 20-*mega*byte hard drive," said the enthusiastic salesperson. After realizing this meant almost nothing to me, he offered a translation for dummies: "You'll never fill it."

Amazingly enough, I never did. In fact, it was barely half full when I sold the machine five years later, prior to departure for another overseas post. And though my students had dubbed it a "Mac Minus" by then, chiding me for clinging to such ancient technology, it still served my purposes. Of course, this was at a time when monochrome monitors stalked the digital landscape, prior to the explosion of memory-hungry applications, not to mention the JPEGs,

GIFs, and streaming audio and video that the World Wide Web would unleash. Five years' worth of text files, including family newsletters with primitive graphics, couldn't fill that hard drive. Nor did the software applications. For the most part, I had resisted software applications that turned this writing tool into a toy. It was reserved for "word processing," and I steadfastly refused to let my 5-year-old son play games with it, despite my wife's prophetic claim that the computer would soon be an "educational tool."

Indeed, it taught me plenty that night the system crashed. Such a painful experience—or a reasonable facsimile thereof—serves as a point of departure for many educators who have reluctantly acquired computer literacy. This is partly explained by the personal satisfaction derived from problem solving, which enables us to fix something today that we didn't know existed yesterday. There's more to this, however, and I suspect it's the part that we don't like speaking about very much. At such moments we realize that, despite our deepening dependency, we really don't know very much about this plastic Cyclops that sits on our desk, staring back at us while monotonously humming along. Like negligent parents, we attend to it, asking forgiveness, sacrificing untold hours, and saying prayers to pagan gods in the hope that the next time we "boot up" a smiling face will greet us instead of some terrifying icon.

So, I dutifully backed up the files on my hard disk, then took a deep breath and began the painful process described by that sterile, clinical term: "reinitialize." It took several minutes, but as soon as I'd flushed the hard disk and installed one—and only one—operating system, my formerly lethargic machine snapped to attention. Now it was time to rebuild the file system, dragging files back onto the hard disk. Data files, that is, and preferably ones without hidden operating systems. This took more hours than I care to recall, primarily because the global backup had saved disparate documents without paying heed to the folders that had previously contained them. This gave me the pleasure of creating new folders and trying to sort through three years' worth of lesson plans and syllabi, personal and professional correspondence, and numerous items that my wife and I had composed. In the meantime, I kept a stern vigil, protecting my refreshed hard disk from stray system folders.

When I had finished reorganizing data it was time to address the issue of the operating system and special effects. I had already installed the original system, the one I had bought nearly four years before. I realized computer jocks would cringe at the thought of working with such antiquated software, but as I launched into this I told myself I didn't need last week's innovations. No one really does, I said, we're just suckered into it by the manufacturers of these contraptions. Yet, despite that sentiment, I couldn't deny my disappointment with the computer's "old" look, which lacked the pizzazz of more recent systems installed at our school in Ecuador. I soon found myself reaching for disks to modify the system, updating methodically to increase my options, which essentially meant adding gimmicks. One system update brought new icons to the screen. Another provided new fonts for fancier printing. Still another system brought the ability to preview pages. The final updates brought further cosmetics. One delivered a prompt that told me I could safely turn off my computer after asking it to shut down, instead of blanking the screen abruptly; another gave me a small watch with a moving second hand instead of a static one while the computer worked; finally, the garbage can bulged when I dumped trash into it, rather than standing passively at the bottom of the screen when I pulled an outdated résumé from a folder and tossed it. That's when I knew it was time to stop.

After acquiring a computer, I learned quickly, but never as thoroughly as I hoped. It was enough, at first, just to set margins, change fonts, and print a letter without making the unit freeze. Yet the computer is a curious thing. It tests one's ability to follow rigid guidelines even as it encourages curiosity and prompts the natural avarice of a human mind. No sooner do you master a small task, such as paginating, than you find yourself trying to import graphics, create spreadsheets, write hypertext, download PDF files, use FTP privileges, decipher CGI scripts, or do scores of other things that didn't exist when my trials took place a decade ago. The machine encourages us, perhaps more than any other, to reach for forbidden fruit. So we reach and acquire, tweaking our technology while tiptoeing along the precipice of disaster. I, like millions of others, borrowed and copied pirated software. This, in turn, led to the discovery of viruses, which I was amazed to learn were caused not by tiny infective agents but by demented computer jocks. That, in turn, led to the acquisition of virus protection software.

WHAT I finally realized is this: the computer encourages endless acquisitions, some motivated by intellectual avarice, others by petty jealousies excited by colleagues who rave about the latest "innovation." We might wish to dismiss each new product as so much hype, but how can we deny the usefulness of course websites, academic discussion forums, telecollaborative research, and online bibliographies? I took solace in the belief that this machine encourages intellectual exploration while merging work with play. After all, no other technology had ever helped me type while providing musical accompaniment or presented 3-D images while printing the finished product.

Nonetheless, I was puzzled by my own infatuation with this plastic box and all the toys that it inspired. I had never suffered a fetish for novelty before. In fact, I was a traditionalist, eschewing aluminum bats for wooden ones when playing American Legion baseball, refusing to use the fax machine that arrived while I was teaching in South America, and burying myself in medieval and Renaissance literature to complete my M. A. at Oxford.

When it comes to computers, though, it's difficult to resist temptations; we become obsessed with the idea that we're "falling behind" if we cling to a familiar system. So we forage for the new and update the old, suffering all the while from the delusion that as we make the computer better we're doing the same to our minds and our lives. At least, we do so until we go just a little too far, too fast, and realize that the pursuit of *computer literacy* and the promise of greater ease and efficiency may have gotten the better of us. Rather than obtain grace, we simply fall from it. In my case, that meant dragging system folders onto the hard disk without installing them properly. With time, the computer wasn't sure where to look for the information it needed. That's when the bomb icon appeared, sending me over the edge, where I fell like Adam with a forbidden fruit in my palm. Unlike Adam, though, the computer hacker can restructure the tree so it will accept the fruit's return and bear still more. The question is, How much fruit does one need in order to be satisfied? The answer, of course, is one that the curious and avaricious have always given: "Just one piece more!"

While the ancient world was spared this particular compulsion, its poets and philosophers knew plenty about the impulses that have carried us from the abacus to the computer chip. Perhaps one of Aesop's fables captures those impulses and describes their consequences best:

> Two neighbors came before Jupiter and prayed him to grant their hearts' desire. Now the one was full of avarice, and the other eaten up with envy. So to punish them both, Jupiter granted that each might have whatever he wished for himself, but only on condition that his neighbor had twice as much. The Avaricious Man prayed to have a room full of gold. No sooner said than done; but all his joy was turned to grief when he found that his neighbor had two rooms of the precious metal. Then came the turn of the Envious Man, who could not bear to think that his neighbor had any joy at all. So he prayed that he might have one of his own eyes put out, by which means his companion would become totally blind. Moral: Vices are their own punishment.[1]

At some point, we must ask ourselves just how much *computer literacy* we wish to have and what other literacies we're willing to sacrifice in order to obtain it. There will always be new temptations, new gadgets, new applications, and new possibilities. As educators, though, we must distinguish what is good and lasting from what is mediocre and ephemeral. I could've stopped pursuing a more extensive vocabulary and more advanced *computer literacy* the moment my digital garbage can bulged, but what if I had? That decision would have limited my acquisition of a literacy that's essential for educators in the 21st century. So I reneged on that vow, allowing my technological avarice (and dare I say professional envy?) to push me into the ranks of cyberwriters at work.

Though hindsight seldom ensures foresight, it does reveal the methods and rationale behind our collective madness. Because of its challenges, not in spite of them, computer literacy enables me to converse in a new language while retaining the power of my native tongue. It allows me to synthesize the often polarized worlds of art and science, humanities and technology. It also provides me with the vocabulary necessary to "read" the social, cultural, and technological events that are shaping the course of human destiny. Nevertheless, it's essential that we pause to ask whether our acquisition of *computer literacy* serves something more than itself. It should go without saying, but I'll say it anyway: educational technology is not about computers. It's about educating our students, serving our communities, and improving our institutions and society. If it's not about those things—first and foremost—then we've got bigger problems ahead of us than the next lethal virus.

I realize, though, that there's no shortage of blind prophets who'd beg to differ.

R. W. BURNISKE is the author of Literacy in the Cyberage: Composing Ourselves Online *(Skylight Professional Development, 2000) and coauthor of* Breaking Down the Digital Walls: Learning to Teach in a Post-Modern World *(State University of New York Press, 2001).*

---

1. Joseph Jacobs, ed., "Avaricious and Envious" in *Aesop's Fables* (New York: Capricorn Press, 1984), p. 66.

Wireless Andrew

On a sunny day, laptop users at Carnegie Mellon University can carry out sophisticated research while lounging around a campus courtyard. They simply log onto the Internet by way of a wireless network.

by Michael Fickes, staff writer

More and more Carnegie Mellon University (CMU) students, faculty members, and staff fail to close their laptops properly before heading to the next class or meeting.

You see it all the time on CMU's Pittsburgh campus. There goes a student with a laptop under his arm, while a magazine protrudes from the folded machine, preventing the latch from engaging. Coming from the other direction, a professor has jammed a scarf into her laptop to prevent it from snapping shut.

Blame it on Wireless Andrew. But don't call it sloppiness. Call it technological progress.

Freedom From Wires

Wireless Andrew, a CMU networking system five years in the making, now enables laptop users to connect to the University's computing network as well as to the Internet without cables. Users can tap into the system anywhere within the range of campus buildings equipped with wireless access points. They will remain connected as long as they don't shut their computers down.

An access point is a receiver and transmitter with an antenna that communicates with properly equipped computers and connects them to the Wireless Andrew network, which then connects to the university network and to the Internet.

"By June, we'll have 31 buildings equipped," says Charles R. Bartel, CMU's director of operations for computing services and project director for Wireless Andrew. Those 31 buildings form the academic core of the CMU campus and include classroom, research and administration buildings, as well as the exterior courtyards and walkways between those buildings. When complete, Wireless Andrew will dot the buildings with approximately 400 access points and provide wireless access to people inside and outside.

From Robots to Laptops

Wireless Andrew's roots at CMU go back more than five years, when researchers involved in the university's world-renowned Robotics Institute began to think about the problems associated with mobile robots.

Reprinted with permission from College Planning & Management magazine. © 2000.

Robots that move from place to place must have wireless capability. The farther the robots go, the more wide-ranging the wireless network must be.

To facilitate its robotics research programs and other mobile computing projects, the university moved into wireless networks in 1995. "We decided that our research programs would benefit from a common wireless infrastructure," Bartel says. "At the same time, we saw that the prices for laptops were falling, while the capabilities were beginning to rival desktops.

"One of the chief benefits of a laptop is that it enables you to take your computing environment with you. In the Internet world, a computing environment is closely tied to the network. So it makes sense that, if you need to carry your computing environment, you also need to carry a seamless network communications capability."

Is Wireless for You?

A wireless network that supports a mobile robotics program makes sense. But extending the program to seamless operation for laptop users across campus seems to stretch the point. Why not shut the computer down, move, plug in and start up again?

"That's a question I'm often asked," Bartel says. "My answer is that I see more and more people moving around campus without shutting their laptops down. So this paradigm has changed."

Some universities may identify a wireless network as necessary support for research programs, just as CMU. But what about a small liberal arts college?

Certainly, university planners must identify a compelling reason to install a wireless network, agrees Bartel. Such a reason, he suggests, might arise as a growing number of institutions require students to purchase laptops for use in class.

How useful will students find their computers if they cannot connect to a network in class? How much will a university pay to install access jacks and cabling throughout classroom buildings with large lecture halls, regular classrooms and seminar room?

Of course, that raises the question of how much a wireless network will cost.

Funding and Functions

Original funding for the CMU program came in 1995, through a $550,000 grant from the National Science Foundation earmarked for the establishment of a mobile computing program.

Working as a partner with AT&T, now Lucent Technologies, CMU designed and deployed a prototype system in five buildings in the years that followed. When the project began, wireless technology offered limited capability. Older wireless systems served as an alternative to cabling between buildings or provided limited mobility for a few computers that might be moved every month or so.

CMU's needs altered the standard concepts of wireless building-to-building communication and limited mobility. "We needed a system that would allow constant movement from point to point," Bartel says. "We worked with Lucent to develop a design based on this view of mobility."

Three years ago, Lucent approached CMU with an offer. Researchers had developed a new standard for wireless networking around the CMU prototype and wanted to prove the standard on the CMU campus. "Lucent granted us 400 access points, 400 pieces of equipment," Bartel says.

Today's Wireless Andrew begins with the 400 access points positioned in campus buildings. Each access point requires a power source and associated cabling. In addition, the access points tie together, using dedicated cabling within each building and tapping into available fibers in existing fiber optic cabling that runs between buildings.

"The architecture of this system creates a parallel wired network for wireless operation," Bartel says. "The wireless network connects to the campus network, which is connected to the Internet. The reason we've done it this way is to facilitate seamless roaming. For reasons related to networking technology, if we tied the wireless network into the campus network at each building, individual users would sometimes have to restart their computers as they moved from building to building to reestablish a network connection. Our parallel network design solves this problem and offers roaming connectivity across the campus."

Bartel hesitates to quote actual costs since they will vary from campus to campus depending upon geography and system architecture. He estimates, however, that preliminary budgets should allow about $1,000 for each piece of access point hardware plus another $1,000 per access point for cabling and system design costs.

System users face minimal costs. Plug-in cards that give computers the capability of logging onto a wireless system range from $100 to $200.

What's next? Someone should figure out how to close a laptop without shutting it down—before students begin breaking their laptop screens.

Unit Selections

Key Points to Consider

❖ What will be the role of interactive technologies within a distance learning environment during the twenty-first century?

❖ To what extent will higher education provide distance learning to business and the community?

❖ Is the intent of distance learning to allow students to work alone, or is it to bring them closer together? Provide reasons for your answer.

 **Links**   **www.dushkin.com/online/**

These sites are annotated on pages 4 and 5.

One of the primary concerns facing distance learning today is finding ways to increase the amount of student involvement and thus maintain student interest. Fortunately technology that can solve this thorny problem has become available. Over the past decade several technologies such as network advances, teleconferencing, wide-band communication, two-way digital video, high-definition video, and Internet 2 have helped make the delivery of high-quality interactive instruction a reality. In addition, software advances such as compression software and management systems are making the job of developing distance learning courseware and presentation more efficient and less time-consuming.

However, when using these more sophisticated technologies, it becomes essential that an adequate infrastructure is constructed and that high-quality, technical support is made available when students and instructors need it. Technology's role in high-quality, interactive distance learning is to create an environment that will promote active learning using higher-order thinking skills such as evaluation, analysis, and synthesis, rather than simple rote learning and memorization. In addition, the technology can be used to promote individual and social interaction for the student during the construction of knowledge and problem-solving skills.

Within a technology-driven distance learning environment, there are two kinds of interaction with regard to learning. One is a student individually interacting with the content. The other is social activity, a student interacting with others about the content. Both types of interaction are necessary for efficient, effective, and affective learning. In distance education, it is particularly important to provide an environment in which both kinds of interaction can occur.

Today's technologies provide an electronic pipeline to reach students at a distance with an instructional delivery system that will involve and interest those who are using it. The articles in this unit demonstrate how educators are riding the backs of current technology and instructional design to meet the need for interaction and involvement in a distance learning environment.

The unit begins with an article by Shayne Russell and Meg Warren, which describes an award-winning multidisciplinary, multimedia unit on Native Americans that was developed through participation in the Earthwatch Institute program. The authors explain the Earthwatch program, collaboration between library media specialists and classroom teachers, and use of the Big6 process for information problem solving and the development of information literacy skills.

Next, Gregory MacKinnon and Lynn Aylward outline an approach for postsecondary educators to improve the quality of electronic discussion groups. Using a template of macros constructed in Microsoft Word, the authors explain a system of coding called cognotes and discuss an evaluation method where higher-order critical thinking skills are given greater value toward higher grades.

In the following article, "Web-Based Portfolios for Technology Education: A Personal Case Study," Mark Sanders describes how students can use Web-based portfolios in technology classes to display class work and project work. Developing effective Web sites gives them an understanding of a range of information-age tools, motivates them to do high-quality work, requires self-assessment and reflection, and teaches design skills.

Finally, in "Seven Tips for Highly Effective Online Courses," Leonard Presby provides a structure for online tools that are useful in helping students learn quantitative methods and analytical techniques. The author recommends hybrid courses that consist of half online and half in-class delivery. His seven steps provide a recipe for building effective hybrid courses.

IT TEAMS:

SAVING THE WORLD THROUGH AUTHENTIC CHALLENGING TASKS

Earthwatch Team Wins 1999 ICPrize

Shayne Russell, library media specialist—Mount Laurel Hartford School, Mount Laurel, New Jersey (be sure to visit her Library Without Walls: http://www.voicenet.com/~srussell/)
Diane Hallisey, library media specialist—Plymouth River School, Hingham, Massachusetts
Suzy Calvert, Gifted & Talented teacher—Maxwell Hill Gifted Center, Beckley, West Virginia
Moacyr Santizo, 2nd Grade Bilingual teacher—Potter Road Elementary School, Framingham, Massachusetts

This team of library/media specialists and classroom educators was awarded the 1999 ICPrize for their "Native American Unit." Using video they filmed at an archeological site in Arizona, the team introduced a multidisciplinary study of Native Americans to students at their respective schools. Five ICPrizes to support the use of Internet technology in the school library media program were announced by the American Association of School Librarians (AASL), a division of the American Library Association (ALA).

The annual ICPrize is awarded as part of AASL's ICONnect technology initiative (see the September/October 1999 *MultiMedia Schools* (*MMS*) at http://infotoday.com/MMSchools/sep99/berger.htm). The I and C represent the basic elements of the ICPrize: Information, Integration, Innovation, Curriculum, Collaboration, and Connection—all integral parts of an ICPrize-winning curriculum unit. Each ICPrize recipient received $1,000 to be used toward the purchase of technology for use in the library media center or to support travel to attend a state or national conference. The applying school library media specialist was required to be an ALA/AASL member and to collaborate with a teacher on the curriculum project submitted. The curriculum project had to include the use of Internet resources. For more information about the ICPrize, visit http://www.ala.org/ICONN/icprize.html.

Shayne Russell

Library Media Specialist & KidsConnect Volunteer
Mount Laurel Hartford School
Mount Laurel, New Jersey

Meg Warren

Manager, Collaborative Technology Projects
Earthwatch Institute

[Editor's Note: We all want to feel part of something bigger than ourselves. Sometimes the challenges we face within our classrooms, our libraries, our networks eclipse the fact that our Earth is in trouble, too! Critics decry the isolating tendencies of technology, as though the computer represents an obstacle inserted between the learner and "real life." However, the Earthwatch experiences of thousands of educators and students speak eloquently to the contrary. There is little more "real" than the field research these students and teachers have conducted with Earthwatch. Their ability to harness technology to translate these life-changing experiences into opportunities for learning breathes new life into the adage "Think globally, act locally." Previously in *MMS*, we've taken the position that by working together, school library/media specialists, classroom teachers, and technology coordinators can change the world. Earthwatch demonstrates that it may even be possible for these teams to save our world—and you can help!]

From *Multimedia Schools*, March/April 2000, pp. 16-21. © 2000 by Multimedia Schools.

Since 1971, more than 8,000 educators have participated in Earthwatch Institute expeditions.

In July, 1997 I worked as an Earthwatch volunteer on an archeological expedition in Springerville, Arizona, with archeologists who were trying to identify ties between the prehistoric people who lived in Casa Malpais (see Figure 1) and the present day Hopi and Zuni cultures. This unique research experience was made possible through Earthwatch's Education Awards Program and generous funding from Bell Atlantic. As part of the project, our team made a commitment to develop a collaborative, Web-based project through which to share our experience with our students back home.

Our team, comprised of two library/media specialists and two classroom educators, planned to provide our students with a valuable research experience, exposing them to online and periodical resources, in addition to the basic print resources

The Big6—Dig It!

The Big6 process is modeled for students at http://www.voicenet.com/~srussell/bigsixdigit.html. At this site, students are asked:

Did you know that the process you use to do research in the school media center is very much like the process scientists use in the field? The "BIG SIX" is a step-by-step method for solving "information problems." If you follow these six important steps, when it comes time to pull that school research project together, you'll have all the pieces you need!

Here's what those six steps might involve if you were an archeologist working on the Casa Malpais/Earthwatch archeological expedition in Springerville, Arizona, as well as what they mean for you in your school media center!

already familiar to them. We wanted to show how information literacy, hands-on science, and collaborative learning can extend the experience of a small group of educators to a potentially limitless audience through the integration of technology and information literacy skills into the curriculum.

Earthwatch Institute is a coalition of citizens and scientists working together to sustain the world's environment, monitor global change, conserve endangered habitats, explore the heritage of our peoples, and foster world health and international

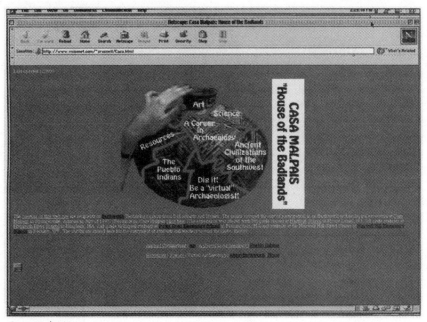

Figure 1

Casa Malpais

WHAT STUDENTS AND SCIENTISTS SAY

"This experience radically changed my views of science. Hands-on participation in research gave me a much clearer picture of what science is all about. I realized I had misunderstood it in school. Science is really about experimentation and thinking creatively and independently. Being a good scientist requires as much creativity and originality as being an artist or writer. I now see science as a method of inquiry rather than a textbook full of facts, and it is suddenly fascinating to me."

Wendy Antibus, Bluffton, Ohio, Student Challenge Award Program Recipient "Rock Art in the Malheur Marshland"

"The students brought unbelievable energy and enthusiasm to the project. Their abilities in math, especially geometry, helped us enormously in our complex mapping needs and facilitated our accurately completing work in a kiva and opening a new area of excavation ahead of time."

Dr. E. Charles Adams, University of Arizona Homol'ovi l: An Ancestral Hopi Village

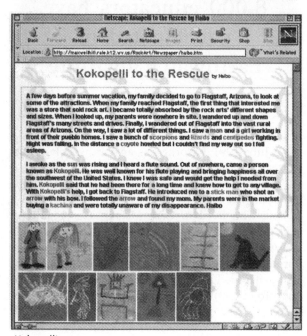

Kokopelli

cooperation. Since 1971, more than 8,000 educators have participated in Earthwatch Institute expeditions. Teachers, library/media specialists, administrators, and high school students make up 20 percent of the 4,000 volunteers who join Earthwatch Institute expeditions each year. In most cases, no special skills are required. The only requirements are a fascination with the Earth, a desire to know how it works, and the drive to help solve its problems.

Knowledge Building Through Information Literacy

I use the Big6 as the research process I teach kids at school and I've taught it through archeology every year since my participation at Casa Malpais in 1997. What a difference it makes! I explain to kids how the process that archeologists use to do their research is exactly the same as the process we use in the media center; then I prove it by showing videos from the dig or using a HyperStudio stack with pictures from the dig to explain each step. Then we compare what we would be doing in the media center. It makes it so "real" to the kids—it's not just "library stuff" anymore.

One of the areas I thought was especially exciting about the project was the way kids were able to reach beyond our own schools (there were four schools involved) to get the information they needed for their particular topics. I had two girls

in my school who wanted to learn about the Zuni language, and we couldn't find anything anywhere. I sent out an e-mail message to someone who had a broken link to a Web page that sounded promis-

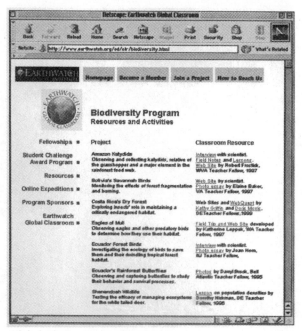

Global Classroom

Figure 4

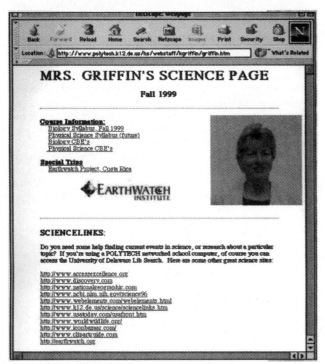

Mrs. Griffin's Science Page

ing, but that person sent a message out to someone else, who passed it on to someone else, etc. In the end, I got an e-mail message from Christopher Lewis, a teacher and a Zuni Indian, in Zuni, New Mexico. His students offered to help my students. They even sent us a great videotape showing us their school and the area it is located in, including in it some of the lessons in which their students were learning to speak Zuni. I had a couple of other students who were researching rock art (see Figure 2). They sent an e-mail message to an Earthwatch scientist I'd met at an Earthwatch conference who leads an Earthwatch project that studies rock art and she answered the students' questions. A few years ago, we would have never had access to resources like that!

Our Earthwatch team shared its excitement and knowledge with students in a constructivist manner. My 18 classes of fifth grade students from Mount Laurel Hartford School, 125 third graders from Plymouth, Massachusetts, 2nd graders from Framingham, Massachusetts, and 6th graders from West Virginia collaborated to create many of our Web pages. From the students, we learn that the dry climate of the American Southwest has helped preserve the antiquities that open the door to our understanding of ancient civilizations. Our student authors were careful to provide bibliographies so

EARTHWATCH BUILDING-BLOCKS FOR KNOWLEDGE CONSTRUCTION

There are three basic aspects to Earthwatch's program: research, conservation and education.

Research

The cornerstone of science is basic research, the gathering of comprehensive data on a subject without regard to how that information might be ultimately used. Earthwatch supports basic research in many fields, from archeology to zoology, learning about rainforests mechanics, ancient civilizations, and dozens of other subjects.

Conservation

Earthwatch's conservation projects have resulted in the creation of eight national parks, several conservation awards, and the rescue of dozens of endangered species.

Education

Every Earthwatch volunteer not only learns a huge number of facts, but perhaps more importantly, gets a context for those facts and a perspective that Earthwatch feels is essential for creating a sustainable future. Because they feel this kind of education is so important, Earthwatch offers scholarships to educators, students, and in-country conservation workers to multiply the effect of their experience through their respective constituents.

How You and Your Students Can Get Involved

Full-time K-12 educators of any discipline and high school students, age 16 and above, are eligible to apply for a fellowship to participate in a variety of Earthwatch research projects, ranging from monitoring Blue Ridge black bears, or tracking Baja sea turtles, to studying Costa Rican caterpillars.

For more information, including an Awards Application that can be downloaded, visit the Earthwatch Institute Web site (www.earthwatch.org) and Earthwatch Global Classroom. Or, contact Brian Barry, Education Awards Program Manager via telephone (800/776–0188 x118) or e-mail (bbarry@earthwatch.org.)

You can also participate online in a Virtual Field Trip or Online Science Expedition through the Earthwatch Global Classroom (www.earthwatch.org/ed/home.html (see Figure 3). Current expeditions include interviews with Earthwatch scientists (Saving Sea Turtles (see Figure 4), Tracking Mexican Wild Cats) and research activity "live" from the field with Delaware and Massachusetts Teacher Fellows (Brazil's Rainforest Wildlife, Wild Dolphin Societies).

Membership in Earthwatch Institute is $35 per year, but teachers may receive a free sample copy of the full-color Expedition Guide.

users know upon what authority the information was based. We also got a glimpse into what it is to be a real-life archeologist.

Chris Adams, one of the archeologists at Casa Malpais in Springerville, Arizona, was responsible for the reconstruction of the site's "Great Kiva" and the enclosing wall. He also discovered that the area once thought to be an animal pen was actually a solstice calendar.

Asked what the most important or interesting part of his discovery and work was, Chris responds, "I would have to say it's the people that I meet along the way, and that's usually the Native American people. Usually when you meet them they don't talk to you very much, but after you gain their trust they will sometimes take you to places that you didn't know existed. That is what I treasure the most. Artifacts are one thing, but it's the people themselves that are tied to these old areas that we go to that's most important—their friendship—and knowing a little bit about them."

---

*Communications to the authors may be addressed to **Shayne Russell**, Library Media Specialist, Mount Laurel Hartford School, 397 Hartford Road, Mount Laurel NJ 08054; phone: 856/231–5899; fax: 856/222–1221; e-mail: srussell@voicenet.com; **Meg Warren**, Earthwatch Global Classroom & Collaborative Technology Projects, Earthwatch Institute; phone: 800/776–0188; e-mail: mwarren @earthwatch.org; Web: http://www.earthwatch.org/.*

Six Steps to Improving the Quality of Your Electronic Discussion Groups

Abstract: This paper outlines an approach for post-secondary educators to improve the quality of electronic discussion groups (EDG's). Using a template of macros constructed in Microsoft Word 7, the authors outline a system of coding referred to as "cognotes." The coding of student's discussion has promoted more substantive engagement of ideas through articulate and logical contributions.

Keywords: electronic discussion groups (EDGs), substantive electronic discussion, communication skills.

Gregory R. MacKinnon and Lynn Aylward

Introduction

Electronic discussion groups (EDG) have been used with limited success in post-secondary education (Harrington & Hathaway, 1994; Harrington & Quinn-Leering, 1994; Kuehn, 1994). In most instances the EDG has been used as a strategy for (1) framing a topic for ensuing face-to-face (Ftf) class time or (2) extending the classroom content when Ftf time is limited. The technology that allows college students to discuss course topics "asynchronously" opens an abundance of possible applications.

The enormous potential of EDG's nonetheless stirs up important questions in educators. How do we promote substantive participation in this communication forum? Our action research (Hemming & MacKinnon, 1999) would suggest that involving students in EDG's that are devoid of formal evaluation can lend itself to poor quality contributions by students. Though educators have traditionally opted for applying EDG participation grades, the pitfalls of this approach are immediately obvious. How can we go beyond token participation and encourage more substantive electronic discussion?

This paper offers a generic approach to maximizing the impact of EDG's in your classroom in the areas of both content understanding and improved communication skills.

Step One

Decide what discussion patterns are most important to you. Table 1 suggests our own preferences. Specifically, we have committed ourselves to nine categories of good discussion based on the work of Knight (1990). These categories include acknowledgement of opinions; questions; compare; contrast; evaluation; idea to example (deductive); example to idea (inductive); clarification/elaboration; and cause and effect.

Step Two

In a simple graphics or word-processor program prepare a set of icons that represent the categories of discussion that you are seeking to promote. We have called

Originally published in the *Journal of Instruction Delivery Systems*, Vol. 13, No. 4. Reproduced with the permission of Learning Technology Institute, 50 Culpepper St., Warrenton, VA 20186.

207

Table 1 Categories and Cognotes

Specific Interaction	Coding Icon
Acknowledgement of Opinions (evidence of participation) 1	
Question (thoughtful query) 1	
Compare (similarity, analogy) 2	
Contrast (distinction, discriminate) 2	
Evaluation (unsubstantiated judgement, value) 1	
Idea to Example (deduction, analogy) 2	
Example to Idea (induction, conclusion) 2	
Clarification. Elaboration (reiterating a point, building on a point) 2	
Cause & Effect (inference, consequence) 2	
Off-Topic/ Faulty Reasoning (entry inappropriate)	

Figure 1 Coding the Student's Discussion Contribution Using a Word 7 Template

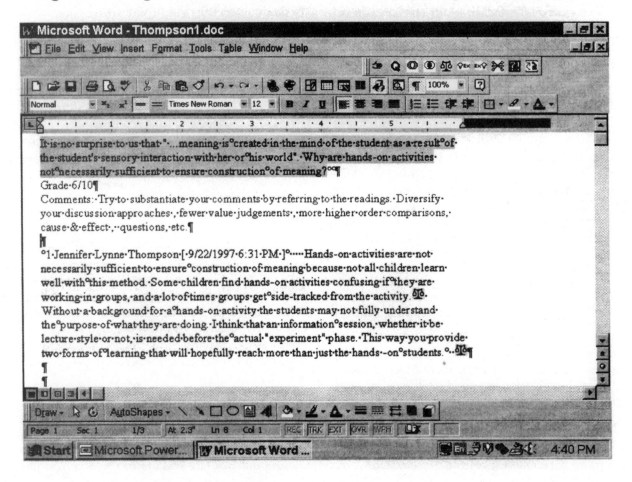

our icons "cognotes" (Table 1). They were created in Microsoft Word 7.

Step Three

The cognotes are ultimately assigned to an electronic discussion. Students must first be taught what the cognote coding icons mean. This is accomplished by having them perform and practice coding exercises on paper copies of sample discussions.

Step Four

Discuss with your students an evaluation scheme whereby higher-order, critical-thinking skills associated with certain cognotes are given greater value in terms of higher grades.

Step Five

In a word-processing program (Word 7) prepare macros that allow you to assign the cognotes electronically to a word-processing file. In our system we prepared a macro for each cognote that highlighted a desired section in colour and then applied the icon at the end of the passage. This set of macros and associated cognotes we then saved as a Word template (Figure 1).

Step Six

After students have participated in the EDG session, capture their discussion as an HTML file and import it into your word-processor. In our case we used Microsoft Word 7. Using the macro template (e.g. Figure 1) assign the cognotes to their work, resave the discussion and send the file to individual students as an attachment via e-mail.

The Impact of This Approach

The greatest improvement in the quality of EDG's can only be recognised over multiple sessions. We found that three successive sessions (of two weeks duration each) provided a notable improvement in students' discussion patterns. Students from the onset of this approach understand that carefully framing and articulating their arguments will be valued and reflected in their grade. It is up to the instructor to clearly delineate the hierarchy of discussion patterns and assign the appropriate grades.

In each successive session students tended to move away from discussion modes such as "acknowledging another's opinion" towards more substantive and analytic engagement using such approaches as cause and effect or compare and contrast.

This approach has the potential to improve communication skills while simultaneously engaging content in a rigorous exchange of ideas. The approach also encourages students to consider the electronic discussion group for more than casual conversation.

References

Harrington, H. L. & Hathaway, R. S. (1994). Computer conferencing, critical reflection, and teacher development. *Proceedings of the Society for Information Technology in Teacher Education*, 543–554.

Harrington, H. L. & Quinn-Leering, K. (1994). Computer conferencing, moral discussion, and teacher development. *Proceedings of the Society for Information Technology in Teacher Education*, 661–665.

Hemming, H. & MacKinnon, G. R. (1999). Developing critical thinking about gender using electronic discussion groups. *Annual Proceedings of the Society for Information Technology in Teacher Education*, 320–325.

Knight, J. E. (1990). Coding journal entries. *Journal of Reading, 34*(1), 42–46.

Kuehn, S. A. (1994). Computer mediated communication in instructional settings: A research agenda. *Communication Education, 43*, 171–183.

Gregory R. MacKinnon, PhD, is an assistant professor of science and technology education at the School of Education, Acadia University, Wolfville, Nova Scotia, Canada, B0P 1X0. gregory.mackinnin.@acadian.ca

Lynn Aylward was the Student Placement Coordinator for student teaching at Acadia University over the duration of the research.

Web-based Portfolios for Technology Education: A Personal Case Study

Mark E. Sanders

A portfolio is a collection of work designed to communicate in various ways about its creator. Art and design professionals have long used portfolios to display their best work for a variety of purposes: to show off their work to prospective employers when seeking admission to colleges and universities; in preparing grant proposals to funding agencies; or seeking approval from a prospective gallery. In addition, art and design educators have long made use of student portfolios for assessment purposes.

The current educational reform movement has generated a frenzy of interest in authentic assessment. As a result, the portfolio has emerged as one of the primary experiments in alternative assessment at every educational level (see, for example, Collins & Dana, 1993; Gordon, 1994; Paulson, Paulson, & Meyer, 1991; Wiggins, 1989; Wolf, 1989). These education portfolios have generally been conventional in nature—containers such as notebooks and folders filled with student work, intended primarily for assessment purposes. In more recent years, portfolios have "gone digital," such as floppy disks on which students store their assignments (Milone, 1995; Moersch & Fisher, 1995; Niguidula, 1997).

Portfolios do, in fact, provide an excellent tool for assessment. This alone would be reason for more widespread use of portfolios in technology education. But the benefits of portfolios in technology education go well beyond assessment, particularly if the portfolio is conceived of and executed as a Web-based portfolio. Web-based portfolios provide an excellent avenue for "Webworking" (Web page/site development), an area

that is not yet, but should be, prevalent in the technology education curriculum.

In the spring of 1995, I began experimenting in my Graphic Communication II class with Web-based portfolios. That semester, I required my communication technology students to represent their course work in a portfolio displayed on the Web. I provided basic instruction in Web page design and development fundamentals and technical specifications, but consistent with Gordon (1994), I intentionally left the details of the execution to the students, rather than provide them with a rigid format. This enabled them to construct and reconstruct their concept of a portfolio as they saw fit—an approach in step with contemporary learning theory. I discovered that the process of designing and producing Web-based portfolios is an exceptional learning experience for students in a variety of ways. This article details the context and findings from this personal case study and offers recommendations and a rationale for the use of Web-based portfolios throughout technology education.

Portfolios in Technology Education

Portfolios and documentation are not really new to technology education. Graphic communication/communication technology teachers have historically required portfolios to display photographs and printing samples, and more recently computer graphics, storyboards for multimedia, and so forth. Students in materials and processing and manufacturing courses have routinely documented their work with such items. Moreover, tech-

From *Journal of Technology Studies*, Winter/Spring 2000, pp. 11-18. © 2000 by Epsilon Pi Tau.

nology teachers have often required students to document their procedures and final products for assessment purposes.

Over the past decade, instructional method in technology education has shifted from the project method to the technological problem-solving method. The latter, often referred to as design and technology, involves substantially more of the design process and a corresponding increase in the amount of documentation required throughout all stages of designing, constructing, and evaluating solutions to technological problems posed. As a result, conventional portfolios have increasingly been used as a way of documenting and displaying student work in the field. Hutchinson, Davis, Clarke, and Jewett (1989) provided a detailed overview of the conventional design portfolio and discussed its purpose, structure, and potential in technology education.

A Web-based portfolio is a transformation of the conventional portfolio to a format that may be displayed on any computer or accessed via the World Wide Web. The development of a Web-based portfolio offers such an array of learning opportunities and benefits that it now makes sense for nearly every student in technology education to develop a Web-based portfolio and continue to add to it in all subsequent technology education classes.

Why Web-Based Portfolios?

The information age is not just a cliché—we're living it! Global networked information systems such as the World Wide Web are changing nearly every aspect of our lives. These technologies should be prominent within our curriculum. Often, they are not. Web-based portfolios offer a meaningful way for technology students to gain a thorough understanding of these critical new technologies beyond mere Web research.

Web-based portfolios provide benefits that can never be realized with conventional portfolios. One vitally important benefit to the future of our profession is the Web and its potential to illustrate the outcomes of technology education programs—especially to those beyond our profession. While the Web is indeed a global medium, the most important audiences are much closer to home: parents, fellow teachers, administrators, and local educational decision makers. We want them to know what technology education is, and there is no better way than to share with them "authentic" evidence of what students are learning and doing in technology education classes.

The Web offers new ways of displaying our work. Conventional portfolios are fine for conventional materials—sketches, drafting, printed materials, and photographs. But the Web allows us new options such as animation, navigation, digital audio/video, virtual reality, and interactivity. In comparison, conventional portfolio techniques limit what's possible.

Everything we create in technology education may be displayed on the World Wide Web, whether it originates in the communication, production, or energy/power/transportation component of the curriculum. Digital graphics can go straight to the Web. Three-dimensional prototypes may be recorded with a digital camera and displayed on the Web within minutes. Projects/solutions with moving parts may be videotaped, digitized, and converted to Web-viewable formats such as animated GIFs or digital video. Digital video (DV) camcorders now make it remarkably simple to create digital video, and technologies such as Apple's QuickTime and RealNetwork's streaming software make video display on the Web an increasingly viable option.

There are no compelling reasons why technology education should not be taking full advantage of the opportunities that Web-based portfolios provide. Technology education should be leading this effort in our schools.

Findings

In the spring 1995 semester, I provided students in my Graphic Communication II course (the second in a three-course sequence) with the option of developing a Web-based portfolio. Two students accepted the challenge and created handsome displays of their course work. I was impressed with how much they learned in the process and how well these portfolios communicated about what they had studied in the course. I had provided the basic fundamentals through conventional instruction, and they learned some "tricks" on their own from resources on the Web, as there were relatively few other sources of information at that time.

That fall, with the assistance of one of my undergraduate students, I established a Web site for the technology education program at Virginia Tech. Initially, it fit on a single floppy disk, though it now consumes several gigabytes of server space. Over the winter break, I set up a Web server to house our new Web site and the student portfolios that I now required (Sanders, 1996). The server proved to be relatively easy to set up, providing both my students and me with a host of new learning experiences. Among other things, students learned to upload data to the server with the FTP (file transfer protocol), basic server set-up, and a good bit about cross-platform compatibility. In short, they began to learn how networked information systems work (Sanders, 1999).

Given these initial successes with Web-based portfolios, I began to require them in my Communication Technology class the following fall (1995) semester. The experiment continued to go very well. About 20% of the students seemed to get "hooked" on the possibilities the Web provided. That very first year, one student created a virtual reality (VRML) component for his "frames" formatted portfolio and included such things as midi audio segments and Java scripts. These were state-of-the-art capabilities at the time, supported only by the latest browser version. I did not teach those tools; he discovered and perfected them on his own. Students immediately began to create Web-based presentations for their in-class presentations in lieu of the more conventional PowerPoint presentations I had been requiring in class. Some students also began making Web-based presentations in other classes when called on to make presentations.

During the semester, students present their Web-based portfolios in class and their classmates and I provide both written and verbal feedback. These reviews cause students to reflect upon their work and upon the structure/aesthetics of their portfolio. Gordon (1994) and Porter and Cleland (1995) have discussed the value of peer feedback and reflection in the development of conventional portfolios. Students have an opportunity to rework their portfolios following these peer reviews, and the results can be dramatic. Moreover, the portfolio presentations often provide students a teaching opportunity, as they explain to their classmates the concepts and technical processes used to accomplish specific aspects of their portfolio.

The Web-based portfolio assignment was rich with problem-solving challenges. Some of the work (e.g., electronic color separations) was difficult to display effectively. Students began to experiment with screen captures, animations, and portable document files (PDF file format) to solve these technical challenges. I began to see the Web as a very powerful environment for the teaching/learning process—better, in some ways, than any I had previously experienced. The Web is the ultimate "facilitative" environment. I discovered, as did my students, that every technological "trick" a student might wish to execute on the Web is documented and often supported (with free tools) on the Web. Thus, motivated students access the information they need to develop innovative portfolios. Some did so voraciously, in a way that I had not previously witnessed in more than two decades of teaching.

In the fall of 1996, I extended the Web-based portfolio requirement "down" to the first course in the Graphic Communication sequence. This allowed students to develop their Web-based portfolios over the three-course sequence, adding to it during each subsequent course. My Web page/site development instruction expanded to include such things as technical and aesthetic design issues, creating and editing PDF files, animations, image maps, frames, copyright, and "fair use" of multimedia. A substantial percentage—perhaps half or more—of my students continue to experiment extensively with Webworking tools beyond those I demonstrate, putting in long hours after class on the assignment.

I continue to extend the offer of free server space (global dissemination) to students whose portfolios meet my expectations for this mode of "publication." People from all over the world regularly access these electronic portfolios from our technology education server (http://teched.vt.edu/).

In April 1999, for example, visitors browsed 15,449 electronic portfolio pages from our technology education server over the course of the month. These Web-based portfolio page "hits" resulted in 61,616 total "requests." Since each graphic on the page represents a "hit," there was an average of 3.99 images/page. This is worth noting, as it gives you some idea of just how "graphically rich" these pages are. Visitors literally get a rich picture of the work our students are doing by browsing these Web-based portfolios. In the process of browsing these portfolios, visitors learn a good deal about technology education and our program. In effect, these Web-based portfolios are the "industrial arts fairs" of the information age.

Elements of a Web-Based Portfolio

A Web-based portfolio is not a "home page"! Home pages that are often required of students in public schools are usually very simple Web pages with links to other "cool" Web pages, illustrated with a variety of "free" graphics copied from the far corners of the Web. Despite the zillions of home pages that have been created in classrooms across America and throughout the world, this exercise is relatively limited in the learning opportunity it provides. There are three fatal flaws to this home page strategy. First, almost no one other than the home page developer is likely to find the linked information to be the least bit interesting or useful. Second, few graphics found on the Web are copyright free, which means the act of copying them to a home page is a violation of copyright law. Finally, there is very little to be learned from creating a list of Web-links and copying/pasting graphics.

Fortunately, there is a very simple solution to all three problems: students should create every component of their Web-based portfolios. By handling the assignment this way, every aspect of the Web-based portfolio—not just the images of class projects—is a demonstration of the student's potential/capability. This simple strategy solves all copyright issues. If students want a nifty animation for their return mail, or a flashy graphic for their main page, or attractive navigation buttons, they simply create these images. That's where most of the learning takes place. With this in mind, the Web-based portfolio might be viewed and characterized more as a learning activity than as an assessment tool.

Web-based portfolios should begin with an original design. In developing their designs, students should review other Web-based portfolios, making note of techniques and design solutions they like. They should also consult some of the many excellent Web sites that discuss and illustrate good Web design as well as conventional literature along these same lines (see, for example, Siegel, 1996; Weinman, 1997; Williams & Tollett, 1997; or more 25 links found at http://teched.vt.edu/gcc/html/Webtools/WebDesign.html). They should then develop rough layout sketches for each section of their portfolio and a "site map" for the overall layout. A house or a gallery offers a useful metaphor for conceptualizing the structure of the Web-based portfolio; both should have a welcoming entrance/main page that provides convenient access to the other rooms/sections of the building/portfolio.

Web-based portfolios should include a resume or, for younger students, a personal statement. But putting the resume alone online does not constitute a Web-based portfolio. One-line listings on resumes offer a concise way of communicating basic information, but they do not begin to portray the range of accomplishment afforded by the rest of the Web-based portfolio. Listing a class taken or software applications used means little compared to a well documented presentation of a project/solution created in a technology education course.

From the onset, my intent with the Web-based portfolio was to provide a venue so that students might display work from all of their technology education classes. While not a particularly difficult task, this takes considerable time and careful planning. Images and documentation must be created/saved as students progress through their various courses. All work, both digital and conventional, must be converted to Web-viewable file formats. Regrettably, many students do not find enough time outside of class to prepare work from all of their technology education courses for display on the Web. This will change as we increasingly use networked information systems (i.e., the Web and whatever supplants it) throughout the entire technology education curriculum. One day in the not-too-distant future, documenting course work on a network will be as commonplace as storing work in a notebook is today.

The following are some of the critical insights I have gathered since my first web-based portfolio class. Navigation tools (buttons and menus that allow "browsers" to go forward, back, return to the main page, etc.) are very important in portfolios. It is best to design a simple layout for these buttons and links. They should appear consistently in the same place on each page, so the user may find them easily. This simple rule of interface design made the Macintosh remarkably more "user friendly" than the DOS environment of the PC for a decade.

Each piece of work displayed in the portfolio should be accompanied by a brief narrative description of the process involved in the creation of the work. This is very important because, philosophically, technology education is more concerned with understanding technological concepts and processes than it is with the actual appearance of the final product. In contrast to artists' portfolios, which focus almost entirely on the appearance of the work of art, technology education portfolios should com-

municate the concepts and processes learned in the process of creating the work being displayed. Technology education is for all students, not just for those gifted in graphic design. Narrative descriptions of process accompanying each work displayed helps to underscore the point to those who view these portfolios on the Web that technology education is about technological understanding. Moreover, writing about the concepts, processes, and techniques employed reinforces the conceptual component of technology education for the students creating the portfolios. This documentation of process is often more telling than the final compressed images of the work completed, since students gain an understanding of technological concepts and processes through the hands-on work, even if the final picture of the work does not make an award-winning design.

Finally, portfolios should include an "About this Portfolio" section. This is a good place for students to explain that the portfolio was developed as part of a technology education course/curriculum. In doing so, they should name the teacher, school, and semester year in which the Web-based portfolio was initiated, keeping in mind that the Web-based portfolio may well continue to develop throughout the students' lifetimes. In addition, students might identify tools used and the unique technologies employed to produce this section of their portfolio.

Copyright protects the creator of any work from improper use by others. Technology educators and students need to be aware that most text, graphics, and so forth found on the Web may not be freely used elsewhere on the Web by all who encounter them! Since the creator has the rights to the work until those rights are formally released—which is generally handled by a written contract—most information encountered on the Web requires permission for fair use.

When students display their own work, they will own the rights, and they will begin to appreciate that copyright laws are written to protect their rights as the creator, rather than as a means to punish copyright violators. If all of the work contained in the portfolio is the student's work, there is not any danger of copyright infringement. For those who feel they must use clip-media, there are a relatively small number of Web sites that offer copyright free images and media. Typically, these sites clearly state that the media is "copyright free," and they provide written permission to use this media right there on the site. For a modest investment, technology teachers may purchase copyright-free graphics, audio, and video, and provide these for student use, thereby solving the copyright dilemma for those students who do not have the time or wherewithal to create their own from scratch.

Invariably, students will find copyrighted material on the Web that they would like to use. The "Fair Use Guidelines for Educational Multimedia" (Subcommittee on Courts and Intellectual Property, 1996) were established to assist educators in making decisions about the use of multimedia for educational purposes. In short, while 10% or less of most multimedia text/images/clips may generally be used in educational presentations, putting these same "clips" on the Web for worldwide dissemination is not considered "fair use." Technology teachers and students should become familiar with these guidelines and share them with their students to avoid unnecessary copyright infringement. The complete set of guidelines is posed on a number of Web sites (see, for example, http://www.libraries.psu.edu/mtss/fairuse/).

Benefits of Web-Based Portfolios for Technology Teachers and Students

One of the most compelling reasons for employing Web-based portfolios in technology education is the outstanding learning opportunities they provide. Just as woodworking projects engaged students in the tools, materials, and processes of the industrial age, "Webworking" involves students with the tools, materials, and processes of the information age. Developing effective Web pages requires an understanding of a wide range of information age tools—design fundamentals, HTML and VRML (both scripting languages used to construct web pages) Java scripts, digital graphics, digital audio, digital video, animation techniques, and so forth. There are Web-development tools aimed at all levels of expertise so elementary technology education students may begin creating Web pages and continue to learn new and more sophisticated tools throughout their middle and high school years.

The Web-based portfolio assignment begins impacting students in significant ways even before they begin to assemble the final portfolio. Just as writing for publication requires more diligence and considerable revision than does writing in one's diary, the possibility of publishing their work on the Web provides students with additional motivation to do quality work in class. Selecting work for the portfolio involves self-assessment. Planning the portfolio requires students to reflect on their work, evaluate it, and revise it for "publication."

Web-based portfolios offer a good opportunity for both teaching and learning design fundamentals. Conventional portfolios cause students to ask and answer such questions as: What is the best way to show off the work? How should the work be ordered and arranged? How might color enhance or detract from the work?

Web-based portfolios require answers to similar questions, but they also provide design challenges that are tempered by the technical specifications and demands of the Web. The opportunities for technical challenges and creative alternatives when developing or converting material for display on the Web are much greater than for conventional portfolios. While basic display of text and graphics on the Web is a relatively simple task, students wishing to go beyond basic Web-portfolio assembly will discover technical challenges as far up the ladder as they wish to climb. Other than the obvious learning opportunities, self-promotion is the primary benefit students will realize from the development of Web-based portfolios. Students may use their portfolios to communicate specific talents and expertise to university admissions officers, scholarship selection committees, and prospective employers. Although providing a marketable skill is not an objective of the Web-based portfolio assignment, significant numbers of students who have created one in my classes have found both part-time and full-time employment as Web-site developers.

Goerss (1993) asked middle school students what they liked about creating conventional portfolios. Among other things, students said portfolios helped keep them organized, allowed them to see personal improvement, provided a glimpse of their best work and past accomplishments, and gave them responsibility and choice.

Web-based portfolios benefit technology teachers in many ways as well. Student-developed Web-based portfolios can and should be used to promote what is happening in the technology education program. This can be accomplished by publishing all or some on the technology education program's Web site. Selected images may be compiled into a "gallery" of best work, in much the same way teachers collect and display work at technology festivals.

Technology teachers are increasingly using the technological problem-solving approach, requiring students to design multiple solutions to problems. The Web-based portfolio provides a means of documenting all of the steps along the way in the design process. Portfolios can be a very student-centered activity, particularly for older students who see it as a means of communicating their expertise to others, such as a prospective employer or college admissions officers.

The portfolio requirement also benefits technology teachers by bringing them "up to speed" with current information technologies. Teachers will increasingly face a credibility problem if they do not have basic competence with Webworking tools.

Benefits of Web-Based Portfolios for the Profession

As school systems continue to ramp up to the Internet, it is critical to the future of technology education that our laboratories be included in the school network. Because our facilities are often remotely located within, or even beyond, the walls of the main school building, leaving our facilities out of the network will be an easy way to shave dollars from the networking budget. When and where that occurs—and there is considerable anecdotal evidence that this trend is occurring—technology education will take a giant leap backward with respect to its role and status in education. It is critical that we request/demand network access in our laboratories—and required Webworking is perhaps the best way for us to make the case.

Webworking is becoming a requirement in education. Virginia's Standards of Learning, for example, require all students to be able to create Web pages by the end of eighth grade. This presents an opportunity for our profession. If all middle school technology education students were required to build Web-based portfolios, students could simply enroll in technology education to learn the basics of Webworking. Imagine what this would do for the status/image of the field. On the other hand, if we fail to seize this opportunity, others certainly will.

Since the Web is accessible to nearly everyone in the school and community, and to many across the planet, Web-based portfolios offer unprecedented public relations potential for technology education. Through the Web we can inform/educate parents of our students, potential new students, fellow teachers, administrators, and curious "surfers" about technology education. Given the multitude of ways in which technology education is misunderstood by the public, it is critical that we develop a presence on the World Wide Web, which would help to educate the public about our field (Sanders, 1995). Student portfolios displayed on technology education program Web sites would go a long way toward educating the public and developing such a presence. The resulting influence is global.

Our field has historically used student projects for public relations purposes. The public's image of industrial arts was linked to the tangible reminders of the "take-home" project and public displays of student work that were so common in our field. The public did not learn of industrial arts by attending our national conference or reading our publications. They learned about us when their children built something tangible and brought it home. By seeing the work of our students in Web-based portfolios, parents and the broader public can begin to understand the content, method, curriculum, and purpose of technology education.

Our field needs the exposure Web-based portfolios provide. We need to share our good work with the public—fellow teachers, administrators, parents, and education decision makers. Without their knowledge and support of our work, we will not achieve what we hope to achieve in education.

Webworking Tools

While the intricacies of hypertext markup language (HTML) once limited Web page development to computer programmers, inexpensive what-you-see-is-what-you get editors now make the process more like word processing than programming. These tools make it easy to display and link graphics and text—the essential skill required for creating a Web-based portfolio. An endless array of freeware and shareware on the Web provides inquisitive and motivated students with the tools they need to create almost any effect that's "do-able" on the Web (see, for example, the Web Tools section of GRAPHIC COMM CENTRAL, http://teched.vt.edu/gcc/). So the tools are readily accessible and cost effective.

Though not absolutely essential, it is desirable for technology teachers to operate or have access to a Web server on which they may post student portfolios. Fortunately, most school systems now operate a Web server. But Web-based portfolios are developed off-line and may be saved on any storage medium (e.g., floppy disk, removable cartridge, CD-ROM, etc.) and displayed/read on any computer, whether connected to the Web or not.

In those cases where technology education teachers/students do not have local server support, there is the possibility of mounting Web-based portfolios on a nonprofit server in the community, on a commercial Web server in the community, on a commercial Web server supported completely by advertising (e.g., www.geocities.com), or on a remote server supported by the profession. The Virginia Technology Education Electronic Publishing Project (Sanders, 1997) for example, hosts Web sites for technology education programs in the state. State departments of education or professional associations can and should provide this service for those who do not have local options in this regard.

Closing Thoughts

Webworking is not yet commonly taught in technology education. My sense is that teacher education programs are not generally teaching or requiring Web-based portfolios of their students, and teachers in the field are likewise shying away from this opportunity. A national study of middle and high school technology education programs (Sanders, 1997a) found that about 40% of the programs had no access to the Internet whatsoever, which would help to explain why Webworking has not yet become a widespread practice in the field.

While many modular laboratories incorporate digital communication activities, most that I have visited were ill-equipped with respect to Webworking—or even Web access—perhaps since Web infrastructure/access cannot be sold/shipped with the other modular laboratory components. My work with the ITEA Section for Communication Technology, GRAPHIC COMM CENTRAL (http://teched.vt.edu/gcc/), and in the field leads me to conclude that relatively little is happening with networked information systems and, more generally, with digital communication technologies of all types in more conventional technology education laboratories/programs.

We do live in the information age. Thus, failure to engage our students in meaningful activities related to networked information systems will have negative ramifications for our profession in the future. The Web-based portfolio is an effective way for technology education teachers, programs, and students to become active and savvy participants in the networked information systems that are transforming our society. Technology teacher educators, public school technology teachers, and curriculum developers should therefore move quickly and decisively to incorporate Web-based portfolios into the technology education curriculum. Doing so would benefit the student, the local technology education program and teacher, and the profession at large. It is an opportunity we should not let pass us by.

References

Collins, A., & Dana, T. M. (1993). Using portfolios with middle grade students. *Middle School Journal, 25*(2), 14–19.

Goerss, K. V. (1993). Portfolio assessment: A work in process. *Middle School Journal, 25*(2), 20–24.

Gordon, R. (1994). Keeping students at the center: Portfolio assessment at the college level. *Journal of Experiential Education, 17*(1), 23–27.

Hutchinson, P., Davis, D., Clarke, P., & Jewett, P. (1989, November–December). The design portfolio: Problem solving. *TIES Magazine,* pp. 17–27.

Milone, M. N., Jr. (1995). Electronic portfolios: Who's doing them and how? *Technology & Learning, 16*(2), 28–29, 32, 34, 36.

Moersch, C., & Fisher, L. M., III. (1995, October). Electronic portfolios—Some pivotal questions. *Learning and Leading with Technology, 23*(2), 10–14.

Niguidula, D. (1997, November). Picturing performance with digital portfolios. *Educational Leadership,* pp. 26–29.

Paulson, F. L., Paulson, P. R., & Meyer, C. A. (1991, February). What makes a portfolio a portfolio? *Educational Leadership,* pp. 60–63.

Porter, C., & Cleland, J. (1995). *The portfolio as a learning strategy.* Portsmouth, NH: Boynton/Cook.

Sanders, M. E. (1995). A proposal for a presence on the Web. *Journal of Technology Education, 7*(1), 2–5. Retrieved December 27, 1999 from the World Wide Web; http://scholar.lib.vt.edu/ejournals/JTE/jte-v7nl/editor.jte-v7n1.html

Sanders, M. E. (1996, March). *Establishing World Wide Web services for technology education.* Paper presented at the annual conference of the International Technology Education Association, Indianapolis, IN.

Sanders, M. E. (1998). *Virginia technology education electronic publishing project.* Retrieved December 27, 1999 from the World Wide Web: http://teched.vt.edu/vteepp

Sanders, M. E. (1999a). Developing Web services for technology education. *The Technology Teacher, 58*(5), 12–18.

Sanders, M. E. (1999b, March). *Status of technology education in the public schools.* Paper presented at the annual conference of the International Technology Education Association, Indianapolis, IN.

Siegel, D. (1997). *Creating killer Web sites* (2nd ed.). Indianapolis, IN: Hayden Books. Retrieved December 27, 1999 from the World Wide Web; http://www.killersites.com/

Subcommittee on Courts and Intellectual Property, and Committee on the Judiciary, U.S. House of Representatives. (1996). *Fair use guide lines for educational multimedia.* Washington, DC: Author, Retrieved December 27, 1999 from the World Wide Web: http://www.libraries.psu.edu/mtss/fairuse/

Weinman, L. (1997). <ldesigning web graphics.2>: How to prepare images and media for the Web. Indianapolis, IN: New Riders.

Williams, R., & Tollett, J. (1997). *The non-designers Web book.* Berkeley, CA; Peachpit Press.

Wiggins, G. (1989, May). A true test: Toward more authentic and equitable assessment. *Phi Delta Kappan, 7*(5), pp. 703–713.

Wolf, D. P. (1989). *Educational Leadership, 46*(7), 35–39.

Mark E. Sanders is an associate professor of Technology Education in the Department of Teaching and Learning, Virginia Polytechnic Institute and State University, Blacksburg, Virginia. Correspondence concerning this article should be addressed to Mark Sanders, 144 Smyth Hall, Virginia Tech, Blacksburg, VA 24061-0432, msanders@vt.edu. He is a member of Beta Chi Chapter of Epsilon Pi Tau.

Seven Tips
for Highly Effective Online Courses

A veteran instructor offers suggestions to make the most of the hybrid course.

by Leonard Presby
WILLIAM PATERSON UNIVERSITY

About two years ago, after 24 years of teaching in the traditional face-to-face format, I sat in on a presentation on online courses. The idea was quite intriguing. I wondered how effective, though, would an online course be and whether students would really get out of it what a traditional course could offer. Would students be disciplined enough? Could one teach an equation online? Could a student understand the concepts involved in forecasting or an inventory model while sitting by his or her computer?

Implicit in the delivery of distance learning at William Paterson University is the provision of access to the various information resources required for an enriched learning experience. These educational services are developed within the mission of the university and delivered remotely via technology, traditionally via an instructor on site in combination with technology, and through the development of new pedagogies looking at how people learn best. About 75 percent of the student body does not reside on campus.

My first exposure to online teaching was in the summer of 2000; the second was fall 2000. I taught an online course for Production and Operations Management which included techniques and methods to plan and control manufacturing and other operating systems. Application of quantitative methods and various analytical techniques were stressed for operating system design, productivity, inventory, quality, and capacity management. Experience taught me that online courses demonstrate a tool useful in helping students learn. However, a hybrid type of course consisting of half class time and half online time proved more beneficial than a pure online course. Finding that many students want to be in

class up to 50 percent of the time, I formulated a list of seven components for a successful online course:

1 *Choice.* Some students thrive in group settings; others prefer working independently. Students should be given choice as to how they learn, as long as they learn. WPU has a great library. Although I didn't want to tie down students to have to go to it unless they wished, I did want them to use the Web.

2 *Up-to-date information.* Material presented in textbooks is often dated. Students are able to read more timely information in newspaper articles. To both provide this material to the students and to have some means to know whether it was read, I required them to respond to questions on each reading assignment.

3 *Virtual company visits.* Students were interested in "seeing" what a company does. Unfortunately, it is almost impossible to organize a class trip to a company. Virtual visits provided some interesting walk-through tours of companies. To be sure that students were taking these "tours," I included questions at the end of each tour that students could e-mail to me.

4 *Textbook link.* A textbook should provide material to supplement the computer. Here again, I created an opportunity to obtain feedback from the students on the chapter through quiz questions. As long as a student answers most of the questions correctly, he or she can earn full credit.

5 *Communication within groups.* In a traditional course, interaction between students is somewhat difficult, especially with shy students who sit in the back. I thought I could overcome this barrier by introducing case studies, which would require input from all. I assigned three case studies to groups of four students each. Each student read and analyzed the case. Each group then communicated in their specific discussion group and shared thoughts. On its due day, one student from each of the groups submitted the answers from the group. We would then actually meet in class to discuss the answers "live."

6 *Interaction between groups.* Another component required each student to interact with someone else in the class by answering the current events questions and commenting and/or adding to other students' answers as well.

7 *Actual class interaction.* Absolutely necessary is a pre-class or first class session, in which the students learn about the delivery technology and are able to ask me "in person" any question about the course. Typically I offer two identical sessions at different times during the first week in order to accommodate students who have scheduling problems.

The face-to-face class is typically reserved for answering technical questions, reviewing discussion questions from the text, discussing exercises from the chapters, and for demonstrating software concepts. Students find this component of the course beneficial, even though it is an online course. When asked, "How valuable do you feel contact time is in this course?" students felt it was important to express feelings and problems at the same time and to get a better idea of how they were doing in the class.

Leonard Presby is a professor in the Department of Marketing and Management Science, William Paterson University. presbyl@wpunj.edu

This glossary of computer terms is included to provide you with a convenient and ready reference as you encounter general computer terms that are unfamiliar or require a review. It is not intended to be comprehensive, but, taken together with the many definitions included in the articles, it should prove to be quite useful.

AECT. Association for Educational Communications & Technology. A national association dedicated to the improvement of instruction through the effective use of media and technology.

Alphanumeric. Data that consists of letters of the alphabet, numerals, or other special characters such as punctuation marks.

Analog signals. Audio/video signals currently used in broadcasting where the signal performs transmission tasks by translating continuously variable signals (physical variables such as voltage, pressure, flow) into numerical equivalents, continuously varying and representing a range of frequencies. Current TV and radio signals and phone lines are analog.

Applications software. Software designed to accomplish a specific task (for example, accounting, database management, or word processing).

Archive. Storage of infrequently used data on disks or diskettes.

Artificial intelligence. Hardware or software capable of performing functions that require learning or reasoning (such as a computer that plays chess).

ASCII. American Standard Code for Information Interchange. (The acronym is pronounced "as-key.") An industry standard referring to 128 codes generated by computers for text and control characters. This code permits the computer equipment of different manufacturers to exchange alphanumeric data with one another.

Audiographics. Computer-based technology that allows for the interaction between instructor and students through a simultaneous transmission of voice and data communication and graphic images across local telephone lines.

AUTOEXEC.BAT. An old MS-DOS file that computers read when first turned on. The file provided instructions for running DOS programs.

Backup. An extra copy of information that is stored on a disk in case the original data is lost.

Bandwidth. The speed at which data can be transmitted on a communications frequency (measured in Hertz).

Bar code. A code that consists of numerous magnetic lines imprinted on a label that can be read with a scanning device. Often used in labeling retail products.

BASIC. Beginners All-purpose Symbolic Instruction Code. A high-level computer language, considered by many authorities to be the easiest language to learn, and used in one variation or another by almost all microcomputers.

Batch processing. An approach to computer processing where groups of like transactions are accumulated (batched) to be processed at the same time.

Baud rate. The speed of serial data transmission between computers or a computer and a peripheral in bits per second.

Binary. The base-two number system in which all alphanumeric characters are represented by various combinations of 0 and 1. Binary codes may be used to represent any alphanumeric character, such as the letter "A" (100 0001), the number 3 (000 0011), or characters representing certain computer operations such as a "line feed" (000 1010).

Bit. Binary digit. The smallest unit of digital information. Eight bits constitute one byte.

Bit-mapped. Any binary representation in which a bit or set of bits corresponds to an object or condition.

Board. Abbreviation for printed circuit board. Can also refer to any of the peripheral devices or their connectors that plug into the slots inside a microcomputer.

Boot (short for Bootstrap). To start the computer; to load an operating system into the computer's main memory and commence its operation.

Browser. A program that allows a user to view the contents of pages and also to navigate from one page to another.

Buffer. A temporary memory that is capable of storing incoming data for later transmission. Often found on printers to allow the printer to accept information faster than it prints it.

Bug. An error in a program that causes the computer to malfunction. *See also* Debugging.

Bulletin Board System (BBS). An electronic message data base that allows users to log in and leave messages. Messages are generally split into topic groups.

Bus. An electronic highway or communications path linking several devices.

Byte. The sequence of bits that represents any alphanumerical character or a number between 0 and 255. Each byte has 8 bits.

CAI. Computer-Assisted Instruction or Computer-Aided Instruction. An educational use of computers that usually entails using computer programs that drill, tutor, simulate, or teach problem-solving skills. *See also* CMI.

Card. Refers to a peripheral card that plugs into one of the internal slots in a microcomputer.

CAT scanner. A diagnostic device used for producing a cross-sectional X ray of a person's internal organs; an acronym for computer axial tomography.

Cathode-ray tube (CRT). *See* Display screen.

CD-I. Compact Disc-Interactive. A format available to personal computer users that allows access to picture databases and large text; a compact disc standard that includes music compact discs (CD audio), static data (CD-ROM), and graphics.

CD-ROM. Compact Disk Read Only Memory. An auxiliary storage device that contains data that can be read by a computer. Its major advantage is that it can store more information than floppy diskettes.

Central Processing Unit. *See* CPU.

Chip. An integrated circuit used in a computer.

Clip art. A collection of ready-made graphics.

CMI. Computer-Managed Instruction. An educational use of computers that usually entails the use of computer programs to handle testing, grade-keeping, filing, and other classroom management tasks.

CMICOBOL. COmmon Business Oriented Language. A high-level language, used mostly in business for simple computations of large data amounts.

Coaxial Cable. A thickly insulated metallic cable for carrying large volumes of data or video, consisting of a central conductor surrounded by a concentric tubular conductor. Typically used in networks covering a limited geographic area. Gradually being replaced by fiber optics.

Command prompt. A symbol used to mark the place to type instructions (commands) to DOS.

Compatibility. 1. Software compatibility refers to the ability to run the same software on a variety of computers. 2. Hardware compatibility refers to the ability to directly connect various peripherals to the computer.

Compiler. A program that translates a high-level computer language into machine language for later execution. This would be similar to a human translating an entire document from a foreign language into English for later reading by others.

Compressed Video. System by which a vast amount of information contained in a TV picture and its audio signal is compressed into a fraction of its former bandwidth and sent onto a smaller carrier. Often results in some diminished color, clarity, and motion.

Computer. Any device that can receive, store, and act upon a set of instructions in a predetermined sequence, and one that permits both the instructions and the data upon which the instructions act to be changed.

Computer Bulletin Board Service (CBBS). A computerized data base that users access to post and to retrieve messages.

Computer literacy. Term used to refer to a person's capacity to intelligently use computers.

Computer program. A series of commands, instructions, or statements put together in a way that permits a computer to perform a specific task or a series of tasks.

Computer-Aided Design (CAD). An engineer's use of the computer to design, draft, and analyze a prospective product using computer graphics on a video terminal.

Computer-Aided Instruction. See CAI.

Computer-Aided Manufacturing (CAM). An engineer's use of the computer to simulate the required steps of the manufacturing process.

Computer-Assisted Instruction. See CAI.

Computer-Based Testing. See CBT.

Computer-Based Training. See CBT.

CONFIG.SYS. This file, which contains information on how the computer is set up and what it's attached to, is read by the computer every time it boots up.

Configuration. The components that make up a computer (referred to as hardware—a keyboard for text entry, a central processing unit, one or more disk drives, a printer, and a display screen).

Control key. A special function key found on most computer keyboards that allows the user to perform specialized operations.

Copy protected. Refers to a disk that has been altered to prevent it from being copied.

Courseware. Instructional programs and related support materials needed to use computer software.

CPB. Corporation for Public Broadcasting. A nonprofit corporation authorized by the Public Broadcasting Act of 1967 to develop noncommercial radio and TV services in the United States.

CPU. Central Processing Unit. The "brain" of the computer consisting of a large integrated circuit that performs the computations within a computer. CPUs are often designated by a number, such as 6502, 8080, 68000, and so on.

Cracker. A person who seeks to gain unauthorized access to a computer system and is often malicious. See also Hacker.

Crash. A malfunction of a computer's software or hardware that prevents the computer from functioning.

Crossfooting. The computer's ability to total columns and rows of numeric amounts. The answers are then placed at the end of each row or bottom of each column.

CRT. Cathode-Ray Tube. See Display screen.

Cursor. The prompting symbol (usually displayed as a blinking white square or underline on the monitor) that shows where the next character will appear.

Cyberspace. The Internet or the total of all networks.

Data. All information, including facts, numbers, letters, and symbols, that can be acted upon or produced by the computer.

Data processing. Also known as electronic data processing (EDP), it is the mathematical or other logical manipulation of symbols or numbers, based on a stored program of instructions.

Database. A collection of related information, such as that found on a mailing list, which can be stored in a computer and retrieved in several ways.

Database management. 1. Refers to a classification of software designed to act like an electronic filing cabinet (which allows the user to store, retrieve, and manipulate files). 2. The practice of using computers to assist in routine filing and information processing chores.

DBS. Direct broadcast satellite.

DDS. Digital Direct Satellite.

Debugging. The process of locating and eliminating defects in a program that causes the computer to malfunction or cease to operate.

Dedicated Line. Communication line leased by a company for its own transmission purposes.

Default format statement. Formatting instructions, built into a software program or the computer's memory, which will be followed unless different instructions are given by the operator.

Demodulation. Process of converting analog signals sent over a telephone line into digital form so that they can be processed by a receiving computer.

Desktop publishing. A layout system that processes text and graphics and produces high-quality pages that are suitable for printing or reproduction.

Directory. A list of related folders (files) that are stored on a hard disk.

Disk, Diskette. A round flat plate with a magnetic coating to store information.

Disk drive. A peripheral device capable of reading and writing information on a disk.

Disk Operating System. See DOS.

Display screen. A peripheral that allows for the visual output of information for the computer on a CRT, monitor, or similar device.

Distance education. Distance learning that includes evaluation by distance educators and two-way communication—computer, telephone, mail.

Document. A file that contains information. Documents can be created or changed within a program.

DOS. Disk Operating System. An operating system that allows the computer to run programs.

Dot-matrix. A type of printing in which characters are formed by using a number of closely spaced dots.

Download. To move a file from another computer.

Downtime. Any period of time when the computer is not available or is not working.

Drag. A four-step mouse process that makes it possible to move objects across the desktop.

Dumb terminal. Refers to a terminal that can be used to input information into a computer and to print or display output, but which lacks the capacity to manipulate information transmitted to it from the host computer. See also Intelligent terminal.

Dump. Mass copying of memory or a storage device such as a disk to another storage device or a printer so it can be used as a backup or analyzed for errors.

Duplexing. The procedure that allows simultaneous transmission of data between two computers.

DV-I. Digital Video-Interactive. Optical storage media that delivers full-motion, full-screen video, three-dimensional motion graphics, and high-quality audio capabilities.

E-lecture: A lecture delivered via electronic mail to individual computers.

Electronic Bulletin Boards. Information services that can be reached via computers connected to telephone line that allow users to place or read messages from other users.

Electronic mail (e-mail). Sending and receiving electronic messages by computer.

Elite type. Any typeface that allows the printing of 12 characters to an inch.

Enter. Adding data into memory via the keyboard.

ERIC. Educational Resources Information Center. An organization sponsored by the Office of Educational Research and Improvement (OERI) that collects and processes printed materials on education that are not available commercially.

Escape key. This function key allows the movement from one program to another program.

Execute. To perform a specific action required by a program.

Exponential notation. Refers to how a computer displays very large or very small numbers by means of the number times 10 raised to some power. For example, 3,000,000 could be printed as 3E + 6 (3 times 10 to the sixth power).

Fan fold. A type of paper that can continuously feed into a printer (usually via tractor feed).

FAQ (Frequently Asked Questions). Used to answer the most common questions that could be asked.

Fax. (n.) Short for the word facsimile. A copy of a document transmitted electronically from one machine to another. (v.) To transmit a copy of a document electronically.

Fiber Optics. Newer, high-tech delivery system using attenuated glass (quartz) fiber hardly thicker than a human hair, which conducts light from a laser source. A single glass fiber can carry the equivalent of 100 channels of television or 100,000 telephone calls, with even more capacity possible by encasing many fibers within a cable.

Field. Group of related characters treated as a unit (such as a name); also the location in a record or database where this group of characters is entered.

File. A group of formatted information designed for computer use.

First-generation computers. Developed in the 1950s; used vacuum tubes; faster than earlier mechanical devices, but very slow compared to today's computer.

Fixed disk. See Hard disk.

Floppy, Floppy disk. See Disk.

Folder. An organized area for storing files. See also Subdirectory.

Format. (n.) The physical form in which information appears. (v.) To specify parameters of a form or to write address codes on a blank disk in preparation for using it to store data or programs. See also Initialize.

FORTRAN. FORmula TRANslation. A high-level programming language used primarily for numerical and scientific applications.

FTP (File Transfer Protocol). Allows a user to transfer files to and from another computer on the Internet network.

Function keys. Computer keyboard keys that give special commands to the computer (for example, to format, to search text).

Gig. Short for gigabyte, it consists of over 1,024 megabytes.

GIGO. Garbage In, Garbage Out. Serves as a reminder that a program is only as good as the information and instructions in the program.

Global. The performance of any function on an entire document without requiring individual commands for each use. For example, a global search-and-replace command will allow the computer to search for a particular word and replace it with a different word throughout the text.

Graphics. 1. Information presented in the form of pictures or images. 2. The display of pictures or images on a computer's display screen.

Hacker. A person who is an expert at programming. See also Cracker.

Hard copy. A paper copy of the computer's output.

Hard disk. A rigid, magnetically coated metal disk that is usually permanently mounted within a disk drive, although there are also removable disks.

Hard drive. A disk drive that is used to read and write hard disks.

Hardware. Refers to the computer and all its peripheral devices. The physical pieces of the computer.

HDTV. High Definition TV. A television with quality resolution that is higher than current international standards.

Head. Refers to the component of a disk drive or tape system that magnetically reads or writes information to the storage medium.

Hex or Hexadecimal. A numbering system based on 16 (digits 0–9 and letters A–F) rather than on 10. Most computers operate using hex numbers. Each hexadecimal digit corresponds to a sequence of 4 binary digits or bits.

High-level language. An English-like computer language (BASIC, Pascal, FORTRAN, Logo, COBOL) designed to make it relatively convenient for a person to prepare a program for a computer, which in turn translates it into machine language for execution.

Highlight. A selected item; a distinguished word or group of words that are singled out for further action.

Home page. Generally the main page of a Web server.

Hotlink. Shared data between programs in which data changed in one program are automatically changed in the other programs as well.

HTML (Hypertext Markup Language). A hypertext document format; this is used on the World Wide Web.

HyperCard. Brand-name for Apple/Mac product. Simple authoring system for lower level interactive computer-based instruction or information management.

Hypermedia. The connecting of data, texts, video, graphics, and voice in an information system that allows a user to move easily from one element to another.

Hypertext. A collection of documents that contains links or cross- references to other documents.

IC. Integrated Circuit. See Chip.

Icon. Refers to the use of a graphic symbol to represent something else. When the user clicks on the icon, some action is performed (such as opening a directory).

IHETS. Indiana Higher Education Telecommunication System. A consortium of Indiana higher education operating voice, video, and data networks, through which its members coordinate distance education efforts.

Indexing. The ability of a computer to accumulate a list of words or phrases, with corresponding page numbers, in a document, and then to print out or display the list in alphabetical order.

Initialize. 1. To set an initial state or value in preparation for some computation. 2. To prepare a blank disk to receive information by dividing its surface into tracks and sectors. See also Format.

Ink jet printer. A class of printer in which the characters are formed by using a number of closely spaced dots that are sprayed onto a page in microscopic droplets of ink.

Input. Information entered into the computer.

Insertion point. Used in word processing, it is the short, blinking (horizontal or vertical) line that indicates where the next typed letter will appear.

Integrated circuit. See Chip.

Intelligent terminal. A terminal that is capable of doing more than just receiving or transmitting data due to its microprocessor. See also Dumb terminal.

Interactive multimedia. Back-and-forth dialogue between user and computer that allows the combining, editing, and orchestrating of sounds, graphics, moving pictures, and text.

Interface. (v.) To connect two pieces of computer hardware together. (n.) The means by which two things communicate. In particular, it refers to the electrical configuration that allows two or more devices to pass information. See also Interface card.

Interface card. A board used to connect a microcomputer to peripheral devices.

Internet. A large interconnected set of networks.

I/O. Input/Output. Refers usually to one of the slots or the game port in a microcomputer to which peripheral devices may be connected.

Joy stick. An input device, often used to control the movement of objects on the video display screen of a computer for games.

Justification. A method of printing in which additional space is inserted between words or characters to make each line the same length.

K. Short for kilobyte (1,024 bytes) and is often used to describe a computer's storage capacity.

Keyboard. The typewriter-like keys that enter input into a computer. Each computer will have basically the same keyboard as a typewriter, with major differences limited to special function keys such as ESCape, RESET, ConTRoL, TABulate, etc.

Kilobyte. *See* K.

Language. Used to write programs; they are characters and procedures that the computer is designed to understand.

Laptop. A personal portable computer that can rest comfortably on a user's lap.

Large-Scale Integration (LSI). Refers to a generation of integrated circuits that allowed the equivalent of thousands of vacuum tube switches to be installed on a single chip.

Laser printer. A high-resolution printer that uses a rotating disk to reflect laser beams onto the paper. As the beam touches the paper, electrostatic image areas are formed that attract electrically charged toner. An image is then formed when the toner is fixed onto the paper.

LATA. Local Access and Transport Area. A contiguous geographical region of the United States for telephone exchanges.

LCD. Liquid Crystal Display.

LEC. Local Exchange Carrier. A local telephone company

Light pen. An input device, shaped much like a mechanical pencil, which, when touched to a display screen, can be used to select or execute certain computer functions.

LISP (LISt Processing). Programming language primarily used in artificial intelligence research.

Local Area Networks (LAN). The linking together of computers, word processors, and other electronic office equipment to form an interoffice network.

Log on. To execute the necessary commands to allow one to use a computer. May involve the use of a password.

Logo. A high-level language specifically designed so that it may be used by both small children and adults. It involves a "turtle"-shaped cursor for much of its operation.

M. *See* Megabyte.

Machine language. A fundamental, complex computer language used by the computer itself to perform its functions. This language is quite difficult for the average person to read or write.

Macro. Refers to the use of a simple command to execute a sequence of complex commands while using a computer program. The use of macros can save the user a considerable amount of time and reduce the chance of typing an incorrect key when executing a sequence of commands.

Magnetic Ink Character Recognition (MICR) devices. Computer hardware capable of reading characters imprinted with magnetic ink, such as on checks.

Mainframe. Refers to large computers used primarily in business, industry, government, and higher education that have the capacity to deal with many users simultaneously and to process large amounts of information quickly and in very sophisticated ways. *See also* Time share.

Management Information System (MIS). A systems approach that treats business departments as integrated parts of one total system rather than as separate entities.

MB. *See* Megabyte.

Megabyte. A disk-storage space unit or measurement of memory. It consists of 1,048,576 bytes.

Memory. Chips in the computer that have the capacity to store information. *See also* PROM; RAM; ROM.

Menu. The list of programs available on a given disk to guide the operator through a function.

Menu driven. Refers to software in which the program prompts the user with a list of available options at any given time, thus eliminating the need to memorize commands.

Merge. A command to create one document by combining text that is stored in two different locations (e.g., a form letter can be merged with a mailing list to produce a batch of personalized letters).

Microcomputer. Refers to a generation of small, self-contained, relatively inexpensive computers based on the microprocessor (commonly consists of a display screen, a keyboard, a central processing unit, one or more disk drives, and a printer).

Microprocessor. (The central processing unit [CPU]). It holds all of the essential elements for manipulating data and performing arithmetic operations. A microprocessor is contained on a single silicon chip.

Microsecond. One millionth of a second.

MIDI. Musical Instrument Digital Interface. A protocol that allows for the interchange of musical information between musical instruments, synthesizer, and computers.

Millisecond. One thousandth of a second; abbreviated "ms."

Minicomputer. Refers to a class of computers larger than micros but smaller than mainframe computers, many of which support multiple keyboards and output devices simultaneously.

Minimize. To shrink a window down to a tiny icon to temporarily move it out of the way.

Mnemonics. A computer's system of commands, which are words, letters or strings that are intended to assist the operator's memory. Abbreviations are used for the command functions they perform (e.g., C for center, U for underline).

Modem. MOdulator/DEModulator. A peripheral device that enables the computer to transmit and receive information over a telephone line.

Monitor. The display screen of a computer.

Motherboard. The main circuit board of a computer.

Mouse. A hand-operated device that is used to move the cursor around on the CRT screen.

Multiplexing. Digital electronics system that allows for the transmission of two or more signals on a single cable, microwave channel or satellite transponder. It doubles the capacity of television transmission and allows for simultaneous feed of independent programs for two audiences.

Multitasking. The ability to run several different programs simultaneously.

Nanosecond. One billionth of a second; abbreviated "ns."

National Crime Information Center (NCIC). A computerized information center maintained by the FBI that serves agencies throughout the United States.

Netscape. A popular World Wide Web browser that features integrated support for electronic mail and for reading Usenet news.

Network. A structure capable of linking two or more computers by wire, telephone lines, or radio links.

Newsgroups. A large collection of groups that include government agencies, universities and high schools, businesses, and other areas, all of which can be reached by an information utility.

Nibble. 1. Half a byte. 2. Refers to copy programs that copy small portions of a disk at a time, often used to copy otherwise copy-protected programs.

Nonvolatile memory. Memory that retains data even after power has been shut off. ROM is nonvolatile; RAM is volatile.

Notebook. A small portable microcomputer. *See also* Laptop.

NTU. National Technological University. A consortium of engineering, science, and technical colleges with a satellite delivery system of graduate and professional courses in the sciences.

Numeric keypad. An input device that allows the user to input numbers into a microcomputer with a calculator-like key arrangement.

NUTN. National University Teleconference Network. Network created to provide a means of information sharing and exchange, primarily by satellite-delivered teleconferences, with approximately 260 higher-education institutions as members.

Offline. An operation performed by electronic equipment not tied into a centralized information processing system.

Online. An operation performed by electronic equipment controlled by a remote central processing system.

Operating system. A group of programs that act as intermediary between the computer and the applications software; the operating system takes a program's commands and passes them down to the CPU in a language that the CPU understands.

Optical Character Recognition (OCR). A device that can read text and automatically enter it into a computer for editing or storage. Linked to a scanner, this software allows already-printed material to be converted to electronic text without having to type it on a keyboard.

Output. Information sent out of the computer system to some external destination such as the display screen, disk drive, printer, or modem.

Parallel. A form of data transmission in which information is passed in streams of eight or more bits at a time in sequence. *See also* Serial.

Pascal. A high-level language, with a larger, more complex vocabulary than BASIC, used for complex applications in business, science, and education.

Password. A code word or group of characters required to access stored material. This provides protection against unauthorized persons accessing documents.

Path. A sentence that tells a computer the exact name and location of a file.

PC. Personal Computer. *See* Microcomputer.

Peripheral. Hardware attachments to a microcomputer, (e.g., printer, modem, monitor, disk drives, or interface card).

Peripheral card. A removable printed-circuit board that plugs into a microcomputer's expansion slot and expands or modifies the computer's capabilities by connecting a peripheral device or performing some subsidiary or peripheral function.

Pica type. Any typeface that allows the printing of 10 characters to an inch.

PILOT. Programmed Inquiry, Learning, or Teaching. A high-level language designed primarily for use by educators, which facilitates the wiring of computer-assisted instruction lessons that include color graphics, sound effects, lesson texts, and answer checking.

Pitch. A measurement that indicates the number of characters in an inch (e.g., pica yields 10 characters to an inch; elite yields 12 characters to an inch).

Pixel. PIXture ELement. Refers to the smallest point of light that can be displayed on a display screen.

Plotter. A printing mechanism capable of drawing lines rapidly and accurately for graphic representation.

Port. An input or output connection to the computer.

Printout. *See* Hard copy.

Program. A list of instructions that allows the computer to perform a function.

PROM. Programmable ROM. A ROM that is programmed after it has been made.

Prompt. A message given on the display screen to indicate the status of a function.

Protocol. A formal set of rules that governs the transmission of information from one piece of equipment to another.

Proxy. A program or computer that performs a service on the user's behalf.

Quit. Exiting or closing a program, which removes the program from memory.

RAM. Random Access Memory. The main working memory of any computer. In most microcomputers, anything stored in RAM will be lost when the power is shut off.

Read Only Memory. *See* ROM.

Reboot. Restart the computer.

Retrieve. The transfer of a document from storage to memory.

RF modulator. Radio Frequency Modulator. Refers to a device that converts video signals generated by the computer to signals that can be displayed on a television set.

RISC. Reduced Instruction Set Computer. A processor that is designed for the rapid execution of a sequence of simple instructions rather than on a variety of complex functions.

Robotics. The science of designing and building robots.

ROM. Read Only Memory. A memory device in which information is permanently stored as it is being made. Thus, it may be read but not changed.

RS-232. Industry standard for serial transmission devices. It specifies the gender and pin use of connectors, but not the physical type.

Run. 1. To execute a program. 2. A command to load a program to main memory from a peripheral storage medium, such as a disk, and execute it.

Save. To store a program on a disk or somewhere other than a computer's memory.

Scanner. An input device that digitizes an optical image into an electronic image (which is represented as binary data). It can be used to create a computerized version of information or graphics.

Schema. The organization of a relational database in its entirety, including names of all data elements and ways records are linked.

Screen. A CRT or display screen.

Scroll. The ability to view a large body of text by rolling it past the display screen.

Search and replace. Locating a character string in a document and replacing it with a different character string.

Second-generation computers. A computer that was built from transistors; smaller, faster, and had larger storage capacity than the first-generation computers; first computers to use a high-level language.

Serial. A form of data transmission in which information is passed one bit at a time in sequence.

SMPT (Simple Mail Transfer Protocol). These are the rules that define how mail may be sent over the Internet.

Software. The programs used by the computer. Often refers to the programs as stored on a disk.

Sort. To arrange fields, files, and records in a predetermined sequence.

Speech synthesizer. Refers to a peripheral output device that attempts to mimic human speech.

Split screen. A type of dual display that allows some computers to view two or more different video images on the screen at the same time. *See also* Windowing.

Spreadsheet. A program that provides worksheets with rows and columns for calculating and preparing reports.

Stack. A list used to keep track of the sequence of required program routines.

Store. Placing information in memory for later use.

Subdirectory. A directory within a directory that is used to further organize files.

System. An organized collection of hardware, software, and peripheral equipment that works together. *See also* Configuration.

TDTD (Telecommunications Device for the Deaf). Frequently referred to as Telecommunication Display Device, this terminal device is used widely by hearing-impaired people for text communication over telephone lines.

Telecommunication. Transmission of information between two computers in different locations, usually over telephone lines.

Teleconference. Simultaneous program distributed via AUDIO only. Some call conferencing via satellite on video a "teleconference."

Telephone Bridge. Computerized switching system that allows multisite telephone conferencing.

Telnet. A service that provides a text-based connection to another computer.

Terminal. A piece of equipment used to communicate with a computer, such as a keyboard for input, or video monitor or printer for output.

Third-generation computers. Computers that are built with small-scale integrated circuits. Refers to the present generation of computers based on microchips. Compare to first generation (vaccum tubes) and second generation (transistors).

Time share. Refers to the practice of accessing a larger computer from a remote location and paying for services based on the amount of computer time used. *See* Mainframe.

Toner. Dry ink powder that serves as the "ink" for a laser printer.

Tractor feed. A mechanism used to propel paper through a printer by means of sprockets attached to the printer that engage holes along the paper's edges.

TTY. A teletype terminal that has a limited character set and poor print quality. It is characterized by a noisy mechanical printer.

Turing test. Proposed in 1950, the "Imitation Game" was offered to decide if a computer is intelligent and to answer the question, "Can machines think?" A person asks questions and, on the basis of the answers, must determine if the respondent is another human or a machine. If the answer is provided by a computer and the questioner guesses a human, the computer is deemed to be intelligent.

Typeover. Recording and storing information in a specific location to destroy whatever had been stored there previously.

Universal Product Code (UPC). A bar code that appears on virtually all consumer goods; can be read by a scanner or wand device used in point-of-sale systems.

URL (Uniform Resource Locator). This provides a standardized way to represent any location or service that is on the Internet. In HTML documents, it is used to specify the target of a hyperlink.

User friendly. Refers to hardware or software that is relatively easy for a new operator to learn, and which has features to help eliminate operator error.

User group. An association of people who meet to exchange information about computers or computer applications.

Usenet. An Internet group discussion service. It is international in scope and is a large, decentralized information utility.

Very Large Scale Integration (VLSI). Describes semiconductor integraded circuits, which are composed of thousands of memory cells or logic elements.

Video conferencing. Allows a video and audio discussion between groups in different locations, using electronic communications.

Video Display Terminal (VDT). A type of terminal that consists of a keyboard and screen. There are two categories—dumb terminals and intelligent (programmable) terminals.

Virtual. Commonly used to describe computer simulations (describes things that appear to be real, but are not really there).

Voice recognition system. A system that allows the user to "train" the computer to understand his or her voice and vocabulary.

Volatile. Refers to memory that is erased whenever the power is removed, such as RAM.

WAN. Wide-Area Network. The movement of data between computers in various areas through high-speed links.

Web. *See* World Wide Web.

Windowing. The ability of a computer to split a display screen into two or more segments so that several different documents can be viewed and several different functions performed simultaneously.

Word processing. Refers to the use of computers as electronic typewriters capable of entering and retrieving text, storing it on disks, and performing a wide range of editing functions.

World Wide Web. A global document that contains hundreds of thousands of information pages. The pages can be distributed across different Internet machines.

Wraparound. A computer's ability to automatically move words from one line to the next or from one page to the next as a result of margin adjustments, insertions, or deletions.

Write protected. A disk in which the write-enable notch is either missing or has had a write-protect tab placed over it to prevent information from being written to the disk.

Write-enable notch. A notch in a floppy disk that, if uncovered, allows a disk drive to write information to it, and which, if covered, prohibits such writing.

Write-protect tab. A small adhesive sticker used to write-protect a disk by covering the write-enable notch.

Sources for the glossary include:

Apple Computer Incorporated, Apple IIe Owner's Manual, Cupertino, CA, 1982.

"Apple II New User's Guide"; B. Gibson, "Personal Computers in Business: An Introduction and Buyer's Guide," *MECC,* Apple Computer, Inc., 1982.

"Glossary of Computer Terms," *Printout,* April 1983.

"Glossary of Computer Terms," Andy Rathbone, *Windows 95 for Dummies,* 1995.

"Glossary of Computer Terms," S. Richardson, *Noteworthy,* Winter 1982, pp. 27–29.

"Glossary of Computer Terms," William A. Sabine, *Gregg Reference Manual,* 1992, pp. 480–490.

Softalk, January 1982, January 1983.

"Using the Computer in the Classroom," *Today's Education,* April–May 1982.

"VisiCalc Glossary," *Apple Orchard,* July–August 1982.

227

Test Your Knowledge Form

We encourage you to photocopy and use this page as a tool to assess how the articles in **Annual Editions** expand on the information in your textbook. By reflecting on the articles you will gain enhanced text information. You can also access this useful form on a product's book support Web site at **http://www.dushkin.com/online/.**

NAME: DATE:

_____

TITLE AND NUMBER OF ARTICLE:

_____

BRIEFLY STATE THE MAIN IDEA OF THIS ARTICLE:

_____

LIST THREE IMPORTANT FACTS THAT THE AUTHOR USES TO SUPPORT THE MAIN IDEA:

_____

WHAT INFORMATION OR IDEAS DISCUSSED IN THIS ARTICLE ARE ALSO DISCUSSED IN YOUR TEXTBOOK OR OTHER READINGS THAT YOU HAVE DONE? LIST THE TEXTBOOK CHAPTERS AND PAGE NUMBERS:

_____

LIST ANY EXAMPLES OF BIAS OR FAULTY REASONING THAT YOU FOUND IN THE ARTICLE:

_____

LIST ANY NEW TERMS/CONCEPTS THAT WERE DISCUSSED IN THE ARTICLE, AND WRITE A SHORT DEFINITION:

ANNUAL EDITIONS revisions depend on two major opinion sources: one is our Advisory Board, listed in the front of this volume, which works with us in scanning the thousands of articles published in the public press each year; the other is you—the person actually using the book. Please help us and the users of the next edition by completing the prepaid article rating form on this page and returning it to us. Thank you for your help!

ANNUAL EDITIONS: Computers in Education 02/03

ARTICLE RATING FORM

Here is an opportunity for you to have direct input into the next revision of this volume. We would like you to rate each of the 42 articles listed below, using the following scale:

1. Excellent: should definitely be retained
2. Above average: should probably be retained
3. Below average: should probably be deleted
4. Poor: should definitely be deleted

Your ratings will play a vital part in the next revision. So please mail this prepaid form to us just as soon as you complete it. Thanks for your help!

RATING

ARTICLE

1. Lamar Alexander: A Transformative Power
2. High-Tech Teaching
3. Technology & Literacy: Raising the Bar
4. Early Childhood Classrooms in the 21st Century: Using Computers to Maximize Learning
5. What Students Want to Learn About Computers
6. Technology Use in Tomorrow's Schools
7. Project TEAMS: Integrating Technology Into Middle School Instruction
8. Using the Internet to Improve Student Performance
9. Working With WebQuests: Making the Web Accessible to Students With Disabilities
10. Designing Instruction for Emotional Intelligence
11. An Illusory Dilemma: Online to Learn or In Line With Standards
12. Computers as Mindtools for Engaging Learners in Critical Thinking
13. Grounded Constructions and How Technology Can Help
14. Kids as Computers
15. Learning to Use Your Mind Effectively in a Technology-Based Classroom
16. Strategies of Successful Technology Integration: Part 1—Streamlining Classroom Management
17. Concept to Classroom: Web-Based Workshops for Teachers
18. Look It Up on the Web: Practical Behavioral Support Information
19. Stages of Virtuality: Instructor and Student
20. Online Mentoring
21. Evaluating & Using Web-Based Resources

RATING

ARTICLE

22. Using Computers to Support a Beginning Teacher's Professional Development
23. Using Personal Digital Assistants in Clinical Supervision of Student Teachers
24. Do It Step-by-Step
25. MindWorks: Making Scientific Concepts Come Alive
26. Designing Instructional Technology From an Emotional Perspective
27. Multimedia or Not to Multimedia? That Is the Question for Students With Learning Disabilities
28. Multimedia Distance Education Interactions
29. Guerrilla Technology
30. Champions of Women in Technology
31. False Promise
32. Symbiosis: University/School Partnerships
33. Who Owns the Courses?
34. Internet 2 and the Next Generation Internet: A Realistic Assessment
35. Intelligent Campus Buildings for the Information Age
36. Web Clippings
37. Avaricious and Envious: Confessions of a Computer-Literate Educator
38. Wireless Andrew
39. IT Teams: Saving the World Through Authentic Challenging Tasks
40. Six Steps to Improving the Quality of Your Electronic Discussion Groups
41. Web-Based Portfolios for Technology Education: A Personal Case Study
42. Seven Tips for Highly Effective Online Courses

(Continued on next page)

NO POSTAGE
NECESSARY
IF MAILED
IN THE
UNITED STATES

BUSINESS REPLY MAIL
FIRST-CLASS MAIL PERMIT NO. 84 GUILFORD CT

POSTAGE WILL BE PAID BY ADDRESSEE

McGraw-Hill/Dushkin
530 Old Whitfield Street
Guilford, CT 06437-9989

ABOUT YOU

Name   Date

Are you a teacher? ☐   A student? ☐

Your school's name

Department

Address   City   State   Zip

School telephone #

YOUR COMMENTS ARE IMPORTANT TO US !

Please fill in the following information:
For which course did you use this book?

Did you use a text with this *ANNUAL EDITION*? ☐ yes ☐ no
What was the title of the text?

What are your general reactions to the *Annual Editions* concept?

Have you read any particular articles recently that you think should be included in the next edition?

Are there any articles you feel should be replaced in the next edition? Why?

Are there any World Wide Web sites you feel should be included in the next edition? Please annotate.

May we contact you for editorial input? ☐ yes ☐ no
May we quote your comments? ☐ yes ☐ no